PRAISE FOR
MARKET RESEARCH IN PRACTICE

'If you are new to market research then this should be your bible. If you hate guessing what your customers are thinking, then this should be your road map. And if you are a marketer, young or old, then this masterly reference piece will serve as a timely reminder that the most effective marketing is still about thinking and planning.'
John Dodds, Global Director Brand and Marketing Communications Excellence Air Products

'We are reminded of the scope of issues that market research helps us with and how exciting market research can be. Grounded in the realities of the product lifecycle along with the core strategic decisions (about products and markets) and management decisions (about the marketing mix) that are made in marketing, this is a very useful explanation and guide to using and undertaking market research.

'Whether you are interested in understanding markets, customers, the offer or positioning, this book offers accessible explanations of methods and applications. With top tips and helpful summaries, this is an excellent handbook for all those seeking to implement data collection and use market research information. It will help those commissioning or undertaking market research to plan to get the best form each project. This book will be useful to those interested in information-based decisions – practitioners and students of management in both the public and private sectors. The book covers both secondary and primary data it encompasses our move to interest in big data as well as making the most of small-sample qualitative studies. In this context, it puts sampling into context and gives insight into the appreciation of validity. The section on analysis suggests practical approaches to presenting results based on descriptive outcomes and multivariate analysis to understand market segmentation.

'The book clearly draws on a wealth of experience; it is credible and understandable, and I would recommend it to anyone undertaking marketing information gathering.'
Prof Gill Wright, Chair of Strategic Marketing, Manchester Metropolitan University

'The world of market research is constantly evolving with new methods and technologies. It's important to have a resource that you trust to remind you of the foundations of research-done-well. A valuable tool for insights professionals of all types, this is the book that I use with my team, whether we're searching for new inspiration or just want to go back to basics.'

Rebecca Cunningham, Senior Market Research Manager, Stanley Black & Decker, Inc

Market Research in Practice

THIRD EDITION

Market Research in Practice

An introduction to gaining greater market insight

Paul Hague, Matthew Harrison, Julia Cupman and Oliver Truman

KoganPage

LONDON PHILADELPHIA NEW DELHI

First published in Great Britain and the United States in 2004 by Kogan Page Limited
Second edition 2013
This third edition 2016

2nd Floor, 45 Gee Street
London EC1V 3RS
United Kingdom
www.koganpage.com

1518 Walnut Street, Suite 1100
Philadelphia PA 19102
USA

4737/23 Ansari Road
Daryaganj
New Delhi 110002
India

© Paul Hague, Matthew Harrison, Julia Cupman and Oliver Truman, 2016

The right of Paul Hague, Matthew Harrison, Julia Cupman and Oliver Truman to be identified as the authors of this work has been asserted by them in accordance with the Copyright, Designs and Patents Act 1988.

ISBN   978 0 7494 7585 7
E-ISBN   978 0 7494 7586 4

British Library Cataloguing-in-Publication Data

A CIP record for this book is available from the British Library.

Library of Congress Control Number

2016932638

Typeset by Graphicraft Limited, Hong Kong
Print production managed by Jellyfish
Printed and bound in Great Britain by Ashford Colour Press Ltd.

For everyone who is fascinated by the question 'Why?'

CONTENTS

For online resources to accompany this book, visit:
www.koganpage.com/MRinPractice

PREFACE

No one at school ever says they want to be a market researcher. It is a job that most people fall into by accident and yet it is arguably one of the best jobs in the world. Where else could someone with a curious mind be paid to find out what is going on? Nowhere else could there be such a variety of work: exploring motivations, finding out what is going on and always seeking the truth.

The four of us just fell into the job and it has kept our interest for years. In fact between us we have 70 years' experience in the profession to share with you. And there's another thing: this often intellectually challenging job doesn't have quite the status of other professions. We market researchers are an aspiring lot, always seeking to be analysts, consultants and advisors rather than authors of yet just another horizontal bar chart.

We would be less than honest with ourselves if we didn't confess that sometimes we find the life of a market researcher difficult. We are increasingly asked to jump over Olympian-high hurdles in the search for some new piece of intelligence that will give our clients a commercial advantage. Perhaps this is what keeps us interested, seeking the Holy Grail and occasionally getting quite close to it.

This book is an introduction to market research. It seeks to give the reader a taste of the whole process from planning a project and executing it, through to analysis and presenting the findings. It is aimed at students who need to understand the theory of the subject as well as people who want to carry out or manage their own surveys. Essentially it is a practical book, hence its title, and it is written by practitioners as this is what we do for our day job. Our aim is to educate you, of course, but also to enthuse you in this most wonderful subject, which we guarantee will absorb, frustrate and mainly satisfy you as your skills are developed.

In order to enliven the subject, the book is laced with examples of studies we have carried out over the last 40 years. This brings us to our first acknowledgement. Between us we have worked on a few thousand projects, each one paid for by a client. A typical project costs an amount equal in value to a new medium-sized saloon car. Commissioning market research is like buying a pig in a poke – the quality of the job is only evident when it is complete. We are ever grateful for these commissions. They are a supreme vote of confidence. They provide a livelihood. Not least they have enabled us to learn our craft.

One thing has remained the same over the years and that is the axiom: good market research is about asking the right question of the right person. In order to do this we need a field force. Market research interviewers use our questionnaires day

in and day out. Sometimes (no, often) these questionnaires are less than perfect –
but the interviewers make them work for us. These people are not in the spotlight.
When we present the findings and bathe in the glory of a successful conclusion
(hopefully), these stalwarts have moved on and their heads are down on the next
survey. The data-processing staff, whose timetable was squeezed because the project
was running late, do not have time to draw breath as they too are working on their
next screamingly urgent deadline. These 'support' staff are the unsung heroines and
heroes of market research, and we salute them.

Market research is almost always a team effort. Most projects involve a small
battalion of people. Indeed, this book is an example of team work. The foundations
of the book were based on publications by Paul Hague and Peter Jackson. Paul was
joined in the Second Edition by Nick Hague and Carol-Ann Morgan. Nick and Carol-
Ann have now stood down and Julia Cupman, Oliver Truman and Matt Harrison
take their turn to share their considerable knowledge on the market research subject.
We must also thank our editor, Jenny Volich of Kogan Page, for her encouragement
and expertise in keeping the timetable on track.

Finally, our greatest debt goes to you, the reader, without whom there would be no
market for our scribblings. Our hope is that we stimulate you to want to learn more
about this fascinating, frustrating and most rewarding subject that occupies our life.

PART ONE
Planning a market research study

Introduction

Who needs market research?

You are walking through a farmers' market where the stalls are full of plump produce. The stallholders have their wares positioned so that they are displayed to best advantage. Some are shouting to catch your attention. There are price tickets clearly displaying the cost of each item. It is busy and very noisy. Business is brisk and sellers and buyers seem to be in perfect harmony – each understands the other. It is highly unlikely that any of the stallholders have ever read a market research textbook, designed a questionnaire or carried out a survey; but they certainly do carry out market research.

Customers comment on the produce and the stallholders listen and respond, adjusting the next day's or week's stock. Each looks at the others' prices and knows instantly if they are out of line. And if they are, a quick adjustment is made. The stallholders watch and listen to each other to see how effective they are at catching the attention of the crowd, and if someone has a good idea, others quickly copy it. The stallholders' antennae are constantly monitoring the market because if they were not, they would soon be out of business.

You are whisked off now to the offices of a global company in Philadelphia. The company has plants in 30 different countries and it employs 30,000 people. It sells through 300 distributors who in turn sell to hundreds of thousands of customers. How does the boss of this company stay in tune with its market?

First, he or she has internal sources. Managers of each territory make their reports. The functional heads compile data on sales, finance and production. And whenever time allows, the boss does his/her own tour. But the position is no way as clear as it is to the stallholder. There are conflicting views from staff. Cultural differences around the world blur the understanding. Customers are distanced by distributors and there are few opportunities for them to express their opinion. What is more, unlike the stallholder who can quickly make adjustments to changing conditions, it takes an army of people weeks and months to make changes in the global company. The cost of a wrong decision is a fall in sales and profitability, resulting in the loss of thousands of jobs and millions of dollars off the share price. This company cannot rely on its antennae to tell it what is going on, it needs a process.

New roles for market research

Market researchers have a tool kit made up of desk research, telephone interviews, face-to-face interviews, self-completion questionnaires, focus groups and observation. They employ special techniques for selecting samples and analysing the data. Much of this book is devoted to these subjects, explaining how each works and how to do your own market research. However, it is equally important to understand what market research is for – why it is carried out. It is helpful, therefore, before we get into the tool kit, to consider the role of market research in decision making as this provides a context for the later discussions of methods and techniques.

We should begin this contextual understanding by reflecting on how young is the subject of formal market research, and how and why it started.

It is said that the first recorded straw polls (incidentally, the term comes from farmers throwing a handful of straw into the air to check where the wind was coming from) took place in the early 1820s when newspapers in the United States carried out simple street surveys to see how the political winds were blowing. By the early 1900s a fledgling market research industry had started there, focusing on advertising testing in one form or another. In those early days there was concern that direct questioning would produce dishonest answers and so some of the first commercial market research relied heavily on observation. The number of baked bean tins was counted on the shelves of supermarkets at the beginning and end of a period, and account was taken of the movement of the inventory. The audit was born. Famous market research companies such as Nielsen and Attwood in the United States and Audits of Great Britain (AGB) emerged. For the first time, managers had objective, accurate data on their sales, the size of the market, trends and their competitors' shares.

In the 1950s and 1960s business competition intensified and market researchers, building on the experience of social researchers, used sample surveys with questionnaires to obtain attitudinal data. The market research interview was accepted as the main vehicle for collecting information, and survey companies blossomed. For the first time, managers had objective and systematically collected data to help them understand what people were doing with or thinking about their products.

In the 1970s and 1980s attitudinal research moved to a different level and surveys were developed to track customer satisfaction.

In the last few years computing power has become cheaper and more powerful and the emphasis has turned to 'squeezing' data for more insights, using modelling such as factor and cluster analysis for segmentation, conjoint analysis for pricing decisions, data fusion to fill in gaps of missing data and geomapping to find the best locations for retailing or distribution.

The effect of regional culture on the use of market research

Managers are always making decisions based on their experience, the facts known to them internally and their intuition. Perhaps the way forward is obvious, or the size of the decision does not merit a huge spend on fact finding. Maybe action is required today and there is no time for formalized research even though it would be welcome. There is nothing wrong with intuition and 'common sense' and these are naturally part of decision making in business. However, where the decisions require large financial resources and where the costs of failure are high, there is a need for decision making based on robust and reliable data. Companies operating in large and international markets that are changing apace cannot rely on anecdotal and intuitive approaches to decision making. The purpose of market research is to reduce business risk.

It is perhaps surprising that major investments and strategic decisions are still made without adequate information. The reasons for this may include some professional failures on the part of market research practitioners such as an inability or unwillingness to be involved in decision making, as well as differences in corporate cultures. In the United States and northwest Europe, market research is almost standard practice as an aid to making large decisions. However in southern Europe, much of Asia and the developing world, market research is used less and there is more reliance on hunch and intuition. This is partly historical in that market research is less established and still finding its feet in these regions. It may also be because of cultural diffidence and suspicion about a methodology that people believe may not be a reliable means of getting to the heart of the matter.

The use of market research in business models and frameworks

Almost all the frameworks that help us understand our businesses and markets require data. Market research is therefore a vital component in many of the marketing paradigms. In Igor Ansoff's products' and markets' matrix there are four business situations, depending on whether the market we are addressing is new or one that is known to us, and whether the product/service we are selling is new or in our existing portfolio (see Figure 1.1). Market research has a role in all four situations. In Theodore Levitt's life cycle, market research plays an important role at each of the stages (see Figure 1.2). The four Ps (product, price, place and promotion) are the pillars of marketing. Each requires market research to help understand how these subjects work (see Figure 1.3).

FIGURE 1.1   Ansoff and market research

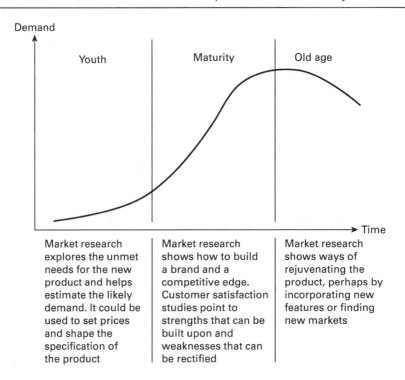

	Existing markets	New markets
New products	Market research can show the likelihood of adoption of new products	Market research can show unmet needs and provide an understanding of unfamiliar markets
Existing products	Market research can measure customer satisfaction to find out how to maintain a competitive edge	Market research can find new territories for products or services

FIGURE 1.2   Market research in the product/service life cycle

Youth	Maturity	Old age
Market research explores the unmet needs for the new product and helps estimate the likely demand. It could be used to set prices and shape the specification of the product	Market research shows how to build a brand and a competitive edge. Customer satisfaction studies point to strengths that can be built upon and weaknesses that can be rectified	Market research shows ways of rejuvenating the product, perhaps by incorporating new features or finding new markets

In this book the emphasis is on market research for business decisions. However, market research is also widely used in opinion polls (for political marketing), social issues and policy making, and personnel management (for example, employee attitude surveys).

FIGURE 1.3   Market research in the four Ps

Product	Price
Market research can test attitudes to products by describing them or showing them in focus groups and hall tests, or placing them in the home and workplace	Market research can show how much people value products and indicate an optimum price
Place	**Promotion**
This is the distribution part of the marketing equation, and market research can help plan the most effective route to market	Market research can help in all aspects of promotion from developing ideas for the adverts through to testing which advert is most effective

Consumer and business-to-business market research

The most fundamental division of markets is between those involving members of the general public and those where people are buying or specifying on behalf of another organization such as a business.

In consumer markets, the number of potential buyers of a product is often a significant proportion of a total population running into millions. Techniques used to research these markets include quantitative methods based on rigorous sampling as well as qualitative techniques that explore complex consumer perceptions and motivations. Consumer markets can be further subdivided between FMCGs (fast-moving consumer goods – food and similar frequent purchases) and other markets – media, travel and leisure, financial, consumer durables and so on. Modern marketing concepts and market research largely grew up in FMCG markets and this sector remains the area where most commercial market research is carried out. Consumer markets – FMCGs in particular – are also retail markets, and anyone marketing through retail distribution needs to know as much about what is happening in the shops as amongst final consumers. What is happening at the store level is, therefore, a major concern and is the information output of some of the largest continuous market research programmes (for example by organizations such as Nielsen).

Business-to-business market research employs the same techniques but in different ways. Many business-to-business markets are characterized by a much smaller population to survey, often measured in hundreds or thousands rather than the consumer millions. What is more, the business-to-business markets are frequently very variable, made up of companies in different industries and with huge differences in size. A researcher may be looking at the market for office equipment and face a sample that could include companies as disparate as General Motors and a 'Mom and Pop' organization providing some form of services to the local community.

Within the businesses there are often complex groups influencing the buying decision (the decision-making unit or DMU). The obvious groups, such as procurement, place the orders but technical and production departments may set specifications and financial departments may impose budgets.

In these complex business-to-business markets with smaller and more varied populations and with tangled decision-making units, we need different research methods. Sample sizes are smaller in number and the researcher may be leaning as much on judgement and interpretation as on the rigour of the method.

Markets (whether consumer or business-to-business) are not confined to single countries. Increasingly, marketing is international with global brands and marketing programmes. International companies may require their market research to cover North America, Europe and Asia in the same survey. International research programmes are logistically more complex and commonly require access to more extensive resources than may be required for domestic-only research. We discuss international market research in more detail in Chapter 25.

The scope of market research information

In consumer and business-to-business markets, the decisions that research is guiding tend to be similar. Whether the product is soap powder or servo motors, research could cover subjects such as the product specification and its relation to consumer needs and requirements, branding, pricing, distribution methods, advertising support, market definition and segmentation, forecast sales levels and so on. Each of these decisions requires information from the market to reduce business risk. Common information requirements met through market research are listed below although this is by no means exhaustive and can of course be classified in different ways. Also no single research commission would cover all or even most areas; as argued later, research that is focused and restricted to what is really crucial to the decision is more likely to be effective.

The applications for market research in Table 1.1 are not exhaustive. Market research can be used specifically to assess the competition, to determine employee satisfaction, to explore the values of a brand, to determine readership, examine sources of purchase – indeed it can be used to obtain a deeper understanding of the dozens of marketing-related decisions faced in business every day. Whether or not it is used depends on the financial implications of the decision and the speed with which a result is required. A decision linked to an investment of a small number of dollars and where the results are required tomorrow is less likely to be researched than one that has massive financial ramifications and where time is available to think about it.

Although information is potentially a requirement in all markets, the characteristics of specific markets mean that there is considerable variation in the detailed coverage sought in each case. Market segmentation, for example, means something rather different for FMCGs than for engineering components. Similarly, in industrial markets there is often a greater need for understanding the structure of suppliers and their organization, while in consumer markets branding issues may be of greater concern.

TABLE 1.1   Information that can be obtained through market research

Market size and structure	**Methods used to assess market size and structure**
The value of the market in currency value and units sold each year	Published market research reports
The historical trends in size of the market	Desk research
The key consuming segments of the market	Market surveys aimed at calculating consumption and brands purchased
The competition and its shares	
The route to market	
Use of and attitude to products	**Methods used to assess use and attitudes**
Awareness of suppliers	Quantitative surveys carried out by telephone, online, face to face
Attitudes to suppliers	
Attitudes to products	Focus groups
Volume and frequency of purchases	
Customer satisfaction and loyalty	**Methods used to assess customer satisfaction**
Ratings of customers (and sometimes potential customers) to show what they think is important in influencing their buying decision and how satisfied they are with their supplier on each issue	Quantitative surveys carried out by telephone, online, face to face

TABLE 1.1   *continued*

Promotion effectiveness	**Methods used to assess promotion**
Key messages for campaigns	**effectiveness**
Effectiveness of adverts and promotions	Focus groups
	Face-to-face interviewing
	Telephone interviewing
	E-surveys
	Pre-and-post quantitative surveys
Brand impact	**Methods used to assess brand impact**
Awareness of brands	Focus groups
Values attached to brands	Telephone interviewing
The influence of brands in the	E-surveys
purchasing decision	Face-to-face interviewing
Pricing effectiveness	**Methods used to assess pricing**
Optimum prices	**effectiveness**
Price values attached to features	Market research in test markets
of the offer	Trade-off analysis using conjoint
	techniques
Product tests/concepts	**Methods used to assess products**
Likelihood of purchasing different	Hall tests
products	Focus groups
Attitudes to products	Quantitative research
Attitudes to new concepts	
Unmet needs identification	
Segmentation	**Methods used to assess segmentation**
Opportunities for segmentation based on	Quantitative surveys with factor and
demographics, behaviour or needs	cluster analysis

The uses of market research are discussed in more detail in Chapter 3 and also in Chapters 17–23.

Quantitative and qualitative research

One important classification of market research information, regardless of the type of market, is between quantitative and qualitative. Quantitative research is concerned with the measurement of a market and can include calculation of the market size, the size of market segments, brand shares, purchase frequencies, awareness of brands, distribution levels and so on. Such quantitative data is required to some level of accuracy (though not in all cases to very high levels) and the methods used must be capable of achieving this. In consumer markets at least, quantitative information is almost always based on extrapolating from a sample to the general population or market, and the research design and particularly the sampling methods must be sufficiently rigorous to allow this.

Qualitative information is rather harder to define but the emphasis is on 'understanding' rather than simple measurement – advert A is recalled better than advert B (quantitative information), but how does A work as an advert and why is it more effective than B? (qualitative information). Much qualitative research is concerned with empathizing with the consumer and establishing the meanings he or she attaches to products, brands and other marketing objects. Another focus is motivation. For example, why does one product rather than another meet consumer needs and what are these needs that are being met? Qualitative research is conducted amongst a sample, but in this case usually a small one, since there is no attempt to extrapolate to the total population. In the case of attitudes to brands, for example, qualitative research may determine that there is a specific view held about the brand, whereas quantitative research would tell us what proportion holds that view.

Quantitative and qualitative research are often complementary, and in a research design both may feature. The qualitative element frequently takes place at the front end of the study, exploring values that need measuring in the subsequent quantitative phase. The 'qual' research may offer a diagnostic understanding of what is wrong, while the 'quant' research provides hard data across different respondent groups that can lead to specific recommendations with measures that can be used as controls to determine the effectiveness of actions.

The market research process

The collection of any facts relevant to a marketing decision can be considered as market research. However, we are concerned in this book with something rather more than an occasional and haphazard use of snippets. We suggest a definition of market research as follows: the systematic collection, analysis and interpretation of information relevant to marketing decisions.

In our definition, the word 'systematic' does not necessarily imply that market research is a scientific discipline, as we often use procedures such as observation and focus group research that are long on interpretation and short on mathematics. In this respect, market research is closer to the social sciences than those such as physics that can be more precise about the laws of nature.

FIGURE 1.4 The market research process

Market research can be carried out as a one-off project to meet a specific requirement, in which case it is called ad hoc research, or it can involve continuous or regular tracking such as the monitoring of the market share held by a product or brand. The purposes for which ad hoc, or for that matter continuous, research is carried out are enormously diverse, but the process followed in virtually any ad hoc (and in principle most continuous) projects is as illustrated in Figure 1.4.

The starting point of any market research project is to have a brief – a background to the problem or the opportunity, and statement of what information is required in order to make a decision. It is especially true in market research that a problem well defined is a problem half solved, as this leads naturally to the definition of the objectives of the survey – what the work is meant to achieve. If this is not done adequately – too often it is not – the effort put into the work will be wasted. Objectives are a statement of what the research will be used for and what specific items of information are being sought.

A plan of how these objectives are to be met and how the information is to be obtained is then required. This is the proposal or research design, and it will cover the use of both qualitative and quantitative methods, detailing who will be interviewed, what number and whether this will be face to face, by telephone or self-completion. The resources needed (especially the money) and the timescale are also important at this planning stage. The planning of a market research project is the subject of Chapter 2.

Fieldwork or data collection is the visible part of market research. Fieldwork normally involves interviewing and completing a questionnaire for each individual or organization in the sample. This may be numbered in tens, hundreds or even thousands. The individual questionnaires and responses are usually of little or no interest; what is required is an aggregation of the whole sample or perhaps groupings within that sample. This larger picture is obtained by analysing the data using proprietary software that allows cross-cuts of the data.

Once an analysis and aggregation of the data has been produced, this needs interpreting and presenting in a meaningful way so that the decision maker can act on the results. This is the reporting stage of the process, and may involve the researcher making recommendations. Data analysis is discussed in Chapter 16 and reporting is the subject of Chapter 24.

Top tips

- Look for a business model or framework in which you can locate your research problem/opportunity.

- Scoping the survey is critical. Think about the different types of people you want to interview and which geographical area should be covered, and be clear about these from the outset.

- Decide what information you want from the research and avoid adding more and more 'nice to have' but inessential questions and subjects. Beware of people who want to hijack your survey and, 'while you are at it', add a lot more questions.

- In consumer quantitative research, make sure you have a sufficiently large and robust sample. A quantitative survey should have at least 200 respondents.

- Different sampling rules apply in business-to-business research. Here the 80:20 rule is important, based on the premise that the largest 20 per cent of companies account for 80 per cent of industry sales. A quantitative survey in a B2B market should ensure that it includes a good number of these large companies so that it covers a good proportion of the market with a relatively small number of interviews.

- Make sure that the processes you use for market research are systematic so that they can be repeated if necessary.

The organization of market research

There are limits to what can be achieved by a lone market researcher. The researcher can certainly carry out desk research, and it is arguable that someone working inside a client organization is the best person to do this (see Chapter 5). The insider will be able to interpret the data far better than an outsider. A market researcher on his or her own could also send out an e-based questionnaire to a sample of customers and analyse the returns (see Chapter 15). However, most market research requires fieldwork of some kind or another, and logistics, budgets and the need to meet timetables require some division of labour and a team approach. Fieldwork options are an important part of the market research process, and we devote a good deal of space to them in this book. They are discussed in detail in Chapters 6 (focus groups), 7 (depth interviews), 12 (face-to-face interviewing), and 13 (telephone interviewing).

The tasks covered in the outline of the market research process can be rather crudely divided between 'thinking' and 'doing'. Thinking-type tasks include planning the research, selecting an appropriate research design, developing questionnaires and similar tools, deciding how the data should be analysed and interpreted, and the communication of the results. These tasks require professional-level skills and a background in the body of theory underpinning market research. However, unlike the doing parts of the process, a large team is not usually required for these parts of the process; in many projects the work can be handled by one person.

The two main 'doing' parts of research are data collection and data analysis. Some types of data collection (for instance, focus group moderation) are best carried out by professional-level staff, but in most cases this would be impractical or unduly expensive since quite sizeable teams are required for the data collection element of even average-sized projects. Consider, for example, a quantitative study of a consumer market in which it is decided that 1,000 face-to-face interviews are required with a nationally representative sample. It may well be decided to plan this as a programme of 50 interviews around 20 sampling points spread around the country. The costs and time of travel point immediately to the need for a team of 20 interviewers (one per point). To keep the fieldwork within an acceptable timetable and to avoid interviewer fatigue, it will be more common to use two to four interviewers per sampling point – 40 to 80 interviewers in total for an 'average' job. These interviewers need to be trained in gaining and carrying out interviews but there is no reason why they should also be proficient in other parts of the process. In practice this is how most market research fieldwork is successfully carried out – by teams of trained but not professional-level staff.

Data processing is the area of market research where information technology (IT) has had the longest-standing impact (IT is also widely used in data collection through online surveys). The data is often entered into computers at the time of the interview by the interviewers, who use laptops in face-to-face interviews (CAPI – computer-aided personal interviewing) or desktops in telephone interviews (CATI – computer-aided telephone interviewing). Not all data is entered directly as the interview is carried out; some is captured on paper questionnaires and transferred to computers at a later time by 'coding' and 'data entry' staff. Again, therefore, the professional researcher needs the assistance of a sizeable team in order to carry out the work effectively. Also, the IT aspect of data processing has brought new specialists ('spec writers') into the market research industry and extended the team required for many types of project.

The complicated logistics required to carry out surveys means that this has to be outsourced to specialized market research companies. In-house research staff act as interfaces with other departments in their organization, helping write the specifications for research, evaluating tenders and controlling the projects. In the mature economies of the Western world there are hundreds of market research suppliers, ranging from small firms offering specialist services of focus group moderation or statistical modelling through to the international giants with offices across the globe.

Possibly one consequence of the organizational split between market research suppliers (agencies) and clients (the companies making the marketing decisions) is that market research does not realize its full potential in contributing to decision making. The researcher, however experienced and skilled, is often remote and a stranger to those making decisions. He or she is also insulated from other factors that may need to be taken into account in decision making – production capabilities, finance and wider corporate goals. In addition, rightly or wrongly, market researchers are often seen as backroom people: valuable in a narrow field but not capable of taking the broader view or contributing to long-term strategy. This is a role that is changing as researchers have the advantage of drawing on experience in the many markets they examine and because they now have access to a much more powerful arsenal of statistical tools that aid their interpretation.

SUMMARY

Market research is the systematic collection, analysis and interpretation of information relevant to marketing decisions. The industry was spawned in the United States in the early 1900s and has been widely embraced by large companies throughout the world. Large companies have a frequent requirement for market research in their marketing planning.

The applications for market research have grown over the years, and increasingly market researchers use modelling to improve the relevance of their data. The most common applications for market research are to assess customer satisfaction and loyalty, to measure the effectiveness of promotions, to show the market size and shares of suppliers, to measure use and attitudes to products, to determine optimum pricing strategies and brand influence, and to determine effective segmentation strategies.

There are significant differences between research with the general public and research with buyers in businesses. Business-to-business market research is characterized by complicated decision-making units, often involving a number of people, whereas consumer research generally focuses on just a single person or the family unit.

There are two important schools in market research – qualitative and quantitative. Qualitative research is often used as a precursor to a larger study and it provides diagnostic data and insights using focus groups and depth interviews. Quantitative research is concerned with larger numbers of interviews, at least 200 and sometimes 1,000 or more. These numbers provide measures of behaviour and attitudes that represent the larger market from which the sample has been drawn.

The market research process begins with a definition of the problem – the brief. This is prepared by the sponsor of the research and it is converted into a proposal by the market researchers. The proposal shows the design of the study, which often involves input from desk research and fieldwork made up of qualitative and quantitative methods. Analysis and reporting concludes the project.

Most market research programmes involve a good deal of labour in the interviewing and analysis. For this reason, large surveys have to be carried out by specialist market research companies organized to carry out the many tasks.

Market research design

What is worth researching?

Market research is the systematic and objective collection of data on a marketing subject. Put another way, it is the map by which we steer our marketing course. It is the intelligence that helps us make the most informed (and hopefully the correct) marketing decisions. You would think, therefore, that market researchers would be continuously occupied providing the intelligence that allows businesses to operate efficiently. This is not the case.

The first thing to bear in mind is that not every business decision requires formal market research. Marketing managers in businesses around the world are confronted daily with decisions on what type of packaging to use for their products, what improvements would make the products more attractive, what prices to charge for their products, and how they should be promoted in the marketplace. (By the way, we are using the word 'products' liberally as they could just as easily be services.) If every decision needed a special market research study, it would take for ever and cost a fortune. It is only necessary to use market research for big decisions and those where there is insufficient knowledge to move forward.

It is necessary to have some knowledge about the capabilities of market research before it can be considered as a possible solution. Most people know something about market research in a general sense. They know it can be used to find out how many people do something or think something. But they may not know that it can be used to work out how much people are prepared to pay for each feature of a product. They may not appreciate that market research can work out the importance of factors that influence customer satisfaction without asking the customer how important each factor is. If you don't know what something can do, you won't think of using it.

Furthermore, there are very few processes in business that say 'before we make that decision, we must carry out market research'. The decision to use market research is entirely judgemental. Some managers use it regularly, others hardly ever.

TABLE 2.1   The gestation period for a market research idea

What happens	Idea, business problem, business opportunity	Internal debate	External debate	Information collection
Who generates it	A manager with an idea or problem	Between the manager and his or her colleagues, sometimes involving a market research manager	Manager or market research manager presents problem to market research companies for their suggested solutions	Market research company is selected and carries out the work
How long does it take	A few days and often a week or a month	A week and more often a few weeks	A week or two	4–12 weeks

In the main, the decision to commission market research is likely to be made by a manager or at least someone senior within a company. After all, it is managers who make decisions, and market research is there to reduce business risk in decision making. The decision under consideration may gestate for weeks before it is brought to the attention of the market research company that is asked to plan and cost a research programme (see Table 2.1). On the way, the business problem may very well bounce between people, including an internal market research manager who helps develop a research brief. By the time that the idea or problem is finally put before the market research company, the timescale for decision making could be under real pressure. Indeed, the time available for the collection of the intelligence could determine the method that is to be used for the data collection.

We will talk later in the book about how long it takes to carry out market research and how much it costs. It is worth bearing in mind that both the timeline for a study and its cost are very frustrating for many managers. Intelligence and information of all kinds surrounds us in our daily life. Every time we watch a news programme or pick up a newspaper we are bombarded with intelligence of one kind or another. A Google search will deliver thousands if not millions of hits on a subject within milliseconds. It seems as if data and intelligence proliferate everywhere and apparently at low or no cost. So why does it take market researchers 10 weeks and the price of a luxury car to complete a study?

This is a legitimate concern. Market research is expensive and it takes a relatively long time to complete a typical study. That said, the real cost of research has declined considerably over the years, aided by technological improvements, particularly in terms of data collection and analysis. Today, it is in theory possible to design a questionnaire within a few hours, launch an online survey and have the results the same day. This is a rarity, if only because most market research requires due consideration at every stage of the process. The questionnaire is developed and discussed between the client and the agency over a number of days until everyone is satisfied that it will do the job. It is then pilot tested and, if everything is satisfactory the fieldwork takes place, during which time the researchers may have to fill quite difficult quotas of respondents to ensure that everyone in the target population is covered. And then the analysis takes place, again over a number of days, as full deliberation is given to every insight that can be wrung from the data.

Market research suppliers

Market research is an industry that involves suppliers of many different kinds. Some offer a full service, with researchers who can design questionnaires, a fieldwork department that can carry out interviews, a data analysis department that can crunch the numbers, and analysts who can interpret the data and prepare a report. In addition, there are many companies that specialize in just one area of market research. There are boutique agencies with a small number of people who are experts in a subject area. There are fieldwork agencies that carry out telephone interviews and others that can organize face-to-face interviews. There are companies that specialize in data tabulations and statistics. There are companies that provide facilities for hosting focus groups. It is a $40 billion business globally. However, this does not take account of all the time and the opportunity cost expended by people within companies and universities carrying out their own market research studies – some of them undertaking primary research and carrying out their own fieldwork, and others basing their studies largely on secondary research or what is already published and available on the internet.

Ad hoc research is the mainstay of most market research companies. Projects are carried out for individual clients and designed as one-offs to meet specific needs and objectives. Because research companies work closely with clients, and involve themselves in the full background of the research requirement, their service shades into management consultancy.

Anyone new to market research always wants to know what ad hoc research costs. The costs could range extremely widely, depending on the number of interviews, who they are with, how they are carried out, and in which countries. However, as a rough indication, the starting level for complete projects is around the US $30,000 mark and can go up to six figures. Most are in the US $50,000 to US $200,000 range.

An excellent starting point for finding a market research company is through one of the trade associations in each country that represents the market research industry (for example, the Market Research Society of the United Kingdom or the American Marketing Association, the Market Research Association or the American Association of Public Opinion Research). An excellent source of market research companies around the world can be found on the ESOMAR website (European Society For Opinion & Marketing Research, **http://www.esomar.org/**), which offers an up-to-date directory of 1,600 research organizations. In the US go to www.greenbook.org or www.quirks.com.

The market research brief: a statement of the problem/opportunity

A research brief is a statement from the sponsor setting out the objectives and background to the case in sufficient detail to enable the researcher to plan an appropriate study. As a general rule, a market research study is only as good as the brief. The brief is important to the researcher: it educates and influences the choice of method. It gives the objective to which the project is geared.

The brief is no less important for the researcher working in-house than for the market research company. The in-house researcher has the benefit of close and constant access to other internal staff who are able to fill in on background and product details. Though the brief may be less formal for the in-house market researcher, it nevertheless needs to cover all the details, such as the decisions that will be made with the information that is obtained, specifically what information is required, and when it needs to be delivered.

Some clients prefer to give their brief orally, developing points of detail during the initial discussion with the researcher. Alternatively the brief may be given in writing. A written brief can be important when a number of research companies are invited to submit proposals providing a standard that is the same for all contestants.

When preparing a brief the following questions should be considered:

1 What action will be taken when the research is completed? What would be the risk of not doing the research?

Answers to these questions will enable the researchers to work out the specific information that will be useful (see item 5 below).

2 What has caused this problem or led to this opportunity?
Here it is helpful to describe the history that has led up to the need for the research. A description of the product/service is important, and it would also be good to talk about the way that the market is changing.

3 What is known about the area of research already?
It can be helpful to market researchers to be aware of what is already known so they can build on existing knowledge and not waste money or time re-establishing it. Also, knowledge on the structure and behaviour of a market allows the researchers to be more precise in their proposals. For example, most sponsors of research have some feel for a market either from internal opinion or possibly from multi-client reports that have been purchased as background to the subject. It is helpful to know that these exist and can be made available to the researchers who are planning a research programme if they need a deeper understanding of the market.

4 Target groups for the research.
The target for interviewees needs to be scoped precisely. Should they be people who have bought a product or who are thinking of buying a product? Should they be buyers or specifiers? Should they be frequent purchasers or not? Questions that most researchers will ask at the time that they are designing a study are: 'Do you have a good list of the target audience? Does this list contain telephone numbers or e-mail addresses? Would we be able to use the list to contact respondents?' A good list (the jargon is a 'sample frame') makes the fieldwork much easier, faster and cheaper.

5 What specific information is needed from the research (for example, market size, trends, buying behaviour, customer satisfaction, customer needs, segmentation)?
The manager requesting the market research almost certainly has key information gaps that need filling. Listing them will help the professional market researchers work out if they can be answered, if there are other specific questions that should be asked and what methods should be used. The market researchers that respond to the brief can be expected to flesh out the information objectives with their own suggestions, as they know better than anyone what can and cannot be achieved by market research.

6 What is the proposed budget?
Seldom are there unlimited funds for research and more often there are very limited funds. It is almost always helpful to know what these are for otherwise a study could be designed that over-delivers and breaks the bank. Many clients hold back from giving the research company a budget in the hope that a lower-cost project will be tendered. It is true that researchers are likely to use

every cent within a budget in order to obtain the most robust result possible. A sponsor seeking three quotes from different suppliers can always choose the one that offers the best research design for the budget. If there is a very limited budget, it is good that the research suppliers know this so they can cut their cloth accordingly.

7 Are there any initial ideas for the research method?

A client who is sponsoring a research project may well have a method in mind. Now is the time to say whether a research method is favoured or distrusted. If focus groups are thought to be the most appropriate method by the research sponsor, it is worth discussing it at this briefing stage.

8 Are there any reporting requirements?

Increasingly the default report in the market research industry is a PowerPoint deck of slides that doubles as the presentation and the report. Researchers have no problem writing a narrative report, but they would typically have to charge an extra three or four days for its preparation – incurring a cost of a few thousand dollars.

The research sponsor may want an interim report or access to specific data such as interview transcripts. It is wise to specify this at the brief, for otherwise it may not be included in the research specification.

9 When are the findings required?

Most research has a demanding timetable and sometimes this can be punishing. The dates by which the research is required should be specified so that even if deadlines are tight, the research supplier can make provision, perhaps with interim debriefs or regular reporting sessions.

The research brief should be a dialogue, and even the most thorough brief, covering all the points that have been mentioned, will generate some additional questions from the researchers. This is healthy and to be expected, indicating that the problem is being thought through and interest is being shown. Sometimes the written brief and a series of phone calls are sufficient for the market research company to get on with its part of the process – the proposal writing – and sometimes there will be justification for a face-to-face meeting. Nearly but not quite always, these briefing sessions are at the research sponsor's offices where it is easier to show the product, look at brochures and reports, and meet with other people who may be able to contribute to the debate.

The market research proposal: the return of brief (ROB)

Having received the brief the researcher, whether in-house or from an agency, must submit a written proposal to the sponsor that states an appreciation of the problem, the objectives, the research method and the timing. The proposal should be in writing and, in effect, is the basis of a contract of considerable financial value.

The nature of market research is such that it is seldom possible to pin down every aspect of the contract in detail. For example, the questionnaire has not yet been developed and this is a key to the survey. The number and type of questions in the questionnaire will have a material influence on the quality of the work.

Flexibility is going to be needed on many aspects of the work, and as the research progresses and information is uncovered, there will be changes made to the original objectives and possibly some changes to the details of the research design. For the most part, however, the number and type of interviews will remain the same, as this is the basis of the price.

Armed with the brief, the researcher now knows what the client is looking for and must balance four factors in arriving at an appropriate design (see Figure 2.1).

FIGURE 2.1   The trade-off between cost, quality and time

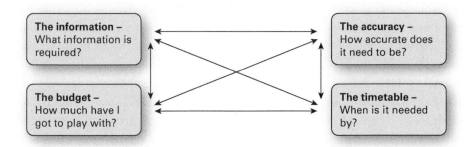

The information required

The researcher must take the various inputs from the brief and play them back in terms of outcomes, objectives and questions that will be asked. Examples of these three levels are shown in Table 2.2.

TABLE 2.2 Outcomes, objectives and questions

Level 1	Outcome	Should we launch a new product?		
Level 2	Research objective	To show product preferences for the new and the old design	To assess trends in buying behaviour	To determine the optimum price of the new product
Level 3	Questions to be answered	Do people prefer the new product to the old one? Do people prefer the new product to the competition's? What would improve preferences for the new product?	Are people buying more of the product? How are preferences for this type of product likely to change over the next five years? What factors are driving the changes in the market?	How much will people buy at different prices? What is the optimum price for the new product? What is the elasticity of demand for the new product?

The researcher must work out what can reasonably be included as an objective in the project as well as what may have to be left out. As the researcher is thinking about the objectives, inevitably there will be consideration of the methods by which these will be achieved.

Consider Table 2.2, which has a range of outcomes, objectives and questions that relate to the launch of a new product. The researcher could use a qualitative tool such as focus groups. However, even with a number of focus groups, that would still result in a qualitative finding that provides a good feel for and understanding of the opportunity but no more than that. If the research is being commissioned to make a decision on the launch of a new product, some quantification is likely to be required. Here the choices are twofold: home placement tests, or mall/hall tests (where the respondent is recruited from the shopping mall and brought to a nearby hall to experience the product). The arguments in favour of one approach rather than another or mixing different approaches will be made in the proposal under the 'methods' section.

The accuracy

When professional market researchers ask their clients how accurate they want the data to be, the answers are often 'very accurate' or 'as accurate as possible'. Quite reasonably the sponsor of the research will want to know in advance a measure of the statistical accuracy of the findings. However, accuracy has a price; as a general rule, increases in accuracy not only cost more but cost disproportionately more.

A high level of accuracy may not always be needed to meet the research objectives. If a company is entering a new market, where common sense indicates that the market is huge, there may be little point in spending lots of money closely measuring its size. An approximation is all that is needed and the money saved may be better spent on some other information requirement. For example, a company that would be happy achieving sales of US$1 million per annum in a new market that is earmarked for expansion need not be concerned to know if the total market size is US$100 million or US$150 million (an accuracy of +/–50 per cent). With modest sales targets, the accuracy of the market-size estimate is not so important. If, however, the objective of a study is to measure the impact of an advertising campaign, it will be essential to have a sufficiently large and accurate sample for both the pre-and-post research campaigns in order to know if any changes between the two are statistically significant.

The required accuracy must, therefore, be linked to how the resulting data will be used – the nature of the decisions that the research will guide. Even if a precise definition of accuracy is not practically possible (as is often the case), some judgement should still be made on the reliability sought from the information. At the very least it should be stated in the research design whether measurements will be obtained (quantitative research) as opposed to insights, description and explanation (qualitative research). Both approaches can contribute to effective marketing decisions but it is important that neither is used for the wrong application. Like information coverage, accuracy levels need to be considered before deciding on appropriate research methods.

The budget

What budget should be made available for the research project? The methodologically pure researcher would argue that the budget should be whatever is needed to meet the research objectives and produce information to the defined accuracy level. However, in practice it is more a question of what funds are available or can be afforded for the project relative to other calls on business expenditure. Furthermore, even if cash is freely available, there are other considerations and especially the amount at risk in the decision that the research is to guide. If the decision entails capital expenditure of US $20 million, a research budget of US $100,000 may be well worth spending. If the research indicates that the planned expenditure is a poor investment, only the research cost will be lost rather than most or all of the US $20 million investment.

At the time of writing the global solar power industry is closing plants and trying to cope with huge overcapacity. Did these investors carry out good and solid market research on both the demand for solar power and the competitive environment? An investment of US $100,000 in good market research might well have saved many millions of dollars in lost assets. However, if the business investment decision has low cost implications, the justification for carrying out the research will be less. Obviously there is no point spending US $50,000 on research to decide whether to invest in a project entailing only this level of expenditure.

We recently carried out a research project examining the effectiveness of a planned promotional campaign for an industrial gas manufacturer. The cost of the research was US $100,000 and the advertising campaign itself was only US $500,000. However, the gas manufacturer runs many such campaigns across its divisions and learning what makes advertising more effective sharpened all its campaigns and will do so for some years to come. The long-term payback will be considerable.

Determining the return on investment (ROI) of market research projects is truly difficult. At least it should be possible to establish some sort of justification for the research based on the questions posed in Table 2.3. If the answer to any one of the questions is a score of 4 or 5, then market research could be justified.

TABLE 2.3   Questions to assess the ROI of market research projects

	5 = high/important; 1 = low/not important
What is the size of the investment for which market intelligence will guide the decision?	
What is the need for market knowledge that does not already exist within the organization?	
What is the risk to the business of taking a decision without market intelligence?	
What is the need for independent research to resolve internal differences on a proposed decision?	

The timetable

A research plan needs a timetable. The research may have a deadline that is driven by external events and time frames such as a business investment meeting or a business plan. A demanding deadline of two or three weeks for a research project may effectively limit it to a quick (and 'dirty') design as there just is not enough time to do the job in any other way. Whether researchers should turn down such jobs is hardly worth debating since, in this commercial world, market research companies will nearly always try to accommodate their clients' needs. To an extent it may be possible to speed up the research to fit such demands. Certainly good research can be carried out within a short time frame, but beyond some point, quality will be compromised.

Most research companies need at least six weeks to carry out a project that accommodates the different events and stages. Getting questionnaires designed is in theory only a day's work for a professional researcher. However, getting it approved and modified to the final version (often it is at version 5 before it is finally piloted) can take three weeks as it bounces like a pinball between the different parties. The timetable given in Table 2.4 is probably realistic for a project involving four focus groups and 500 interviews with the general public.

Top tips

- When commissioning market research it is most important to prepare a good brief. The brief should state the background to the study, what will be done with the research findings, the scope of the study, the specific objectives of the study, the timetable and any budget limitations.

- The proposal is the return of brief from the market research consultants. Proposals should give answers to all aspects of the brief (ie the information that will be sought methods, the timetable and cost). A good proposal is one that is clear and logical, and carries conviction that the brief will be achieved.

- Discuss the potential project with a number of market research agencies before you send them a brief to find out their capabilities. Then obtain three or four proposals from companies that are able and qualified to carry out the project.

- The quality of the proposal will have a major bearing on your choice of agency. Other factors to take into account are the experience of the agency in the subject of study, and the reputation of the company in producing reliable and creative solutions.

TABLE 2.4   A typical market research timetable

	Week 1	Week 2	Week 3	Week 4	Week 5	Week 6	Week 7	Week 8	Week 9	Week 10
Commissioning meeting	x									
Focus group recruitment	x	x								
Focus groups			x	x						
Qualitative debrief				x						
Questionnaire design				x	x					
Sample composition				x	x					
Fieldwork					x	x	x			
Analysis								x	x	
Presentation development									x	
Presentation										x

What to expect in a proposal (return of brief)

The proposal is one of the most important documents a researcher ever writes. It is the equivalent of an architect's drawing. It is the plan, the schema, that shows what will be achieved and how it will be achieved. The proposal is usually submitted in PowerPoint or Microsoft Word.

The content, structure and quality of the proposal may account for well over 50 per cent of the decision to place the business with a market research company. Within the client company, the proposal will do the rounds, winning or losing approval with its many readers, without the accompaniment of the author. It is therefore a vitally important weapon used by market research companies to win business.

The proposal is more than just a research design with a price; it is a statement of the company that has prepared it. In the proposal, the research company will state the aims of the study to add clarity to the brief and a deeper understanding of the subject. It will show what can be achieved and how it can be achieved. It will provide assurances on the quality of the information and offer testimonies from previous clients who have commissioned similar types of work. It could include a description of the team that will carry out the research and it will have a timetable and a detailed breakdown of the cost.

The devil is in the detail in a document of this kind because it indicates to the reader the quality of work they will receive. Spelling and grammatical errors could flag up concern that there will be lack of attention to detail in the project itself.

The research company will typically be given about a week to prepare the proposal. This is not to say that a full week will be spent on the document; rather an elapsed time of a week will be required to get the proposal together whilst other work is being carried out.

Inevitably there will be some standard parts of a proposal document that can be cut and pasted. However, if the document looks to the reader as if it has been pieced together without much forethought, that will again be indicative of lack of interest from the research company.

In the sections that follow we present some thoughts as to the different chapters that could be included in a proposal.

The introduction

The proposal should have a title page and table of contents. In a lengthy proposal, the first section could be a summary, but more usually the first page of text will state the background and circumstances that have led to the research project being considered. The introduction will resonate if it contains information that the research company has found from initial research on the internet or through preliminary interviews. These insights and demonstration of interest in the subject will be highly effective in selling the proposal to the reader.

The scope

Before describing the objectives of the study it will be necessary to define its scope, and here we would expect to see a statement of which geographical areas will be covered and who the target respondents will be. Sometimes it is important to state what will not be covered in the study.

The objectives

Next is the section on objectives. This is important for the research sponsor as it is a statement of what they will receive from the investment. Typically the research would be given an overall goal such as: 'to assess the market for weather forecasting services amongst electricity generating, transmission and distribution (retail) companies in the United States'.

A more detailed listing of the many research objectives would then follow. For example, here are just three specific objectives that were listed in a weather forecasting services study.

1 To gain an understanding of how weather affects business operations of energy companies in the three target markets and their key weather information needs (that is, the perceived importance of the weather to their business and business planning processes and the type of products/services they need).

2 To gain an understanding of the extent of weather information usage and the nature of that use (that is, what they use it for, how and why). This would include: where they get their existing weather information from, how it is delivered, the problems they encounter, how much they spend, and if they do not use weather information, why not.

3 To assess the perceived future demand for weather information products and services in the target energy markets (including, do respondents perceive they will use weather information more or less in the future?).

The methods

To the researcher, the methods section of the proposal is vitally important. If the researcher gets the methods wrong, the objectives will not be achieved. The client will certainly be interested in the methods but much will be taken on trust. If the researcher says that 200 telephone interviews will answer the questions, the client may well accept this, as the research company is supposed to be the expert.

In the methods section the researcher may begin with a brief overview of the approach and the factors that have influenced the design. It is not unusual in a research programme to have an eclectic range of methods, including secondary research (desk research) that supports the primary fieldwork. The fieldwork could have a qualitative phase, perhaps comprising depth interviews or focus groups. If there is a quantitative stage it will be spelled out in detail, arguing the reasons for choosing online over telephone or face-to-face interviews. The size of the sample and any quotas for certain groups of respondents will be stated.

The research team

It is usual to describe the credentials of the research team that will carry out the project. Typically the proposal provides a summary of each person's qualifications, their experience in the field of study and their responsibilities in the project.

Timing and costs

By the time the research sponsor arrives at the section laying out the timetable and the costs, the project will most probably be won or lost. Of course the price of the research is important, but market research is not a commodity product. There are significant differences among research suppliers and this is recognized by clients. It is not a business where the cheapest product always wins. It is quite normal to give a detailed breakdown of the costs to show how they have been built up.

SUMMARY

The idea of carrying out market research may ferment within a sponsoring company for a number of weeks before a commitment is made to obtain proposals. In briefing an agency the client should try to give answers to a number of questions:

- What action will be taken when the research is completed?
- What has caused this problem or led to this opportunity?
- What is known about the area of research already?
- Who are the target groups for the research?
- What specific information is needed from the research?
- What is the proposed budget?
- Are there any initial ideas for the research method?
- Are there any reporting requirements?
- When are the findings required?

The market research supplier will prepare a proposal (the return of brief) after weighing up what information is required, the accuracy of information required, the budget and the timing. With these four factors in mind, a written proposal is prepared that covers the following issues:

- an understanding of the problem;
- the scope;
- the objectives in broad terms and in detail;
- the method that will be employed to achieve the objectives;
- the credentials of the researchers;
- the timetable;
- the fee.

The quality of the proposal plays a large part in whether or not the market research supplier wins the project.

Uses of market research

All companies and organizations need intelligence to survive and grow. Intelligence is obtained in many different ways and is not always received at the same central point within an organization. This is one reason why market research is so valued, as it is systematic, organized and specific to a goal. Good market intelligence can have a huge return on investment. A market research study costing between $40,000 and $200,000 (a typical expenditure range for many market research studies) can generate or save many times that amount in extra customer revenue or the avoidance of a bad investment decision.

There are many reasons why market research is used; however, the most fundamental is to help an organization better understand its markets so that it can make sound decisions about future direction. Research reduces risk and leads to more informed decisions. It is very easy for an organization to make assumptions about its markets, its competitive position and its customers. A systematic analysis of the market will challenge or confirm internal anecdotal knowledge and, because it is objective in the sense that it is collected independently, it should be more believable.

Market research can be used to help almost any business decision. What changes should we make to the workforce? (An employee attitude survey would be a good starting point.) How can we increase profitability? (A pricing survey would be extremely useful.) What sales budget should we have for next year? (A survey of customers' views on the market would help.) Market research has a role to play almost anywhere there is a substantial question to be answered in an organization. There are, however, four important applications that account for most of the market research surveys that are carried out, and these we discuss in this chapter:

- understanding markets;
- understanding customers;
- understanding and developing the offer;
- positioning the brand and communications.

Understanding markets

It is surprising what scant knowledge many companies have about their markets. It isn't essential that a company knows the precise size of the market into which it sells its products but it is certainly helpful, if only in broad figures. Without an understanding of market size, it is difficult for a company to understand its position within a market and to know how much potential remains available for it to attack.

The term market size comprises two elements – the served available market (SAM) and the total available market (TAM). In most markets, the number of ultimate consumers has not reached a ceiling and there will be an opportunity to grow. Take for example the market for bottled water; it competes in the wider market of soft drinks and even competes against water from the tap, which is drunk for free. The served available market in this case is the current market size for water sold in bottles. The total available market is the broader potential, assuming that inroads for bottled water are possible into other types of drinks consumed.

Without knowledge of the market size, a company cannot plan its future with confidence. Market-size data provide an understanding of the potential for expanding sales and for increasing market share. Market-size data tracked over a number of years indicate trends in the market. Understanding market size becomes especially important when a company is entering a new market as this will determine whether the investment and risks of entry are justified.

Market size is seldom a single figure. Markets are made up of segments or groups of different products and it is important to show the breakdown of the market size according to the different products that constitute the market, the gender of buyers, their age, the geographical regions where they live, and in the case of business-to-business markets, the industry verticals and size of companies that buy the products.

There are many sources of intelligence on market size. Government statistics, trade associations and published reports can provide instant figures. Computations can be developed to estimate the size of a market, for example by obtaining statistics on the number of consumers of a product and multiplying by their average consumption of that product in a year. Alternatively, estimates of market size can quickly be arrived at by assessing and summing the sales of the major suppliers. A rough and ready figure will usually suffice in the first instance as it can be refined and improved over time when more intelligence is obtained.

Market-assessment studies are commonly used to explore opportunities in new geographical regions or new segments of the market where the product hasn't been sold before. Equally, they could examine a completely new opportunity such as the market for a new product that is being sold to completely new customers. These are occasions when a company needs objective intelligence to make informed decisions about the levels of risk, the likelihood (and timescale) of rewards, and to make a more accurate evaluation of the level of investment that will be required for a venture to succeed.

Understanding customers

There have been times in the past when, with products in short supply, customers have been taken for granted. This can still be the case today if a supplier has a monopoly and doesn't feel the need to care about its customers. More enlightened companies know the importance of putting customers at the heart of their business because:

- Two-thirds of customers say a positive customer experience results in them spending more with the company.
- Eight out of 10 customers say that they would pay up to 25 per cent more for a superior customer service.
- Three-quarters of those who switch suppliers/brands claim that this is due to a poor customer experience and service.
- More than half of those who recommend a company do so because of the customer experience rather than other factors such as price or product.
- Almost all of those who have had a bad customer experience tell others about it, mainly to warn them or stop them buying from the supplier.

Market research that focuses on customers is often referred to as 'the voice of the customer' (VOC) and can take many forms, from one-off surveys providing feedback on specific issues through to trackers that provide regular feedback from planned studies.

Customer-satisfaction programmes are among the most common types of VOC surveys. They have evolved over the years to include more than the simple measurement of satisfaction, looking especially at factors affecting customer loyalty and retention. The rationale for conducting customer feedback programmes can be seen in Figure 3.1, showing the link between loyalty and satisfaction outlined by JL Heskett.

Heskett suggests that only those customers that register the highest overall customer-satisfaction scores will stay loyal. These customers are not likely to switch to another brand/supplier and are most likely to be advocates through their own positive experience.

Crucially, customers who think a company or its products are acceptable (but not particularly special) and who give satisfaction scores in the moderate range of 7 or 8 out of 10, are vulnerable and could take their business elsewhere. These customers occupy 'the zone of indifference'.

FIGURE 3.1   The link between loyalty and customer satisfaction

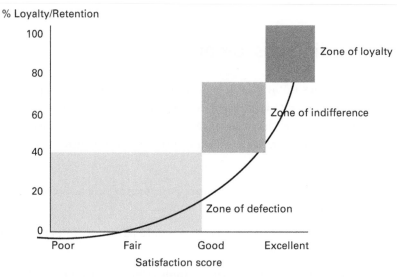

After JL Heskett (The service-profit chain)

Quite clearly if customers have had a bad experience and give a low customer-satisfaction score, they are certain candidates for defection to a new supplier if and when the opportunity arises.

Customer-satisfaction programmes usually include a range of measures to collect data about customer experiences at various points in the customer journey. A customer journey refers to all the occasions on which a supplier touches the customer. The journey usually begins when a promotion makes a customer aware of a supplier, and continues with many more touches as the customer makes enquiries, visits websites, engages in phone calls, tries the products and on some occasions tests its warranty. Customer satisfaction can be measured at any or all of these touch points or 'moments of truth'. The most common measures are:

- satisfaction with individual issues related to the product/service at different points on the customer journey;
- overall satisfaction score;
- likelihood to recommend score;
- ease of doing business score (most common on B2B markets).

A wide range of traditional research methodologies can be applied, depending on the type of insight required. Increasingly, consumer behaviours and perceptions can be monitored electronically through the use of web-based tools, and social media

FIGURE 3.2 Three levels of customer segmentation

monitoring can sometimes be employed to identify informal opinions and percep-tions from potential or current buyers. Read more about using market research to improve customer satisfaction and loyalty in Chapter 19.

While on the one hand every consumer is an individual in his or her own right, on the other hand groups of consumers have similar characteristics in terms of their demographics, their behaviour and their needs. Voice-of-the-customer surveys col-lect intelligence that can be used to group customers in different ways to see if a company's product or services can be more closely aligned to them. This is market segmentation and it is at the heart of all good marketing. Segmentation allows a company to understand which groups of customers it should be targeting and, of equal importance, to identify those whom it is not worth targeting, either because they have no interest in the products or because to do so would be unprofitable.

Segmentation can be carried out on three different levels (Figure 3.2). The most basic is demographic segmentation (referred to as firmographics in business-to-business markets) and is based on age, gender, income, the geographical location of the customer – the easily recognized physical aspects of a customer.

The next level is behavioural segmentation, more difficult to recognize because information about behaviour is not necessarily public knowledge. For example, if you run a supermarket it would be good to know when people buy wine because you would then be able to send them marketing communications at exactly the right time. It would be good to know if people who buy wine also buy other types of foods at the same time because this would help position these products close to the wine racks. It would be good to know if people are loyal to a certain brand of wine or switch between different brands as this would influence how the wine is laid out in the supermarket to encourage sales. Behavioural segmentation gets us closer to customers than simply knowing their age, their gender or their income group and can be a powerful means of better serving their needs.

The most difficult segmentation is based on understanding people's needs and unmet needs. If these needs can be recognized and customers can be grouped according to them, it can be a most effective way of positioning a company's products to sell more. Most people who drive cars have different needs from their cars. Some need a people wagon, others want fuel economy, and yet others may want their car to reflect their status in life. These needs will be many and varied and no doubt each car owner will have a mixture of requirements. Now, imagine that a car manufacturer understands these needs to the point it can direct powerful marketing messages that resonate with different groups of people: this surely would be more successful than a broader promotion aimed at appealing to everyone. Needs-based segmentations are most commonly used in consumer markets. In business-to-business markets, segmentations are likely to combine elements of firmographics and behaviour as needs are more difficult to recognize because of the complex decision-making units. Read more about using market research to segment markets in Chapter 17.

Understanding and developing the offer

The development of new products requires significant investment. For this reason the testing of customer reactions to new products and the gauging of their likely acceptance or rejection is an important use of market research. Market research can range from the testing of an idea or concept through to product trials. It also addresses the competitive environment, identifying and evaluating alternative products within the market that offer similar benefits to the buyer. Research can be used to establish acceptable competitive price points and to test marketing messages and key product benefits, delivering intelligence that will be more likely to ensure success.

Key issues that need to be identified in product development research are:

- competitor products, including their price, features, distribution and market share;
- likely customer acceptance or rejection of new or modified products;
- forecast of use of products;
- threats and barriers that will inhibit the products' success;
- optimum pricing of new products;
- reaction to packaging concepts;
- customer benefits derived from features and promotional messages.

It seems obvious that new product research will tap into the views of customers, and this is certainly important. However, there are occasions when the general public may not be able to contribute to product development so easily because people don't understand what technology can deliver. Imagine the difficulties Mr Sony would have had in the 1960s when testing attitudes to his Walkman. The only hi-fi known to the general public at the time was a stack of components and speakers that took up a whole wall of their lounge. They would have had difficulty imagining their need for music on the go as they walked or jogged around town. It is difficult for members of the public to suggest how they would like their needs fulfilled by new technologies when they have no idea whether things are possible. Telling a car company that they would like a vehicle that runs on fresh air is not particularly helpful.

However, there are more prosaic ways in which the general public can inform manufacturers about the products and services that they want. They could tell a detergent manufacturer that it is a nuisance measuring out the amount of detergent that is required in each wash, and this could lead to the development of detergent in dissolving capsules.

Product research often requires a methodology in which the consumer can experience the new product. For this reason qualitative methods such as focus groups and hall tests have traditionally been important. Today, the web presents the opportunity for respondents to view new products online and experience them visually, if not in the flesh. In this way, both qualitative and quantitative data on people's attitudes to new concepts and products can be collected quickly and inexpensively.

Market research is also used when there is a need for the testing of factors surrounding a product, such as pricing, packaging and promotions, even though there may be no new product to be developed. There are several specialist research approaches that can be used to identify the key product benefits and the value attached to those benefits. Conjoint and SIMALTO are two trade-off research tools for this purpose and are discussed in Chapters 11 and 16. The key component of these approaches is that they ask respondents to evaluate realistic product profiles incorporating a range of the product features and price options and choose which they would buy. These approaches are more sophisticated than traditional lines of questioning that simply ask people which they would prefer. Read more about using market research to launch new products in Chapter 23.

Positioning the brand and communications

In recent years we have seen huge changes in the importance of different communications media. Digital advertising has grown exponentially in the last few years and, according to PwC, will account for a third of total advertising revenue by 2018 (not far behind the amount spent on TV advertising). Decisions must be taken as to where to place advertising to meet the target audience, what messages will resonate and how to extract the most value from the advertising spend. Market research can be used to measure the effectiveness of advertising, whether this is related to the drive for sales or increasing awareness of the brand.

A significant amount of research is carried out to establish the most effective advertising media. Specialist market research companies such as AC Nielsen offer syndicated research on audience measurement, testing how many people watch television, read newspapers or notice billboards in the street.

Market research companies also help in the planning and execution of campaigns. Qualitative market research provides insights into what type of messages make sense to an audience and is also used to pre-test advertising copy and the adverts themselves. Quantitative research can be used to judge the effectiveness of a campaign if a study is carried out before a campaign begins and another after it is finished. In addition to pre-and-post market research campaigns of this kind, internal sales data and web analytics provide market intelligence that can show the impact of a campaign.

The use of market research in an advertising campaign quite clearly depends on the expenditure of the campaign itself. There would be little point in spending $100,000 on a pre-and-post study if the total expenditure of the campaign is only around $200,000.

Market research plays a role in making brands more effective. Brands distinguish one seller from another. A strong brand carries emotional attributes that come from the awareness and knowledge that people have acquired either through real experience or through word-of-mouth and promotions. These emotional attributes have values, and in a strong brand the customer will pay a significant premium for them, possibly insisting on the brand to the exclusion of all others. It is for this reason that a brand is often described as 'a promise delivered'.

Brands position companies and products in their markets, drawing customers to them according to their 'promise'. Brands can build strong positions in luxury and premium products just as they can in cheap and economy ones. Branding strategies incorporate the development of strong brands and the alignment of all activities, including advertising and communications.

In an overcrowded marketplace brands have become particularly important in determining a company's success. Brands help people choose products. Market research provides valuable insights on brands, from the development of their position through to decisions about their future. The purpose of brand research is to:

- identify brand perceptions, performance and uniqueness;
- position brands competitively;
- measure the effectiveness of brands;
- measure the effect of brand promotions in attracting customers;
- test brand positions and promises;
- track brands over time.

Identifying the current position of a brand is likely to involve all stakeholders. Customers are of course central to this research, but it may also be important to canvass the views of employees because everyone, both customers and employees, should be aligned to the same understanding of the brand position. At this early stage, the market research may use qualitative and quantitative methods to explore the brand position and arrive at measures amongst the wider customer audience. From the research, brand strengths and weaknesses will be identified as well as opportunities and threats. Following the development of the brand image, market research is used to test the new position and any promises that have been developed for credibility and 'best fit'. It is also useful to explore this in the competitive landscape to ensure the brand position is not already owned by a competitor. Finally a brand-tracking programme enables a company to measure the effectiveness of its brand and ensure that it is achieving the desired levels of awareness, interest and loyalty. Read more about using market research to test advertising effectiveness in Chapter 22.

Top tips

- There are two measures of market size that matter: the served available market (the SAM or actual market size) and the total addressable market (the TAM or notional market size). Try to get measures for each.

- When assessing a market size, get a fix on it from as many angles as possible – the supply-side as well as the demand-side. These cross-checks will raise everyone's confidence in the result.

- Remember when asking customers about their levels of satisfaction that the range of responses for 90 per cent of people will be ratings of between 7 and 9 on a scale from 0 to 10 (where 10 is completely satisfied). This means that a difference in satisfaction scores of 0.2 or more between one group and another is usually significant.

- When carrying out new product research, remember that the predictions of future sales are made difficult by two factors. On the one hand, people can be generous with their estimations of how likely they are to buy the new product because they don't have to actually do so. On the other hand, they haven't been subjected to the promotions and conditioning that will ultimately affect their likelihood to buy.

- Measuring the influence of a brand on the buying decision is hard because many people understate its effect. Use market research to assess the strength of brands by measuring levels of awareness and values associated with the brands.

SUMMARY

Market research is the systematic collection and analysis of intelligence to help inform business decisions and to reduce business risk. Every day, business decisions are made that require managers to have a general understanding of the markets in which they operate. Many companies are moving beyond their home territories into new markets and for this they require independent and accurate intelligence to guide their expensive investments. Market research has a role to play in all business decisions, but particularly in:

- Market assessment: Understanding the market size and structure enables companies to determine their market share and that of the competition. Measurement of the different segments of the market enables companies to identify opportunities and threats.

- Voice-of-the-customer research: Understanding customers is critical to all businesses, and market research shows how to build customer satisfaction and loyalty. The results of customer-satisfaction surveys can be used to segment the market and find groups of customers with behaviours and needs that are most aligned to a company's products and services.

- New product research: The word 'new' is one of the most important in the marketing vocabulary encouraging people to buy and test products. Market research plays an important role in identifying unmet needs and testing attitudes to new products, new pack designs and new ways of reaching customers.

- Communications and brand research: Market research plays an important role in helping businesses identify how to make the most of their promotional budgets. Media research points to the effectiveness of television, press, posters and, most recently, the internet as places to advertise. Market research can test advertising concepts and campaigns, and help develop and track the effectiveness of brands.

PART TWO
Qualitative research

Qualitative research

What is qualitative research?

Most market research projects can be described as either qualitative or quantitative. A qualitative project, as the name suggests, seeks depth and quality from the usually small sample in contrast to quantitative research which is very much about larger samples and measurements.

There are no hard and fast numbers that identify the break between qualitative and quantitative research. In general anything with less than 30 to 50 respondents is qualitative and anything over 100 respondents is moving into quantitative territory. There is something of a grey area in between.

Researchers can use focus groups or extended interviews to obtain insights that may not be possible in a larger, more structured survey. Open-ended questioning that explores behaviour and attitudes enables a moderator (that is, the interviewer) to test hypotheses and seek explanations. The ability to dig deep and use probing techniques is made possible with qualitative research.

Depth interviews can use laddering in which the interviewer keeps asking the question 'Why?' until it is felt that the real answer has been given. Projective techniques, videos and products can be shown. Such interviews and discussions are engaging because they are more conversational and as a result can easily last 30 minutes or an hour without a respondent feeling bored or strained. Respondents can take their time and think about the subject. They have the time to talk things through or tell a story that could not be accommodated in a tighter, structured, quantitative study.

The small samples mean that qualitative researchers cannot state the accuracy of their results. This does not mean that qualitative researchers cannot arrive at the truth. Very often the answer becomes clear after just one or two focus groups even though it isn't possible to express this result within statistical bounds.

There is a high level of dependency in qualitative research on the moderator as they do most of the interviewing, building a capital of knowledge and adjusting the questions as the research progresses. The findings are based on the moderator's interpretation and this means that he or she plays a much more important role than in quantitative research. In quantitative research the roles of the interviewers and the data analysts are quite separate.

The tools of qualitative research

The moderator has access to three important tools for qualitative research – the depth interview, the focus group and ethnography.

Depth interviews

Depth interviews or extended interviews require discussion guides similar to those used in focus groups. The discussion guide is a relatively unstructured list of topics which acts as an aide memoir. If, during the discussion, interesting comments and experiences are shared, it may result in a temporary diversion which is not scripted in the questionnaire. The moderator plays a huge part in determining the success of the qualitative research.

During the depth interview the moderator takes some notes but more likely the interview will be recorded for subsequent transcription. This is another reason why it is difficult to carry out a large number of such interviews. Transcribing and analysing open text from more than a dozen or so interviews is tedious. The emphasis in qualitative research is always on the quality of the understanding rather than the precision of the result.

Depth interviews are discussed in detail in Chapter 7.

Focus groups

Focus groups comprise between 5 and 10 people who take part in a discussion led by a moderator. The respondents are carefully selected because they represent a target audience – this is the focus. The discussion takes place in a special venue with viewing and recording facilities. The interaction of the members of the group creates a sharing experience which encourages people to mention things that wouldn't otherwise surface. Respondents have the opportunity of listening to the answers of others which gives them time to reflect and make insightful comments of their own. It could also result in a debate if people take opposing views and this in itself can help build an understanding of the subject.

There are potential problems in running focus groups. Bias can be introduced if someone makes a comment and they are articulate on a subject or perceived as an authority by other group members. In these circumstances there is much pressure on the group to acquiesce and fall in with the views that have been expressed. Some respondents can dominate the discussion while others sit back and say little. All this requires careful handling by the moderator.

The findings from two, three or four focus groups can sometimes provide a clear response so that there is no need to proceed further with a quantitative study.

Focus groups are discussed in detail in Chapter 6.

Ethnography

There has been a surge in interest among market researchers in ethnography. Ethnography borrows from anthropology, which is the study of humans in a specific environment. The ethnographer seeks to understand the behaviour of a group by living close to it so that they can observe and listen, as if a fly on the wall. We know that direct questioning can sometimes elicit acquiescence or answers that respondents believe are socially desirable. Behaviour can give more honest answers but we have to be prepared and able to observe the target in their home or workplace for some period of time for the truth to emerge. Cameras and prying eyes can bias behaviour as people are self-conscious about being closely monitored in this way. Over time the ethnographer hopes to melt into the background and be forgotten allowing the target audience to act normal.

Ethnography is discussed in more detail in Chapter 8.

When to use qualitative research

In a research project which explores a subject for the first time, researchers may need a qualitative stage to build their understanding. A small number of depth interviews, even as few as a dozen, may give a feel for the subject, the terminology which is used, constructs that need testing, how the audience sees the world and so on. This is vital information for designing a questionnaire in a subsequent quantitative stage. Qualitative research is very often phase 1 of an extended study.

Qualitative research sometimes stands alone. It could constitute a programme of depth interviews or focus groups commissioned to explore or test concepts such as new products or ideas for an advertising campaign. In the practical world of business, budgets and timetables may not stretch to a full quantitative programme and qualitative research may be all that is possible. This puts pressure on the researchers as they have to hope that the findings from the qualitative study are reflective of the findings that would be obtained from a much wider audience. A cautionary note is needed here. Qualitative research should not be used as a low-cost dipstick which is an alternative to quantitative research.

The uses of qualitative research

Exploring attitudes and behaviour

A good deal of qualitative research is the first stage of a wider research programme in which the initial depth interviews or focus groups are to understand attitudes, delve into behaviour and examine the overall hypotheses.

Testing adverts

Advertising agencies frequently use focus groups or in depth interviews (IDIs) to get ideas for campaigns or to test advertising messages. The focus group is an ideal opportunity to show different ads and generate a discussion as to which has impact, relevance and communicates the appropriate brand position.

Developing concepts and new products

Focus groups are an excellent tool for exploring ideas for new products or getting reactions to prototypes of new products. The moderator is able to watch how people react to the concepts or new products, especially if they are able to pick them up and touch them. Focus groups can be used to show if the design of a product generates an intuitive reaction or if people need more information to use it. Questioning can be directed to specific aspects of the new product to find out attitudes to the feature.

New product research is discussed in more detail in Chapter 23.

Building a picture of a market

Qualitative research can be used to build a picture of the market through depth interviews with experts. A small number of open discussions with people who have an overview of a market can yield an understanding of its size and structure, the competitive environment, its growth prospects. Each of the people interviewed in this type of project could require a different checklist of questions depending on their interests and knowledge. For example, a manufacturer of products will see the market in a different way from retailers and distributors. A trade association will have a different view from a government regulator. However, all could contribute knowledge to a study and build a picture of market size and opportunities.

Carrying out qualitative research

It will be apparent from the above discussion that qualitative research requires a special skill. Qualitative researchers are empathetic and able to engage easily with respondents. They have a questioning mind and an ability to pose questions without creating offence. They have the skills of the chat show host but they are also highly commercial as most of the projects will be testing some business opportunity or problem. Many focus group moderators have studied psychology though this isn't a prerequisite for the job.

It goes without saying that qualitative researchers must be able to develop appropriate questions to guide the interviews. They must be able to pose those questions in a non-threatening manner. Most importantly they must be good listeners, all the time looking for answers that require further probing.

Once the interviews are completed the qualitative researcher must be able to make sense of a morass of data. The challenge in analysing qualitative research is coping with the myriad of pieces of unstructured intelligence which must be categorized and classified so that a picture emerges. The grouping of data into relevant classifications is the process of moving from the general to the specific. A balance must be kept between having a few groupings which are too broad through to a great deal of detail which may be too confusing.

The grouping of data will help simplify the findings but it may not produce a successful report. It is important to locate the data in a framework or model which will guide the research sponsor as to the most appropriate course of action. There are many theoretical models and frameworks which the researcher can use and finding the right one can be critical to the success of the qualitative project. Sometimes the best models are those developed specifically by the researcher from first principles. This movement from unstructured data to structured reporting requires critical thinking skills on the part of the qualitative researcher.

Good qualitative researchers may work within market research companies running a qualitative research department or the market research company may be a specialist in qualitative research. In the case of the latter, the company is likely to be relatively small compared to those research companies carrying out quantitative studies. Indeed, small is beautiful in qualitative research and there are many excellent freelance qualitative researchers for hire.

The emphasis in this chapter has been placed on the moderator, the qualitative researcher who carries out the interviews and prepares the report. Supporting the qualitative researcher throughout the process are focus group venues. These independent centres have facilities for recruiting people to the venue and rooms where the respondents can assemble and ultimately sit comfortably while they are led through a discussion by an experienced moderator. The rooms have cameras and recording equipment for capturing the event and a one-way mirror which allows the client or the sponsor of the study to sit in a darkened room and watch the proceedings without the focus group delegates being able to see them. The moderator would explain that observers are watching the proceedings behind the mirror and that the findings are for market research purposes and will remain confidential.

Top tips

- When you know very little about a subject or market, consider focus groups for a quick education.

- Use focus groups to generate ideas, especially for new products.

- Use focus groups to test new products and advertising concepts but beware of bias that can arise from dominant respondents.

- Use in-depth interviews (IDIs) when you want to follow the complete story of a single respondent.

- Use IDIs when you want uncontaminated views on a subject.

- Use ethnography when you believe that important aspects of behaviour may not be disclosed in interviewing. Use it for new product development, packaging research, and understanding the context in which products and services are used.

- When commissioning qualitative research, look beyond the company and focus on the moderator – he or she will determine its success.

SUMMARY

The market research industry recognizes two very different approaches to research problems – qualitative and quantitative. Qualitative research uses small samples, sometimes involving only a handful of respondents. However, the interviews are in-depth, unstructured and aimed at obtaining insights. Focus groups are another important tool of qualitative research and they are used where debate and discussion can flush out interesting answers. Ethnography is a third tool for the qualitative researcher and brings about a deep understanding through the carefully planned observation of people's behaviour.

Qualitative research is often used as a first stage in an extended market research programme. It helps researchers understand the nature of the people who will be interviewed in a subsequent quantitative study. Their attitudes and the factors which influence their choice of supplier will be flushed out and can be built into a more structured questionnaire at a later stage.

Qualitative research can also be used in its own right to test new products, to develop ideas for new products, and to test advertising and promotions.

Carrying out qualitative research demands a special skill. The qualitative researcher often takes on the whole project from the design of the discussion guide, moderation of interviews, through to the analysis and presentation of the findings.

Desk research

A veritable gold mine

We are great fans of desk research. The trouble is that desk research sounds so boring compared to primary research. Primary research is about new discovery and exploration, asking questions and coming up with answers that no one has heard before. However, our role as market researchers is to discover the truth and collect data and intelligence on any subject that helps the marketing task.

Desk research is the study of secondary sources of data – information that is already available either in the public domain or within the private confines of an organization itself. It is always surprising that this goldmine of intelligence can sit underneath our noses and yet be ignored while preference is given to carrying out a specially tailored survey. There is no reason why desk research shouldn't be every bit as exciting as primary research. There is much satisfaction in building a complex jigsaw from the many bits of disparate information that is commonplace in desk research studies.

The expert desk researcher can quickly and inexpensively dig out data from a wide variety of sources to answer many research objectives. So why do we spend so much on primary research? It may be that we are suspicious of the secondary sources because we had no involvement in their compilation. It may be that the data we are looking for is not in quite the form we require. It could be that we have not searched long enough or dug deep enough to see if this information is already available. Sometimes, desk research seems too easy. A big decision surely needs a lot of money spending on it and merits an original piece of research. It is not necessarily so.

If desk research is such a valuable tool, why isn't it offered more frequently by market research suppliers? The answer is twofold. First, it is very difficult for a market research supplier to commit to meeting the objectives of a brief by proposing a desk research project. Until the desk research is carried out, the research supplier cannot know exactly what is available and it is not in a position to expend time and money to find this out until commissioned. So desk research as a stand-alone research method is a risk to a market research company. Second, and perhaps cynically, there is far less money in carrying out a desk research study than a fieldwork survey.

Market research suppliers are survey organizations and are organized to carry out interviews, which they do very well.

Desk research on the other hand is an ideal task for the in-house or do-it-yourself researcher. In fact, if more desk research was carried out, it could negate the necessity for many an expensive fieldwork survey. A couple of days of desk research can have a very big yield.

Desk research is a term that is used loosely, and it generally refers to secondary data or that which can be collected without fieldwork. To most people it suggests published reports and statistics, and these are certainly important sources. In the context of this chapter the term is widened to include all sources of information that do not involve a field survey. This most certainly will include searching the internet, but it could also include digging into and analysing internal sales statistics, tapping into private archives, speaking to people at trade associations or carrying out interviews with experts.

Before we talk about public sources of desk research, it is worth emphasizing that much useful information sits in the computers and files of the very companies that are seeking the data. This information could be in sales reports, in sales statistics or in a customer-relationship management system (CRM). With some imagination, this data could be re-worked to produce a valuable picture.

One of the most important sources of data within a company is the customer database (which could also be extended to include potential customers). This source of intelligence is always worth analysis, especially if it is populated with sales data. Questions that can be answered from such a simple source are:

- How many customers do we have?
- Where are they located?
- How much do they buy?
- How regularly do they buy?
- What do they buy?
- What is the average price they pay?

If the database is more sophisticated it may include information on how long particular customers have been buying from the company, how frequently they are visited by the sales team and which competitors also supply them. Our first plea is to make sure that there is no desk research lurking undetected inside the sponsoring company before moving the search to the wider and more expensive outside world.

An important principle of desk research

Before we begin to explore the different sources of desk research, it is worthwhile establishing an important principle. Although Google has made our desk research task so much easier, we cannot assume that what we are looking for will be handed to us on a plate. Let us imagine for example that we want to find out 'how many organizations in the United States carry out leadership training'. If we pose this as a simple question within Google it will deliver over 5 million results in 0.7 seconds. If we then lock the same search string with inverted commas (by doing that Google will only look for any reference for this specific request as it is stated in its entirety) we get no results. We can play about with the search strategy by searching for 'number of organizations' + 'leadership training' but we still won't find what we are looking for. Does this mean that desk research has failed us in answering this question? What it does mean is that what we are looking for is not going to be provided in a simple and obvious form and we will have to search for it in a more sophisticated way.

After some further research we may find that the organizations that are most likely to carry out leadership training are those employing more than 1,000 people. We may even get an estimate as to how many large organizations send their managers on leadership training courses. We can then begin to explore how many organizations there are in the United States employing more than 1,000 people and use this as a basis for estimating how many might use leadership training. Our finding will be an estimate but it will be one based on reasonable assumptions that may be good enough to give us the answer that we are looking for.

The principle we encourage market researchers to think about when using desk research is: believe the answer is out there somewhere; it is simply a question of thinking through as many search strategies as possible that will deliver the answer. We also encourage market researchers to obtain as many different fixes as possible on the answer so as to check it out and make sure that it is a very good estimate. Just because something is in print in a publication mentioned on the internet does not necessarily mean that it is correct.

Sources of sources: the high-level view

At the top of many a Google search is a link to Wikipedia. This amazing encyclopaedia provides excellent background on subjects that the researcher may be exploring. It is written collaboratively by anonymous internet volunteers and, therefore, some would say it has to be treated with caution. However, it does enjoy public scrutiny, which means that if anything is seriously wrong, it will be rectified or removed before long. There are nearly 5 million articles in the English language and 36,000,000 pages of information. If *Encyclopædia Britannica* required its own bookshelf for the complete set, Wikipedia would need a whole house. Wikipedia is a treasure trove of information and is an early stopping-off point on most studies.

The United States has led the world in the collection and dissemination of business information for many years. The Central Intelligence Agency uses its expertise on our behalf to bring together basic intelligence that began as the National Intelligence Survey and is now an online Factbook that can be examined country by country (**www.cia.gov/library/publications/the-world-factbook/index.html**). This website provides summaries of 267 countries in the world. For most countries there is a description of the geography, the people and society, the government, the economy, energy, communications and more. For market researchers looking at a global picture, it provides an excellent starting point for understanding the different geographies of interest.

Industry experts

The downside of having the internet as a research tool means that we all too often fail to pick up the phone and speak to a person – which was essential only a few years ago. This very obvious and simple device for getting a quick answer to a question is too little used nowadays and we encourage it as a source.

In any industry there are people who are living repositories of intelligence because of their involvement over years. These experts can readily be located through the internet as they write articles on the subject, make presentations, sit on committees and advise on legislation that might affect the industry. These people are knowledgeable and passionate about their subject and an intelligent discussion, especially one that rewards them with some titbits of information in return, will be very well received. Their contact details can be found by straightforward internet searches or on LinkedIn.

The internet

Accessing information via the internet is the modern alternative to hours spent in libraries. For market researchers, the internet has two important sources of information: the sites that companies, organizations and individuals have created to promote or communicate their products, services or views, and user groups made up of people who have an interest in a particular subject.

The World Wide Web is estimated to contain 5 billion pages of indexed accessible information. The problem is not the volume of information but finding the tiny bit that is needed in this ocean of data. Fortunately for researchers, search engine technology has increased by leaps and bounds, and an appropriate word string in a search engine such as Google, Bing, Yahoo or Ask will usually deliver thousands of hits. This too is a researcher's problem, for who ever looks beyond page three of these listings? Although Google rules as a search engine in most of the Western world, it does not enjoy dominance in China, where Baidu is the leading player, or in Russia, where the largest search engine is Yandex.

Search engines use programs based on a spider or a crawler that looks for key words or a word string in the billions of pages. The results are copied into a huge database (an index or list of information) and we are presented with the summary contents of the search at each site together with a hyperlink, from which a click takes us to the reference. Metasearch engines such as Dogpile or Excite use several search engines all at once, and then blend the results into a convenient form, such as listing the references in declining order of appropriateness to the search request.

In this massive sea of information it may be difficult to find what we require because:

- We are using the wrong search strategy – a different word or arrangement of words may yield more precise hits.

- We are using the wrong search engine – even the very best search engines do not cover all the pages on the net so the vital piece we are looking for may never be uncovered. A different search engine could produce a different result.

- We are using the wrong word – the use of the American spelling of 'tires' would miss out on web references to the British spelling of 'tyres'.

- The information we are looking for may not be available in the precise form we are hoping for. A search for the volumes of tyres bought as original equipment by Ford may come to naught, but it would be easy to derive the figure by finding out the number of Ford cars produced per year and multiplying by five (one per wheel plus the spare).

A search strategy with a suitable arrangement of words may well hit the bullseye and locate the information that is being sought. When typing in the search string, it may be helpful to use quotation marks to enclose the phrase so that 'world health organization' will only deliver references to those three words in that combination. Without the inverted commas, most search engines look for each of the three words separately and would deliver hundreds of thousands of irrelevant references to world, to health and to organizations. (Note that the internet is indifferent to capital letters.)

As we have mentioned earlier in this chapter, thinking laterally is an important principle of desk research using the internet (see section above). Avoid using very common terms (for example, internet or people) as this will lead to thousands of irrelevant hits. Where possible, use a phrase (in inverted commas) or proper name to narrow the search and therefore retrieve a smaller number of more relevant results. If too many results are generated, it is easy to refine the word string in the search box and carry out an advanced search, or simply renew the search since, given the speed of delivery, new results will be on the screen in fractions of a second.

The most experienced researcher will still learn a lot from the advice provided on 'How to search on Google', where Google shares tips and expert advice to help improve an internet search.

For example, we researchers are often interested in data that can be found in Excel spreadsheets. Let's say that we were seeking statistics on employment in the construction industry. We could limit our search and make it more useful by using the word *filetype* followed by the type of file. In this case, filetype:xls + 'employment in the construction industry' would yield only a small number of hits but every one of them would have an Excel spreadsheet that contains statistics on employment in the construction industry.

Equally, if we are carrying out a study on the future of the automotive industry and we believe that there could be a good PowerPoint presentation on the subject, we could try to narrow our search by using filetype:ppt + 'future of the automotive industry'. In the same way, the word *filetype* followed by :doc, :pdf, will collect only files that feature a Word document or a PDF.

More often the search will start a trail that follows the links between related sites. The researcher must learn to surf from one site to another, bookmarking those that are useful for downloading or copying into a work file. Here it is worth emphasizing that a crucial rule of desk research is always to note the reference of the data. Referencing data allows its credibility to be judged and it facilitates re-examination.

Online market reports

There are a number of companies producing reports on a range of products and markets that are available for purchase by anybody. These multi-client reports can be a useful and inexpensive introduction to a subject.

The tables of contents of the multi-client reports are available free and there are many synopses, which may be sufficient for those requiring just an overview. The charges made for bought-in reports and similar sources range from the nominal to levels comparable to commissioning ad hoc research. Most fall within the $500 to $5,000 bracket. A good source of market research data, offering full or part reports, is **www.marketresearch.com,** which allows access to a collection of over a million market research publications from over 700 research firms.

Material such as abstracts, statistics and large directories are increasingly available on websites, though for anything useful you will probably have to pay a fee (for example information on the chemical and rubber industry can be obtained from RAPRA – the Rubber and Plastics Research Association – on a subscription basis).

Mintel provides reports on a range of fast-moving consumer goods (FMCG), financial services, media, retail, leisure and education. The company publishes hundreds of report titles covering the UK, Europe, United States and international consumer markets.

The press

The general, business and trade press are key sources for the desk researcher. As well as 'news' these sources include much background material, including special supplements on industries and markets. In the past, researchers relied on the clippings services of libraries and archive agencies but today's work is made easier by online search facilities on some newspaper sites. One of our favourites is the *Financial Times*, which has an archive facility available to everybody for simple searches and power searches of a wider archive for a fee.

Company data

Researchers need company data for competitor benchmarking, sourcing suppliers or building profiles of customers and potential customers. Only a few years ago company literature was a mainstay of product searches. Today company websites are brimming with useful information. They contain pictures of products, lists of distributors, data sheets, company histories, press releases and sometimes financial background. The information is nearly always more extensive and current than printed brochures and it is available in an instant. A request for information about a competitor could be put together in couple of hours and contain an impressive amount of material.

The US Securities and Exchange Commission (SEC) requires all US public companies (except foreign companies and companies with less than $10 million in assets and 500 shareholders) to file registration statements, periodic reports and other forms electronically, and anyone can access and download this information for free from its Edgar database on **www.sec.gov**. Searches can be made for individual companies or those within a standard industrial classification (SIC). The database allows access to all the reports that have been filed, including the most useful 10-K financial statements and directors' reports.

Financial information on companies is available in the United Kingdom from Companies House (**www.companieshouse.gov.uk**). The website of Companies House offers a searchable index that gives access to information on 3.2 million companies. Of these about 11,000 are public companies (PLCs), which issue shares, and of the PLCs about 2,000 are quoted on the Stock Exchange. Smaller companies file only limited information, and this can reduce the value of company accounts in niche markets.

Financial data can also be accessed via specialist websites such as DueDil in the UK and Hoovers throughout the world.

Government statistics

In most projects, the desk researcher will seek hard statistical data, and sooner or later this will point towards a government source. These cover most areas of business and social life.

A visit to the US Department of Commerce site on **www.commerce.gov** offers a vast source of information, from industry sector statistics to economic analysis to demographic data and research publications. There is a good search engine to help navigate through this very large site.

The United Nations has a very good statistics division and a number of databases that can be accessed for free. One of the web services provided by the United Nations Commodity Trade Statistics is called UN Comtrade (**http://comtrade.un.org/**), which provides import and export statistics for countries throughout the world. (There is a charge for some detailed drill downs.)

The Organization for Economic Cooperation and Development (OECD) has a Statistics Department (**http://stats.oecd.org**) that enables users to search for and extract data from various databases showing gross domestic product (GDP), labour market statistics, economic indicators and the like.

For the European Union, Eurostat is the office responsible for statistics (**http:// epp.eurostat.ec.europa.eu/**).

In the United Kingdom, the National Statistics website (**www.statistics.gov.uk**) contains a range of official UK statistics that can be accessed and downloaded free. The site allows searching by themes such as agriculture/fishing/forestry, commerce, energy, industry, education, crime and justice, the labour market and population.

One of the cornerstones of any government's statistical service, and a massive source of data for market researchers, is the Census of Population. The US Census Bureau (**www.census.gov**) has a site covering every aspect of the population, including all key demographics such as age, education, labour, computer ownership and use, and income (to list but a few subjects). Marketers use census output for segmentation by demographics and for survey planning (for example, setting quota samples). The census is also the basis of geodemographic analysis systems.

Trade and industry bodies

Almost every trade, no matter how obscure, has some collective body to represent its interests (and often publish trade publications). To meet members' needs, and for PR purposes, most of these bodies make available (sometimes to members only) considerable information about their industry. The organization and sophistication of these bodies and the volume of the information offered varies enormously.

Wikipedia lists over 400 industry trade groups in the United States and over 200 in the UK. Very often the easiest approach is to search for a specific trade association in a region, using a search engine such as Google. For example, a study of the Chinese automotive market could start with a visit to the association that represents Chinese automotive manufacturers. This is quickly found on Google (China Association of Automobile Manufacturers – **http://www.caam.org.cn/english/**) where there are up-to-date statistics on the outputs of cars and motorcycles.

Directories and lists

As market researchers we spend a lot of time on questionnaire design, and a whole chapter is devoted to it in this book. However, working out who should be interviewed and making sure that the right person is interviewed is sometimes overlooked or at least not given enough attention.

In a consumer market research survey this task can be sorted out by screening questions in an online questionnaire. The choice of the panel company will also have a very strong bearing on whether the right people are available for interview.

There are still a large number surveys that require lists of respondents to be prepared. A customer survey is usually dependent on a list of customers provided by the sponsor of the research. In many business-to-business surveys it is necessary to find target respondents by using directories or specialist list suppliers. Spending time on making sure that the list is a good one will speed the survey up, keep the cost down and ensure that the right person is interviewed. A market researcher therefore needs to be fully familiar with all potential sources of lists.

Directories are the staple diet of market researchers. They provide details of companies that either supply or consume goods and they are the usual source for preparing sample frames (lists of companies or people to be interviewed). The directories may also provide a profile of a company, detailing its size by giving the number of employees, or whether it is an agent or producer.

One of the most comprehensive general directories is Yellow Pages (**www.yellow-pages.com** in the United States and **www.yell.com** in the United Kingdom) because every company with a telephone number is given a free entry. These directories form the most comprehensive listing of small and medium enterprises (SMEs). Lists of companies entered in Yellow Pages can be bought for relatively small fees from Experian (**www.experian.com/**). By way of example, in the United States Experian offers lists of 110 million households and 40 million businesses. Lists can be ordered in hard or soft copy filtered by Standard Industrial Classification, company size (number of employees) and geographical region.

Other general directories that include larger companies than those in Yellow Pages include Kompass and Hoovers. The online facility of these directories allows entries to be abstracted using filters such as location, size of company and industry specialization. The directories can be extremely useful for carrying out counts of how many companies of a certain classification exist within a country. The search can usually be carried out on the website for no fee. Fees are incurred when data on a company is downloaded. As well as these general sources, most industries have their own specialized directories, which may have a better listing of suppliers and buyers.

If building lists from directory sources sounds too onerous, the task can be given to a specialist company such as SSI (Survey Sampling International) that is able to source lists of most types of people and companies in many parts of the world (**www.surveysampling.com/**).

The range of information available from desk research

Sources such as those outlined above can be used to obtain data on a large majority of the subjects likely to be covered in a market research project. These include those mentioned below.

The marketing environment

Markets do not exist in isolation and are shaped by environmental factors such as the state of the general economy, demographic trends, the legislative framework and various social factors. An understanding of these external factors is likely to be part of any full analysis of a market. The marketing environment is generally well documented, and desk research (rather than primary research) is the only practical source available. The economy, demographics and key social variables are all well covered by governments' statistical services and the many publications they produce. Other sources in this area include special reports (government and private) and press commentary.

Market structure and size

The structure of most business and industrial markets can be fully analysed through desk research. Sources include the general and trade press, directories, company financial data, published reports, trade association output and government statistics. We have already pointed to the rich sources in the government statistical sites of the United States (Department of Commerce) and Europe (for example Eurostat, UK National Statistics, DeStatis for Germany). Government statistics sites provide time series of data that are a basis for historical and future trend analysis.

These sources may not provide market-size estimates of the specific category of interest but, with ingenuity, approximations can usually be derived from top-down analysis (making estimates from a wider classification that includes the one of interest) or bottom-up estimates (aggregating sub-classifications). The skill in this sort of work includes bringing together disparate pieces of data from separate sources. For example, if a researcher has a reasonable idea of a market size in one country, it may be possible to make estimates for other countries by relating the known market size to readily available statistics on population, gross domestic product (GDP) or some other proxy that indicates the relative size of the market, such as electricity production. This type of data is widely available for nearly every nation state in the world.

Suppliers and brands

Data on suppliers and brands can be thought of as an extension of the sort of market structure analysis considered above, and may include profiles of major suppliers and their brands, marketing methods and advertising tactics, and factors making for success. Company websites are an obvious first source to be examined when researching suppliers and their brands. So too is the press (including trade journals), directories, company accounts and published reports. Advertising and trade literature (especially in technical markets) can usually be collected free and could add to the information obtained from websites. One important area of information that is usually outside the scope of desk research is consumers' attitudes to and satisfaction with suppliers. Generally this can only be obtained through primary research, although in some industries published reports may have relevant data.

Distribution and retailing

Retailing is one of the largest industry sectors and, as might be expected, is well covered by many online sources. Mintel produces comprehensive market research reports on retail and apparel. Forrester produces an annual report on The State of Retailing Online and a series of articles on online retailing. The large consultancy groups such as Deloitte and KPMG publish annual reports on the retail industry. Nearly every government statistical site has copious data on retailing within its country.

In most industries, distributors play an important role as they provide a cost-effective means of supplying and servicing small (and sometimes not so small) accounts. Distribution structures can vary considerably and some have many tiers, ranging from importers through to main distributors and local dealers. Sources that provide an analysis of these structures are much the same as those on companies and markets in general.

Products

Desk research can provide detailed product information. Websites are a first port of call as they usually provide illustrations and specifications of products that can be captured and downloaded. Trade publications in some markets compare products from alternative suppliers. Amazon and online retailers are another source of product details and prices. Product literature is often particularly relevant in technical markets and is a valuable source for analysing product features.

Visits to exhibitions and trade fairs to collect this literature are an example of 'near' desk research that can be used before moving into primary research. Pricing information may also be available from the sources just mentioned, although the difference between list prices and what is actually paid may reduce the value of such information.

Desk research is not usually thought to have a role in new-product evaluation, and certainly consumer reaction to a new product has to be established through primary research. However, the fate of other new launches can provide very useful information and can be accessed from the trade press and other sources.

Planning, recording and evaluating desk research

A plan is needed if the search for published data is to be efficient. A written plan is a help to desk research, whether it is utilizing library or online sources. Before logging on, you should specify the information sought in some detail, although flexibility and some ingenuity are also needed (for instance, looking for relevant data under wider or narrower classifications and creatively making connections).

The desk research plan should also include a timetable. How long should be spent on the desk research part of a project? This will depend on the breadth of the information sought, the type of data and the resources to be used. It is difficult to generalize. However, what can be said is that diminishing returns apply and after quite a short time the extra information gained falls in proportion to the time spent searching. Two or three days of focused concentration on a subject should yield a good deal of whatever can be found.

Once found, data needs downloading into files. The source of any data should always be recorded, so that its accuracy can be both evaluated and, if necessary, retraced. In long projects and repeat work, this will provide useful short cuts to the most valuable sources and ensure that the same blind alleys are avoided.

Information needs not only collecting but also evaluating. In part this is a matter of making judgements about its validity. We are often fooled into trusting information that is published. Once it is there in black and white, we assume that it must be correct. The experienced desk researcher learns that market-size figures that are published need to be cross-checked by using two or three sources, and frequently there are some serious anomalies.

Most secondary data accessed through desk research was originally generated through primary research. Thorough validation requires going back to the source and understanding the methodology used: was the market-size figure based on some sort of census, on a sample survey, on some crude formula using a ratio, or merely on anecdotal evidence? Where possible two or more sources for the same data should be compared. But some sense of proportion has to be kept. It is simply not possible to validate all the data thoroughly and nor is it necessary to do so – as previously mentioned, market researchers can work within quite wide bands of accuracy for practical purposes.

As well as validating the information, evaluation also includes its integration into a meaningful whole. Looking for linkages and patterns can and should be part of the desk research process, with initial material often pointing to other sources and subjects. That is why we stated earlier that although planning is needed in desk research, flexibility should be retained. Subsequent analysis and integration of data will be facilitated by good note and record keeping when the material is collected and, if this is voluminous, by reasonably organized filing.

The limits of desk research

Desk research can be very fruitful. However, it has its limits and it may only provide part of the information sought in a project. As previously suggested, where a mix of desk and primary research is required, there is everything to be gained by carrying out desk research first and then filling the gaps through interviewing. In this way, the more expensive primary sources are used only where they are essential.

One limit of desk research is its unpredictability. At least for the novice or where the subject area is unfamiliar, there can be no certainty of what the desk research will yield and what gaps will remain. For this reason, desk research is often a DIY task for the in-house researcher. At worst a short desk research exercise will cost very little, and it may save on much more expensive fieldwork. Unlike a market research company, a do-it-yourself researcher can live with little to show for the desk research stage.

Some information is also in principle not available from desk research, and with experience this is obvious from the start. Generally this includes attitudinal data such as opinions on a company's service, attitudes to novel product or views on specific adverts.

SUMMARY

There have always been volumes of data available to market researchers via secondary data (that which is already in the public domain). The internet has considerably expanded the sources and the ease of accessing the data. There are many sites that are rich in data for market researchers, and government statistical agencies or trade associations often own these.

A quick search on the internet will show if there is a published report on a subject, usually supported by a synopsis that could give sufficient information for a quick assessment of a market.

In addition to becoming familiar with favourite websites, the market researcher should develop search strategies that deliver useful information.

Desk research is an excellent tool for piecing together pictures of a marketing environment – showing the market size, suppliers, the products that they make and the trends in the market. It is also a rich source of data on company information, and therefore useful for profiling both customers and competitors.

Often the market researcher must piece together disparate information from desk research to provide a picture of a market. This requires skill in searching as well as lateral thinking – to work out how one piece of information provides an answer to another.

The internet has revolutionized desk research. However, the market researcher should also remember that valuable sources of secondary data could be found in conventional libraries, in trade associations and from industry experts.

Focus groups

The focus group

The focus group is a research technique used to collect data through group inter-action on a topic. Essentially, it is a group experience comprising a small number of carefully selected people who are recruited to discuss a subject on the basis of their shared experience.

Focus groups have four key characteristics:

- They actively involve people.
- The people attending the group have an experience or interest in common.
- They provide in-depth qualitative data.
- The discussion is focused to help us understand what is going on.

Focus groups have traditionally taken place in a face-to-face environment, with all participants brought together in one location for a given period of time to discuss the research topic. However, technological advances have made it possible to bring groups together online, overcoming the barrier of participant proximity to the focus group venue. Online groups tend to adopt one of two styles: the 'live chat' forum or the 'bulletin board' group, which tends to remain open and live for several days but does not require participants to be logged in during the whole period.

The people that make up a focus group

Focus groups typically are made up of 5 to 10 people. The group needs to be small enough to allow everyone the opportunity to share insights, and yet large enough to provide group interaction and diversity of experience. Larger face-to-face groups inhibit discussion, as some delegates shy away from venturing opinions, while smaller groups may be limited in their pool of ideas. Bulletin style online groups afford the opportunity for a larger number of participants.

Commonality of experience and interest

Focus group participants have a degree of homogeneity, and this is important to the researcher. This similarity is the basis for recruitment, and indeed, specific requirements are usually necessary for attendance at the group.

It is common for researchers and clients to jointly identify the criteria that point to the individuals for focus group discussions. For example, a focus group examining people's attitudes to websites would almost certainly require them to have access to the internet and to use it fairly regularly (this would need defining).

Depth of information

Focus groups deliver qualitative data that is rich in words and descriptions, rather than numbers. The group provides the forum for discussion, and the group moderator (the researcher guiding the group) uses his or her skills to get the discussion going in order to flush out ideas, attitudes and experiences. The focus group is more than a group interview. The key is the interaction between the group members.

Online groups can be just as rewarding in terms of their output as a face-to-face group. The word count of an online discussion group can easily reach 10,000 words, which is as much as from a face-to-face discussion group and likely to be more focused on the subject (there is less pontificating and puffery when people write things down rather than speak them). The depth of insights from an online focus group is therefore very good, although there is inevitably less spontaneity than in a face-to-face group. Furthermore, it is impossible to see the interaction between people in an online focus group.

The topic for discussion

Questions in a focus group are carefully designed to elicit the views of the participants. A discussion guide is prepared prior to the group meeting and the group moderator uses this as an aide memoir of what must be covered. Careful design of the guide ensures a logical flow of conversation around the topic area and a clear focus for the discussion.

The topic guide is reflective of how groups operate. Groups always start with an introduction from the moderator explaining the purpose of the meeting and what can be expected to happen. Encouragement will be given to people to speak their mind but to try not to speak over each other so that the recording picks up everyone's comments. Participants are then asked to introduce themselves and perhaps say a few words about their experience with the subject in hand. This serves to get people talking and comfortable enough to speak about their opinions and experiences as the discussion progresses. Questions are tossed in by the moderator and the group members are encouraged to comment, debate and adjust their views so that the subject gets covered from all angles, and points of dispute are reconciled as far as is possible.

In online groups it is necessary to be more prescriptive about the questions that are posed. There are a smaller number of questions posted in bulletin style groups and a maximum of 15 questions can normally be covered in a day's session. The bulletin-style online group can have a larger number of participants (up to 30 can be accommodated) and quick mini polls can be used to generate debate in addition to the posted questions.

When to use focus groups

Focus groups are used to identify and explore behaviour, attitudes and processes. They are best used to throw light on the 'why?', 'what?' and 'how?' questions. They can be used in three ways in the research design:

- Stand-alone method: where the focus groups are the sole data collection method and they serve as the principal source of data.

- Supplementary to a survey: where focus groups are used to enhance alternative means of data collection. Typically this would be as a precursor to a quantitative stage – determining the issues to be covered in the structured interviewing and giving insights into the problems or opportunities that are being researched.

- As part of a multi-method design: where studies use several sources of data collection and no single method determines the use of the others.

When focus groups are used as the sole source of data, the objectives will be explorative and diagnostic (what is the problem, how can we solve it, how will the market react?). When it is important to also get a fix on the number of people that think or behave one way or the other, a multi-method design will be required with a quantitative stage to follow.

Focus groups are especially useful for researching new products, testing new concepts or determining 'What would happen if...?'. They work because the participants can consider the points raised by other members and, as they think about the implications of issues raised, further ideas may be sparked off that would remain untapped in a one-to-one interview. This interaction creates a 'dynamic', as if the eight or nine separate brains have been wired together, with ideas bouncing from one to the other in an easy fashion and issues being challenged until a general consensus is achieved.

Typical applications for focus groups are:

- to unravel complex processes from the basics, for example a complicated buying process;

- to identify customer needs, that is, where there is a complex interaction of factors influencing motives;

- to identify how products are used;

- to test new products, that is, where something needs showing to people;

- to explore a concept, perhaps with stimulus aids so that people can visualize what it would look like;

- to explore and identify issues of satisfaction (or dissatisfaction) for customers, staff or suppliers;

- to explore perceptions of brand and service elements associated with the brand.

The decision to carry out focus groups or individual depth interviews is based on several factors. Focus groups are not always practical, and within the business community it has to be accepted that geography often precludes the bringing together of participants. For this reason depth interviews are and will remain (until multiple verbal/visual link-ups become feasible) the most widely used qualitative research technique.

In general, focus groups are not the preferred option where:

- measurement of size and distribution is required;

- the sample base is widespread and small;

- there is a need to protect participants from possible bias introduced by others;

- the topic area is sensitive, for example requiring disclosure of sensitive issues that could be an embarrassment in the company of others;

- participants require preparation to answer knowledgeably;

- participants need to be able to show the researcher something in their home or business.

Areas of special consideration

The biggest potential problem of focus groups is the bias that can occur from the small number of people taking part, their interaction with each other and the subject of discussion. These need not create problems if they are considered beforehand.

Culture

In many cultures, particularly in Western countries, people have less difficulty sharing their views with others and engaging in debate even though their views may differ from those of others within the group. The West has a culture of free speech and therefore group discussion comes naturally. However, this cannot be assumed for all cultures. In many Asian countries it is considered rude and inappropriate to openly criticize products, services and suppliers. The natural response is to be polite and present a view that is expected. It is also more difficult to get a group dynamic amongst some Asian participants as the culture is to take everyone's views into consideration and to defer to the most senior person. We were reminded of these difficulties by an event in a focus group in Japan that was exploring attitudes to showers. Towards the end of the focus group the moderator (a Japanese lady) left the room to check with the client if any subjects needed further coverage. During her absence from the room, for nearly five minutes, the members of the focus group did not speak a word to each other. This would be unthinkable in similar circumstances in a Western focus group.

Sensitivity of the focus topic

Focus groups are an excellent tool for getting people to open up and for flushing out ideas. However, there will be subjects where the sensitivity of the topic is an issue.

There are many subjects related to personal hygiene, sexual habits or the bathroom that people may not want to discuss in groups. Such sensitive and potentially personally embarrassing topics are best discussed in a private, non-threatening setting, perhaps with the researcher being distanced from the participant through the use of self-completion questionnaires.

The effect of the group hierarchy

Every researcher has to recognize the inherent imbalance of authority in a group situation. In general, if people feel equality between the group members and the group moderator, they are more likely to be at ease and share their views in lively debate. For example, if you were tasked with researching the needs of people using hearing protection in the workplace (earplugs and ear defenders) and had chosen to use focus groups, you would have to think about the consequences of mixing plant workers, supervisors and purchasers in the same group. Plant workers may find it difficult to discuss their experiences in front of supervisors, particularly if some of their actions contravene company policy. Therefore, in planning focus groups, keeping participant types as similar to each other as possible facilitates more open and candid discussion.

Difficulties with disclosure

Some people find self-disclosure more difficult than others. People can experience self-doubt and lack confidence in expressing their views. Listening to others who are articulate and confident may make them still more fearful of showing themselves up. The group moderator needs to be sensitive to the differences among the group participants and help draw these out.

For example, focus groups with installers of central heating boilers may reveal practices that are considered sub-standard by other members of the group, and this may cause a group member to remain silent about his or her practices at work. Intimidation by more skilled, knowledgeable and confident plumbers may inhibit some group members and give a skewed view of plumbing practices.

Match of moderator

The role of the moderator is crucial to the success of the focus group. A skilled moderator uses social skills to settle people down and get them to open up. In face-to-face groups the body language of the moderator will help this process, including his or her attire. In most consumer groups the moderator dresses smart/casual to create a feeling of professional informality. However, if the focus group comprises accountants or members of the legal profession it might be more appropriate to wear a suit.

The match between the moderator and the group participants has been the subject of much research on how the credibility of the moderator is viewed by the group participants and how much this affects the group dynamics. The key point is that the moderator needs to be accepted by the participants and must have the ability to create a 'safe' environment where participants feel comfortable and confident to freely express their own viewpoints.

The age, gender and experience of the moderator may be an influence in some topic areas. In general, the moderator's standpoint will be one of a researcher, not an industry expert, and usually his or her detachment from the topic area is an advantage. However, in some sensitive topics, it may be necessary to match the moderator to the group participants – a female moderator for discussing feminine issues, a male moderator for a male group of heavy beer drinkers.

Planning and recruiting groups

Between 5 and 10 members normally constitute a group, though there are no precise rules as to the ideal number. If there are more than 10 people, and everyone has their say, over the hour and a half of the group each member, allowing for comments from the moderator, would contribute no more than 10 minutes of talking time.

As few as five participants can still be effective in a focus group since even with this small number there is sufficient scope for a dynamic to build and for the cross-fertilization of ideas to take place. These small groups (mini-groups) can be used where respondents are thin on the ground and the brainstorm effect of the focus group is still required.

In online focus groups, the number of people can be considerably more flexible. Online bulletin style groups can have as many as 30 contributors, whereas live chat groups will need to be limited to a maximum of 10–12, rather like the face-to-face group. The number of participants may limit the degree to which each participant feels engaged with the group, and certainly the volume of output each participant can be expected to read and consider when making their own contributions, but this should be balanced against the objectives of the research.

Number of groups

There are no hard and fast rules for deciding how many focus groups are needed to cover a subject. One focus group could give the right answer but who would know? Two focus groups is on the light side as there could be differences between the two groups that would raise doubts as to which was correct. To obtain a better feel and counter the possibility of a biased response, it is advisable to conduct three or four groups. If the number of groups goes beyond six or eight (with people of the same characteristic) the output from the groups becomes difficult to draw together and analyse.

With online groups, it is not unusual to conduct a one-off bulletin board style or even a series of groups that are distanced in time and have content that develops as each new group is launched.

Venues of groups

The venue for a focus group is only a consideration for the face-to-face group, and groups can take place in a in a number of different settings. It is common for specially designed viewing centres to be used for both consumer and business groups. Sometimes business groups take place in hotels, at conventions or at trade exhibitions, if these prove more convenient.

Venues need to be chosen to match the participants and should suit the expectations of the participant group. Specialist centres have many advantages. They provide facilities for good-quality audio and video recording of the proceedings. They are used to hosting groups and they have holding rooms where delegates can assemble before being seated. Not least, they have viewing rooms from which observers can see and hear the group through a one-way mirror.

The venue must be easily accessible, preferably well known in the area and with good car-parking facilities. The memory lingers of holding a group for independent pharmacists at a hotel in a city centre location where the directions to the hotel were poor and the local parking was an expensive public car park with no concession for hotel users. Focus group participants arrived late and annoyed, presenting an additional challenge to the moderator.

The room in which the group is held should be small and intimate. A consumer focus group may have a layout similar to a lounge, with easy chairs in a semicircle and a coffee table in the centre. A group of business participants is likely to be set up in boardroom style. The aim is to make the environment appropriate to the proceedings while at the same time being easy and relaxed.

The audio and video equipment for recording the groups should be checked beforehand. If the group is being conducted in a viewing centre, this will be taken care of by the venue; otherwise, the moderator will take responsibility for this.

Whilst we have stated that the online group location is not an issue for consideration, the location and availability of the participants are. Care has to be taken to ensure that participants can all speak the same language (online focus group aren't bound by country boundaries) and that they have the time and relevant technology to take part in the group. This is particularly important for the live chat-style group where all participants are required to be online at the same time for a given time. Using the bulletin-style group gives greater flexibility to the participants to log on at times convenient to them.

Getting participants to attend

Because focus groups rely on such a small number of participants, it is essential that care is taken to recruit the correct profile. The criteria for attendees must be decided at an early stage and turned into screener questions for a recruitment questionnaire.

Once commitments to attend the focus group have been received from participants, it will still be necessary to chase them up closer to the day of the event to confirm attendance. Bad weather, illness and other emergencies can always affect the turnout, so sometimes 12 people are recruited to ensure that 10 turn up. If by chance everyone turns up, a couple may be 'paid off' with their incentive and asked to leave as otherwise the group would be too big to generate an intimate discussion.

It always helps if the subject of the discussion sounds inviting. A good 'hook' helps. Of course, the recruiter needs to communicate enthusiasm for the event and to make the participants feel that the success of the group is dependent on their attendance.

For online groups, it is usual to send e-mail reminders to the participants just before the group is due to begin and to encourage any member of the group if he or she has not contributed within a given period of time after the group has gone live.

It is usual to give an incentive to participants to encourage their attendance. The incentive is usually financial and will vary according to the expectations of the audience, usually amounting to around a half a day's pay (in cash).

Top tips

- Use focus groups when you need answers to questions that you believe won't or can't be answered in more structured interviews.

- Don't assume that you can get all your answers from one or two focus groups. Sometimes focus groups provide the answers that you need, but in the main they offer insights that need quantitative research as a second stage.

- Spend time and thought on the recruitment guide for screening and inviting respondents to the focus groups. There is nothing worse than moderating or observing a group and finding out that some attendees shouldn't be there.

- Only consider a focus group if there are sufficient potential respondents within striking distance of the venue (around half an hour's travel time). You will need at least 50 prospects within this radius to get eight people at a venue at an appointed hour and date.

- Take care in choosing the moderator of the focus group. A successful focus group is heavily dependent on a skilful moderator. Good moderators put people at ease. They control dominant respondents and draw out those who are less forthcoming.

- One of the observers of the focus group should be a note taker. His or her notes will be available to you immediately after the focus group and you won't have to wait for the full transcription.

- Consider online focus groups whenever respondents are geographically scattered or thin on the ground.

The group moderator

Groups are led by a researcher whose role differs considerably from that of an interviewer. The group moderator's role is:

- To steer the discussion through a range of topics. There is usually an order to the 'unfolding' of these topics but there is sure to be some influence created by the spontaneity of the group itself.

- To act as a catalyst to provoke responses or introduce ideas. Sometimes the researcher should play devil's advocate or feign ignorance.

- To draw a response from those who are less responsive and curb those who attempt to monopolize.

In online groups, some packages allow the moderator to send a 'nudge' to a participant or trigger an e-mail in order to provoke a response to something someone else has posted. The challenge for the online moderator is to generate an environment that encourages all participants to read the posts of other group members.

The way questions are asked in a focus group is quite different from a conventional interview. Empathy must be created with the members, relaxing them and generating a lively discussion. A brief introduction explains the proceedings, including the recording on film (there is little chance of the moderator taking notes as he or she will be busy keeping eye contact with the group). It is then necessary to break the ice by asking members to introduce themselves and their experience with the subject.

Working from the topic guide developed prior to the group, the researcher moves the discussion from the broad to the particular. Members of the group are continuously encouraged to express their viewpoints and challenge the views of other group members. In this way all the issues unfold, supported by a discussion that gives a deeper understanding of the subject being researched.

Managing the group dynamics can be made difficult by a dominant personality who may attempt to take charge of the conversation or whose views colour those of other members. Equally there may be slow thinkers, introverts, wits, compulsive talkers and the indifferent. Bringing out the best from each without insulting or embarrassing anyone requires authority and tact.

Face-to-face groups and online live chat groups generally take around 90 minutes to administer, depending on the complexity of the subject and interruptions from videos or product presentations. Bulletin-style online groups can be spread over a period of a couple of days, though there is no requirement for simultaneous logging in by participants.

Tools of the group moderator

The group moderator will establish the stimulus materials prior to the group. The line of questioning will be defined through the topic guide, and any additional stimulus materials will be introduced at particular points in the discussion. This sounds easy, but it requires skill to ensure that the questions deliver the necessary answers. For example, although the main aim of using a focus group may be to find out why people do certain things, the way to do this may be by asking 'How?' and 'When?' or 'What?' This is because the question 'Why' may not have always been fully thought through and posing the question why may generate an answer that is a self-justification rather than the truth. Using how, when, what (as well as why) may get behind the question and help the researchers arrive at their own interpretation. As with any depth interviewing approach, most questions are 'open', to keep the conversation going and to get the fullest answer.

We have already explained the importance of asking people to give personal introductions to ease themselves into a conversational mode. It is also important to ensure that early questions are non-threatening so that participants feel comfortable. Good questions are conversational in nature; they use the vernacular of the participant and are easy to understand.

Group members are not always kept interested and stimulated only by questions. Stimuli of one kind or another may be introduced, such as:

- visual stimulus materials (for example, video, story boards, photographs, advertisements);
- auditory stimulus materials (for example, recordings and sound files);
- web interaction (for example, website navigation and searching patterns, electronic product simulations);
- product trials and demonstrations.

In addition to stimulus materials, there are a number of specific techniques that can be used in focus groups. Many of these are termed 'projective techniques' and are borrowed from the field of psychology. They are used to seek information on a topic by asking about a different or easier topic. They work because they circumvent potential barriers to expression and tap into different ways of thinking.

Brainstorming is a common technique used in many business meetings in which a long list of ideas is encouraged – anything goes, and the more the merrier. One of the ideas may offer something that can be developed and built upon. An important principle of brainstorming is saying what comes to mind without too much forethought. It is also closely linked to word association, where participants are asked to think of words associated with a product or brand.

Sentence completion is a development of word association where the moderator presents the group with an incomplete sentence that they are asked to finish. This can be carried out individually and introduced into the group for discussion, or the group can engage in discussion to complete the sentence jointly.

Word sorting is a technique where the groups are presented with a number of words or sentences and asked to sort them into groups according to the attributes of a product, brand or need. This is commonly used in advertising research for identifying associations with brands.

Developing a process is a group activity in which everyone would work together to come up with a process or campaign around an issue, for example getting people like themselves to buy a product. This method is also used to identify a customer's journey through interaction points with the company/brand.

Some subjects are difficult to express in words and picture drawing can be used to stimulate discussion. In a focus group with undergraduates, participants were each asked to draw a heraldic shield and divide it into four quadrants, each with a simple drawing to describe their life before coming to university, something that characterizes their disposition, what it feels like now they are at university and where they see themselves in the future. The foetus and the armchair in the drawings by two of the students (see Figure 6.1) were strong expressions of their feelings of safety and security at the university.

FIGURE 6.1   Drawings showing attitudes to a university

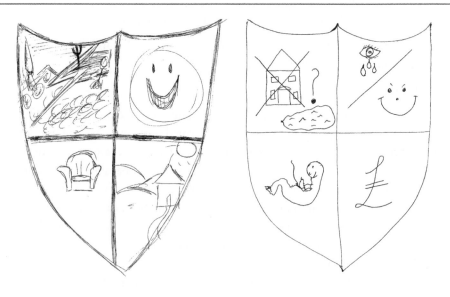

Other projective techniques that can be used in the focus group include:

- Creating fantasy: for example, if you had a magic wand and could change anything about the way you do your weekly shop, what would you change?

- Creating analogies/questions: for example, if this brand was a car, what would it be?

- Personification: for example, if this brand was a person, what would it be like, what gender, how would it behave? What would it look like?

- Futuristic imagination: for example, looking forward to the next five years, how do you think things will change in the way people book their holidays?

- Role play: for example, if you were the CEO of this company, how would you promote your products to people like yourself?

- Zaltman metaphor elicitation technique (ZMET): based on the theory that humans think in images, participants are asked to select a set of pictures that represent their thoughts and feelings about the topic of interest. The pictures are then important non-literal devices for uncovering deeply held, often unconscious, thoughts and feelings.

SUMMARY

Focus groups are typically carried out face to face and comprise 5 to 10 participants who have been recruited to join in a discussion on a subject of common interest. Developments in technology have overcome one of the greatest hurdles of the face-to-face focus group – participant locality. Focus groups can now be carried out online under several different formats – the longer-running bulletin board and the live chat forum. It is now possible to interview groups with participants based in different parts of the country or even across continents.

Whichever method is used, the critical element of a focus group is the steering of the discussion to generate meaningful debate around the research topic, with or without the input of other stimulus material. Under the guidance of a skilled moderator, ideas are flushed out and developed in a way that is not possible in one-to-one interviews. It is the group interaction that makes focus groups special.

The findings from focus groups, whether conducted online or face to face, enable us to obtain a deep understanding of behaviour, motivations and attitudes. Although they are based on smaller samples, the insights that come from group interactions almost always facilitate an understanding of the real issues. Quantitative measures may still be required to judge their importance.

A small number of focus groups with a target audience, typically four, will ensure that all the issues have been aired and that the possibility of bias in a group is minimized.

The three most important ingredients for successful focus groups are the recruitment of the correct participants, a skilled moderator and a well-designed discussion guide.

Careful screening at the recruitment stage ensures that people with the right characteristics are recruited.

The skills of the moderator will be used to open and direct the discussion so that everyone is included and all of the points of the debate are fully aired.

Depth interviewing

Interviewing implies formality, structure and purpose. It suggests that there is a list of questions to be asked and answered. It is, of course, a dialogue between people, so to that extent it is a conversation. Ordinary discourse need not take you anywhere, whereas an interview needs to elicit information. The asking of questions through interviewing is central in our lives, and it is therefore no surprise that it is one of the most common methods of enquiry in market research.

In this book, we divide research methods into the two traditional paradigms: qualitative and quantitative. Where the research sets out to measure and quantify, the interview will be structured with precise questions, a strict order of asking the questions, and answers that have been anticipated and accounted for with pre-coded responses. This type of questioning is covered in Chapter 13.

The depth interview gives a different perspective from the highly structured interview used in quantitative designs where numbers and spread of response are crucial. In practice, many market research studies lend themselves to a multi-method design, incorporating aspects of both qualitative and quantitative methodologies (see Figure 7.1). A customer-satisfaction survey might require depth interviewing at the front end of the survey to establish issues that people should be questioned about. A survey on product development might begin with focus groups to explore

FIGURE 7.1   Different types of interviews in market research unmet needs, followed by structured interviewing to measure the size of these needs, and conclude with depth interviewing to test the concepts.

Where insights and exploration are required, the interview will be more loosely structured, with flexibility in the construction of the questions themselves and the order they are asked, and plenty of scope for respondents to answer in their own words without having responses boxed into pre-set classifications. This is the subject of this chapter.

The format of the depth interview is loosely structured, allowing freedom for both the interviewer and the interviewee to explore additional points and change direction if necessary. These interviews incorporate a good deal of the respondent's perspective into the findings, and therefore increase the validity of the information collected. This is a very important feature where the research issues are not known, or where there is a feeling that decisions have been driven by assumptions that may or may not be an accurate reflection of the views in the marketplace.

Why use depth interviews?

Depth interviews are generally (but as we will see, not always) carried out face to face so that the interviewer can create a relationship with the respondent by taking the time to open up the subject, respond to body language and build trust that results in the truth coming out.

A small number of depth interviews increase our understanding of the issues faced by the respondents and can reveal practices that were previously assumed. By using depth interviews in a research design, the validity of the research is increased as the respondents' own perspectives are incorporated into the research agenda.

Depth interviews can be carried out individually or in pairs. A husband and wife may be interviewed as a pair about banking choices. Two teenagers may be interviewed to find out what they think of parental controls.

Depth interviews compete with focus groups as a qualitative research method and are preferable in a number of circumstances:

When to use depth interviews rather than a focus group

- Respondents are geographically scattered and it is not possible to convene a group.

- There can be no contamination of other people's responses in the discussion.

- Each respondent's story needs to be followed from beginning to end, as in a case study of behaviour.

- Significant comment is required from each and every respondent (in a 90-minute focus group each person only gets to talk for a maximum of around 10 minutes, whereas in a 45-minute depth interview respondents have the floor to themselves).

- Individuals' behaviours and responses need to be tracked over time, as with new product trials.

- The topic area is sensitive, such as personal wealth (or debt), personal hygiene topics, drug or alcohol use.

Depth interviews therefore are useful in market research designs where:

- Research issues are not known.
- Issues, attitudes and motivations need exploration.
- Processes need describing in detail.
- Contamination from other people's views is to be avoided.
- Complex explanation and understanding is required.
- Individuals need to test things and give their reactions to the products.

Depth interviews in market research design

As with focus groups, depth interviews can stand alone or be used as part of a multi-method design:

- Customer-satisfaction studies: often in conjunction with a quantitative survey. Depth interviews can be used at the start of the study to identify satisfaction issues, or at its end to explore subjects that have emerged from the main survey.

- Market structure: key respondents with a bird's-eye view of the market can be selected for depth interviews on the basis of their expert knowledge.

- Product testing: individual cases can be tracked through a trial of a new product through staged depth interviewing.

- Needs assessment: a small number of depth interviews can be used to identify current behaviours and identify unmet needs.

- Advertising research: testing of advertisements in many formats can be carried out using depth interviews. This allows the material to be shown and avoids the inevitable contamination from other respondents that occurs in focus groups.

How many depth interviews are needed?

The number of interviews that are to be carried out is determined at the research design stage. In qualitative research we are more concerned with the quality and depth than the proportions of people that gave one response or another. As few as 10 depth interviews can be enough and 30 would almost certainly draw out all the factors pertaining to the research topic.

Carrying out and analysing 30 depth interviews can be very costly. A face-to-face depth interview costs around 10 times as much as a comparable interview conducted on the telephone. The actual cost depends on the spread of the interviews, the ease of travel to the respondent, and the ability to combine other interviews in the same vicinity.

Questions to ask about the number of interviews to be used

- Are the interviews the sole data collection method?

- How specialized and unique are the practices or attitudes that are being researched?

- What is the variability of the respondent types in the population – will 30 interviews cover all of them?

- How important is it that the range of responses sought is exhaustive?

- How important is it that the research diagnoses the problem rather than measures its size?

- How large is the population?

- Who is going to analyse them? (Thirty transcripts or recordings of depth discussions would be difficult to wade through and interpret.)

The role of the telephone in depth interviewing

There can be no doubt that face-to-face interviews offer advantages over the telephone in building rapport, watching body language and allowing time to pace the discussion. The telephone is a restrictive tool demanding quick responses to questions and abhorring the vacuum of silence. In this respect it limits the time that someone can think about answers to questions. It may also be difficult to keep a respondent's concentration on the telephone for more than 30 to 40 minutes (although there are examples of discursive, unstructured, conversational-type interviews that have lasted 90 minutes).

However, face-to-face interviews are not without their disadvantages. They are expensive to set up. Normally they are preceded by a phone interview at which time the project is explained, some qualifying questions are asked and an appointment for the visit is made. So the cost of the initial telephone interview should be added to the cost of the face-to-face interview when comparing the total cost.

Just because a face-to-face interview has been set up does not mean that it will happen. The logistical problems of sickness, absence and crises interrupting interviews should not be underestimated. 'No shows' occur frequently in face-to-face depth interviewing programmes and they raise the cost of the project if a wasted journey is made.

Since the telephone is such an efficient medium for carrying out interviews, it is used widely for depth interviews and proves highly successful for a number of reasons. Nowadays, when time is at a premium, many respondents may prefer to carry out the interview using the phone. It can be argued that when visiting respondents on their territory there are many potential distractions that could disturb the interview such as phones ringing, people interrupting, or distracting chitchat about the weather and the neighbourhood. Although these could be social niceties that lubricate the interview, they also burn up the interview time. In contrast, people with a telephone glued to their ear may be more likely to give their undivided attention.

There is, therefore, a trade-off that researchers have to make when deciding their medium for the depth interviews.

Winning cooperation for the interview

We live in a world of information seeking and information gathering, and this has undoubtedly affected compliance with market research studies, particularly where the interview requires a significant investment of time. Compliance with depth interviewing can be a problem where there is no 'buy in' with the topic area and seemingly no advantage to the respondents in giving up their valuable time. Where respondents already have a relationship with the research sponsor – that is, customer or consumer – the compliance will be higher, and a financial incentive either to the respondent or to a selected charity can sometimes help.

The principles of interviewing

We have described interviewing as a conversation with form and purpose, where usually the interviewer and the interviewee talk for the first time. This presents special problems beyond those that would be met in normal social interactions among friends. The interviewer has limited time to get the respondent to talk freely and openly about a subject. Some guidelines can help this process:

- Listen rather than speak. The role of the interviewer is to ensure that the questions facilitate rather than close down conversation. A transcript of the recording should demonstrate this, with a significantly smaller proportion of time given to the interviewer's words.

- Adopt a clear line of questioning. The interview should have a flow that makes sense to the respondent. Questions should be non-threatening, but can still be challenging and straightforward, and most of all should avoid confusing respondents or making them defensive.

- Facilitate a permissive tone. Any suggestion of 'correct' responses should be guarded against. It is easy for respondents to feel there is a 'right' answer and that the interviewer is seeking to elicit this from them. Questions that might be leading and body language encouraging certain responses must be avoided. Equally, there will be situations where the interviewer deliberately challenges or even provokes respondent in order to obtain a reaction. The depth interview is a choreographed conversation in which the interviewer can choose to play different roles to achieve a desired effect.

- Demonstrate engagement with the respondent. The interview will flow better if the respondent feels that the interviewer is part of the process. The interviewer's facial expressions, voice tone and intonation and body language can convey all kinds of messages to the respondent, including interest and encouragement.

Top tips

- Use depth interviews when you want to obtain deeper insights on how and why people do things. Depth interviews provide responses that are not contaminated by other people's opinions (which is a danger in focus groups). You also get more output per respondent in depth interviews than from focus groups.

- Depth interviews are useful for following an individual's thought processes or actions right the way through from start to finish. In a focus group you will only get a snapshot of each person's thoughts and actions.

- Use depth interviews when the target audience you want to speak to is geographically scattered and would be unable to attend a focus group.

- If you are carrying out more than 10 depth interviews make sure that you have some structure, especially recording what people have said. Analysing more than 10 free-ranging recorded conversations is difficult. Structuring the responses on to a paper questionnaire and taking notes during the interview will speed up the analysis.

- As with focus groups, find interviewers who are good listeners and capable of probing interesting lines of enquiry.

- Don't spread the interviews too thinly across a number of different interviewers. Rather use one or two interviewers who can build up a deep understanding of the subject.

The interview itself

Interviewing is a matter of style, and what works for one interviewer does not necessarily work for another. A businesslike approach with an aura of confidence and control will transmit positively to the respondent. Enthusiasm will help develop interest in the topic. There really is nothing worse than the uninterested interviewer.

At the beginning of the interview it is to be expected that respondents will feel a certain anxiety, not knowing what to expect, perhaps concerned that they have let

FIGURE 7.2 The emotional state of respondents in different stages of the interview

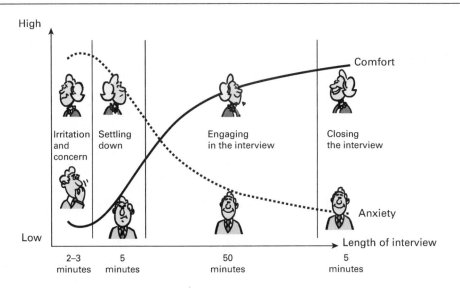

themselves in for something they would have preferred to avoid. Informing them that their words are being recorded could heighten this tension. They do not know what questions are in store or how long it will take, and they could fear the worst. They may even be unsure of their ability to answer the questions. Most of these feelings are rooted in ignorance – the anticipation being worse than the experience.

Skilled interviewers will create a rapport with respondents as quickly as possible and put them at ease. They will be assumptive about the recording device rather than making a big issue out of it. The sooner the interviewer gets the respondents talking, the sooner they will settle down and the greater will be the cooperation level. After the briefest of introductions, an easy question will start the ball rolling.

The line of questioning

There is no correct line of questioning in an interview, and much will depend on the topic matter. However, the stages in the interview need to be borne in mind at the planning stage. There is little point in launching into detailed questions in the first five minutes. The interview works because of the relationship between the interviewer and the respondent. The line of questioning must facilitate the development of the relationship and gradually build up to more searching questions.

As with focus groups, depth interviews are conducted around a topic guide. This is not set in stone; it is, as its name suggests, a guide for the interviewer with sufficient freedom to allow the development of the interview at the respondent's pace and incorporate the needs of the research as well as of the respondent.

The guide serves to ensure that all the research topics are covered in the discussion, but this does not mean that it is followed to the letter. The skilled interviewer will hold the discussion guide in his/her head and make a mental note of coverage in the interview. In this way, the interview flows as a 'guided conversation' and appears 'natural'. Topics of discussion will arise naturally and can be followed. Issues that have not surfaced can be raised by the interviewer. The discussion will be improved if subjects are raised by respondents in the natural course of the conversation.

We cannot emphasize strongly enough the importance of listening to the responses, as many nuggets can be lost by the failure of the interviewer to pick up on issues either raised by the respondent or implicit throughout the interview.

Developing the discussion guide for the interview

The depth interview, being a qualitative data collection method, uses a loosely structured discussion guide similar to that used in the focus group discussion. This is in contrast to the highly structured questionnaire that is used in a quantitative inter-view. It should follow a sequence that conventionally is:

1 Introduction.

2 Warm-up questions.

3 Main body of interview.

4 Thank and close.

The main body of the interview will be characterized by a number of specific sections relating to the research objectives, and these are broken down into specific questions with probes and prompts that can be used to develop the discussion and flush out answers.

As with the focus group discussion, open-ended questions are at the heart of the depth interview. They allow the flexibility to probe so that the interviewer may go into greater depth if required. They facilitate the development of a rapport between inter-viewer and respondent, encouraging cooperation and sharing of information. They also allow the interviewer to test the limits of the respondent's knowledge and experience, and as such can result in unexpected answers that may challenge the researcher's assump-tions. A study commissioned to identify what prompted the referral of work to accountancy firms revealed that a practice previously thought to be standard proce-dure was no longer operating and had not been for some time. These assumptions had been a major brake on the development of new business within the accountancy firm.

Probes and prompts

A probe is a way of getting a respondent to expand further on his or her answer. The decision by the interviewer to probe further may be left to his or her discretion, or built into the discussion guide with reminders to prompt. Cues from the voice, body language and general tone of the interview can indicate that there is more that the respondent could and is willing to say. Silence itself can be a prompt as it encourages people to jump in and fill the space. An encouraging gesture and an enquiring look may be all that is needed. However, specific phrases and questions relating to the topic area can also be used:

- And what do you think about that?

- Can you talk me through that again?

- What more can you tell me?

Whereas a probe seeks the enhancement of an answer, prompts introduce a subject that has not been raised. In most market studies, there are certain issues that need to be brought to the attention of the respondents to obtain their views. It may be necessary to remind a respondent about brands that have not yet been mentioned. It could be important to obtain respondents' views on a process that has not been talked about.

The general rules for the development of the discussion guide are to follow a sequence of questions that appear natural, building the conversation in depth, and using questions that open rather than close down the discussion. Types of questions to avoid are:

- Long and complex questions causing respondents to become confused about what they are responding to, such as 'What do you think about the range of product available to you now, in the DIY stores and the supermarkets compared with a few years ago?' This also, in turn causes confusion at the analytical stage about which part of the question the respondent is referring to.

- Vague questions, such as 'What do you think will happen in the future?' The future in this question is open-ended and vague. Do we mean the next year, 5 years or 10 years?

- Questions using technical jargon or company jargon that is not the language of the respondent, such as 'Have you got any use for SMS or GMS telemetry?' It is easy to forget that terminology used by the client is not always that used by the respondent.

- Leading questions, such as 'So you think Shell is a good supplier of LPG?' You will never know if the question led people to respond as suggested or if they rebelled at the suggestion, regardless of their viewpoint.

- Aggressive or threatening questions or comments, such as 'You seem to be avoiding answering me.' This may be the approach of the political interviewer, but in most marketing research, these questions serve to alienate the respondent and break down the rapport between interviewer and respondent.

Example of an interview discussion guide

Interviews with bankers and other lenders about using business recovery services and choosing suppliers of these services. Commissioned by Argent Fait accountancy company.

1 Personal information. Your job/responsibilities/position within the company.

2 The market. Overall how has the economy changed in the last couple of years? PROMPT: chances of recession, and impact on businesses if there is a recession. How has the lending market changed in the last couple of years? Have you seen any changes resulting from the move towards a more rescue-oriented culture? What are these? PROMPT: fees, relationships, insolvencies.

3 New legislation. What has been the impact of the new Insolvency Bill? What will be the future ramifications?

4 Suppliers of business recovery services. What services are the most commonly used/most infrequently used? Who are the major players in business recovery service provision? What companies would you think of to use for these types of services? How do you get to hear about providers of such services?

5 Choosing a business recovery service provider. How do you make the decision about which supplier of business recovery services you use? PROMPT: who is involved, how long does it take, company policy, relationships in the field, 'approved' suppliers. How many suppliers would you be able to choose from and how would you go about selecting one supplier over another? What factors might cause you to select?

6 Dealing with suppliers. As a percentage of your total workload, how much time, on average, do you spend dealing with business recovery suppliers? Thinking of all the suppliers of business recovery services you have used, can you describe to me an excellent example of service? Use a case history. And similarly, can you describe to me the worst-case scenario you can recall?

7 Magic wand. Let's now imagine you have a magic wand that you could wave to change the way business recovery services are commissioned. What would you do? How would that affect you? And also for the way business recovery services are organized, what would you use it for there?

8 Argent Fait services. Thinking again now to the services of Argent Fait's business recovery team, how do you think they compare against other suppliers? What are their strengths/weaknesses? What do you think they could do better than they are currently doing to make usage easier and more efficient for yourself? PROMPT: contact, response times, availability, keeping to deadlines, clarity, knowledge, dependability, enthusiasm, efficiency. What do you value in their services over any of the other suppliers you use? PROMPT: fee levels, added value, creativity of solutions. If you had the ability to change three things about the service Argent Fait provides, what would you change?

9 Future trends. In the longer term, thinking about the next two years, can you see any changes that might influence the market for business recovery services? If you were the manager of the business recovery services department in a company, what would you expect to have to do over the next couple of years to keep your current level of business/increase the business you have?

10 Anything else you want to raise about business recovery services and providers?

THANK AND CLOSE.

SUMMARY

Depth interviews are a qualitative data collection method that offers the opportunity to collect rich, descriptive data about people's behaviours, attitudes and perceptions, and to unfold complex processes. They can be used as a stand-alone research method or as part of a multi-method design, depending on the needs of the research.

Depth interviews are normally carried out face to face so that rapport can be created with respondents and body language can be used to add a high level of understanding to the answers. The telephone can also be used by a skilled researcher to carry out depth interviews with little loss of data and at a tenth of the cost.

The style of the interview will depend on the interviewer. Successful depth interviewers listen rather than talk, have a clear line of questioning and use body language as a cue to building a rapport. The interview is more of a guided conversation than a staccato question and answer session.

The interview is conducted using a discussion guide (as in focus groups) that facilitates the flushing out of the respondent's views through open-ended questioning. As with focus groups, projective techniques can be incorporated into the interview.

Observation and ethnography

Observation: a research method you can believe

Watching people is not only interesting, it tells you a huge amount about them. Imagine that you were to ask people how they make a cup of coffee. They would most likely tell you that they get a cup out of the cupboard, a spoon out of the drawer, they put a spoonful of coffee in the cup, add boiling water and a drop of milk to taste. However, if you were to watch them you might see other interesting things. What size cup do they choose? Do they have a choice of different jars of coffee, and which of these do they choose? How high do they heap their spoon with coffee? Do they spill the coffee off the spoon? What do they do while the kettle is boiling? Do they stir the coffee after they have put in the boiling water and the milk? All these questions and observations may in themselves be trivial but they could provide a clue to a manufacturer of coffee who is looking for a way of helping the customer prepare a better cup of 'Java'.

It is worth reflecting on the important role that observation has played in the formative years of the market research industry. In the 1930s companies such as AC Nielsen and Attwoods in the United States and Audits of Great Britain (AGB) began carrying out audits of product sales through retail outlets by counting stock levels in stores at periodic intervals and accounting for deliveries to the store during that same period. There were no questionnaires in the sense we know them today; the market researcher's role was simply to count stock and record purchases. As long as the recording was diligent and the sample of stores was representative, the result would be accurate.

Prior to the Second World War, the British government sponsored the Mass Observation Project to provide an anthropological study of the nation. A national panel of volunteers kept diaries and tracked the mood of the war-beleaguered country. They sat in pubs, watching and listening. They stood at bus stops and watched. They later captured their observations in diaries ready for analysis. A legacy of this approach was the title of the market research company Mass Observation, which existed for about 30 years until being subsumed within a larger group. Video Research, located in Tokyo, is now one of the largest market research companies in Japan and began life in 1962 (as its name suggests) by measuring TV audiences based on observational reporting.

When to use observation

Since its origins in the 1930s the market research industry has moved on and the administered interview – either face to face or by telephone – has become a common method of data collection. But there is still a role for observation, and indeed there has been something of a revival in its use, though usually as one of a mix of methods that form part of the whole research design. So, for example, the video camera and mobile phone have found a role for the market researcher. That camera positioned discreetly in the corner of the supermarket ceiling may not be there just to stop pilfering; it can also observe shoppers and their behaviour. It can watch our procrastination as we buy our beans and collect behavioural patterns that may be autonomic and that would not be recalled in a conventional interview. Do we deliberate over our purchase of a can of beans? Do we read the label? What influence and pressure comes from the accompanying kids? Do we pick up other brands and examine them or do we just fly down the aisles throwing cans in the trolley without even checking prices?

For years anthropologists have researched tribes by using observation. They seek to become a part of the tribe until their presence is taken for granted and the actions and behaviours of the people they are observing are as normal as can be. Market researchers have drawn on this experience and ethnography is now in common use as a market research tool. It works particularly well when trying to figure out how people buy or use products. Typical examples of ethnographic research would be accompanying someone on a shopping trip and watching them as they browse or choose their products. Sometimes the respondents may be asked to speak aloud their thoughts as they do their shopping. This 'stream of consciousness' is recorded or notes are taken and these provide another insight, beyond the visual, into the shopping process.

Ethnography in the workplace and the shopping mall requires the full cooperation of respondents, who must try and act as normally as possible – which may be difficult knowing that their every move is being observed. The researcher therefore takes time before the observation begins to get to know the respondents and make them comfortable. This means that ethnography can be a lengthy process and relatively expensive. It is qualitative research and a handful or a dozen ethnographic observations may be sufficient to provide interesting insights. Working through a few hours of notes and video following just one ethnographic event can take as long if not longer than the observation process itself.

There are, of course, many occasions when what we do is very personal, and it may be difficult to organize ethnographic research. Our behaviour in the bedroom and during ablutions may make interesting observation but most of us would be too reserved to agree to be filmed at this time. In business-to-business situations it can be tricky getting agreement to observe behaviours. Recently we were involved in researching how people use workplace gloves and needed to watch bricklayers on building sites. Building site managers were extremely reluctant to allow researchers onto what could be a danger zone.

A project of a similar kind worked for a manufacturer of hand tools. The company carried out research amongst electricians and watched them during their daily chores, climbing ladders and fumbling in their tool belts to find the right screwdriver for the job. This led to the simple solution of printing a slot on the top of the handle of the screwdriver to indicate either a flat blade or a cross in the case of a Philips screwdriver. This small innovation was an improvement for the workmen who can now look at the top of the screwdriver handle in the tool belt and spot which should be used.

Observation can play an important supporting role in many different types of market research projects, and it is these that we describe in the sections that follow.

The audit: a major application for observation

Traditionally, researchers visiting stores on a particular date collected data for audits. At this time they would record the stock levels of all products of interest and check on delivery notes and purchase documents. They would return in one or two months' time and repeat the exercise. The data could then be used to calculate the sales of products by adjusting the retailer purchases by the difference between the two stock levels. Once the information had been collected from all the stores and pooled for analysis, it offered considerable insights into brand share movements over time, by retailer, by geography and average prices.

Today the data is collected by electronic means using bar codes (EPOS, or electronic point of sale) and there is no requirement for a field worker to visit the store, though the principle remains the same. The key to audits is to set up systems for regular and continuous recording over years so that trends are measured accurately. This is a quantitative research tool and therefore the sample must be chosen with care to reflect the trade outlets that sell the products that are being tracked. Since just a few companies and outlets so heavily dominate the retail landscape, every effort must be made to be as inclusive as possible. If a leading outlet refuses to take part, it may scupper the whole scheme. As compensation for providing the data, the retailers either get paid or they get the data fed back to them against an aggregated figure for the rest of the contributors so that they can benchmark and track changes in their position.

An extension of this type of research is for retailers to encourage their customers to sign up to a loyalty clubcard that is swiped every time they visit the store to make a purchase. Companies can then track the purchases of customers and find patterns of products that are bought together or at a certain time of day. This silent observation allows the retailers to design their stores and present their goods in a fashion that will be most conducive to sales. The market research firm Dunnhumby developed a new loyalty card for Tesco in the late 1990s and, through sophisticated analysis of customers' buying habits, this is credited as providing one of the components of the retailer's growth over the following decade.

Observation in shopping surveys

Mystery shopping is a form of ethnographic research in which respondents are unaware that they are part of a research programme. In a mystery shopping survey, a fieldworker plays the role of a member of the public buying or enquiring about the product, and records the experience in as much detail as possible on a questionnaire (usually at a later time so as not to be obvious). This is common practice in hotels, restaurants and car dealerships. Because they are unaware that the shopping enquiry is not real, respondents are not biased in their behaviour.

There are codes of conduct that researchers adhere to in mystery shopping. If the target of the mystery shop could lose out financially (as in the case of a car showroom where the fieldworker has no intention of buying a car) then the contacts are limited to members of the sponsor's outlets. In other words, only dealers within the research buyer's group are covered. Mystery shopping hotels involves paying the going rate for a room, and so allows the researchers to widen the net since a fair price has been paid and nobody's time has been wasted.

There are many more complex buying situations where observation can be used. Take for example the visit of a prospective customer to a car dealer's showroom. What do customers do when they enter the showroom? Are they purposeful and walk to look at one of the cars on display? Do they look around for help? Do the salespeople offer help and do they do so in an appropriate manner? How successful are the car salespeople in dealing with questions and helping move the sale forward? How do they deal with the tricky business of giving a price for the car? Do they follow up the enquiry?

The camera (or conventional observation) could be used to capture customers' reactions as they check in to hotels, airports or restaurants. How friendly is the meet and greet? How efficiently does reception deal with the check-in process? Are customers offered all the information and help they require?

A key part of any shopping study is the measurement of footfall – that is the number of people passing an outlet or an advertising hoarding. Observation is an obvious means of recording shopping traffic, and it can be measured by fieldworkers counting heads. (Rather than keep a literal head count they are likely to use 'clickers', which are simple mechanical counters that are activated by squeezing/clicking the device.) Equally, the footfall may be measured electronically using optical scanners (more difficult than you might think in a busy thoroughfare with people pushing in crowds and not walking in an orderly manner).

Observation plays a very obvious role in shopping surveys, where a researcher can easily walk into a store to check if products are in stock and take note of their ticketed price. In this case there is no communication with the retail staff (other than perhaps to ask if the product is sold at the store). The research task becomes more complicated if the researcher seeks to photograph the in-store display. For this, permission would be required from the manager and it cannot be assumed it will always be granted.

Observation in product research

The traditional interview, especially one-to-one depth interviews in the home, mall intercepts or focus groups, is an important contribution to product research. Such interviews provide occasions for respondents to evaluate products and talk about what they like and dislike. There is, however, always the danger that a 60-minute interview discussing a product will end up splitting the atom, yielding a great deal of information but not in the context of how real decisions are made. The decision to choose a particular brand of toothpaste may be complicated by a history of loyalty to that brand, but it is made in seconds in the superstore. It is not something that consumers agonize about a great deal and yet the interviewer asks them to do just this. There is always a danger that this extreme focus on a small decision achieves a result but that it is 'overcooked'.

A video camera in a store would capture the consideration given to choosing a brand of toothpaste. However, if it were possible, observation in the bathroom would also establish if the tube is squeezed at the bottom, in the middle or at the top. We would see if the top of the toothpaste is replaced after use. We would see how much paste is squeezed onto the brush. A toothpaste manufacturer interested in packaging and product development might find value in all these observations.

Video cameras trained on the feet of runners in a marathon are played back at slow speed and accurate market share data can be determined for the different models and brands of shoes. In another piece of observational research adidas noticed, almost by accident, that kids were leaving the laces of their trainers undone and this prompted them to launch a highly successful shoe with a Velcro strap.

Grohe, a German manufacturer of mixer showers, ran workshops in which installers were observed fitting different makes of showers. The exercise prompted the development of an easy-fixing kit to simplify and speed the work of the installer.

Marks & Spencer uses its Oxford Street store to watch how consumers react to new designs, and through observation of this type quick decisions can be made to launch or kill a product.

Observation in poster checks

One of the problems of poster research is determining how many people see them. Posters form part of the backcloth of our streets. People seldom study them deliberately but take them in subliminally as they move around on foot, in the car or on public transport. Observation plays a role in providing answers to important questions: what is the traffic count that passes the poster, how visible is it, and what condition is it in?

In order to obtain answers to these questions, visits must be made to the poster sites. From the traffic measures that are taken at the sites, researchers can develop predictive models to show the likelihood of viewing. These gross viewing opportunities are then adjusted by a visibility index assessed from cars, the sidewalk and taking account of any obstructions. This type of data is important to advertisers and their clients when setting charge rates for posters. A specific campaign would normally be tracked in the conventional way by interviewing a sample of people to determine their recall of the posters.

Observation in checking television viewing

The television is an integral part of the lives of people worldwide. In most Western societies, 98 per cent of households own a television, and many have two or more. Commercial television is financed by adverts costing thousands of dollars for a 30-second slot. Not surprisingly, the measurement of television audiences is taken very seriously.

In the early years of television, viewers were given a diary and physically recorded the shows they watched. This self-reporting approach was not particularly accurate because viewers failed to note programmes they had viewed or just were not diligent in the task. A more sophisticated approach was required. Early electromechanical systems were devised that worked out from the heat of the television whether it was on and recorded the event on long streams of paper tape. However, it measured television use and not television viewing, and more advanced methods have evolved.

In any country where TV viewing is measured, a sample of up to 5,000 households are recruited to have a 'black box' computer and modem attached to their TV. This modem sends information on viewing patterns back to a central computer every night.

Small electronic boxes placed near the TV measure who is watching by giving each member of the household a button to turn on and off to show when their viewing begins and ends. These 'people meters' know the age and gender of each member of the household and guests can participate in the sample by recording their age, sex and viewing status into the system. People who take part in this audience research are chosen to be representative of the population at large.

This is not observation in the classical sense as discussed earlier and is almost Big Brother watching you watching them.

Top tips

- Use observation when you believe that people's behaviour may provide insights that can't necessarily be obtained through direct questioning. Observation works well with product tests.

- Make sure that you get consent from the respondents and any other parties who are involved in the study before committing to the observation programme. Don't assume that you can walk onto a building site and watch a bricklayer at work without permission.

- Devise a systematic process for capturing the observation – a diary or questionnaire for the moderator or respondent to complete, photographs and videos of what they have been doing, and instructions for the observers on how long to spend on each task.

- Become a good ethnographic researcher by developing the skills of an intelligent detective, spotting clues and watching for reactions that tell a hidden story.

Setting up observation programmes

Using observation requires imagination. Most of the occasions when we use observation occur in an artificial environment such as an ethnographic accompaniment, a focus group, a hall test or a clinic. These contrived occasions may be perfectly acceptable for simple checks. However, there is no substitute for watching consumers in the real world. The small instructions on a pack may be perfectly visible in a well-lit hall or focus group venue but illegible in a gloomy domestic environment. Installers of showers might be at pains to use screws for all parts of their installation when they know they are being watched in a clinic, whereas in the privacy of their own work environment the same installation might be put together with nails.

It is not easy to organize a fly-on-the-wall camera to capture everything that goes on in domestic or business life. There are obvious issues of privacy to consider, and in any case fixed-head cameras may not give the detailed picture that is required. However, video and cameras are superb ways of capturing a feel for the ways that products are used. A manufacturer of electrical cable reels (extension cables) believed that the display of his products in stores materially affected sales. He commissioned a store check that involved researchers visiting outlets and taking photos of the displays. Pictures came back of reels that were in jumbled heaps, and usually at floor level, because the flanges of the reels were not flat and would not stack. A small redesign resulted in a reel that worked just as well for the consumer and could be displayed to best advantage in the store.

Consumers can be asked to save their used discarded packs in a 'bin test'. The old wrappers, boxes or cans are thrown into bin-liners and saved for collection by the researchers. The trash is then examined to see how it was opened and used.

Reporting observational data

In this discussion of the use of observation, it is clear that there is a high level of subjectivity (excepting audits and people meters that record television viewing). There may only be a relatively small number of data sets to interpret. The observations may be capable of interpretation in different ways. The picture of what was observed may not be absolutely clear.

Despite the high cost of capturing and interpreting observational data, its impact can be considerable – it is said that a picture is worth a thousand words. A large ship repair company commissioned a survey to find out why it was losing share to South East Asian yards. On conclusion of one of the depth interviews, a researcher asked permission to take a photograph of the respondent, a manager of a large shipping company. The photograph showed the respondent at his desk, on which were two quotes: one was a few pages held together by a paper clip, the other was an impressive bound document. The impressive bound document was the bid that won, and it was from a Japanese competitor. The market research study contained 15,000 words of worthy analysis, but it was the single photo of the ship owner and his two bids that had most impact.

SUMMARY

Observation was one of the first methods used by market researchers to collect data. It has been superseded by interviews but there are nevertheless many opportunities where observation can provide valuable insights.

Observation was originally used to carry out audits of products in supermarkets, but today data is collected by swiping bar codes at the point of sale.

Mystery shopping is an important form of observation in market research, and is used to test customers' experience in buying situations such as at car dealerships, hotels or restaurants.

Ethnography has become an important tool in market research in which market researchers seek to understand social meanings and behaviour by placing themselves in a naturally occurring setting. In this way researchers can uncover things that would not have been found from conventional interviewing.

The video camera can be used to observe customers in supermarkets to find out how they choose products for their shopping basket. It is used in focus groups to watch the body language of the participants. It can be used to check on traffic flows or brands used.

The applications for observation in market research are increasing, helped by digital cameras and optical devices. It makes a very powerful supplement to other forms of more conventional research.

PART THREE
Quantitative research

Quantitative research

What is quantitative research?

The term speaks for itself. The word *quantitative* implies quantity – data based on large samples that allow measurement and statistical analysis. This raises the question: when does qualitative research end and quantitative research begin? Statisticians tell us that when around 30 people have been asked an open-ended question (for example, why they like or dislike something), almost all the possible answers will have been received. When more people are interviewed there may be an occasional mention of another factor but the main ones will have been mentioned. There is no hard and fast number of interviews that separates qualitative and quantitative research but we can say that we are moving into quantitative territory with sample sizes greater than 30.

Determining the size of the sample

A question that is frequently asked prior to a quantitative study is 'How big should the sample be in order to be accurate?' In answering this we first of all have to decide how accurate we want the results to be. Most market researchers are happy with a result where we can be 95 per cent certain that if we repeated the survey again and again, any results we obtain would be plus or minus 5 per cent of what would be achieved if we interviewed absolutely everybody.

Working on this assumption that plus or minus 5 per cent is a reasonable level of error, we can now think about how many people we should interview. Imagine that we wanted to carry out a survey to determine the attitudes to political leaders among the voting population in the US, Ireland and the UK. In the US there are just over 200 million people eligible to vote. In the UK the figure is around 45 million and in Ireland it is just over 3 million. There is clearly a wide variation in population size in these audiences. Is this of relevance to us when deciding how many people we need to interview?

Where a target audience is large, and by this we mean anything over 10,000, the size of the target audience has little relevance. We are not going to take a 10 per cent sample of each of these audiences. What we need is a sufficiently large sample in each country to give a valid result. It is the absolute size of the sample that matters, not the proportion that the sample is of the total population.

If we wanted to determine how many people we should interview in these three countries with an accuracy of plus or minus 5 per cent, we would use a sample size calculator such as the one shown on page 116. Here we can see that a sample of 400 people in each country would give us an answer within the limits of statistical error that we have set (ie 95 per cent certain the result will be plus or minus 5 per cent).

There are a number of caveats we should bear in mind when making this statement. Everyone within the sample must have an equal chance of being selected – that is, the sample must be random. Furthermore, if we want to analyse the results by state or county or gender or any other demographic, we would lose this level of accuracy. This means that for all intents and purposes a sample size of just 400 would give us an overall snapshot of people's views but it would not allow us to analyse it in any depth. If we want to slice and dice the data and look at smaller cells of respondents, we would have to think about how big those cells of respondents would be. For example, if we wanted to look at male versus female respondents and each made up around half of the sample, we would need a sample of 800 in total if the sub-samples of males and females are to give us a result where we can be certain they are plus or minus 5 per cent. Researchers wanting a reasonably accurate view of attitudes, behavior or consumption in any country often choose a sample size of between 500 and 1,000 respondents knowing that this will give an acceptable result. Read more about sampling methods in Chapter 10.

It should be clear by now that a quantitative survey begins with a minimum of 30 questionnaire completes but more normally 200-plus. The ultimate size of the sample depends on the number of sub-cells that may need analysing, bearing in mind that we like a minimum of 30 in each cell.

With this sample size we have a reasonable degree of confidence in the result being representative of the total population and so can measure consumption rates, attitudes and behavior so as to understand the markets which we serve or would like to serve.

The tools of the quantitative researcher

Face-to-face interviews

In the early days of market research almost all surveys were carried out face to face by interviewers armed with clipboards and questionnaires. Some face-to-face interviews are still appropriate, for example in shopping malls, at exhibitions or even in busy streets. But there are only a limited number of large face-to-face surveys carried out for quantitative purposes, not only because of the high cost, but also for the security of the interviewers.

Telephone interviews

In developed countries, as households prospered and most acquired telephones, telephone interviews quickly replaced those carried out face to face. A 10-to-15-minute interview over the telephone yields what might take 20 to 30 minutes face to face – usually for a lower cost, particularly so in business-to-business surveys. However, over the last decade many householders have chosen not to be listed in telephone directories and so are not available for sampling. At the same time, hard-wired phones are rapidly being replaced by mobiles, again removing potential respondents from the sample frame as there are no publicly available lists of mobile phone numbers. Today telephone interviews account for just over a tenth of all the interviews that are carried out by the industry, and many of these are for business-to-business studies.

Online surveys

Today, online surveys have taken over as the dominant source of quantitative research. These self-completion surveys can be received on mobile phones, iPads and computers and can be administered quickly and efficiently in a matter of minutes. They have made significant strides in reducing the cost and improving the speed of completion of quantitative research. Read more about online surveys in Chapter 15.

What quantitative research is used for

The public face of market research is surveys carried out and published in the press either reporting on political opinion or some aspect of social attitudes. However, this is a very small part of the overall spend on quantitative research. Most quantitative studies are sponsored by private firms or government departments that need the insights for their own planning.

As the word *quantitative* suggests, this type of research is used for market measurements. These measurements are required to determine proportions of people who use products (and services), who are aware of products, to establish which brands are known and which would be considered. The data are likely to be used in some form of analysis such as segmenting the market or determining the likelihood of buying products and services. Data could also feed the assessment of the size of markets providing a measurement of opportunity.

Nearly all quantitative studies will have specific objectives and these could be various such as guiding decisions on price, promotion, the channel to market or assisting in product development. Many quantitative studies are repeated each year (sometimes more frequently) in order to track changes in data. These studies are particularly important for measuring changes in awareness to brands and people's attitudes to brands.

The applications for quantitative research are covered in more depth in Chapters 17 to 23.

Analysing quantitative research

Quantitative research provides market researchers with raw data for drawing conclusions and taking action. Quantitative market researchers are now data analysts. At its simplest, data can be presented as counts showing what proportion of respondents gave certain answers. This is useful but not necessarily insightful. The data analyst is looking for links between different answers to see if a relationship exists between two or more variables. Cross-tabulation will show the results for different groups of respondents and highlight variations from the norm. Simple XY graphs are frequently used to show the relationship between two questions. All the time the analyst is mindful that the measurements must be significant – that is, in sufficient numbers to be accurate and representative of the population as a whole.

Market research survey companies have specialist data processing teams who can produce cross analysis tables. They have statisticians who can apply various tests to the data. Although the quantitative market research is supported by the specialists, market analysts need to be comfortable with numbers and especially basic programs such as Excel. There is often no substitute for a quantitative researcher getting his or her hands dirty in the data itself in a spreadsheet. Being able to produce pivot tables of data is a daily task for the quantitative researcher. Examining the spreadsheet may well highlight rows of data that need cleaning up or individual responses that give an enlightened result.

In addition to Excel there are a number of programs that can be used by the quantitative market researcher to analyse the data. SPSS (Statistical Package for the Social Sciences) is a widely used program, taught at universities and frequently used by market researchers and survey companies. Variations on SPSS are programs such as Q, R or SAS which are attuned to the needs of market research. When the data is required for more specific purposes such as conjoint analysis, software such as Sawtooth may be appropriate.

Top tips

- Quantitative research can be expensive when based on large samples. Only carry out the research when you are absolutely sure what questions you want to ask and for what purpose the answers will be used.

- There are diminishing returns in having a large sample size. Doubling the size of a sample from 500 to 1,000 interviews improves the accuracy from plus or minus 4.5 per cent to plus or minus 3.2 per cent. Ask yourself whether the extra cost of the larger sample is worth it.

- Look for relationships among quantitative variables to see if they indicate cause and effect.

- Use XY graphs to explore the different relationships between answers to questions.

- Even though you are interested in aggregated responses, it is important to get your hands dirty in the data and look at line-by-line responses to see if any data stands out as being peculiar or are outliers.

- Learn how to use pivot tables in Excel.

SUMMARY

Quantitative research deals with large numbers of interviews. Usually a quantitative study has more than 200 interviews and many studies of the general public have 1,000. The numbers of interviews carried out and the random selection of these data points govern the accuracy of a study. It is the absolute size of the sample that determines accuracy, not the proportion that the sample represents of the total population. Surveys of the general public often have around 1,000 interviews as this produces results which are plus or minus 3.2 per cent of what would be achieved if a census was carried out (we can be 95 per cent certain of this). Also, a sample of this size is sufficiently large to allow the analysis of sub-cells of respondents, each of which must be of a sufficiently large size for the results to be statistically significant.

In business-to-business surveys the total size of the population is much smaller than in consumer surveys as frequently there are much fewer members of the population. In surveys of markets such as this, a sample is chosen based on judgement (the larger companies in the sample often accounting for a disproportionately large number of interviews). Business-to-business surveys may have fewer than 100 interviews but they are still quantitative as the analysis is very much concerned with measurements of various kinds.

Today, quantitative surveys are mainly carried out online or by telephone. They are used to show the size and structure of markets, to measure and track brand awareness and to show the proportions of the population that have certain attitudes or behave in a particular way.

Sampling and statistics

The principles of sampling

When we discuss the principles of sampling with new market research recruits who haven't had any training in the subject, it is good to ask them to think about the following question: 'There are 320 million people in the United States. If we wanted to know how many eat breakfast every morning, how many people would we need to interview to get a reliable answer?' Intuitively the new researcher might think that we need to interview a certain proportion of the population – say 10 per cent. However, if we were to do this within such a large population, this would require us to interview 32 million people. As we reflect on this we might come to the conclusion that this would be way over the top and unnecessary. So what is the answer?

It often amazes people that it is possible to arrive at an accurate answer addressed to a large population from a relatively small sample of people. In a country such as the United States we can randomly interview just 2,000 people and determine that the results we achieve will be within 2.2 per cent of what we would have discovered had we carried out a census of the whole population. At least we can be 95 per cent sure that this would be the case. Being able to interview such a small number of people and obtain such a reliable result is extremely valuable to market researchers who do not have the time or the resources to carry out a census.

What can be confusing is to extend the question. For example, let us now address the same question to Ireland where the population is 4.6 million. What size sample would we need in order to determine the number of people who eat breakfast in that country? Intuitively we would imagine that because the population is so much smaller, the sample size could equally be reduced. However, the answer is that we would still need to randomly interview 2,000 people to obtain a result that is + or –2.2 per cent from what would be achieved if we carried out a census (again at the 95 per cent confidence level). From this brief introduction you will have learned that it is the absolute size of the sample that determines the accuracy of the results to a question, not the proportion that the sample is of the total population.

The theory of sampling frightens many would-be market researchers. There are all those formulae and so much science. Certainly the market researcher needs a good grasp of how to choose a robust sample, but in truth serious mathematics is seldom required. Standard software and statistician colleagues do the heavy work.

Readers who want the mathematical side of the subject spelling out to them should read one of the many books that are devoted to this subject. In this chapter we will talk practically about how and why we choose samples in the way that we do.

The sampling that takes place in consumer markets is very different from that in business-to-business markets. We will take each separately.

Random sampling in consumer markets

Consumer markets tend to be massive, with target audiences measured in hundreds of thousands or millions of people. Interviewing everyone, or indeed most people, in such large populations would be inordinately expensive and take a considerable amount of time. However, if we take a carefully chosen subset, then we do not need to interview many people at all to achieve a reliable picture of what the result is for the whole of the population. This subset is a sample; a group of people selected to represent the whole.

If the sample is chosen randomly, with everyone in the population having an equal and known chance of being selected, then we can apply measures of probability to show the accuracy of the result. If there is no random selection (we will come to this later), then there must, by implication, be an element of judgement or bias in determining who should be chosen, in which case it is not possible to measure the accuracy of the sample result. A random sample is often called a probability sample as we can determine the likelihood or chance of the result being within bounds of accuracy.

Random need not mean that the whole database of people we are surveying has to be in one single pot. It is still random if the population is broken into smaller databases and a system is devised of selecting randomly from these. For example, surveys of a national population are more conveniently chosen by first breaking that population into districts such as states, counties or boroughs, and carrying out a first cut to randomly choose a number of these districts. Areas that are chosen in this way are then used as the next level of a pool from which to carry out a random selection. This multi-stage or stratified random sample has all the principles of randomness and therefore qualifies as a probability sample from which the accuracy of the result can be determined.

If the selection of the sample is carried out manually it demands some systematic approach such as choosing every nth number. In fact, we seldom need to worry about making the random selection in this way as the computer does it for us.

Choosing the size of the sample

We now have to decide on the size of the sample. As was discussed in the introduction to this chapter, what matters is not what percentage the sample is of the whole population but its absolute size. In other words, as long as the sample is big enough, it will give us a picture that accurately reflects the total. But what is big enough?

Imagine that you had to test the quality of the water in Lake Michigan. How much water would you have to take out to do the test? There must be millions of gallons in that lake and you certainly would not want or need to take out 10 per cent. In fact, if you assumed that the water was well mixed, and you took a few bucketfuls from various points around the lake and from its centre, you would get a very good picture of its water quality. It is the same with populations: only a few bucketfuls of people are required to give us a good picture.

Let us now return to the earlier question that we posed in which we wanted to determine how many people in the United States eat breakfast every day. The first half-dozen people that we interview (randomly) could give results that are highly variable and the picture may not be clear. However, after a surprisingly small number of interviews, in fact around 30, a pattern will emerge. This is only a pattern and in no way allows us to predict the likelihood of whether the next respondent we are about to interview will eat breakfast or not. However, by the time we get to 200 or so interviews, we will find that the result begins to settle at around 80 to 90 per cent of people saying that they eat breakfast every day. Even though we may go on and interview hundreds more people, the result will not change a great deal. The way in which the variability of a sample stabilizes as the sample size increases is illustrated schematically in Figure 10.1.

FIGURE 10.1 Variability of response and sample size

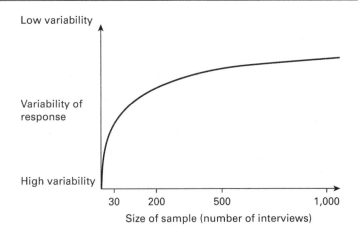

It will be noted from the figure that once our sample becomes larger than 30, the consistency of response (that is, it is less variable) markedly improves. Beyond the number of 30 we are moving from qualitative research into quantitative research, and once the sample size reaches 200 we are very definitely into quantitative territory. The area between 30 and 200 interviews is somewhat grey.

Sampling error

It is worth repeating this very important principle of random sampling – the sample size required to give an accurate result to a survey bears no relation to the size of the whole population; it is the absolute size of the sample that matters. It does not matter if we are researching breakfast-eating habits in a small country like Ireland with a population of just 4.6 million or a large country like the United States with a population of over 300 million, a random sample of 2,000 people in each country will give us the same, very accurate result that is plus or minus 2.2 per cent of the true result (at 95 per cent confidence levels).

What does very accurate mean? Because we have chosen the sample randomly, the accuracy of the result can be stated, at least within limits. These limits are expressed in terms of confidence or certainty. In most market research sampling, confidence limits are given at the 95 per cent level, meaning that we can be 95 per cent certain that if we carry out this sample again and again, choosing different people to interview each time, we will get a similar result. The result will only be similar – it will not be exactly the same. This is because there will be some degree of error from what would have been achieved had we carried out a complete census. However, with 2,000 interviews that error is only plus or minus 2.2 per cent of what the true figure would be from the census, which in the circumstances – not having to interview all those millions of people – is very good.

Hopefully, this is clear. A large, randomly selected sample size is all that is needed and it does not matter how many people there are in the total population. It now gets slightly more complicated because the error level is not always plus or minus 2.2 per cent for a sample size of 2,000; it varies depending on the actual response that is achieved. The point is that when we set out to measure the proportion of people that eat breakfast, we do not know what the result will be – that is the very point of carrying out the survey. It could be that everyone (or no one) eats breakfast, in which case this would very soon become clear. For example, let us imagine that we interviewed 500 people and asked them the stupid question, 'Do you take a drink of one kind or another every day?' When all 500 tell us that they do, we can be fairly certain that the next person we speak to will also tell us that he or she has a drink of one kind or another every day.

Now imagine that we interview 500 people and ask them 'Do you drink tea every day?' and from a survey we determine that half do; when we get to the 501st interview we cannot be certain whether this person will drink tea or not. This 50/50 split in an answer to a question is the worst case, whereas 100 per cent giving the same answer every time (or 0 per cent) is the best in terms of sampling error.

Before we carry out a survey we do not know what the result will be, and so we have to assume the worst case and quote the error assuming that 50 per cent will give a response to a question. And the plus or minus 2.2 per cent referred to for a sample of 2,000 is just that – it assumes that a response to a question from a survey will be 50 per cent.

So, we choose a sample size based on the worst case scenario (50/50). Once the survey is complete we have a result. In the case of the 'Do you eat breakfast?' question we find that 90 per cent of the people in the survey say that they do eat breakfast. We can then look up in tables or calculate using a formula what the error is around that specific figure of 90 per cent. Figure 8.2 shows a 'ready reckoner' that can be used to check the sample error at the 95 per cent confidence limits. Look along the top row to the percentage that says 10 per cent or 90 per cent (the proportion that say they eat breakfast). Look down the left-hand column to where it says the sample size is 2,000. Where the row and columns intersect you will see the error is given as plus or minus 1.3 per cent. In other words, we can be 95 per cent certain that the true proportion of people that eat breakfast (if we were to interview absolutely everybody) is between 88.7 per cent and 91.3 per cent.

If we interviewed only 500 people, the error on the 'Do you eat breakfast?' answer would be plus or minus 2.7 per cent, and it would be plus or minus 1.9 per cent if we interviewed 1,000 people. It is clear that the more people we interview, the better the quality of the result, but there are diminishing returns. Quadrupling the sample will usually double the accuracy for a given sample design.

The other important thing to remember about sample sizes is that they must always be judged in terms of their accuracy on the number in the group of people being examined – even if it is a subset of the whole. For example, the 2,000 people we interviewed to find out if they eat breakfast gave us a result that we are happy with plus or minus 1.3 per cent at the 95 per cent confidence level. However, if we get interested in the possible differences between children and adults or males and females, we have to take each subset separately. We may look at the female respondents in the sample (we will assume there were 1,000 females of all ages in total) and see that adolescent women appear less likely to eat breakfast than women over the age of 18. Let us say that the results show that only 70 per cent of adolescent girls eat breakfast compared with 90 per cent of the non-adolescent females in the total sample. Can we be sure that the difference between these two responses is significant – that the difference is a real one that would show every time if the survey was

FIGURE 10.2 Sample size ready reckoner

Sample size	1% Or 99%	2% Or 98%	3% Or 97%	4% Or 96%	5% Or 95%	6% Or 94%	8% Or 92%	10% Or 90%	12% Or 88%	15% Or 85%	20% Or 80%	25% Or 75%	30% Or 70%	35% Or 65%	40% Or 60%	45% Or 55%	50%
							% giving a response to a question										
25	4.0	5.6	6.8	7.8	8.7	9.5	10.8	12.0	13.0	14.3	16.0	17.3	18.3	19.1	19.6	19.8	20.0
50	2.8	4.0	4.9	5.6	6.2	6.8	7.7	8.5	9.2	10.1	11.4	12.3	13.0	13.5	13.9	14.1	14.2
75	2.3	3.2	3.9	4.5	5.0	5.5	6.2	6.9	7.5	8.2	9.2	10.0	10.5	11.0	11.3	11.4	11.5
100	2.0	2.8	3.4	3.9	4.4	4.8	5.4	6.0	6.5	7.1	8.0	8.7	9.2	9.5	9.8	9.9	10.0
150	1.6	2.3	2.8	3.2	3.6	3.9	4.4	4.9	5.3	5.9	6.6	7.1	7.5	7.8	8.0	8.1	8.2
200	1.4	2.0	2.4	2.8	3.1	3.4	3.8	4.3	4.6	5.1	5.7	6.1	6.5	6.8	7.0	7.0	7.1
250	1.2	1.8	2.2	2.5	2.7	3.0	3.4	3.8	4.1	4.5	5.0	5.5	5.8	6.0	6.2	6.2	6.3
300	1.1	1.6	2.0	2.3	2.5	2.8	3.1	3.5	3.8	4.1	4.6	5.0	5.3	5.5	5.7	5.8	5.8
400	.99	1.4	1.7	2.0	2.2	2.4	2.7	3.0	3.3	3.6	4.0	4.3	4.6	4.8	4.9	5.0	5.0
500	.89	1.3	1.5	1.8	2.0	2.1	2.4	2.7	2.9	3.2	3.6	3.9	4.1	4.3	4.4	4.5	4.5
600	.81	1.1	1.4	1.6	1.8	2.0	2.2	2.5	2.7	2.9	3.3	3.6	3.8	3.9	4.0	4.1	4.1
800	.69	.98	1.2	1.4	1.5	1.7	1.9	2.1	2.3	2.5	2.8	3.0	3.2	3.3	3.4	3.5	3.5
1,000	.63	.90	1.1	1.3	1.4	1.5	1.7	1.9	2.1	2.3	2.6	2.8	2.9	3.1	3.1	3.2	3.2
1,200	.57	.81	.99	1.1	1.3	1.4	1.6	1.7	1.9	2.1	2.3	2.5	2.7	2.8	2.8	2.9	2.9
1,500	.51	.73	.89	1.0	1.1	1.2	1.4	1.6	1.7	1.9	2.1	2.3	2.4	2.5	2.5	2.6	2.6
2,000	.44	.61	.75	.86	.96	1.0	1.2	1.3	1.4	1.6	1.8	1.9	2.0	2.1	2.2	2.2	2.2
2,500	.40	.56	.68	.78	.87	.95	1.1	1.2	1.3	1.4	1.6	1.7	1.8	1.9	2.0	2.2	2.0
3,000	.36	.51	.62	.71	.79	.87	.99	1.1	1.2	1.3	1.5	1.6	1.7	1.7	1.8	1.8	1.8

Range of error at 95% confidence limits

repeated with new samples? Before we can answer this we need to know how many adolescent females were in the sample. In fact, there were only 150 adolescent females interviewed compared with 850 non-adolescent females (there being 1,000 females and 1,000 males making up the 2,000 total sample). Look on the error tables and see what the range of error is on these results.

We see that for the adolescent females the range of error for this result is plus or minus 7.5 per cent, or between 62.5 per cent and 77.5 per cent eat breakfast. The range of error for the non-adolescent females is plus or minus 2 per cent, or between 88 per cent and 92 per cent eat breakfast. Because the ranges of error do not overlap between these two results, we can say that the difference is statistically significant – we can be certain that the survey has shown a real difference in terms of breakfast eating behaviour between these two subgroups of the sample. It is because we most probably will want to interrogate the sample to compare and contrast the responses from subgroups that we need a substantial total sample. Each subgroup has to be regarded as a sample in its own right when we calculate the sample error, so we need enough numbers of respondents in the sub-cells to give us a statistically significant response.

A final word on error: it will be recalled that we said that very few samples are drawn from the total mass of population; rather the samples are selected in stages by randomly choosing a region (for example a state or political area) and then a random sample of sub-areas within that political region until finally the households are drawn randomly from the electoral register. As a result of this procedure, the sample of households will be clustered into small areas that can be far more economically contacted and interviewed. Because multi-stage sampling is much less costly to administer than a true random sample, it is widely used in market research wherever random samples of the whole population are sought. The technique can be used with other sample frames as well as the electoral register. A problem with the technique, however, is that sampling error is always increased. Effectively, additional sampling error is introduced at each stage of the sampling process and needs to be allowed for when selecting the size of sample.

Random sampling and non-response

From a sampling perspective, non-response is a major source of bias in the achieved sample. For one reason or another it is in practice impossible to collect data from every individual making up a sample. Some will not be contactable, some may have moved away or died and some will certainly refuse to participate. If respondents live in certain parts of an inner city it may be impractical to even approach them – interviewers increasingly will not go into some notorious areas. If for a random sample the response rate achieved is say 80 per cent (in practice now considered to be very high), the achieved sample from 500 people originally selected will be only 400, and possibly the accuracy levels with this smaller sample will be too low. Of course the problem can be solved by sample replacement – take a supplementary sample and make contact until the desired 500 interviews are achieved. However, we are back to problems of bias. The non-respondents may in some way or another differ significantly (in relation to the aims of the study) from those who were interviewed and the results may not, therefore, be representative of the whole population. Certainly some non-respondents differ from respondents in that they refuse to participate in surveys, and this may well be very relevant in political polling or attitude research (that is, non-cooperators may be a certain personality type who hold more critical attitudes in general).

Non-response is a major problem for market researchers, particularly because average response rates to surveys are falling year by year. One advantage of random and pre-selected samples in relation to non-response is that at least the level of response achieved in a survey can be quantified – with a complete list of the sample the results of contact with each potential respondent can be logged. Also, because of contact records, rigorous call-back procedures can be enforced to increase response: interviewers can be required to return up to three times at different times of the day to attempt the interview. Such procedures cannot be used in quota sampling (or at least their implementation cannot be assured), the subject to which we now turn.

Quota samples

In reality, very few samples in market research are truly random in the way that we have described so far. This is because random samples are quite difficult and expensive to administer. In order to have a random sample, we must have the whole population available to us from which we can make our selection. In Europe, interviewing amongst households may be carried out face to face, calling at dwellings that have been identified in some systematic and random fashion. Typical of these is a random walk in which a street is randomly selected, a house is randomly selected on that street and then the interviewer has instructions to then interview every nth house and to alternately choose an intersection to turn down. Special rules will cover blocks of apartments and what to do when buildings are non-residential. Already you can see that it is getting complicated and there is scope for the instructions to go wrong.

Choosing the sample from an electoral register overcomes this nth number and left–right problem but there could still be quite some distances between the calls, making them very expensive.

And then who do you interview when the door is answered? The old-fashioned notion of there being a 'head of household' has long since been abandoned and today it would be more relevant to include screening questions to find out who has most influence on a specific activity such as shopping for food, buying a car or whatever is the subject of the study.

In the United States there are very few door-to-door surveys. The size of the country and the possible dangers associated with knocking on strangers' doors in city areas are two very good reasons this is so. Instead, the phone is more likely to be used for the interview or the survey will be online. However, there is neither a perfect database of phone numbers nor a perfect panel of online respondents. Significant numbers of people are ex-directory and they could represent a group of respondents with special characteristics – older and wealthier, more likely to be female. Overcoming these deficiencies of sample quality leads to inventive methods such as random digit dialling for phone surveys (eventually a real number is found and starts ringing) or the selection of a number at random from the white pages and changing the final digit by increasing it by one number (say the randomly selected number from the directory was +1 972 735 0537 then it would be changed by adding one to the last digit to become +1 972 735 0538). Both random digit dialling and 'plus 1' dialling involves high costs of wasted calls – to non-residential subscribers and non-existent numbers. Also, since among the reasons why people choose to be ex-directory undoubtedly is that they do not want to be bothered by people such as market research interviewers, response rates will be even lower than among listed households. (Response rates in consumer phone interviewing are low in any case.)

These problems of telephone sampling and face-to-face sampling are becoming somewhat irrelevant as online surveys take over. Online now dominates as a fieldwork method in almost every developed country. Here the problems are more to do with the quality of members of the online panels (who are these people who sign up to panels and seek rewards from filling in questionnaires?).

We will set aside the problem of online panels for the time being (see Chapter 15) and return to the subject of sampling. Many of the problems associated with random sampling are avoided if we carry out 'quota samples'. The demographic structure of most populations is known. Previous surveys and census data tells us the splits by gender, age, income groups (or social grade), geography and many other key selection criteria. Therefore, a simpler and cheaper means of obtaining a representative sample is to set a quota for the interviewers to achieve a picture that mirrors the population that is being researched. Filling the quota will provide a mix of respondents that is reflective of the population being targeted.

Most fieldwork nowadays is controlled by computers that hold the sample, which is in turn coded according to the different characteristics of the quota. In the case of telephone interviews the sample that is contacted is fed to the interviewers through

TABLE 10.1   Example of interlocking quotas

Numbers of people to be interviewed in each income group

Age	High income group	Medium-to-high income group	Medium-to-low income group	Low income group	Total
18–24	2	12	8	11	33
25–44	12	19	18	16	65
45+	17	24	25	36	102
Total	31	55	51	63	200

the computer-aided telephone interviewing (CATI) programme. When the number of interviews required for a certain group of respondents (ie the quota) is achieved, the computer closes down the delivery of samples for that group. In consumer research, demographics such as gender and income groups (or social grade) are common quota parameters, and they are often interlocked (for example, age group quotas for each income group). Table 10.1 illustrates this. In research using these quotas, respondents would be selected by the interviewing team to match the characteristics of each cell (for example, 12 respondents of the medium-to-high income group and aged 18 to 24), until all cells are filled. In Table 10.1, the quotas shown are for a total sample.

One practical problem with quota sampling is that the numbers required within a subgroup (for instance, higher-income groups) may be sufficient to meet the needs of the total sample size but too small to provide reliable results about a subgroup that may be of particular interest. The common solution to this problem is to 'oversample' the subgroup (for example, instead of 10 per cent of the sample being in the 'heavy consumers' group, this is increased to 25 per cent) and the results adjusted back to the true profile of the population at the data analysis stage through the use of weighting techniques.

Quota samples are very commonly used in market research. Their chief practical merit is low cost: there are no clerical costs of pre-selecting the sample, the interviewers' productivity (interviews per day) is higher because they are not following up initial non-responses and the technique can be used with online interviews or low-cost mall or street interviewing (where obviously pre-selection is a non-starter). The theoretical disadvantages are, however, considerable. There is the bias of respondents being selected by interviewers, who may consciously or otherwise reject potential respondents who appear 'difficult'. Also, since initial non-responders are not followed up, there is a bias against those respondents who are less accessible – for example, people working long hours.

Then there is the problem of non-computable sampling error. Quota samples, like random samples, are of course subject to sampling error but in this case there is no simple way of calculating what it is. Often the sampling error is calculated as if the sample was random but there is no theoretical basis for doing this. A number of studies have compared results from quota surveys with those from random probability surveys and it is claimed that data from quota and random probability samples are, in the main, comparable – most showing only small differences between sample types.

As well as its application in quantitative research, quota sampling is widely used to recruit qualitative samples for focus group discussions and depth interviews. In a fairly loose sense the intention is to cover a sample that is broadly representative of the target population in terms of demographics, product usage or even attitudes to critical issues. However, since there is no attempt to quantify from the research in any rigorous sense, questions and problems of sampling error do not apply. Problems of interviewer bias in selection, however, still need to be considered.

Sampling in business-to-business markets

Business-to-business research is concerned with populations not of individuals but of organizations (companies, not-for-profit organizations, government departments and the like). Surprisingly, there is no universal sample frame, or even comprehensive ones for most sectors, that is anywhere complete. Lists of companies can be bought from many sources, including such large directories as *Hoovers*. Although they are reasonably comprehensive, these directories miss out many smaller businesses and include names of businesses that are in unrelated fields. Also where research is of an industry sector (commonly referred to as a 'vertical'), the definition of the sector relevant to the research objectives may not match the classifications used in sample frames.

These comments may suggest that reliable sampling is not possible in business-to-business research but this is to overstate the problem. In practice, samples taken from such directories, and built from several sources, while not completely free from bias, are good enough for most purposes. There are also other issues important in business-to-business research apart from sample frame limitations, and particularly those relating to the fact that the companies in the population are not of equal size. Take for example the chemical industry. At one level there could be a small company employing one or two people and mixing chemicals with a bucket and a stick,

FIGURE 10.3 Domination of companies in business-to-business markets

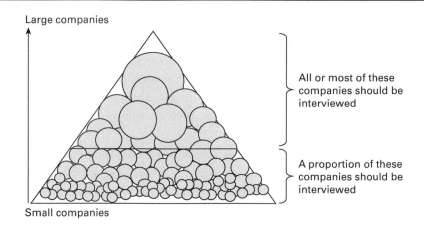

through to huge companies such as DuPont, BASF and Dow. In most business-to-business markets the distribution of companies follows the 80:20 or Pareto rule: that is, 20 per cent of the units account for 80 per cent of the market being studied. The domination of most industries by a small number of large companies means it is crucial that they are included in the sample. In fact, the researcher may seek (so far as cooperation levels allow) to carry out a census of the largest companies, and a sample of the rest (see Figure 10.3).

This singling out of specific companies to interview is judgemental, although there will be some guiding principles such as the number of employees, the revenue and its domination of an industry vertical.

Not only does the business-to-business researcher have to contend with wide differences of company size, there are also complications caused by the intricate nature of the decision-making unit (DMU). Whereas decisions in most households are made by the partners and the children (or even by just one person), in businesses there are inputs from purchasing, technical, production, and possibly finance and marketing. These inputs change over time. At the point where a product is being specified or evaluated for the first time, the technical team is likely to have a strong voice. Once the product is in the routine re-ordering stage, the purchasing and production people have more influence. So who do you select to interview? In theory you may set out to build up a picture across the board by selecting people from each group. However, since many business-to-business samples are small (200 interviews is quite a respectable size), the sub-cells of respondents in a particular job responsibility end up being too small to analyse separately. For these reasons business-to-business researchers may compromise and decide to concentrate the interviews on just one group such as the key decision maker (thankfully there is usually one person who holds most sway in a business-to-business decision).

Using statistics to derive importance of factors

The discussion so far in this chapter has been on the subject of sampling. The availability of statistical-processing software tools such as SPSS means that researchers are constantly looking for means of squeezing the data for more meaning. One common application that researchers should be aware of is the use of regression techniques to work out the importance of the various factors that are rated in customer-satisfaction surveys.

Customer-satisfaction surveys have two important components: measurement of the importance of the many factors that are part of the offer from a company (for example, delivery on time, consistent quality, technical support) and satisfaction with these factors or attributes. However, researchers are constantly plagued by the measurement of importance, because what people say is important when choosing a supplier may not be what makes them satisfied with that supplier. This we know because when we attempt to correlate all the attributes with the score given to overall satisfaction, we find different drivers of satisfaction from those that people stated were important in their choice of brand or supplier. For example, we find strong correlations between the 'softer' service and people-related factors and overall satisfaction. This high level of association between certain individual factors and overall satisfaction implies that they are a significant influence on that overall figure.

Some researchers believe measures of derived importance are more relevant than the answers to direct questions on what is important (stated importance), as the derived-importance figures show where improvements will raise the overall satisfaction score. However, there are dangers in ignoring the stated importance. Although these may not be a complete guide to what drives satisfaction, they are basic requirements that are so important they have to be provided, at an acceptable level, by every supplier. In effect they are hygiene factors and typically include product quality, value for money and quick delivery. They may not drive satisfaction, but they do determine whether you 'play in the game' and whether your company is chosen as a supplier in the first place. These hygiene factors are important in enabling a supplier to win business, while the softer factors that drive satisfaction are the ones that determine whether the business is retained.

Using statistics to arrive at needs-based segmentations

Segmentation is concerned with ascertaining the size and nature of subgroups of a population and it may be based on any number of characteristics. Consumer segments can be recognized according to demographics such as gender, age, income or where people live. We may also recognize groups of consumers by their psychographic differences, not just their demographic differences and behaviour.

The classification data on questionnaires provide demographic data, while questions in the body of the interview determine aspects of behaviour and needs. Cross-tabulations of data on these criteria allow us to see the different responses among groups of respondents. This is segmentation at its simplest level, and every researcher uses the computer tabulations of findings to establish groups of respondents with marked differences.

However, we can use statistical techniques, in particular multivariate analysis, to allow more sophisticated segments to emerge. In a segmentation study (or even in a customer-satisfaction study), respondents are asked to say to what extent they agree with a number of statements. Or points may be allocated to a range of factors to indicate their importance. Answers to these questions determine the needs and interests of the respondents. The possible combination of different groupings of the many questions in a questionnaire from 1,000 interviews is literally millions of millions and we need some means of creating combinations that have a natural fit.

Using a technique known as factor analysis, statisticians can work out which groups of attributes best fit together. After this grouping has taken place it is usually possible to see common themes such as people who want low prices with few extras, people who want lots of services or add-ons and are prepared to pay for them, people who are concerned about environmental factors and so on. Factor analysis reduces the large number of attributes to a smaller but representative subset. These subsets are then given labels such as 'price fighters', 'service seekers' and any other such terms that help the marketing team know exactly who they are addressing.

The groupings of needs that have been worked out by factor analysis are now run through further computations using a technique known as cluster analysis. These factors are inserted into the cluster analysis, whose algorithms rearrange the data into the partitions that have been specified and so determine how neatly the population fits into the different groupings.

The statistical approach to a needs-based segmentation has become extremely popular, and it is certainly an important objective means of finding more interesting and possibly more relevant ways of addressing the customer base. However, the tastes and needs of populations are constantly changing, and we should always be mindful of new segments that may not show up as more than a dot on the current radar screen. For example, even if Guinness had carried out a needs-based segmentation amongst its (mainly elderly) customers in the 1960s, it might not have recognized the opportunity to reposition the drink as being young and trendy. This segment was developed by a series of astute marketing campaigns.

Top tips

- Check with the sponsor of the study how accurate the survey needs to be. There is no point commissioning a large and expensive survey if they are looking only for directional pointers.

- Recognize the difference between sampling in consumer markets and business-to-business markets. In business-to-business markets you will be interested in sampling buyers and specifiers within companies of different sizes and in different vertical markets. In consumer markets you will be more interested in obtaining a representative group of consumers or potential consumers.

- When deciding on the overall size of the sample, build it up from the sub-cells of respondents that are of interest and ensure that you have enough people in each of these cells. A minimum size for a sub-cell in a quantitative survey is around 50 people. So, if you want to interview men and women in four different age groups you will need a total sample size of not less than 400 people in all.

- Use statistics wherever you can to squeeze more understanding from the data.

- Make use of the statistical functions in Excel that allow non-statisticians to do simple tasks like correlating two sets of data. For example, correlating the overall satisfaction score of respondents with the scores that they give for individual aspects of a product or service will show the 'derived importance' of each of those individual factors. This could save having to ask people how important things are when choosing a brand or supplier.

SUMMARY

Every market researcher needs to understand the basics of sampling. The only surveys that can be measured in terms of their accuracy are those based on a census or a random sample. Sampling enables us to take a small proportion of the total population and to establish a result that is representative of the whole.

The variability in the responses to a survey question begins to settle down once there are more than 30 completed interviews. The more accurate the required result, the larger the sample needed. It is the absolute size of the sample that matters. A random sample of 500 people will produce a survey result that we can be almost certain (95 per cent confident) will be plus or minus 4.5 per cent of what would be achieved had we interviewed everyone in the population. A sample that is four times larger will deliver a result that is twice as accurate because there are diminishing returns from increasing the sample size.

There are practical problems associated with random samples. Most market research surveys are based on quota samples, which ensure that the composition of the sample is the same as the overall breakdown of the population.

Industrial and many business-to-business markets require a different approach to sampling because the members of the population are (unlike in consumer markets) of widely differing size. Lists are built up of the companies that make up the market, and they are stratified on the basis of size or their industrial classification. In most industries a small number of companies dominate and so as many of these are interviewed as possible because they represent a disproportionate consumption within their sector.

Statistical modelling is used widely in market research to derive the importance of factors that drive customer satisfaction. This type of analysis often shows that softer issues such as friendliness of staff and good communications affect customer satisfaction in a more positive manner than some of the hygiene factors such as price, product quality and delivery.

The analysis of findings almost always involves comparing the results of different segments (groups of respondents). More sophisticated statistical techniques are used to discover needs-based segments. Factor analysis is used to distil the many attitude ratings into groups of common themes. Cluster analysis is then used to find out the size of these segments within a population.

Questionnaire design

What is so difficult about designing a questionnaire?

Asking questions and getting the right answers is not always as straightforward as it may seem. Someone beginning their market research career may presume that questionnaire design is a clear-cut process – ask questions of the right respondents and you will get the right answer. How hard can it really be? It is true that anyone can string some questions together, and normally you will get an answer in some shape or form, but it may not be the answer you were looking for.

Questionnaire design is one of the hardest and most important parts of market research. It is the equivalent of the architect's plan when designing a building – if the plan is wrong in any way, the building will fail to satisfy. However, just as two architects could submit quite different designs for a building, two researchers would probably never design the same questionnaire. Questionnaire design allows licence to the creator. The guidelines that set the framework for individuals to design questionnaires are outlined in this chapter.

The role of questionnaires

The questionnaire plays a number of important roles. Its primary purpose is to facilitate the extraction of data from a respondent. It serves as an 'aide memoire' to the interviewer so that there is no need to learn the questions off by heart. It provides consistency in the way the interview is conducted, especially as frequently a number of interviewers are working on a project at the same time. Without a questionnaire, questions would be asked in a haphazard way at the discretion of the individual. Questionnaires also play an important part in the data collection methodology. They allow responses to be recorded in a consistent way to facilitate data analysis.

Different types of questionnaires

A questionnaire can be administered in three different ways: by phone, face to face or self-completion (through mail or online). These three incongruent methods require different forms of questionnaire (Table 11.1).

TABLE 11.1   The three different types of questionnaire

Questionnaire type	Area of use	Method of administration
Structured	Large, quantitative studies	Telephone/face to face/online
Semi-structured	Qualitative consumer studies, business-to-business studies	Telephone/face to face
Unstructured	Qualitative studies	Depth telephone/face to face/ group discussions

Structured questionnaires consist of closed or prompted questions (with predefined answers – see next section) that require the designer to be aware of or to anticipate all possible answers. They are used in large interview programmes (anything over 30 interviews and more likely more than 200 in number) and may be carried out over the telephone, face to face or by self-completion depending on the respondent type, the content of the questionnaire and the budget.

Semi-structured questionnaires comprise a mixture of closed and open questions. They are used in business-to-business market research where there is a need to accommodate a large range of different responses from companies. The use of semi-structured questionnaires enables a mix of qualitative and quantitative information to be gathered. They can be administered over the telephone or face to face.

Unstructured questionnaires are made up of free-ranging questions that allow respondents to express themselves in their own way. They list questions in an apparent order but they are not so rigid that the interviewer has to slavishly follow them in every detail. There is enough flexibility to go down separate lines of questioning and to probe, or even construct new lines of unscripted enquiry. Unstructured questionnaires are used in qualitative research for depth interviewing (face to face, depth telephone interviews) and they form the basis of many studies into technical or narrow markets.

Different types of questions

Questions can be classified in different ways. An important distinction is made between open questions and closed questions.

Open questions gather free responses that are usually collected exactly as they are spoken by respondents. Since respondents have the freedom to express answers in any way they like, this type of questioning is highly appropriate for exploratory research. Open questions are also used where the range of possible responses is not known in advance and cannot be tightly classified into pre-codes.

Open questions present problems for researchers. First, they are difficult to evaluate as they must be grouped together before any statistical analysis can take place. Second, comments must be captured verbatim, which means that interviewers must try to take down every word as it is spoken by writing or typing into a computer. If a recording is taken of the interview and it is typed up later, the penalty will be the huge amount of time required for this purpose. It can take three times as long to type up the answers to an interview from a recording as it takes to carry out the interview itself. In most administered interviews the notes taken by interviewers will suffice. Here we rely on the skills of the interviewer to be able to capture the essence of the response in as much detail as possible without adding their own interpretation of what respondents really meant.

The second style of question is the closed question. These take the form of single or multi-response questions. Single response questions can, as the term suggests, have only one possible answer. Typical of these is the dichotomous question that has just two possible options 'yes' or 'no' (a legitimate response could also be 'don't know'). Many attitudinal questions are single response in that respondents have to choose an answer from a predetermined list of attributes or on a predetermined scale.

Multiple response questions allow respondents to offer more than one answer and are typically about awareness and use, such as which brands are known and which brands are used. A number of brands may well be mentioned.

Most closed questions are prompted in that respondents are given a list of potential answers from which they can choose the one most appropriate for themselves. The predefined answers are worked out by common sense and industry knowledge, or following qualitative research or a pilot study. It is an important principle of questionnaire design that the market researcher should think about all possible answers to the question before the survey is carried out. Not only should all possible answers be considered, the way these are worded as choices for respondents is also critical. The omission of a possible answer in the list that is presented to the respondent, or the incorrect framing of the answer in the questionnaire, could affect the quality of the survey.

In general, closed questions offer efficiencies to researchers. They are easier to analyse and are usually quicker to administer and ask. For this reason they are used in large samples and in self-completion interviews. The consistency in the response categories allows trends to be tracked over time if the same questions are used.

Questions can also be classified by their purpose. Questions are designed to collect three different types of information: information about behaviour, information about attitudes, and information that is used for classification purposes. Table 11.2 summarizes the three different types of information that can be gathered and the surveys in which they are used.

TABLE 11.2   The three different types of questions

Question type	Information sought	Types of surveys
Behavioural	Information on what respondents buy, where they buy it from, how much they buy, how frequently they buy, to what extent they switch their buying patterns etc.	Surveys to find out market size, market shares, awareness and usage.
Attitudinal	What people think of products and suppliers. The image and ratings of products and suppliers. Why people do things.	Image and attitude surveys. Brand studies. Customer satisfaction and loyalty surveys.
Classification	Information that can be used to group respondents to see how they differ one from the other, such as their age, gender, social class, location of household, type of house, family composition.	All surveys.

Behavioural questions

Behavioural questions are designed to find out what people (or companies) do. Such questions are extremely important in market research because they are a strong indicator of attitudes. Answers to behavioural questions can be more robust and believable than answers to attitudinal questions. For example, we could ask somebody why they choose a certain type of car and they could respond by telling us that they choose it because they seek reliability above all else and they want a car that holds its value. If we then ask them what sort of car they own and they tell us that they own a Lamborghini, we may believe that their behaviour is a stronger indication of what is driving this person than their stated answer.

As the term suggests, behavioural questions are designed to understand what people do. For example, do people go to the movies? How often do they go? What type of films do they watch? Who do they go with? Behavioural questions determine people's actions in terms of what they have eaten (or drunk), bought, used, visited, seen, read or heard. They record facts and not matters of opinion and on these grounds they are important because opinions can change whereas behaviour is more stable.

Linked to this subject is the growing importance of behavioural economics in market research. Behavioural economists believe that decisions are not necessarily made on logic alone but on heuristics – experiences that give people a rule of thumb by which to make their decisions. These non-rational decisions may explain why people don't always do things in the way that we thought they would. Of course, this could also be due to market inefficiencies in that we cannot assume that everybody is fully aware of all suppliers, of all their prices and the products that they supply.

Behavioural questions can be extremely important for segmenting customer groups. Because behaviour very strongly reflects attitudes and demographics, it provides a solid base on which to group customers so that the products we sell and the communications that support them are more closely targeted to people's needs.

Behavioural questions address the following:

Have you ever...?

Do you ever...?

Who do you know...?

When did you last...?

Which do you do most often...?

Who does it...?

How many...?

Do you have...?

In what way do you do it...?

In the future will you...?

Attitudinal questions

People hold opinions or beliefs on everything from politics to social precepts, to the products they buy and the companies that make or supply them. These attitudes are not necessarily right, but this is hardly relevant since it is perceptions that matter. People's attitudes affect their behaviour. Even though attitudes are more ephemeral than behaviour, we need to understand them as they are the litmus that tells us about emotions.

Many people are in denial about the degree to which emotions affect their behaviour, claiming that they are rational consumers driven by hard fact and reality. In practice, emotions have a huge influence on buying behaviour and even the most hardened business-to-business buyers do not leave their emotions at home when they go to work. People vote for politicians that they think are attractive. They choose products that they believe will reflect well on them. They buy from suppliers that they think will not get them into trouble.

Researchers explore attitudes using questions that begin with who? what? why? where? when? and how? as well as other exploratory phrases such as 'would you explain ...?' Attitudinal questions address the following:

Why do you...?

What do you think of...?

Do you agree or disagree...?

How do you rate...?

Which is best (or worst) for...?

Scales are commonly used to measure attitudes. Scalar questions use a limited choice of response, chosen to measure an attitude, an intention, an opinion or belief or a respondent's behaviour. Scalar questions may involve numbers for measurement. The numbers help communicate to respondents their agreement or disagreement with a posed question, as well as facilitating statistical analysis of the final data.

We now discuss different types of scales that can be used to measure attitudes:

- numerical rating scales;
- verbal rating scales;
- semantic differential scales (using adjectives);
- ranking.

Numerical rating scales

In a numerical rating scale respondents are asked to indicate their attitude with a number. Scales usually range from 0 to 10 or anything in between. The lower score is usually deemed to be a low association and the higher score indicates a high level of agreement or association with an attitude. These scales are particularly useful for market researchers as they nail a respondent's attitude to a specific number, avoiding vague verbal statements such as 'I like it very much.'

Q. How would you rate the pack on the following?				
Very convenient				Not at all convenient
5	4	3	2	1

Even though numerical rating scales aren't the way we would usually indicate to our friends or colleagues what we think of something, most respondents are able to relate to them.

There is much debate in the research community about which scales should be used, whether 4-point, 5-point, 7-point or 10-point.

A 5-point scale is commonly used because it is simple, has a midpoint, and reflects the five-point Likert Scale, which uses words and ranges from strongly agree through to strongly disagree. So too, 10-point scales are frequently used in customer-satisfaction surveys as they offer respondents a higher degree of sensitivity, there being more numbers they can choose from.

In some questions a 4-point scale is preferred as it doesn't have an option for sitting on the fence or a middle-of-the-road answer.

It is important that the researcher chooses a scale that suits the questions and can be used again and again if a tracking study is planned. Switching from a 5-point scale in one survey to a 10-point scale for the same question in the following year's survey may mean that the results aren't directly comparable. It is also good practice to have some consistency in the scales used in a questionnaire so that respondents don't have to keep switching between scales with different anchor points.

In Germanic-speaking Europe a score of 1 is usually considered best (or good) since this is the convention in marking schoolwork. There is no problem using scales where a high number is considered good, but the nature of the scale would need to be strongly emphasized at the time of the interview.

Verbal rating scales

Verbal rating scales are known as Likert scales, named after Rensis Likert, the American psychologist who popularized a psychometric scale that typically presents five choices. For example:

Q. To what extent would you agree or disagree that the government has inflation under control?

Strongly agree

Agree

Neutral

Disagree

Strongly disagree

Equally, a verbal rating scale could ask about the likelihood of doing something. For example:

Q. And how likely would you be to try this product?

Very likely

Quite likely

Neither likely nor unlikely

Quite unlikely

Very unlikely

Answers to a hypothetical question such as this cannot necessarily be believed. When someone is asked in a market research survey to say how likely they are to try or buy a product it is very different from a real buying situation where money is exchanged. In general the answers to such a question are likely to be over claimed as people find it much easier to say they are very likely to try or buy a product in a market research interview than they are when confronted with a real buying situation. However, the answers can still be useful as they show which group of respondents are more likely to be disposed to the product than others and so guide us to where the best target lies. We can also use such questions for tracking the degree to which attitudes are changing – are people showing a greater inclination to try the product now than they did in an earlier survey?

A variation on the verbal rating scale is to present respondents with a number of statements to which they have to say whether they agree or disagree. For example:

Q. I will read out some statements that people have said about the xxx car. Would you give me a score out of 5 to say whether you agree or disagree with the statement? A score of 5 means you agree strongly and a score of 1 means you disagree strongly. Score 6 for don't know/cannot say.

	Strongly disagree				Strongly agree	Don't know/ cannot say
A car that is a pleasure to look at	1	2	3	4	5	6
A car I hope says something to others about me	1	2	3	4	5	6
A car that is distinctive but not flashy	1	2	3	4	5	6
A rational choice of car	1	2	3	4	5	6
An emotional choice of car	1	2	3	4	5	6
The cheapest suitable car I could find	1	2	3	4	5	6
A car I enjoy driving fast	1	2	3	4	5	6
A car that doesn't attract too much attention	1	2	3	4	5	6
A car with a happy personality of its own	1	2	3	4	5	6
A car that tells people I am different	1	2	3	4	5	6

Answers to these questions could be used to segment customers according to their psychographic attitude to cars.

Semantic differential scales (Osgood scales)

A variation on the verbal/semantic scale is to ask respondents which words best describe a company or a product. The adjectives can be both positive and negative and very often they are opposites. Such scales are commonly known as semantic differential scales and were introduced by Charles Osgood, an American psychologist who hypothesized that we can understand emotional connections and associations by asking people to choose between opposing words. For example:

Q.	I would like to read out some words that describe people. You have to choose one word from each pair to describe yourself. If you think neither fits, you must choose the one which is closest. Would you say that you are:			
	Introvert	1	or extrovert	2
	Traditionalist	1	or an experimenter	2
	Stylish	1	or unfashionable	2
	Ambitious	1	or content	2
	Unsociable	1	or gregarious	2
	Intellectual	1	or not intellectual	2

This type of question is used by market researchers to find out people's emotional attachments to brands. Here is an example:

Q. For each pair of words below, please indicate whether you believe the logo of this product more strongly communicates one word over the other. The closer the scale to the word, the stronger that word is communicated. The neutral point in the middle means that neither of the words is communicated more strongly than the other through the logo.

				NEUTRAL				
Specialized								Broad
Classic								Modern
Bold								Humble
Premium								Value for money
Products								Services
Dynamic								Stable

Ranking questions

Researchers often need to find out what is the order of importance of various factors from a list. Typically this is achieved by presenting the list and asking which is most important, which is second most important and so on. In ranking questions it is usually not valid to ask respondents to rank beyond the top three factors, because the less important the factor, the harder it is to assign a level of rank.

Q. I will now show you a card on which is listed a number of factors that could be important to you when choosing a combined weedkiller and fertilizer. Would you look at the list and tell me which is the most important factor in influencing your choice? READ LIST. ROTATE START. RANK JUST THREE FACTORS.

And what would be the second most important factor?

And what would be the third most important factor?

Factor	Rank
Available in the garden centre	_____
A competitive price	_____
Works at any time of year	_____
Kills weeds and moss	_____
Not poisonous to children or pets	_____
Made by a well-known company	_____

Ranking questions that are read out must not be too long or the respondents will forget what has been asked. Six factors in the list is about the maximum when the interview is administered and read out to respondents.

Ranking is a simple means of determining the importance attached to items and it works well for the most and second most important factors. However, it can be misleading for the lower-ranked issues because although they may appear towards the end of the list, they could still be important to some respondents.

Classification questions

Very often clients will tell us that they want a quick survey carrying out and they have only three or four questions that need asking. Almost certainly they will have forgotten about the need to ask classification questions. These are the Cinderella questions that are critically important as they allow us to classify and cut the data.

Classification questions are used to build profiles of respondents by determining their age, their gender, their social class, where they live, their marital status, the type of house they live in, the number of people in their family and so on. In business-to-business surveys they are used to classify the size of company that has been interviewed, the industrial vertical to which it belongs, the occupation of the respondent, the geographical location of the company and so on. The same classification questions may also be used to control the quota of people or companies that are interviewed. Most classification questions are factual or behavioural.

A number of standard classification questions crop up constantly in market research surveys. These are:

- Gender – Male or female.
- Age – In a survey of the general public we always would want to know the age of the respondent.

Q. In which of the following ranges does your age fall?

Under 18	
18–24	45–54
25–34	55–64
35–44	65+

These bands of age fit with most countries demographic analysis of their population.

Marital status

This is usually asked by simply saying 'Are you ...'

Single
Married
Widowed
Divorced
Separated

Socio-economic grade (SEG)

This is a classification peculiar to UK market researchers and was developed for the National Readership Survey to classify readers of newspapers. Respondents are pigeon-holed according to the occupation of the 'head of the household'. Thus, it combines attributes of income, education and work status. In addition to social grades, researchers sometimes classify respondents by income group or lifestyle. Socio-economic grades were in widespread use in 20th century British surveys but they are less popular today as the occupation of the head of the household has become much less clear.

In summary the socio-economic grades are:

A: Higher managerial, administrative or professional
B: Intermediate managerial, administrative or professional
C1: Supervisory, clerical, junior administrative or professional
C2: Skilled manual workers
D: Semi-skilled and unskilled manual workers
E: State pensioners, widows, casual and lowest grade workers

The grades are often grouped into ABC1 and C2DE and these are taken to equate to middle class and working class respectively.

Alternatively, a question may be asked about the income of the respondent or the combined income of the household. The question can be desensitized by using income bands (these will need to be changed depending on the audience that is being interviewed and which country they are in).

Q. What is the collective annual income of your household?

Under $25,000	$75,000 to $99,999
$25,000 to $49,999	$100,000 to $150,000
$50,000 to $74,999	Over $150,000

Industrial verticals

Countries have standard classifications for business types. In the United States the NAICS (North American Industry Classification System) was specifically introduced in 1997 (with revisions in 2002) for governmental regulations and census reports. In Europe companies are classified according to their Standard Industrial Classification (SIC). Often researchers condense the many divisions into more convenient and broader groupings such as:

professional services (eg law, accounting, architecture, recruitment etc);

financial services/investment/real estate/insurance;

marketing/market research;

advertising/design/media;

non-food manufacturing/engineering/processing/packaging;

food manufacturing/processing/food services/catering;

entertainment/restaurants;

IT/software/telecommunications/electronics;

government/public sector (excluding education & healthcare);

education;

healthcare/medical/pharmaceutical;

retail;

distribution/logistics/transport/wholesale;

utilities/energy;

agriculture/mining/forestry;

voluntary sector;

construction and building trades.

In surveys of the general public, it may be relevant to establish the level of employment of the respondent. For example:

working full time (over 30 hours a week);

working part time (8–30 hours a week);

housewife (full time at home);

student (full time);

retired;

temporarily unemployed (but seeking work);

permanently unemployed (for example, chronically sick, independent means and so on).

Number of employees

The size of the firm in which the respondent works can be classified according to the number of employees:

sole proprietor (no employees);

1–9;

10–24;

25–99;

100–249;

250+.

Location

Depending on the scope of the survey, this can be a country, a state or a broader region such as East Coast, Central, West Coast.

We have described the different types of questionnaires and the different types of questions that are used to create a questionnaire. Figure 9.1 is an example of a questionnaire. The questionnaire was administered by telephone and the interview took less than five minutes to complete.

Three steps in questionnaire design

There are three steps to successful questionnaire design:

- formulate the questions;
- arrange the questionnaire layout;
- pilot and test the draft.

Formulating the questions

The researcher should begin by making a rough listing of all the points to which answers are required in the survey. When building this list of questions the starting point should be the proposal document, which will indicate the objectives of the survey and specific questions that need to be asked. The brief from the sponsor of the study may also provide a list of key questions.

FIGURE 11.1   Sample customer satisfaction survey

Good Grub Restaurant – Customer Satisfaction Survey

Good Morning/afternoon. My name is ...., I am phoning from B2B International, a research agency in New York. We are carrying out research for Good Grub restaurant and we are contacting all recent visitors to the restaurant. Do you have five minutes to help us with a few questions about your visit?

Q1   Have you visited the restaurant in the last month?

Yes..........☐
No ....☐   THANK AND CLOSE

Q2   When did you last visit the restaurant?

DAY	DATE	MONTH

Q3   How often on average, do you visit this restaurant?

At least once a week ....☐
At least monthly ....☐
Less often than this ....☐

Q4   How many people were in your party on the last occasion you visited the restaurant? ENTER NUMBER

Adults .... ☐
Children (under 15yrs) ... ☐

Q5   What did you, personally, order from the menu?

Pasta ....☐
Steak ....☐
Chicken ....☐
Pizza ....☐
Salad ....☐
French Fries ....☐
Ice Cream ....☐
Coffee/tea ....☐
Soft drink ....☐
Other ....☐

Q6   In total, how much did your party spend on this visit?

ENTER TOTAL: | $ |

Q7   Based on your last visit, how do you rate the following?

	Very Poor	Poor	Neither good nor poor	Good	Very Good
Speed of service	☐	☐	☐	☐	☐
Cleanliness ...	☐	☐	☐	☐	☐
Quality of the food	☐	☐	☐	☐	☐
Choice of the food	☐	☐	☐	☐	☐
Value for money	☐	☐	☐	☐	☐

Q8   How do you rate the overall performance of the restaurant, using a scale of 1 to 10, where 10 is excellent and 1 is very poor

| |

Q9   Are there any other comments that you would like to make about the restaurant?

| |
| |

And finally, a few questions about yourself ...

Q10 How old are you?

Under 18 ....☐
18–24 ....☐
25–44 ....☐
45–60 ....☐
Over 60 ....☐

Q11 What is your zipcode?

| |

Q12 CODE gender

Male ....☐
Female ....☐

THANK AND CLOSE

If one of the objectives is to assess the position of a product in the marketplace, a question must be asked about the awareness and use of different brands. If the objective of a study is to establish the satisfaction that people have with products, questions must be devised to find out how important various factors are when choosing a product and how satisfied people are with the product on each of these factors.

In preparing the list of questions, it is important to include classification questions that will be required for slicing and dicing the data.

Each of the questions in the rough list should be scrutinized to establish whether it is vital to the survey. It is very easy at the questionnaire design stage for things to get out of hand and the questionnaire to grow and become gargantuan in size. A reasonable maximum for a questionnaire that takes around 15–20 minutes to complete would be 30–40 questions.

Questionnaires tend to expand as they are reviewed by the market researcher and the research sponsor, and once a question finds its way into a questionnaire it is quite difficult to remove it. Long questionnaires threaten the quality of the study and can lead to people failing to complete the interview, or to 'flat lining' whereby respondents give the same answer to questions just to speed up the interview and get it out of the way. It pays to start the questionnaire with as tight a list of questions as possible knowing that it almost certainly will grow as it is reviewed.

Once the questions have been roughly drafted, they can be developed into a more precise form taking into consideration the points below.

Ensure that questions are without bias

Questions or answers should not be worded in such a way as to lead the respondent into the answer. A bad question:

Q. How would you rate your recent experience from the service provided by company X?

Excellent

Very good

Quite good

Fair

(Respondents are not allowed the opportunity to say that they think the experience was poor or very poor.)

Make the questions as simple as possible

Questions should not only be short, they should also be simple. Questions that include multiple ideas or two questions in one will confuse and be misunderstood. A bad question:

> Q.   What do you know about company X and what do you
>   feel they do well?

(The respondent may not answer both parts of the question, and in any case, the responses will be difficult to analyse.)

Try to keep the questions and the sentences short. It is not always possible but set yourself the target of 20 words as a maximum for each question.

Make the questions very specific

Words such as 'usually' or 'frequently' have no specific meaning and need qualifying. A common mistake is to be vague about time periods. A bad question:

> Q.   How often do you visit your local supermarket?
>
> Very often
>
> Quite often
>
> Every now and then
>
> Very rarely
>
> Never

(We will never know how often the respondent visits the supermarket, as 'very often' to one person could be every day, and to someone else it could be every week.)

Avoid jargon, shorthand and uncommon words

It cannot be assumed that respondents will understand words commonly used by researchers. Trade jargon, acronyms and initials should be avoided unless they are in everyday use. If the research is to taste test a new ice cream aimed at kids, then the language used by children should be that of the questionnaire.

A questionnaire is not a place to score literary points, so use words in common parlance. Colloquialisms are acceptable if they are used widely (some are highly regional).

Avoid questions with a negative in them

Questions are more difficult to understand if they are asked in a negative sense. It is better to say 'Do you ever ...?' than 'Do you never ...?'

Do not use words that could be misheard

This is especially important when the interview is administered over the telephone. On the telephone, 'What is your opinion of different sects?' could yield interesting but not necessarily relevant answers.

Do not ask questions that are outside the frame of reference of the respondent

One of the keys to good questionnaire design is to think through every possible response at the time of designing the question. For example, if an objective is to work out consumers' annual milk consumption it is better to ask 'How many litres/pints of milk do you buy in a typical week?' than 'How much milk do you buy each year?.' The researcher can do the 52 times calculation much easier than the respondent.

Use response bands

Most numeric data that is collected in market research surveys is analysed in bands, and so it may be easier to ask the question in bands. For example, 'How many litres of milk do you buy each week?' could be made easier by putting in response bands such as:

None

Less than 1 litre

Between 1 and 4 litres

Over 4 litres.

The response bands should fit the context of the survey. For example, the simple split on milk consumption may need to be broken into more bands if such level of detail is required in the analysis.

Questions that are sensitive can be desensitized with response bands; for example questions about income or age, or in a business-to-business interview, company size. For example:

> Q. Please indicate what band your company's annual revenue falls into from the following choices.
>
> | | |
> | --- | --- |
> | Less than US $200,000 | US $1,000,000–3,000,000 |
> | US $200,000–500,000 | US $3,000,000–10,000,000 |
> | US $500,000–1,000,000 | More than US $10,000,000 |

The categories that are used in fixed response questions should be sequential and not overlap.

It is quite probable that the pre-coded bands do not allow for every conceivable response. It is good practice therefore to allow the option for other/additional responses. For example:

> Q. Can you tell me which brand of dog food you normally buy?
>
> Barko   Wuf   Yummy   Other (STATE)

Top tips

- Before designing the questionnaire, look at the proposal and the brief and make a list of all the questions that need to be answered.

- At the beginning of the questionnaire make sure that you have screener questions that exclude anyone who isn't relevant for the interview.

- Now start to think about the formulation of the questions. Remember that some questions will need to be broken into three or four separate questions in order to obtain an answer.

- As you are developing a question, think very carefully about all the potential answers that could be given. The potential answers could become response codes for the question. If you can't think of the answers, you probably have the wrong question.

- Give yourself time to develop the questionnaire. Sleep on it if you can. You will return to the questionnaire with fresh thoughts that your brain will have worked on while you were away from the task.

- Try to make the questionnaire interesting. Avoid too many rating scales, which can be tedious for respondents and cause them not to think sufficiently about the answers.

- Be prepared for the questionnaire to move through various versions until you and the research sponsor are satisfied. Even then, make sure that you test it in a soft launch amongst a few people before it is fully launched into the field.

- Check routing instructions, recognizing that questions may have been added or removed.

Arranging the questionnaire layout

The questionnaire will require screener questions to ensure that only relevant people take part in the survey. For example if the survey aims to find out people's attitudes to using a particular product it will be necessary to ensure that they buy it regularly. In such a case screener questions could be such as:

Have you heard of product X?

Do you buy product X?

How frequently do you buy product X?

How much product X do you buy per month?

In the case of interviews that are done on online panels it isn't possible to obtain personal name and address details on respondents. This means that contextual and classification data should be collected to make sure that they are valid respondents. It may be appropriate to build in to the questionnaire questions that ensure that respondents are who they say they are.

Questionnaires that are administered by telephone or face to face require space to collect standard information such as the name and address of the respondent, the date of the interview and the name of the interviewer. Where possible, it is useful to capture contact details for the respondent so that quality checks can be carried out (eg phone-backs to check that the interview was done correctly). In a telephone survey there is no problem collecting this information and the name and address of the respondent, their telephone number and other details can be easily recorded.

Some researchers prefer to place the 'boilerplate' information at the beginning of the questionnaire, while others position it at the end.

The introduction and first question are key elements of any questionnaire, as they address the hurdle of achieving cooperation. Once an interview is started there is a very good chance that it will be completed. The introduction should be designed to quickly and concisely communicate the legitimacy of the survey and win cooperation.

Sometimes the classification questions are asked at the beginning of the interview to ensure that respondents qualify (in other words they act as screener questions). If the classification questions are not needed for screening purposes and there are lots of them, they may be better placed at the end of the questionnaire for otherwise they could annoy respondents who do not understand why they are being asked.

The flow of questions should be logical and make sense to the respondent. Where a mixture of open-ended and closed questions is asked, it would be normal to start with the open question and then follow with the prompted or closed question. For example, Open question: 'What do you like about this brand of coffee?' Closed question: 'I will now read out some features of this brand of coffee that other people have said they like. After I have read them out I would like you to tell me which one of these features has influenced you most in your choice of the brand.'

Open questions sometimes follow closed questions, the most common one asking for more feedback on the respondent's answer – typically, 'Why did you say that?'

A mixture of question types and styles, such as open-ended questions, closed questions and scales, gives texture to an interview and could help maintain a respondent's interest.

Many telephone interviews are carried out using screen-based questionnaires (CATI or computer-aided telephone interviewing) and the computer program neatly arranges the formatting. Routing questions are taken care of and different responses automatically bring up different questions. However, many paper questionnaires are still used, and the layout and format of the questions needs to be designed with the interviewer in mind. This means clear instructions as to what to do at and after every question. These instructions are normally written in capital letters to distinguish them from the questions themselves that are read out.

Response codes should be clearly laid out close to the pre-coded answers.

There should be adequate space for writing in the answers to open-ended questions. The amount of space that is provided is an indication to the interviewer of the depth of response that is expected.

Piloting and testing the draft questionnaire

At last the questionnaire is ready for piloting. In many surveys, half a dozen to a dozen interviews will be sufficient to establish whether the questionnaire really does work. So far as is possible, the pilot should be carried out in the same conditions as the survey proper. A telephone interview should be tested over the phone; an online questionnaire should be thoroughly tested by the researcher and dummy respondents before it is fully launched.

During the pilot the researcher is looking for:

- comprehension (do the questions make sense as they were intended?);
- language and phraseology (are there any words that are creating difficulty?);
- ease of answering (are the answers within the capability of respondents?);
- cooperation (will all the questions be answered?);
- flow (does the interview flow easily from one topic to another?);
- instructions (does the interviewer or respondent know what to do next?);
- aesthetics (in the case of an online questionnaire, does it look attractive and is it easy to read? Will the layout of the online questionnaire work on a mobile device as well as a computer?);
- practicality (is the formatting easy for the interviewers?);
- the length of the interview (does it take too long and overtax the respondent?).

All too often there is not time to carry out a proper pilot, but at the very least, the questionnaire should be tried on someone in the office, preferably someone not involved in the survey. Someone who was not involved in the design of the questionnaire should play the role of interviewer while the questionnaire designer looks on.

The person who is in charge of analysing the questionnaire should also be allowed the opportunity to sign it off before it goes into the field, as he or she may well spot coding or routing problems.

Special questionnaires: conjoint analysis

Conjoint analysis is concerned with understanding how people make choices between products or services, and is used to identify what combinations of features people like and are prepared to pay for. If we ask people what they want in a conventional way, the response is likely to be the first thing that comes to mind and may not necessarily reflect what they actually do want. All choices involve compromises and trade-offs, as the ideal is rarely attainable, so we need an approach that allows us to simulate this decision making in the questions we ask.

Conjoint analysis provides the framework for asking these questions. In order to develop appropriate questions, we need to break the products and services down into their features and benefits, which we call attributes. These attributes can be offered at different levels – high quality/low quality; delivered in an hour/delivered in a week and so on. It is these attributes and the levels of the attributes that we show to respondents, and we ask them which they would choose.

Conjoint analysis takes these attributes and level descriptions of products/services and combines them in numerous ways that are put before respondents for their consideration. People are asked to review the different choices and concepts and say which they would buy (if any). In the following example there are two concepts (envelope A and B) with three attributes and a price at two levels. Which would you choose?

	Envelope A	Envelope B
Colour	White	Brown
Sealing	Glue	Self-seal
Window	No window	Window
Price	$1.00	$1.20

We could easily add more concepts, such as envelope C, which is the same as concept A except that it is brown. Concept D would be the same as A except it would be self-seal and so on. Each would have a different price. The design of the concepts is a crucial step in a conjoint project, and time is required to narrow these down to those that do really reflect buying decisions.

In order to arrive at reliable results in a conjoint survey it is advisable to carry out at least 100 interviews, and 200 plus would preferable. Most conjoint surveys are carried out online, at which time respondents view the different concepts on the screen of their computer. They make their choices, and specific software is able to calculate a utility value for each level of attribute by comparing the choices and therefore the trade-offs that respondents make in their answers.

A total utility figure can be calculated for envelope A and B, and thereby tell us which is preferred and by how much. (The utility values in the example are in brackets and are simply an index – they do not add to 100). Notice that a lower price has a higher utility as we typically prefer cheaper goods.)

	Envelope A	Envelope B
Colour	White (25)	Brown (15)
Sealing	Glue (5)	Self Seal (15)
Window	No window (10)	Window (15)
Price	$1.00 (30)	$1.20 (20)
Overall	(70)	(65)

The example that we have provided of the envelope study is known as choice-based conjoint as the respondent is considering which concept with all its attributes they prefer. There are a number of different versions of conjoint analysis, including adaptive conjoint, which would be used when the number of attributes is too long for the traditional approach. Adaptive conjoint focuses on the attributes that are most relevant to respondents by taking just a few attributes at a time.

Another trade-off technique that is commonly used to find out what is important to people shows groups of factors that are being considered; respondents are asked to indicate which within this group is the most and least important to them. They are then shown more and different factors and asked similarly which is most and least important to them when choosing a product. The subsets of factors are presented in this way until all have been answered in different combinations. This approach is known as Maximum Difference Scaling (MaxDiff) and was developed by Jordan Louviere in 1987 while on the faculty at the University of Alberta. An example of the way such questions would be presented on a computer screen is taken from the Sawtooth website:

When considering different fast food restaurants, among the four attributes shown here, which is the most and least important?

Most Important		Least Important
○	Reasonable prices	○
○	Healthy food choices	○
○	Has a play area	○
○	Clean bathrooms	○

A MaxDiff question has the advantage of being simple to understand, and the results give a greater discrimination of the importance of factors, especially when there is a long list. The weight of importance attached to each item is also easy to interpret as they range from 0 to 100 and sum to 100.

The Sawtooth website at **www.sawtooth.com** is useful for further information on conjoint analysis.

Conjoint analysis is discussed further in Chapters 14 and 16.

Trade-off grids (SIMALTO – simulated multi-attribute level trade-off)

Trade-off grids are an approach to collecting information from respondents that recognizes that an individual customer cannot have everything. A trade-off is inevitably made in order to get the best product someone can buy. The classic trade-off is between price and quality, but in practice when considering most purchases we make trade-offs between different features and service levels, and even emotional factors such as brands. The trade-off grids are easier to administer than conjoint as they do not require a respondent to look at 30 different screens, each with four or five choices on them. The trade-off grid can be completed online or the interview can be carried out on the phone if the grid is e-mailed through to the respondent. Once the respondent has the grid in front of him or her, the interviewer can run through the questions. A simplified example of a trade-off grid is shown in Table 11.3. The technique, developed by mathematician John Green, is referred to as SIMALTO, which is an acronym for Simulated Multi-Attribute Level Trade-Off. In other words, respondents are given lots of different attributes with different levels of performance. They are asked to say which they prefer and to trade them off one against the other, so simulating what they would do in a buying situation.

In a trade-off grid a product or service is described in terms of attributes and levels in much the same way as in conjoint. An attribute describes a generic feature such as the delivery times or how long it takes a supplier to answer the phone. An attribute is then made up of levels: for instance, time to answer the phone has four levels in the example shown in the table. A typical product or service can be broadly defined in terms of as few as 10–15 attributes but can sometimes run to over 50.

The respondent then completes a number of tasks related to the grid. Typically respondents are asked what level of service they are receiving at the present. They would then indicate what level of service they would like to receive and finally they would be given a number of points to spend to indicate, across all the improvements that have been requested, which are the ones that are really valued.

TABLE 11.3 SIMALTO trade-off grid

Attribute	Levels			
Time to answer the phone	Phone can ring and ring	Always answered before 10 rings	Always answered before 6 rings	Phone always answered before 3 rings
Delivery on promises	Only meet 30% of promises	Meet 50% of promises	Meet 80% of promises	Always live up to promises
Knowledge of my business	Take no interest in knowing about my business	Know nothing, but seem keen to learn	Understand business in general	Very familiar with the detail of my business
Quality of advice	Advice is poor and can be incorrect	Advice is factually correct but limited in helpfulness	Advice is accurate and useful, but can miss bigger opportunities	Advice is accurate and identifies new possibilities for my business

One useful aspect of measuring performance by levels described by words is that it is very clear what is required. The outcome is a detailed understanding of where people would like improvements and what those improvements should be.

SUMMARY

Questionnaires are at the heart of market research surveys. They are the means by which we can find out behaviour and attitudes to products and services. Questions are always required to classify respondents for the purpose of analysis.

Questionnaires can vary from those that are highly structured and used in large surveys through to unstructured topic guides used in depth interviews and focus groups.

Questions that can be included in the questionnaire may be open or closed. Closed questions are the norm in structured questionnaires and they are used to capture behavioural, attitudinal and classification data.

▶

A number of special types of questions are used for testing the values people attach to different attributes, and these can use different types of scales. Numeric scales, verbal scales and ranking are frequently used to determine the importance of different attributes.

Conjoint analysis uses sophisticated modelling to compute the utility or value that is attached to different product scenarios. Trade-off grids can be used in a simpler way to find out where improvements can be made to products and services, and how much would be paid for those improvements.

In summary, there are 10 things to think about when designing a questionnaire:

1 Think about the objectives of the survey: this will ensure that the survey covers all the necessary points.

2 Think about how the interview will be carried out: the way that the interview will be carried out will have a bearing on the framing of the questions (online questionnaires need a different construction from an administered interview).

3 Think about the introduction and screener: this is very important in ensuring that the right person is interviewed and capturing the respondent's interest in taking part in the survey.

4 Think about the formatting: the questionnaire should make effective use of white space so that it is clear and easy to read. Questions and response options should be laid out in a standard format, and where appropriate there should be ample space to write in open-ended comments.

5 Think about the respondent: questions should be framed in a respondent-friendly manner and the questionnaire should not be too long or tedious.

6 Think about the order of the questions: the questions should flow easily from one to another and be grouped into topics in a logical sequence.

7 Think about the types of questions: a mix of different styles of questions will create interest throughout the interview.

8 Think about the possible answers at the same time as thinking about the questions: if you cannot fully anticipate what the respondents may say, the question needs redrafting.

9 Think about how the data will be processed: how will the data be lifted from the questionnaires and analysed? (This could vary from proprietary software used by market research agencies to an Excel spreadsheet.)

10 Think about interviewer and respondent instructions: whoever is involved in the interview needs clear guidance what to do at every stage.

The design of a questionnaire should be in three stages – first of all laying out the questions that need to be answered, then developing specific questions in the form that they will be asked together with the appropriate response codes, and finally testing the questionnaire to make sure that it works in terms of flow, logic and sense.

Face-to-face interviewing

Interviewing the general public in person is the traditional – and is still a very common – method of collecting market research data. It competes with telephone and online research as a mainstream quantitative data collection method, although it has lost ground in the last few years to online and telephone interviewing. In the United States, the problem of interviewer safety has wiped out the traditional street and in-home interview, which nowadays is largely confined to the security of special rooms in or close to shopping malls.

Whether face-to-face interviews are carried out in special venues, or in the home, they have a number of distinct advantages over the major alternative method of the telephone.

Advantages of face-to-face interviews

Better explanations

In a personal interview, the interviewer can gain a deeper understanding of the validity of the response. In a face-to-face situation, better explanations are possible as the interviewer is able to develop a rapport with respondents, engaging with them to make the interview more like a conversation than an interrogation. Respondents' body language offers additional clues to the answer. Longer explanations are possible. There are many occasions, particularly associated with advertising and product research, when the interviewer needs to show samples or advertisements, and this demands face-to-face contact.

Depth

Following on from the above point, it is easier to maintain the interest of a respondent for longer if the interview is face to face. The interviewer can use social niceties to maintain interest in the discussion if there is eye contact with the respondent. There is less chance of mishearing or misunderstanding. Deeper explanations can be offered to answers.

Legitimacy

Respondents need to feel that the time they devote to the interview is justified. If someone takes the trouble to meet with them face to face, that implies that they take it seriously. Face to face with the respondent, it is possible to give a more comprehensive explanation about the purpose of the survey. Concerns about confidentiality can be more readily satisfied than with an 'anonymous' person at the end of a phone. An interviewer in the high street can show his or her identity card. Furthermore, it is more difficult for a respondent to decline to take part in an interview when they have to look into the eyes of the interviewer rather than bark a 'no' down the phone.

Greater accuracy

In a face-to-face interview the respondent has time to reflect on the questions and so give a more considered reply. If required, products can be shown, and in a business-to-business interview a colleague could be consulted to confirm a point. The interviewer is in a better position to judge the accuracy of the answer. There are other body language and non-body language clues that add to the answers. If the interview is in someone's home, the surroundings will tell a story about the respondent. If the interview is in the workplace, the respondent's office will be surrounded by accoutrements that provide excellent background material and possibly add to the authenticity of the responses.

Disadvantages of face-to-face interviews

Although there are advantages to face-to-face interviewing, there are also a number of disadvantages.

Organization

Face-to-face interviews are more difficult to organize than those undertaken from a central location by phone. A consumer face-to-face survey of 1,000 interviews needs around 50 interviewers spread around the country. If the subject of the study is complex, a personal briefing of the interviewers may be necessary, and it is time-consuming and expensive to bring them together. On completion of the interviews the questionnaires must be safely despatched to head office on time. A batch that does not arrive on time will hold up the analysis. Computer-aided personal interviewing (CAPI) overcomes the problems of collecting paper, but the method has the added complication of dealing with laptop computers and downloading data.

It is more difficult to supervise face-to-face interviews than telephone interviews. Face-to-face interviews must have a supervisor in attendance for part of the time and check-backs have to be made to ensure quality. For the most part, face-to-face interviewers work on their own, and the quality of their work depends largely on their conscientiousness. Telephone interviewing, carried out from a central location and with constant supervision, eliminates these problems.

Cost

Face-to-face interviews are nearly always more expensive than those carried out by phone. Household interviews that are based on pre-selected addresses are in turn more expensive than those related to a quota. In general, street interviews cost the same as telephone interviews. In some cases, street interviews offer advantages by allowing show-cards and visuals, while at other times the telephone would be preferred as it facilitates sampling a wider audience.

A comparison between face-to-face and other methods of data collection must take into consideration all of the costs. Face-to-face interviewing may use interviewers employed at the same rates as (say) telephone interviewing, but work in the field incurs more expenses. Allowances also have to be made for bringing people together for briefings, additional supervision costs plus out-of-pocket expenses for lunches, travel, parking and post. These 'extras' will, in some cases, equal the cost of the labour.

In business-to-business surveys the difference between the cost of telephone and face-to-face interviews is even greater. A face-to-face interview with a respondent in business needs setting up by telephone and this, in itself, is similar in cost to a telephone interview. In business-to-business research it is not unusual to have to travel (there and back) a few hours to obtain an important interview that may only last an hour. The cost of travel is considerable compared with the cost of a phone call.

Normally a good average for business-to-business face-to-face interviews is one or two completed interviews a day, though this figure could rise to four or five if they are concentrated in a conurbation. Allowing for the time taken to set up the interviews, carry them out, write up the scripts and make the necessary travel arrangements, visit interviews cost 10 times as much as those carried out by telephone – and this is assuming that the same grade of interviewer does both. In reality, telephone interviews are usually carried out by specially trained staff working at lower labour rates than business-to-business research consultants who travel to carry out the interviews face to face.

Street interviews

The market research industry, when it first began, employed low-cost labour to carry out interviews in the street. Very few houses had telephones and the computer hadn't been invented. It was a common sight in busy high streets to see interviewers, clip-boards in their hands, eagerly watching the streams of the passing public as they looked for someone to interview and fill their quota. Street interviews are still an important research method in Europe. They are used:

- Where the people in the street are likely to be the target group: if the subject of the survey is food or shopping, it makes sense that the interviews are carried out close to a busy shopping area. Shopping surveys cover each day of the week, including weekends and late nights in order to catch all groups of shoppers. Although not quite 'the street' these interviews on the feet also take place at airports, railway stations, motorway service stations and shopping malls.

- Where the questionnaire is short and simple: using a short questionnaire (five minutes), and assuming that the questions are applicable for most of the passers-by, an interviewer can achieve 30 and sometimes more completed interviews in a day.

- Where the questions appertain to a local issue: a survey investigating a local issue could be suited to street interviewing – there simply may not be enough people in online panels to provide a localized response. Interviewers positioned in a busy town centre would be able to collect the views of local people as they travel to work or go shopping.

- Where cost and time are vital issues: wherever there are serious time and budgetary constraints, street interviews have an advantage. They are relatively quick and easy to organize compared to house-to-house visits and can be cheaper than phone interviews.

There are some limitations to street interviews:

- Where the interview is long or complicated: the street is no place to carry out interviews that take more than 5 to 10 minutes. Shoppers with their arms laden or dashing home are unlikely to be at their most cooperative. The interviewer-avoidance factor is impossible to measure, but at times it is obvious from the space surrounding the interviewer that many people are crossing to the other side of the street.

- Where it is necessary to show many visuals: it is difficult to show visuals or prompt cards in a street interview. Respondents could be caught without their glasses, the light may be poor, the rain or wind could cause problems, and if the shopper's hands are full, the show-cards cannot conveniently be held.

- Where the targets for interview are not likely to be around: the street is not the best place to obtain interviews with working people who, by definition, are likely to be at their desks or in their offices when the shops are open. Old people who cannot easily get about, people who are ill and people who dislike shopping are not going to be in the street and eligible for interviewing.

- Where it is necessary to calculate the accuracy of the results: street interviews may not provide a representative cross-section of the population. As noted above, those in full-time employment could escape the net of street interviews. It is usual, therefore, for street interviews to be carried out against a quota to ensure that all groups are included in the correct proportions. Quota samples do not allow the calculation of sampling error.

Household interviews

The advantages and disadvantages of household interviews are, by and large, the corollaries of those for street interviews. They are nevertheless worth stating to high-light the strengths and weaknesses of the method. Home interviews (or those carried out in an interview/viewing centre) are suited to certain situations:

- Where the interview is long and complicated: an interview of more than 10 minutes needs to be carried out in a specialist interviewing centre or at the respondent's home.

- Where there are products or visuals to show: visuals (show-cards, advertisements, storyboards and products) need to be shown in a controlled environment. Similarly, demonstrations of products sometimes have to be made in the home.

- Where a probability sampling method is used: random sampling demands the selection of households or people from the electoral register, or can be done by a random walk.

- Where special addresses form the sample: a special list of people may be used as the sample. These could be customers who have returned a guarantee card, people who have enquired about a product, or people who read certain magazines. As the sample is made up of pre-selected addresses, the interviews must be carried out at the household (although telephone interviews would also be a possibility and in many cases the better option).

- Where the questions are of a sensitive nature: if the questions are personal or sensitive in any way, they require an environment where people can settle down and feel safe and secure in their answers. There may not be enough time to build up a rapport and to settle people down in street interviews or over the phone.

- Where the interviewer needs to check out something in the house: research into what has been purchased may require the interviewer to actually see the product. A serial number may have to be noted, a brand name checked, or a receipt examined. If, for example, the interviewer needed a sample of people with solid fuel appliances, then these people could be easily identified by walking around housing estates looking for houses with chimneys. Owners with double glazing, specific models of cars, certain types of garage doors and burglar alarms can all be spotted from the road.

Home interviews have limitations:

- Where time and cost are paramount: household interviews are time-consuming and costly to carry out. Interviewers have to find the householder at home or otherwise they have to call back a number of times until successful. Expenses run high, and the number of interviews that can be carried out in a day is much less than is possible in the street. Seven home interviews per day would be a good achievement.

- Where the home environment could influence the response: a survey carried out in the home, exploring teenagers' attitudes to drugs, could be swayed by fear of an eavesdropping parent. Some people may not wish to discuss personal matters such as sex, finances, politics or religion if they are within earshot of others – even their partners. The street is a public place but in certain circumstances it can offer more privacy than the home.

Questionnaire design

The subject of questionnaire design was covered in detail in Chapter 11. Face-to-face interviews, as discussed here, are a quantitative research technique and they need structured questionnaires with clear routing and interviewer instructions.

The formatting of the questionnaire is especially important for street interviews where laptops and CAPI (computer-aided personal interviewing) are not possible. Questionnaires should be designed so they are easy to read and complete in the dark and dingy lighting that may exist in the street, on the doorstep or in people's homes.

The questionnaire must be piloted prior to use. Ideally this should be done in the field so that problems can be identified in the environment where the interviews will be carried out. Since field piloting is so expensive, a thorough office pilot usually suffices, although it helps if the interviewer is someone who has not been involved in the design of the questionnaire so that he or she can more readily pick up problems that could be missed by those too close to the subject.

Response rates to surveys: an industry problem

One of the most serious problems faced by the market research industry is the falling level of cooperation with surveys. Each survey has a 'strike rate' that measures the successful interviews against the failures. The reason for non-achievement could be that the person was not at home or there was a straight refusal to take part. Strike rates vary survey by survey, with some groups of the public being more heavily researched than others. However, in many surveys the strike rates are below the 50 per cent level. This causes researchers to be concerned about the validity of the findings. Busy people who are never in when the interviewer calls, or those that refuse to take part in the survey, could have different behaviours and attitudes from those that are interviewed.

Interviewers attempt to make contact with respondents by calling at different times of day on different days. The convention is that these attempts should be made up to three times before abandoning the interview with that particular respondent. Once contact is established, the interview is won (or lost) depending on a number of factors:

- *Acceptability*: respondents need to understand the reason why research is being carried out. The more they can justify it to themselves, the more likely they are to see the validity of the survey and their role in contributing to it. Surveys are more likely to be seen as legitimate if the sponsoring company or organization is made known. The interviewer also needs to be seen as legitimate and for this purpose, most carry identity cards issued by official market research trade organizations.

- *Financial incentives*: respondents may be offered a financial incentive (honorarium) to take part in a survey. Members of the medical profession and people attending focus groups would nearly always receive a financial incentive. This said, there are strong indications that more and more people in business find it difficult to accept an incentive and are more likely to accept a charitable donation.

- *Interviewer approach*: an interviewer who sounds confident, assumptive and businesslike is more likely to achieve cooperation than one who is diffident or apologetic.

Survey introductions are best if they are short so they quickly communicate why the research is being carried out. They need to involve respondents as quickly as possible for we know that once the first questions have been answered, most people will finish the interview.

On completion, respondents deserve a thank you. Sometimes they are handed a card that explains who carried out the interview and why. When interviews are carried out in the street it is normal practice to ask respondents for their name and addresses so that a quality check can be made on a small percentage of the responses (usually 5 to 10 per cent). Diplomacy and a special explanation may be needed as many people are reticent about giving their address to a stranger.

The interview may be complete but the interviewer has not finished. A final check is needed on the basic details. All questions should be legible and have been answered. The name of the interviewer, the date, and the respondent's name and address should be checked to ensure that they are filled in. Finally the completed questionnaires must be parcelled up for despatch. The postal instructions should be carefully followed. The field force administration at the office is unlikely to believe stories of recorded delivery or registered post slips that disappear along with a batch of questionnaires – they have heard the excuses too often.

Hall tests (mall intercepts)

Mall intercepts (hall tests or central location tests) are used when it is necessary to test reactions of people to a product or concept that it is impractical to take to homes or into the street. For example, food and drink products need to be carefully prepared and presented at the right temperature and in the right conditions if a fair reaction is to be obtained.

Hall tests (as they are commonly known in Europe) are so named because they involve hiring a suitable hall or venue close to a busy shopping centre. In the United Kingdom many of these venues are church halls, hence the term. This contrasts with the United States where special facilities in shopping malls are owned by research companies and hired out together with interviewers. Such special facilities are becoming increasingly available throughout Europe.

'Clinics' refer to a similar method in business-to-business markets where a viewing centre (and sometimes a hotel) is rented so that respondents can observe, try and comment on products.

At a typical mall test, half a dozen interviewers recruit people from the busy mall or streets and persuade them to come to the venue where they can taste or comment on the product. Sometimes they are recruited in advance. The number of interviews that can be completed in a day depends on the screening criteria for respondents and the length of the interview. If 50 people per day are interviewed, the test would probably run for three or four days in order to achieve a sample size of around 200 and so be statistically robust. The tests may be carried out in different cities to overcome regional bias.

Central to the purpose of holding a hall test is the need to show something to respondents. Usually this is a product, and hall tests and product testing are often regarded as synonymous. However, this is not necessarily the case. Hall tests are also used to test packs and advertising material. Mall intercepts or focus group locations are the normal venue for conventional face-to-face interviews in the United States.

When a product is the subject of a hall test, the objective is usually to establish consumers' acceptance, preference and attitudes. Often the product is new and the respondents have not seen it in the shops. The market research is carried out to measure overall liking plus some limited evaluation of the products. In many food tests, reactions to the product rather than to the brand are required, and so the test is often 'blind' with the respondents unaware of which brands are being tested. This type of taste testing is very different from the sensory evaluation carried out by panels of specially trained tasters who have learnt to feed views back in such a way that the formulation of the product can be changed.

In real life, products are bought in a context of choice. A person goes into a shop and chooses one chocolate bar rather than another. However, people normally only eat one chocolate bar at a time and so it can be anticipated that there will be problems if they are asked to taste a few, one after the other. For this reason, testing a product by itself (monadic testing) is considered to be the best method when food or drink is involved. However, monadic testing is expensive because it is necessary to have a large sample, especially if a comparison is to be made between two different products. In this case half the sample would taste one product and half the other. If each respondent could taste two products sequentially (a paired comparison) it means that a sample of half the size (and significantly less cost) could be used.

Products tested in a hall should be capable of being evaluated in this artificial environment, and most items of food and drink fall into this category. Eating a chocolate biscuit in a hall is no different from eating one at home. Similarly, products whose key characteristics can be seen or smelt, or that can be used in a simple way, can all be objects of a hall test. Products inappropriate for hall tests include personal hygiene products (for instance, deodorants), products that have to be used over time (for example, a soap powder) or in a fairly complex way (for example, a window cleaner), or when used would simply be impractical in the hall (for instance, shampoo).

Beer testing used to be carried out in halls but the drinking environment was so different from the norm it was considered a bias to the test. As a result, most of the tests are carried out in pubs or clubs where the researchers can control the quality of the drink and the atmosphere is more convivial for drinking beer.

Similarly, products where a conditioning process is necessary to gain acceptance may not be suitable to hall tests, and this presents problems for certain drinks and foodstuffs. For example, sweet and gassy drink formulations tend to score quite well in hall tests, but a beer that scores well in such a test could rapidly lose appeal if drunk in quantity, night after night. When a hall venue is not appropriate, it is necessary to consider testing the product in the place of normal consumption (the home, the pub and so on).

Hall tests are a quantitative technique, and use structured or semi-structured questionnaires with answers fed directly into computers at the time of the test so that the data is captured immediately. The aim is to make specific measurements on:

- *Acceptance*: will the product be considered?
- *Preference*: which product is preferred?
- *Attitudes to attributes*: a product can be considered as a collection of attributes: colour, texture, smell, taste and so on (and each of these can be further subdivided). What are the attitudes to these different attributes in terms of satisfaction or preferences?

As well as product testing, hall tests are often used for pack testing. For many consumer products the pack is a major element within the purchasing decision. Indeed, it may be the only way in which it differs from competitive brands. Getting the pack right is therefore critical.

Generally, pack tests are carried out for a new product or when an established product is being changed. The object is usually to compare a few possible pack designs, either with each other or with competitors. This is done by showing mock-ups that are as near the finished packs as possible. As in product testing, packs are tested for specific attributes – colour, legibility, perceived appropriateness to the product and so on. The specific questions asked about the pack are structured and usually closed. If required, any qualitative probing of the pack concept will have been carried out in group discussions prior to the hall test.

Hall tests also have a role in advertising research. Again, the aim is to obtain quantitative responses to specific aspects of an advertisement such as the impact of its headlines and the communication or memorability of the copy and visuals. If the advertising medium covered is the press, a hall test might be used for speed and convenience although alternative methods could be chosen (for example, home or even street interviewers).

- Use face-to-face interviewing when you believe that it is the most convenient method because the people you want to interview will be congregated in a certain place (eg in a shopping mall or at an exhibition).

- Don't consider face-to-face interviewing if it will take interviewers into an area where they could be at personal risk.

- Make sure that you have a process for carrying out quality checks. You will need supervisors to do spot checks to ensure that the interviewers are in the right place, interviewing the right people and asking all the right questions.

- If the interviews are carried out in the street, in a shopping mall or at an exhibition, make sure that there is a maximum of 20 questions otherwise interviews will be truncated as respondents abandon the interview or refuse to take part.

- Keep the questions simple.

- Consider the circumstances in which the interviews will take place. In certain places (such as a wet and windy street) it is not practical to use CAPI (computer-aided personal interviewing) and paper questionnaires will be more appropriate.

- When estimating how many interviews can be achieved per day per interviewer take into consideration that interviewers need comfort breaks and rest periods. About 20 to 30 interviews per day with a short questionnaire is a reasonable maximum that can be achieved in the street or at an exhibition. Four or five interviews per day is a reasonable number for home interviews.

SUMMARY

Face-to-face interviews are considered the gold standard in the market research industry. They have the advantage of rapport with the respondent. Eye contact and the observation of body language can provide many clues that add to the verbal answers. They are excellent for depth interviews. However, face-to-face interviews in the home are relatively rare nowadays. Large-scale surveys are generally carried out online or by telephone and, if depth is required for qualitative research, face-to-face interviews take place in specialist centres.

Street interviewing was the traditional method of collecting data from consumers for many years but today it has been superseded by the telephone and online surveys, which are much quicker and less expensive. Street interviewing involves numerous logistical problems, not least persuading respondents to spare time as they are busy in their daily round.

Face-to-face interviewing is still quite common in airports and shopping malls where as many as 30 interviews per day can be carried out if they take as little as 5 to 10 minutes each.

Face-to-face interviewing in special venues such as halls, close to shopping malls, is still widely used for product tests.

Telephone interviewing

Why interview by telephone?

The world in which we live today is very different from the world we knew just half a century ago. The majority of homes and businesses in the developed world are connected to a telephone network, and in some countries the density of mobile phone penetration is reaching saturation point. It is hardly surprising, therefore, that telephone interviewing has become commonplace and has superseded face-to-face interviewing as a data collection method for market researchers.

Telephone interviews are, in the main, used for uncomplicated, structured interviews. It is common for most interviews with the general public to last around 10 minutes and in the case of business-to-business respondents to last around 20 minutes.

The telephone has become the medium of choice for administered interviews. It allows us to gather information quickly over a wide geographical area at costs that are much lower than those for face-to face interviews. Telephoning is carried out from central units, which facilitates easy monitoring, rapid feedback to interviewers and the ability to capture information directly into computers at the time of the interview.

The greatest advantages of the telephone compared to personal interviewing are its speed and low cost. These are most evident in business-to-business market research. In favourable circumstances up to five telephone interviews can be completed in a day over the telephone compared to just one or two interviews if they were carried out face to face.

In consumer research an accomplished interviewer may be able to achieve 10 to 15 10-minute interviews in a day, but the time and cost advantages of telephone interviewing are not quite so clear-cut. If the comparison is between street/mall interviewing and telephone interviewing, then there is probably little difference in either time or cost – in fact, mall interviewing might even be cheaper. However, when compared with in-home interviews, the telephone is both quicker and cheaper since there is no time wasted in travel between interview points.

CATI: computer-assisted telephone interviewing

Computers have replaced the clipboard and questionnaire in telephone interviews. Interviews carried out by telephone are normally guided by a questionnaire displayed on the screen of a computer. The interviewer records answers via the keyboard, entering numbers that correspond with pre-coded responses displayed on the screen. CATI is therefore the bringing together of computer technology and the telephone to improve performance and quality in market research data collection. The considerable advantages that CATI interviewing offers are:

- The interviewer is left free to concentrate on the interview as the routing instructions are taken care of by the scripting and programming.
- Data is entered directly and the subsequent transactions of data processing are eliminated. Costs and punching errors are reduced.
- The whole process is speeded up because data is entered as it is obtained.
- The software program manages the sample so that quotas are adhered to.
- At intervals during the survey, the researcher can interrogate the computer to examine the results.
- An analysis of results can be obtained immediately after the last interview has been completed.

There are some disadvantages to CATI interviewing. A conventional paper questionnaire can be drafted in no time and without the help of specialist scripters who, in the case of CATI, are required to make the conversion onto the computer screens. Getting a questionnaire up and running, fault free, on a CATI system can take a couple of days. It is doubtful if it is worth using CATI if the project is a small study involving fewer than 30 interviews.

Capturing open-ended responses on a CATI system requires interviewers with good typing skills. Flexibility is lost as it is not so easy to refer back to an answer on the screen as it is to turn back a couple of pages of a paper questionnaire. In general, CATI is best suited to structured interviews carried out in large numbers, especially surveys where all the possible answers have been worked out and can be listed as pre-coded responses.

The art of telephone interviewing: carrying out a successful interview

Whether the interviewer uses a paper-based questionnaire or a CATI system, the principles of successful interviews are the same.

The introduction – beating the 'brush-off'

The general public is suspicious of unsolicited calls, especially following years of cold calling by financial services or double-glazing salesmen. It is understandable that someone whose reverie is interrupted by a market researcher wanting to ask questions about an obtuse subject may be reluctant to help. Respondents are asked to give up their valuable time, usually for little in return. Persuading people to take part in a survey is therefore critically important for, as we have stated, response rates of less than 50 per cent could mean that a significant part of the population with different views and attitudes has been neglected.

Studies of interviewee cooperation show that interviewers who are enthusiastic, confident, clear and pleasant have the greatest success. Achieving this on the telephone in just a second or two is a challenge. Indeed, the opening moments on the phone are critically important in determining whether the interview will be won or lost. It helps to have a hook that interests respondents, and to communicate this as quickly as possible. There are usually other points to get across and this can mean that the introduction drags on.

At some stage before the interview begins the interviewer should give an indication of how long it is expected to take, mention that all that is said will be kept confidential and that there will be no attempt to sell anything. The more the interviewer tries to pack into the introduction and the longer it takes, the more time respondents have to think of reasons that they do not want to take part. A fast engagement is vital. The interviewer's approach really does make a difference:

- *Always be assumptive and confident*: respondents like to feel that they are in the hands of a professional, someone who is businesslike without being pushy.

- *Create trust*: respondents will talk to people they trust. Building trust in a few seconds is difficult when the interviewer has only a voice and words. However both can be powerful ordnance if they are used correctly. The wrong ones will result in a brush-off. It does help to have a script prepared before phoning to ensure that the introduction is, as near as possible, the best one to win trust and cooperation.

- *Respondents do not like to feel like they are being singled out unfairly*: they may feel better if they know that they are part of a nationwide survey but that their response really does matter.

- *Allegiances promote cooperation*: if an earlier phone call resulted in contact with another member of the family (or a business colleague in the case of a B2B survey), it may help to make this reference.

Despite the most polished approach, difficulties will be encountered:

- *The person is always out or does not have the time*: actually people are not always out, it just seems that way. There are certain times when a few minutes could be found for an interview. Family members or (in business-to-business interviews) a colleague could suggest the best time to catch the person.

- *The respondent is survey weary*: some people (especially respondents in particular businesses) are constantly disturbed by market researchers. This leads to 'no survey' policies or a brusque 'Sorry, I'm not interested.' Market researchers have a special responsibility to make interviews as interesting as possible. An attempt should be made to communicate to respondents as convincingly as possible that their cooperation will lead to the improvement of products and services.

The best of planning cannot guarantee success every time. It requires interviewers of considerable skill and tenacity to make the appropriate number of calls and win cooperation. The ratio between the number of phone numbers dialled and the number of interviews achieved will vary considerably, depending on the type of survey and the quality of lists. In a short survey of the general public with a good list, it may be possible to achieve one interview for every five dialled calls. In a business-to-business survey it is likely that at least 20 dialled numbers must be called to achieve one interview. It is clear therefore that a telephone interview programme requires a clean and up-to-date list of potential respondents if it is to be successful.

The interview – keep the interest going

In most cases, once respondents have started the interview, they will see it through to completion. However, we are not suggesting that compliance through the interview is a foregone conclusion; a different set of skills is needed for the execution of the interview itself.

The crucial requirement of any interview is to know the questionnaire thoroughly. The interview is, of course, a script of a kind and the questions have to be read out exactly as stated. Good interviewers develop their own style, speaking at a moderate pace and with good clarity and diction. Although it may be the last interview after a busy and tiring day, the interviewer must sound interested. In fact, he or she will need to be interested because a good interviewer really does have to listen.

Although the questionnaire is a script and must be adhered to, there is scope to build in the social lubrication and verbal encouragements that indicate we are listening and are interested. The body language of the voice becomes even more important, given there is nothing else to create rapport.

The close

By the time the interview is finished a relationship will have been created with the respondent. Respondents deserve to be thanked for their time and effort, and it may be appropriate to ask permission to call again should it be necessary to clarify any of the answers. (This is more important in business-to-business interviews.)

Top tips

- Use telephone interviewing whenever you need to get hold of special groups of people or when you have a list of good contact names and telephone numbers.

- Spend time and money building good lists of potential respondents. A good list of respondents will lower the cost of the telephone interviews by yielding a much higher hit rate.

- Be aware that there can be a huge variability in responses from different telephone interviewers. It is most important that all the interviewers are trained to a standard and carefully monitored for quality.

- There are two different skills required by telephone interviews – one is required to persuade people to take part in the survey and the other is to administer the interview itself. Make sure that the telephone interviewers are trained in both skills.

- Brief the interviewers personally at the beginning of the project. Stay in touch with them throughout the project, asking them how it is going and what they are finding out. This will not be seen as interference; rather it will be appreciated that you care.

- Consider motivating the telephone interviewers with a bonus for completing interviews but be careful that this doesn't jeopardize quality.

- Keep a constant check on the quality of the interviews. Read interviewer scripts soon after they have been completed. This is easy with paper questionnaires but it is still possible with CATI. Do this especially at the start of any survey and give constructive feedback to the interviewers.

Limitations of telephone interviews

We have seen how the many positive attributes of telephone interviews have resulted in them becoming the main method used in administered interviews (where interviewers ask the questions as opposed to online surveys where respondents self-complete). However, there are occasions when it is not appropriate to use telephone interviews.

There are many occasions in market research where we need a respondent to see something. It could be an explanation of a concept that is too lengthy to read out. It could be a picture of a new product. It could be a long list of factors that could influence the respondent's decision to choose a product. When there are more than five or six factors on a list, it is a lengthy task for these to be read out and difficult for the respondent to hold them in their mind. Researchers attempt to overcome this problem by 'recruiting to web'. During the phone call respondents are given a web address to visit where they can view the material. Of course, this presupposes that respondents have easy access to a computer. In a recent survey that sought to find out people's attitudes to new types of cleaning cloths, respondents were invited to view a page on the web. The survey failed miserably because people in charge of cleaning may be reached by phone (with difficulty) but are seldom sat in front of a computer.

The fax machine does not suffer heavy use in most businesses and yet nearly every business has one. It may be possible to fax show material if the respondent cannot or does not want to view it on a computer. Once respondents have the show material in front of them, the interview can continue. In the case of 'recruit to web' there is usually no break in the interview. When material is faxed to respondents it may require a second phone call and this always presents the risk of losing the momentum of the interview.

It is easier to say 'no' on the phone. It is easier for someone to say 'I have to go soon' and put pressure on the respondent to rush the final questions. Telephone interviews are always susceptible to distractions from television programmes, people knocking at the door, or in the case of business interviews, interruptions from colleagues or prearranged meetings. Telephone interviews are normally carried out in an impromptu fashion, while face-to-face interviews are prearranged and so allow the respondent to set aside some time to participate.

The telephone can present problems as an interviewing medium in certain Asian countries. Japanese respondents may feel that an unannounced intrusion from an unknown interviewer asking personal and direct questions is unacceptable. In this case, online surveys may be preferable even though they cannot provide the depth that would come from a telephone interview.

Throughout the world we are changing our use of telephones. Hardwired phones are being replaced by mobile phones. White page directories that used to list every one with a phone are rapidly being eliminated or reduced in size. There are no directories of people on mobile phones and so random sampling using telephone interviews as the survey medium is much more difficult nowadays and is becoming restricted to customer surveys where lists are available.

Things are different in business-to-business surveys where company phone numbers are published and lists can be easily acquired. People in business may not be sitting waiting for a call from a market research interviewer, but on the other hand they do understand that it is a valid part of business communications.

SUMMARY

Telephone interviews offer benefits of speed and cost, and their quality is easier to control than face-to-face interviews. However, all things have a life cycle and telephone interviews are fast being replaced by online interviews.

The telephone will remain important in business-to-business research and with the general public where customer lists with telephone numbers are available.

The telephone interviewer requires special skills. He or she needs to be enthusiastic and knowledgeable about the subject in order to win cooperation from respondents. Once an agreement has been achieved to carry out the interview, the interviewer must follow the script and use all their social skills to make the interview work. Tenacity is required by the interviewer as a large number of dialled calls have to be made to achieve a single interview.

Key requirements of a successful telephone interview are:

- Understand the subject and the questionnaire before picking up the phone.
- Check that the person on the other end of the phone is the right person to interview.
- Adopt a friendly, professional introduction that gives the survey legitimacy and a hook.
- Be clear and concise in the questioning.
- Listen, and make this evident with words of interest and encouragement.
- Capture what has been said in writing rather than relying on recording instruments.
- Ask questions to clarify responses and probe for a deeper understanding of the answers.
- Complete the questionnaire thoroughly, cross-checking responses where appropriate.
- Thank respondents for their time and valuable input and leave the door open so that it is possible to return should this be necessary.

Self-completion questionnaires

The ubiquitous self-completion questionnaire

Self-completion questionnaires face us everywhere we go. They sit in our hotel rooms. They are thrust at us in airports. They drop through the letterbox. We have all been subjected to self-completion questionnaires at one time or another, whether it is checking on satisfaction with a newly purchased car or the local utility company asking for views on its service. How many times have you actually filled one in? More importantly, how many have you ignored? We will discuss the pros and cons of self-completion questionnaires in this chapter, but we know that their major weakness is a low (and often unpredictable) response rate. Our focus for the time being is on hard-copy self-completion questionnaires that are sent by post, or inserted in magazines, or left alongside the menu in a restaurant or hotel. There are many principles in the design and execution of these questionnaires that overlap with e-based surveys. However, because e-surveys have some special considerations they are considered separately in Chapter 15.

When to use and when not to use self-completion questionnaires

Self-completion questionnaires are a perfect tool for the DIY researcher. A lone researcher sitting at a computer can mail out a questionnaire to hundreds of people for the cost of a stamp (or for nothing if it is sent by e-mail).

From the respondents' point of view, self-completion questionnaires may be a preferred method if they have difficulty finding the time to get to the phone or if they value privacy in their responses. A dentist or doctor can fill in the questionnaire in his or her own time. An employee of a company can complete the 'employee satisfaction' questionnaire at home and be confident that the reply is confidential and anonymous.

Long, laborious rating questions unfortunately are a central theme of many satis-faction surveys and in self-completion questionnaires they can be completed much quicker than in an administered interview where each attribute and statement has to be read out. A self-completion questionnaire also presents a chance to use pictorial explanations, or it can be brightened up with scales of smiley and frowning faces.

Self-completion questionnaires are a useful means of collecting data from more than one respondent in a household or company. For example, a survey that seeks to find out weekly food consumption in households would enable two partners of the household to consult and ensures greater accuracy in the completion of the question-naire. People can take their time. They can reflect on questions that need extra thought. There is a more considered response than the spontaneous and off the cuff reply that is received in an administered interview.

Despite their many advantages, there are disadvantages with self-completion questionnaires. The biggest shortcoming is that they generate low and uncertain response rates if the audience is not highly engaged or required to complete the ques-tionnaire by law (as is the case in most censuses). This means that response rates from many mailed or self-completion questionnaires are well below 10 per cent of all those that are sent out. This being the case, it is disconcerting to know that 90 per cent of people who have been targeted in the survey have not replied. How certain are we that the people who did respond are representative of the total? Are the replies from complainers? This we will never know unless we carry out control checks using conventional interviewing with a sample of non-respondents, and that is a luxury that is seldom afforded. If a very low response rate is anticipated, then nearly always this suggests the survey would be better carried out using an adminis-tered interview.

Self-completion questionnaires are not suitable for all respondents, such as the very young, people with learning difficulties, people with literacy problems, or the very old.

The questionnaires have to 'stand on their own' – there is no interviewer on hand to sort out a question if it is not fully understood. The questions must be as near perfect as possible, with clear wording and instructions and adequate room to write in answers. 'Tick box' questions are easier to fill in and so are likely to dominate the questionnaire. Typically there are only one or two open-ended questions and these generally receive poor responses because writing a free response takes longer and more effort than speaking it.

Clarity is also important in the formatting and layout of the questionnaire. A professionally typeset questionnaire manages to squeeze more questions on to the page and still maintain the white space that makes it look clean and neat.

We have suggested that self-completion questionnaires are a suitable instrument for the DIY researcher. However, there is a good deal of time required for the organization of the paperwork, printing, envelopes, the stuffing of the envelopes and the franking. Folding, stuffing and dispatching 1,000 postal questionnaires is a significant manual task.

Principles of designing self-completion questionnaires

The importance of the introductory letter

Self-completion questionnaires require an introduction and this is often in the form of a cover letter. The cover letter is as important as the questionnaire itself. It sets the scene for why the research is being carried out and plants the hook that encourages the response. The introductory note, like any good sales letter, is seeking to persuade the respondent to take action. It must do so quickly so that, just as in the administered interview, the respondent is motivated to pick up a pen and start answering. Once started, there is a good chance that the questionnaire will be completed.

A letter that is addressed to a person by name will have more impact than one that is simply addressed to 'The householder' or the 'Chief buyer'. A personalized letter is more powerful in motivating someone to complete a questionnaire than one that is without a name. Ensuring the right name is on the note and making sure that it is spelt correctly is a challenge as there is nothing that annoys respondents more than getting their names wrong – easily done as databases are often out of date.

The first paragraph of the introductory note should provide assurance that the survey is legitimate. The respondents need to believe that their time will not be wasted and that the survey will be used for bona fide purposes. It may help to say that the survey is being carried out in an attempt to improve products and services and it is worthwhile emphasizing that the respondent's reply is critical to the success of the survey, so creating a small burden of obligation. Even these promises may ring hollow if respondents have taken part in previous surveys with no noticeable effect. Many surveys that are sent unsolicited to respondents require a material incentive to encourage a reply. Small gestures such as enclosing a pen can help, but prize draws or monetary rewards are more powerful.

The cover letter that accompanies the questionnaire should give an assurance about confidentiality and give clear instructions on what to do next. (Almost always a reply-paid envelope is included with the cover letter and self-completion questionnaire, and reference should be made to this in the closing lines.)

> **Golden rules for writing good cover letters**
>
> - Write in an engaging style. Personalize the letter as much as possible. Be clear. Be brief.
>
> - Explain the purpose of the survey and why the respondent has been selected – legitimize it and offer a hook (if necessary a material incentive).
>
> - Give an assurance that completing the questionnaire is easy.
>
> - If it is possible to do so, give an assurance that replies will be confidential.
>
> - Give instructions as to what should be done – how to fill it in and how to send it back.
>
> - Thank the respondent.

An example of a cover letter for a postal survey is provided in Figure 14.1.

Deciding on the questions

The starting point of all questionnaires is to determine what questions need to be answered. If a study is being carried out to find out how much people value a product or service, it should not be assumed that this can be dropped in as a simple question, 'How much do you value this product?'. Such a question would need to be broken into a number of component parts such as:

- Do you buy such a product?
- How frequently do you buy the product?
- Which products do you consider at the time of purchase?
- Which products do you choose?
- What are the reasons for your choice?
- Why do you reject certain products?
- How much do you pay for the product?

These questions will together answer the bigger question, 'How much do you value this product?'. Of course they wouldn't be asked in the simplistic way that they have been listed here and would need careful scripting and formatting, which is the subject for the sections that follow.

FIGURE 14.1   Sample cover letter for a postal survey

Self-completion Questionnaires

University of
HUDDERSFIELD

Date

Dear Student,
It has become increasingly important that Universities understand their student population in order to help them tailor the services and courses they offer to their students. The University of Huddersfield would like to find out why students choose Huddersfield University as their place of study, and what they think of the University when they get there.

To do this, they have commissioned us, B2B International Ltd, a specialist research agency, to carry out an independent study for them. The first stage of the research involved listening to the views of students through focus groups to find out the main issues that are important to students. Some of you may have been involved in these. We would now like to measure these issues across the whole University population and to do this we are seeking your co-operation.

I am enclosing the student survey questionnaire that we have developed from our discussions with students for your completion. We hope that you will use this opportunity to tell us why you chose Huddersfield and to have your say about what is important at the University, how it affects you and whether particular things should change. By spending ten minutes completing this questionnaire you can influence how the University develops.

The data from the survey will be used to build up a picture of the University and identify how the University can improve to meet the needs of the students who attend Huddersfield to study. Completed questionnaires should be returned **directly to B2B International by Monday 13 January** using the reply-paid envelope enclosed.

To thank you for taking the time to complete the questionnaire, there will be a prize draw with seven prizes of £100 (one for EACH School). To enter the draw, please complete the slip below and enclose this with your completed questionnaire. The prize draw will take place in January and winners will be notified personally and results posted on the University website.

Thank you for taking part.

Carol-Ann Morgan
B2B International Limited
Telephone 0161 440 6000

✂ -

GRAND PRIZE DRAW Detach and enclose with your completed questionnaire.
NAME ....
CONTACT ADDRESS ....

....

CONTACT TELEPHONE NUMBER ....
SCHOOL ....

Question types, wording and sequencing

The golden rule of all questionnaire design is to think of all the possible answers at the time of designing the question. Most questionnaires fail because the researcher does not see the questions from the respondent's point of view. For example, it would be difficult for a respondent to answer the question 'How often do you buy a battery for your watch?' without giving any guidelines as to the frequency interval that is considered reasonable. However, if respondents are asked how frequently they buy a battery for their watch and provided with pre-codes for answers, they would find the question much easier. For example:

How often do you buy a battery for your watch?

At least every six months ☐

Between six months and a year ☐

Between one year and two years ☐

Over two years ☐

Technically these response codes overlap but in the context of the question they would work because they fit the approximate timescales with which people buy watch batteries.

Once respondents have answered the first question there is a good chance that they will finish the whole questionnaire. Simple routine questions lead respondents into the main body of the questionnaire.

Open-ended questions are badly answered in self-completion surveys. Questions that ask for free-ranging explanations get inadequate (and often illegible) answers. Typical replies are 'Because it is good,' 'We have always bought it,' 'It does its job' and so on, and there is no opportunity to find out why it is good, why people always buy a product or in what way the product does its job.

Nor is it possible to ask complicated questions. It will be difficult for householders to say how much they spent on leisure activities over the last year. It seems obvious that the question embraces holidays but does it also include meals in restaurants, visits to the cinema, a trip to the seaside, a visit to the library? The subject is too vague and householders do not keep annual expenditure figures of this type in their heads. The researcher stands some chance if a question asks about the frequency with which people indulge in specific leisure activities (and then the researcher can do the maths to arrive at an estimated expenditure).

We have already emphasized that successful self-completion questionnaires should be easy to complete. This means that wherever possible questions should have pre-coded answers that just require a box to be ticked or a number to be circled. Pre-coded questions are suited to self-completion questionnaires as they save the respondent time writing in the answers. Scalar questions are highly applicable because they can be completed quickly by ticking boxes.

Complicated routing can create confusion and can lead to errors.

Finally, with self-completion questionnaires it is not possible to disclose information in a controlled fashion as in a telephone or visit interview, because respondents may read ahead and become aware of forthcoming questions.

Top tips

- When writing a self-completion questionnaire, keep everything simple.

- Use clear and straightforward instructions so that people know what to do and which question to answer next.

- Have a logical sequence to the questions.

- Questions should be short and couched in the respondent's language.

- The first questions in the survey should be engaging and easy.

- Avoid all possibilities of ambiguity.

- Measures of quantity or time should be easy to understand.

- Wherever possible, follow a question with pre-coded (appropriate) response codes.

- Response codes should be easy to complete, such as boxes to tick or numbers to circle.

- Avoid complicated grids.

- Leave sufficient space to be able to tick the correct box or write in the answer.

- Make sure you know who has completed the questionnaire by including appropriate classification questions.

Enhancing the appearance of the questionnaire

Most people view market research questionnaires as 'just another form to fill in', and since there is no compulsion to respond there is a danger that the form will end up in the waste-paper basket unless it catches the respondent's interest. A clear and attractive layout is more important in a self-completion questionnaire than one used in an administered interview.

It is worth considering having the questionnaire professionally typeset. An attractive layout and the interesting use of space will encourage the response. The use of colour and graphics will brighten the questionnaire and make it more fun to complete. There are always exceptions to prove a rule and a simply formatted questionnaire, as if typed by a student on an old-fashioned typewriter, could engender sympathy and interest, and may encourage response.

Figure 14.2 shows part of a sample self-completion questionnaire for a postal survey.

Good practice in self-completion questionnaires

Pre-testing and piloting postal surveys

All questionnaires should be piloted and this is especially important in self-completion questionnaires because once printed and dispatched, there is nothing that can be done to rectify a mistake or omission. At the very least the researcher should have a friend or colleague complete the questionnaire, sitting next to the tester and watching them as they work through the questions.

Project management and administration – planning, costing, timetabling

The starting point of any survey is to work out a timeline of what should be done, by when and by whom. Postal surveys depend on suitable databases containing the correct names and addresses of respondents. If lists are out of date, if they contain inaccurate addresses, or if all the people on the list are not target respondents, the questionnaires will fall on stony ground and the response rates will be low. The database needs to be up to date, accurate and de-duplicated. Part of the study findings will be an analysis of the quality of the database measured by 'return to sender' envelopes or, in the case of e-surveys, failed deliveries.

If many thousands of questionnaires are sent out, it may be worth using a mailing house to run the campaign.

Most people who fill in self-completion questionnaires do so shortly after receiving them, so the bulk of the returns will arrive within a few days of mailing. A reminder will boost the response but a respectable period should be left between the mailings (a week to two weeks). This will add a couple more weeks to the survey timetable. It is preferable that the reminder mailings miss out those who have already returned a questionnaire. This may not be possible if replies are anonymous.

FIGURE 14.2 Part of a sample self-completion questionnaire for a postal survey

---

SECTION 2 – YOUR EXPERIENCE AT HUDDERSFIELD UNIVERSITY
This section is about what you think of Huddersfield University.

I.   YOUR PROGRAMME OF STUDY

Year of your course: 1 ☐1   2☐2   3☐3   4☐4   5☐5   6 or more☐6   (46)

Type of course: Full time ☐7   Part time ☐8

Level of course: Undergraduate☐9   Postgraduate ☐0

Does your course involve a work placement?   Yes☐1   No ☐2   (47)

Which type of award are you studying for?   (48)

Foundation Year	☐1	Postgraduate award, eg MA, MSc	☐4
Pre-Degree, eg HND, HNC, WITS course	☐2	Other programmes, eg ACCA, Cert Ed	☐5
Undergraduate degree, eg BA (Hons) BSc	☐3	Postgraduate award, eg PHD	☐6

On average, how many days per week do you come into the University? (please circle)

        0   1   2   3   4   5   6   7   (49)

Please rate the extent to which you are satisfied with the following issues in relation to your PROGRAMME OF STUDY (COURSE) and then rate how important it is to you.

(6) COURSE ORGANISATION	SATISFACTION			IMPORTANCE		
Not applicable	Totally Dissatisfied	Neither Nor	Totally Satisfied	Not at all Important	Neither Nor	Very Important
a) ☐1 course induction	1 2 3 4 5 6 7 (7)			1 2 3 4 5 6 7 (11)		
b) ☐2 information about your course (eg course handbook)	1 2 3 4 5 6 7 (8)			1 2 3 4 5 6 7 (12)		
c) ☐3 notification of alterations to the timetable	1 2 3 4 5 6 7 (9)			1 2 3 4 5 6 7 (13)		
d) ☐4 how you are kept in touch with what is happening on your course	1 2 3 4 5 6 7 (10)			1 2 3 4 5 6 7 (14)		

(15) COURSE CONTENT						
a) ☐1 content of your course	1 2 3 4 5 6 7 (16)			1 2 3 4 5 6 7 (23)		
b) ☐2 opportunity for work related placements	1 2 3 4 5 6 7 (17)			1 2 3 4 5 6 7 (24)		
c) ☐3 availability of placements	1 2 3 4 5 6 7 (18)			1 2 3 4 5 6 7 (25)		
d) ☐4 extent to which your course motivates you to study	1 2 3 4 5 6 7 (19)			1 2 3 4 5 6 7 (26)		
e) ☐5 extent to which your course meets your needs	1 2 3 4 5 6 7 (20)			1 2 3 4 5 6 7 (27)		
f) ☐6 extent to which your course prepares you for work	1 2 3 4 5 6 7 (21)			1 2 3 4 5 6 7 (28)		
g) ☐7 recognition of your course in the job market	1 2 3 4 5 6 7 (22)			1 2 3 4 5 6 7 (29)		

(30) THE TEACHING STAFF						
a) ☐1 reliability of the academic staff (ie don't cancel classes, punctuality)	1 2 3 4 5 6 7 (31)			1 2 3 4 5 6 7 (38)		
b) ☐2 teaching ability of the academic staff	1 2 3 4 5 6 7 (32)			1 2 3 4 5 6 7 (39)		
c) ☐3 knowledge and skills base of the academic staff	1 2 3 4 5 6 7 (33)			1 2 3 4 5 6 7 (40)		
d) ☐4 the use of a range of teaching methods	1 2 3 4 5 6 7 (34)			1 2 3 4 5 6 7 (41)		
e) ☐5 helpfulness of the academic staff	1 2 3 4 5 6 7 (35)			1 2 3 4 5 6 7 (42)		
f) ☐6 the use of 'Blackboard' by lecturers	1 2 3 4 5 6 7 (36)			1 2 3 4 5 6 7 (43)		
g) ☐7 supervision of your dissertation	1 2 3 4 5 6 7 (37)			1 2 3 4 5 6 7 (44)		

(45) ASSESSMENT						
a) ☐1 flexibility of dates for handing in assignments	1 2 3 4 5 6 7 (46)			1 2 3 4 5 6 7 (53)		
b) ☐2 information about assessment criteria	1 2 3 4 5 6 7 (47)			1 2 3 4 5 6 7 (54)		
c) ☐3 consistency of marking standards	1 2 3 4 5 6 7 (48)			1 2 3 4 5 6 7 (55)		
d) ☐4 methods of assessment used (eg essay, exam, practical, etc)	1 2 3 4 5 6 7 (49)			1 2 3 4 5 6 7 (56)		
e) ☐5 speed of return of course/assessment results	1 2 3 4 5 6 7 (50)			1 2 3 4 5 6 7 (57)		
f) ☐6 usefulness of academic staff feedback about assessments	1 2 3 4 5 6 7 (51)			1 2 3 4 5 6 7 (58)		
g) ☐7 information about dissertation submission	1 2 3 4 5 6 7 (52)			1 2 3 4 5 6 7 (59)		

FIGURE 14.2 *continued*

If you feel there are any questions which are not relevant to you, please tick the 'not applicable' box

(60)   THE TEACHING RESOURCES   **SATISFACTION**   **IMPORTANCE**

Not applicable	Totally Dissatisfied		Neither Nor		Totally Satisfied			Not at all Important		Neither Nor		Very Important	
a) ☐₁ provision of course material (ie handouts, technology based material)...........1	2	3	4	5	6	7 (61)........		1	2	3	4	5	6	7 (65)
b) ☐₂ equipment available for learning and teaching purposes..1	2	3	4	5	6	7 (62)........		1	2	3	4	5	6	7 (66)
c) ☐₃ the teaching facilities available, ie rooms, labs, etc.......1	2	3	4	5	6	7 (63)........		1	2	3	4	5	6	7 (67)
d) ☐₄ 'Blackboard' learning support.......................................1	2	3	4	5	6	7 (64)........		1	2	3	4	5	6	7 (68)

(6)   ACADEMIC AND PASTORAL SUPPORT

a) ☐₁ your access to academic staff outside lecture time......1	2	3	4	5	6	7 (7)........		1	2	3	4	5	6	7 (13)
b) ☐₂ guidance and support from academic staff................1	2	3	4	5	6	7 (8)........		1	2	3	4	5	6	7 (14)
c) ☐₃ support whilst out on placements..............................1	2	3	4	5	6	7 (9)........		1	2	3	4	5	6	7 (15)
d) ☐₄ support for learning disabilities (eg dyslexia)...........1	2	3	4	5	6	7 (10).......		1	2	3	4	5	6	7 (16)
e) ☐₅ support for disabled students (eg physical disabilities)...1	2	3	4	5	6	7 (11)........		1	2	3	4	5	6	7 (17)
f) ☐₆ support for part-time students...................................1	2	3	4	5	6	7 (12)........		1	2	3	4	5	6	7 (18)

2.   **STUDENT ADMINISTRATION**
  Please rate the extent to which you are satisfied with the following issues in relation to <u>student administration</u> both before and since you arrived at the University, and then rate how important it is <u>to you</u>.

(19)   BEFORE YOU ARRIVED AT THE UNIVERSITY   **SATISFACTION**   **IMPORTANCE**

Not applicable	Totally Dissatisfied		Neither Nor		Totally Satisfied			Not at all Important		Neither Nor		Very Important	
a) ☐₁ the open day..1	2	3	4	5	6	7 (20)........		1	2	3	4	5	6	7 (26)
b) ☐₂ information contained in the prospectus.....................1	2	3	4	5	6	7 (21)........		1	2	3	4	5	6	7 (27)
c) ☐₃ admissions process.......................................1	2	3	4	5	6	7 (22)........		1	2	3	4	5	6	7 (28)
d) ☐₄ information through clearing.......................................1	2	3	4	5	6	7 (23)........		1	2	3	4	5	6	7 (29)
e) ☐₅ availability of part-time courses at Huddersfield.........1	2	3	4	5	6	7 (24)........		1	2	3	4	5	6	7 (30)
f) ☐₆ university website..1	2	3	4	5	6	7 (25)........		1	2	3	4	5	6	7 (31)

(32)   STUDENT ADMINISTRATION SINCE YOU ARRIVED AT THE UNIVERSITY

a) ☐₁ student handbook...1	2	3	4	5	6	7 (33)........		1	2	3	4	5	6	7 (40)
b) ☐₂ efficiency of the enrolment process...............................1	2	3	4	5	6	7 (34)........		1	2	3	4	5	6	7 (41)
c) ☐₃ timeliness and accuracy of invoicing for your course fee 1	2	3	4	5	6	7 (35)........		1	2	3	4	5	6	7 (42)
d) ☐₄ method of payment of the course fees (ie instalments)....1	2	3	4	5	6	7 (36)........		1	2	3	4	5	6	7 (43)
e) ☐₅ administration of student loans..............................1	2	3	4	5	6	7 (37)........		1	2	3	4	5	6	7 (44)
f) ☐₆ handling of general enquiries within your school/department...1	2	3	4	5	6	7 (38)........		1	2	3	4	5	6	7 (45)
g) ☐₇ procedure for handing in assignments/assessments....1	2	3	4	5	6	7 (39)........		1	2	3	4	5	6	7 (46)

3.   **COMPUTING FACILITIES**
  Which <u>University</u> computing facilities do you <u>MOST</u> frequently use?
  (Please tick only <u>ONE</u> box. If you use more than one facility, please tick the area you want to rate in the following questions.)

Central Learning Centre ☐₁		School facilities ☐₂	(47)
Do you have access to a computer at home?	Yes ☐₁	No ☐₂	(48)
If yes, is it connected to the Internet?	Yes ☐₁	No ☐₂	(49)

Most self-completion surveys could be cut off after three weeks and, although stragglers will come in over the next weeks, 95 per cent of the replies that are ever going to come back will have been returned (see Figure 14.3).

FIGURE 14.3   Response rates over time from self-completion questionnaires

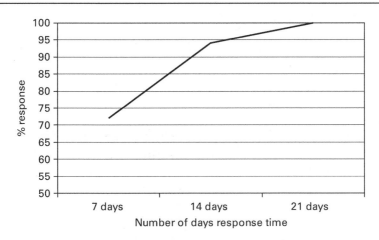

Christmas, Easter and the August holiday period are difficult times to send out self-completion questionnaires. It is also worth thinking about when the mailing will land on respondents' mats. Friday could be a bad day to land a business-to-business mailer but a good one for a householder.

A summary of the project planning tasks in a mailing programme is shown in Table 14.1.

Boosting response rates

There are a number of checks to follow that will boost the response rates in any postal survey.

Interest

The one factor that influences the response rate of a postal survey more than anything else is the interest that respondents have in the subject. A postal survey of customers is likely to achieve a higher response than one of non-customers because there is an interest in and a relationship between customers and the sponsor of the study. We have witnessed response rates of over 50 per cent when questionnaires are sent to highly engaged (and satisfied) customers.

Furthermore, response rates can be high when the subject is about a new car or on behalf of a company with some apparent authority, such as a utility company.

TABLE 14.1   Summary of key tasks in planning a self-completion postal survey

Key tasks	Things to check
Buy or build the list of respondents.	Can it be obtained electronically?
Obtain quotes from printers for typesetting and printing the questionnaire, cover letter and reply-paid envelopes.	Check printing costs. Check on turn-around time.
Design questionnaire and cover letter.	Get sign-off from the client.
Test questionnaire by watching half a dozen colleagues complete it. Amend the questionnaire.	Do they understand the questions? Do they follow the instructions? Did they find it easy?
Order stationery and printed material: outward envelopes, letterhead, reply-paid envelopes, questionnaire.	Check licence number for reply-paid envelope. Check that envelopes are of the right size for holding the return questionnaire and assembly of outbound pieces.
Book a mailing house for folding, inserting and franking mail or ...	Check cost of outsourcing. Check on turn-around time.
If carrying out in-house, arrange for the franking machine to be filled and brief staff who will be helping with typing, and stuffing envelopes.	Note that the Post Office offers a franking service for large quantities of mail. Arrange for checking a sample of each person's work to see it is being done correctly.
Mail the questionnaires.	Response rates are highest for questionnaires received on Monday, and lowest for those received on Friday.
Brief staff who deal with incoming mail on requirements for opening (or not opening) the returned questionnaires.	Is there a need to check the franked return questionnaire to determine the domicile of the respondent?
Track numbers of responses each day to determine when to close the survey.	Consider data processing after two weeks or re-mailing with a reminder.

Staff satisfaction self-completion surveys generally achieve response rates of over 50 per cent. In contrast, respondents receiving unsolicited questionnaires through the post enquiring about a product of generally low interest would most probably yield a response of less than 5 per cent.

Keeping it brief

The shorter the questionnaire, the more likely it will be completed and returned. Carefully laying out 40 questions on two sides of A3 (folded to make four pages of A4) can give the appearance of a shorter questionnaire than one with 20 questions spread over six pages. However, the number of questions does not influence responses as much as the interest factor, and there are many examples of long, 12-page questionnaires obtaining high response rates.

Anonymity

Self-completion surveys that offer anonymity usually have a higher response than those where respondents must identify themselves, although much depends on the circumstances. In many business-to-business surveys, respondents may be happy to be identified as long as they are confident that the research is bona fide and not a surreptitious attempt at selling.

Householders like to be assured that their names will not be sold on to a mailing house, and that there will be no sales pressure to follow. The ever-increasing problem of 'spamming' has resulted in people becoming very suspicious about disclosing their e-mail addresses (see Chapter 15: Online surveys).

Advance publicity

An advance letter alerting people that a survey is planned and will shortly be on its way will boost the response. Other publicity can also help; for example, in staff satisfaction surveys, replies are boosted by posters around the company asking people to respond. A company newsletter could be an excellent vehicle for pre-publicity about the survey.

Second mailings

A second mailing can boost response rates. If, for example, the first mailing yields a 25 per cent response, a second one could draw a further 10 to 15 per cent. The researcher needs, therefore, to consider whether it is better to send a second mailing to the non-respondents and accept a fall-off in response rate, or mail to a fresh sample from which a further 25 per cent response could be obtained.

Incentives

The use of incentives improves response rates. Incentives can take the form of a promise of better products, improved service or a prize draw for a gift such as a sum of money, a holiday or car. In business-to-business surveys, charity donations may be more appropriate in some countries. In general lotteries work better than personal rewards as an incentive. Lotteries cost the same regardless of how many people take part in the study, whereas personal rewards rise linearly with the number of participants and may be difficult to predict. Also, a few big cash prizes or a few big gifts keep transaction costs lower for the market research company as few people need to be contacted and sent their prizes. The difference to overall response rates from using lotteries rather than individual rewards is minimal. For more information on this subject visit the Market Research Society website and look up MRS Regulations for Administering Incentives and Free Prize Draws.

SUMMARY

We live in a world that is awash with surveys and many of us feel victims of questionnaires that don't make sense or are boring or too long. It is not surprising, therefore, that people receiving self-completion questionnaires ignore them and that response rates are low. Where there is a strong relationship with a target audience, the response rates will be high, and in employee satisfaction surveys they often exceed 50 per cent.

Nowadays online surveys have replaced many of the self-completion paper questionnaires. However, paper questionnaires are still widely used in checking customer satisfaction among hotel guests, airline passengers and attendees at seminars and events. Workers on the shop floor don't have access to computers, and if they are testing a product in the workplace, a paper questionnaire is one of the best ways of collecting their views.

Self-completion questionnaires are ideal for the solo researcher as there is no requirement for a field force of interviewers. They are best suited to surveys with lots of rating scales that would be tedious in an administered interview.

The key to designing good self-completion questionnaires is to imagine the difficulties the respondent will face during completion and take these into account when formulating the questions. Clear and simple questions with closed responses and tick boxes are ideally suited to self-completion questionnaires.

An engaging cover letter that creates interest and offers of an incentive for replying are as important as the questionnaire in generating a high response.

The organization of a postal survey requires strong project management skills to ensure that the administration and mailing goes to plan.

Online surveys

The life cycles of research methods

The reader of this book will have noticed how interviewing techniques, like most other products, have a life cycle. Market research began with observation. Face-to-face interviewing then became the norm. This was superseded by the telephone and now we have online research. Observation, telephone and face-to-face data collection have found their métiers, but online research is in the ascendancy.

Using computers to contact respondents began with the growth of e-mails in the late 1990s. The first application for online surveys began around the turn of the 21st century when lists of e-mail addresses became widely available. Researchers were quick to see that this was a novel and inexpensive way of contacting respondents, effectively sending them an online questionnaire to complete. All that the researcher needed to do to carry out a survey was obtain a reasonable list of e-mail addresses, design a self-completion questionnaire, send it by e-mail and await the responses.

The novelty of the medium meant that in the first instance response rates were relatively high. The cost of such surveys was virtually nothing and they could be completed within days. No wonder they took off with a vengeance. It wasn't long before the medium was abused and people were drowned by request after request to take part in online surveys. DIY tools allowed anyone and everyone to design their own e-survey that could be mailed to an online database. Response rates plummeted and a researcher is now lucky to get 2 per cent response to an unsolicited request to take part in an e-survey. Within less than five years, the e-survey mailed to a general database was just about dead.

Sending out e-surveys

The ability to collect information quickly and cheaply using an e-survey is of considerable value to the 'do-it-yourselfer', and if this is used in the right way, the response rates may be acceptable. The task has been made easier for the DIY researcher through the availability of inexpensive software packages designed especially for e-surveys such as SurveyMonkey. These packages allow virtually anyone, with no training, to design questionnaires for e-surveys. The software facilitates the design of the questionnaire with different formats for the questions and the replies and a 'submit' button at the end of the questionnaire that, when clicked, delivers the completed questionnaire back to the researcher and into a 'pot' for analysis. From here the pooled data can either be analysed using the software resident within the package (most allow quite comprehensive analysis facilities) or exported into Excel or SPSS for statistical analysis.

Using tools of this type, e-surveys are an ideal method for internal staff surveys. Most people in companies have an e-mail address, and with the quick delivery of an e-questionnaire and the easy means by which it can be completed and returned, an e-survey makes much more sense than using paper questionnaires. In such circumstances an e-survey to staff to measure their satisfaction on working in a company could easily achieve a 50 per cent plus response rate.

It is the strong engagement of a respondent with the subject of study that drives response rates. This means that a list of e-mail addresses of valued customers could elicit a respectable response. The e-mail addresses are likely to be accurate and the respondents may be convinced that a few minutes of their time feeding back thoughts on how the supplier is performing will be to their own benefit.

The problems occur with e-surveys that aim at a wider audience and where the e-mail addresses have been bought from a list broker. It is likely that a good half of these addresses will be inaccurate and therefore cannot generate any response. There is no easy way to build a large and comprehensive e-mail database if it doesn't already exist. People are very reluctant to share their e-mail addresses, knowing that to do so may subject them to a barrage of unwanted mail in the future.

The growth of online panels

It isn't surprising that there has been a consumer backlash to the storm of surveys that have been generated by the DIY researcher. As people have become resistant to taking part in unsolicited surveys, the opportunity has been opened for companies to recruit and foster participants who agree to provide information on a continuous basis. At the time that respondents are invited to join the panel, they are asked a series of profiling questions so that the online panel company can characterize them on their demographics, job title, gender, age, lifestyle preferences and habits. This then allows careful targeting of future questionnaires to those who are likely to have an interest and experience in a subject.

The privacy of panel members is protected by the owners of the panels and respondents receive rewards for each survey in which they take part (usually in the form of points that can be converted to travel or shopping rewards). These online panels are among the most important sources of respondents for market researchers today.

An industry has grown up around the panel providers. Some are panels of the general public. Some are specific to certain geographies. Some specialize in certain trades such as business-to-business respondents or medics. Panel companies charge their customers (normally market research agencies) a fee agreed in advance for the completion of a number of questionnaires. The panel companies know the profiles of their members, and at the time they are asked to provide an indication of cost they can make a reasonable estimate as to how many of their panel members will reply and what incentive they will need to be offered as an inducement to do so.

In effect, the panel companies are acting as fieldwork organizations, providing completed questionnaires to market research agencies. The market research agencies design the questionnaires and prepare them in a form that can be launched on to the panel, and the panel company releases the questionnaire in batches to its members until the required number of completed questionnaires is achieved.

The advantages and disadvantages of panel research

There has probably been more scepticism about the quality of online panels than to any other data collection medium. Market researchers from the outset were concerned about the natural bias of online panels. By definition, members of the panel have to own a computer and be computer literate. This therefore distinguishes them from those members of the public who are computer shy.

The very fact that members of a panel sign up to carry out market research surveys makes them different, in that most people probably seek to avoid invitations to participate in research studies. The fact that panel members are rewarded for taking part in research posits that these are not typical members of the public, but rather are people seeking to boost their income in some small way by completing online surveys.

All these concerns have some validity and yet online panel studies have shown themselves to be reliable in their results. The predictions of political polling are nearly all carried out online and are generally quite accurate. When surveys are carried out using mixed methods such as telephone and online, the results prove to be very similar. Online panels appear to work.

There are many means by which researchers can test the quality of panel respondents. Researchers know approximately how long it should take for a respondent to complete an online survey. If the survey is timed at 20 minutes and some responses come back that can be seen to have taken only 5 to 10 minutes to complete, they can be regarded with suspicion. Researchers may build in cross-checking questions into their questionnaires. At some part in the questionnaire respondents may be asked for demographic details and these can be checked at a later time to see if they have changed. It soon becomes very clear when individual responses are examined whether someone has made up their answers or been honest. And finally, responses can be easily spotted where people have crashed through the survey, clicking the same response every time to quickly get to the end and earn their reward points. 'Flatlining' (providing the same responses time after time) becomes very obvious and these replies can be discarded.

In this way, market researchers examine the responses from the online panel as they are completed and returned into the pot. Even though the identity of individuals taking part in the survey is not known to the market researchers, it becomes clear whether a response is valid or not and those that are suspect are rejected.

Online surveys using market research panels offer considerable advantages:

- They are relatively inexpensive. The cost of a completed online interview from a panel company is likely to be less than half that of the next cheapest method (which is usually telephone interviewing).

- Responses are generally well considered and of a high quality. An online survey eliminates interviewer bias. Respondents read the questions, taking as long as is necessary to think about their answers. This stands in contrast to an administered interview where there is always the chance that the question may not be read out in full or it could be misheard by the respondent. In an online survey the respondent can look over a long list of points of consideration that would be difficult if not impossible to read out over the telephone.

- They are quick to carry out. In most cases the responses from an online survey come back within days and sometimes within hours. Compare this to an administered interview, which requires possibly a dozen telephone interviewers diligently dialling telephone numbers, hoping to get through to respondents and persuade them to take part in an interview. Fieldwork time for telephone surveys can sometimes take three weeks if respondents are hard to contact, whereas panel respondents return their questionnaires within days.

- They do not require huge resources to carry out. Tapping into an online panel is like using a fieldwork organization. A lone market research consultant can design and carry out a substantial survey without large infrastructure or resources.

- International surveys are easy to carry out. Organizing an international survey using telephone interviews is complicated, requiring native speakers who may need to work across different time zones. Controlling the quality of these different interviewers can be a problem for market research companies. Panel companies are extending their databases to cover multiple countries. It is no problem to carry out a study simultaneously in the United States, Russia and China and have the results within a few weeks.

Organizing an online survey

As with any market research study, there has to be a sponsor, a client who requires the data that will be the subject of study in the online survey. Anyone commissioning an online survey should be aware of the limitations of the tool for otherwise expectations will not be met.

Online research cannot be used where there are a limited number of respondents. It is more suited to research with the general public than with specialist business-to-business buyers. Online research would not be the best approach for interviewing the very old and the infirm, who most likely would not have access to a computer. On the other hand, online would work well in a survey to find out what people eat for breakfast, as this is an activity indulged in by 90 per cent of the population.

So too, online studies will not provide deep insights. They are a self-completion tool suited to tick box answers. However, if the subject of the research can be broken down into a series of questions that provide insights, an online study could do the job. For example online research would be a perfect approach for finding out what drives people's choice of certain products by using a MaxDiff question – where respondents are asked to review a number of screens that show a dozen factors or more that could influence their choice of a product (see Chapter 11). Such questions are tedious to read out on the telephone but they are ideal for an online survey where the respondent can quickly read the question, choose an answer and move on. So too, online surveys are ideal for conjoint studies where respondents need to look at screen after screen of offers and choose the ones they think are most suited to their taste.

The market research company will advise the research sponsor what can and cannot be achieved in the online survey. Thereafter it becomes the responsibility of the market research company to design an appropriate questionnaire for the study. The questionnaire will begin as a Word document so that it can be discussed and amended by all parties until everyone is happy. The design of the questionnaire will follow the principles of self-completion questionnaires that are discussed in Chapter 14.

The questionnaire is now ready to be scripted into HTML, a format suited to displaying on a computer screen. Proprietary software tools are used to make this conversion from Word, and the programmers require a day or two to prepare the first draft of a questionnaire containing 40 or so questions.

The scripters will also be required to program the routing of questions that allow respondents to skip through the questionnaire according to how they have given their answers. These routing questions work extremely well in online surveys as they tailor questions specifically to people's needs. From the respondent's point of view the questions are seamless and logical. From the researcher's point of view the routing allows small excursions of study into questions that might be quite specific to only a few people. However, the scripting of routing questions can be tricky and the final version must be tested again and again to make sure that every permutation of answer takes respondents to exactly the right place in the questionnaire.

The scripters must also format questions to make them look attractive. For example, a question could seek to find out how much people are prepared to pay for a particular product. An easy option is to present respondents with a series of prices ranging from a low to a high figure with boxes that can be ticked to indicate which price would be paid. The scripter could make the questions easier to complete and more attractive in appearance by using a sliding scale that allows the respondent to drag a point across the scale to the price that they have chosen. Scripters know what can and cannot be achieved in programming design and their advice in the final questionnaire design is important.

If the survey is multinational and covers a number of different languages, the scripters would also be involved in overlaying the translations into the different questionnaires. One of the first questions in the survey would then deliver to the screen the appropriate language of the questionnaire.

Once the scripting has been completed, the market researcher must test the online version of the questionnaire again and again to check that there are no errors in the questions themselves, and particularly in the routing. This means repeatedly completing test interview after test interview, making different choices of answers in order to ensure that it will work in every situation. This rather tedious aspect of the research design must not be skimped.

The questionnaire is now ready for a soft launch. It is sent to the panel company, which sends an invitation to complete the study to a small number of members to check that all aspects of the questionnaire work and, most importantly, to get a fix on the proportions of panel members that will respond. At the time that the panel company quoted a price for the job it would have made an estimate of the incidence (ie the proportion) of respondents that would be eligible to take part in the study. Until the study is actually carried out this remains an estimate, and different prices for the interviews may be given at different incidence levels. Once the questionnaire is sent out to members of the panel, a true fix on the incidence will be obtained.

The soft launch is an opportunity to make final tweaks to the questionnaire, though most of these should have been done at the editing stage. It is the occasion to make sure that everything works as it should. Only a day or two is required for the soft launch, after which the survey goes live. The panel company releases the questionnaire in batches to its many thousands of members and the returns will flow in usually very quickly. In a matter of days the survey quotas will have been achieved and the results will be available for analysis. During the course of this fieldwork the market researcher can export the data at any time into Excel or some other tool to carry out preliminary analysis.

Understandably, the research sponsor and the market researcher will have a heightened interest as the results come in, and for this purpose the IT members of the team could design a dashboard with various dials that show key measurements as the fieldwork proceeds.

Online focus groups

Carrying out conventional focus groups is difficult if the target audience is small and widely scattered. This is especially the case in some business-to-business markets. These hard-to-get-at populations may come together for conventions or to attend exhibitions, and this can provide the right circumstances to convene a group. However, the timing of the exhibitions and the conventions is seldom synchronous with the research timetable, and so for the most part we are precluded from using face-to-face focus groups.

Now imagine a chat room on a website where a moderator brings together this scattered audience. The audience would be recruited either by telephone or online and requested to join the online focus group on a given date. Usually two days are set aside for the discussion, during which time respondents visit the forum to see what questions have been posed and what answers have been given by other delegates, and to add their own views. In this respect it is a forum of shared views that builds over time.

Other types of online focus groups could be convened in real time. In these real-time focus groups participants are recruited to join and go online at the same time as everyone else. A moderator then poses questions in real time and people give their answers there and then. In this respect these 'real time' focus groups are more spontaneous but they are limited as people wait for responses to be made. It is more difficult to have everyone available at exactly the same time, which means these groups are more difficult to organize than the online focus groups that stretch over a day or two.

The costs of carrying out online focus groups are very similar to those of face-to-face focus groups. Although there isn't a venue to be paid for, moderators have to supervise the forums over the two-day period and this incurs an extra labour cost. Also, respondents need incentives to attend the e-focus group just as they do for face-to-face focus groups.

Clearly in a 'virtual' group, logistical restrictions linked to geography do not apply. Respondents can be gathered from all over the country (indeed all over the world) to take part in the discussion. This means that in markets with a sparsely spread audience (and this applies to many business-to-business markets) there is a new opportunity to bring together respondents with a similar interest.

Experience shows that, once respondents have agreed to join the discussion, they are happy to log on two, three or more times over the duration of the group (typically a couple of days), providing perhaps two hours' worth of comment each. Compare this with a conventional 90-minute focus group made up of eight respondents where each respondent will average only a 10-minute contribution.

An online focus group typically generates around 10,000 to 12,000 words and this transcript is available immediately on completion of the group. This is a similar output to the number of words from conventional focus groups although there is a significant difference – the output from an online focus group has more pertinent comment. People give more consideration to words that are typed than words that are spoken – there is far less waffle!

Online groups allow reflection time when it comes to considering questions and topics introduced by the moderator. Whereas a face-to-face group takes no more than two hours, putting pressure on the moderator and respondents to cover issues quickly, the online focus group takes place over the course of a couple of days, with respondents entering and leaving the discussion as they choose. This provides valuable reflection time, increasing the chances of respondents saying 'what they really think' rather than making rash statements.

Also important, online focus group software allows respondents to be individually identified far more easily than in a face-to-face group. Respondents of a different genre (eg customers and non-customers) can be mixed into one group, while researchers and clients watching the debate know who is who. Indeed, at the end of the group, the transcript can be sorted by respondent or by company, meaning that online focus groups provide far more granularity of response than their face-to-face counterparts.

More respondents can take part in on online focus groups (often up to 20, and sometimes more), which means that an element of quantitative questioning and analysis can be incorporated. Online focus group software allows 'polls', which are effectively mini-surveys of chosen questions, in which respondents can only see the responses from other people when they themselves have contributed.

It must be acknowledged that there are limitations to the variety of stimuli that can be used in online discussions. Essentially, we are limited to displaying the stimuli on the computer screen (stimuli can then of course be printed out by respondents), but for physical objects that we want the audience to touch, feel or smell, some kind of tangible contact between the respondent and the stimulus must be arranged.

Nevertheless, online focus groups are extremely effective at providing on-screen visual stimuli to respondents. Questions can easily include embedded images, links to websites and uploaded documents; indeed they can include links to video clips, sound files and other multimedia files. As with the questions themselves, respondents can look at the stimuli for as long and as frequently as they wish, taking time to consider their views before expressing them.

Top tips

- Be very cautious about carrying out an online survey using a database of e-mail addresses that has been acquired from a list broker. You will be lucky to get a 2 per cent response.

- Panel companies have access to good respondents and the size of their panels is growing all the time. However, be prepared for up to 20 per cent of the completed responses to be poor quality and these will need rejecting. Spot poor quality by noting how long it has taken people to complete the interview, whether they click the same answers for all their responses, and whether they have inconsistencies in their responses.

- Keep a daily check on the completed interviews as they are delivered back to you. Delete those that are suspect quality and return the ID numbers to the panel company asking for replacements.

- Panels are an excellent means of carrying out international research quickly and efficiently.

- The questionnaires used in online interviews must be flawless. (You can get away with the odd error in an administered interview because the interviewer will take care of it.)

- Make the online questionnaire interesting. The more interactive it is, the more you will keep the respondent tuned in to the subject.

- Take care with the routing. You don't want to get to the end of the fieldwork and find out that a number of respondents were incorrectly routed and missed a load of relevant questions.

- Make sure that you impose quotas on the number of respondents you need of a certain type and that these are accurately screened by early questions.

Collecting information from a website

Surveys using panel companies aren't the only way that data can be obtained online. There is much that can be learned from visitors to a company's website. Google Analytics can track visitors to a website, providing statistics that show where they have come from, which pages of the site they have visited and how long they stayed. This most useful information can easily and freely be obtained by marketers and not just IT specialists. It has obvious applications for market intelligence, pointing to areas of the website that are most and least popular, as indicated by the number of hits and the time that people spend on each page.

Although web analytics tell a story, they do not enable us to profile the visitors in great detail or obtain feedback on what people like and do not like about the site. For this we need a more conventional questionnaire.

We are all very much aware of the pop-up questionnaires that ask for just a couple of minutes of our time when trying to view certain websites. These questionnaires are completed by very few people (a 2 per cent response rate to these pop-ups would be considered quite good) but they can provide useful feedback at a low cost. They do not need to be in place all the time and can be used periodically as a dipstick to help understand how the site could be improved.

Google and the rise of the DIY researcher

Online surveys are undoubtedly going to shape the future of the market research industry. They have reduced the importance of labour-intensive fieldwork agencies and put power in the hands of the market research designer. A single market researcher can now control and manage a huge multinational fieldwork programme, tapping into the resources of other organizations such as panel companies that can provide access to respondents.

DIY researchers are likely to be helped in the future by Google consumer surveys. With its access to billions of people, Google has given researchers the facility to run very short surveys (a maximum of 10 questions) that achieve excellent results at a very low cost. At $0.10 to $3 a response, 1,000 completed questionnaires means that the $2000 survey is now a reality.

Mobile surveys

In the above discussion about online surveys, it has been assumed that respondents will complete the interview on a computer. In fact, anyone with access to a tablet or a smartphone can take part in an online survey, the main problem being one of ensuring that the page format fits the small screen on the phone. Simple questionnaires delivered by wireless to smartphones are likely to be increasingly important in the future.

Questions can also be posed to mobile phones in SMS format. Again, this presents difficulties because of the small size of the screen and the limitations on how easy it is to answer questions. Also there are no lists of mobile phone numbers that are freely available and there are many restrictions on the use of mobile phone numbers covered by data protection laws. However, students joining a university may give their mobile phone numbers on registration, and these could be used for quick and simple surveys by the university.

Using the net to pose questions

In a recent survey we carried out into the future for biomass energy (think wood-burning power stations) a trawl was carried out of the subject on the internet. This is a well-documented story with many interested parties who want to push biomass energy because it is a sustainable energy source. Contacts were identified from the internet in organizations around the world and 'conversations' were carried out by e-mail. People proved eager and willing to join in the e-conversation, and many went to a great deal of time and trouble to provide supportive information. This is not interviewing in the conventional sense, but it is a useful tool to researchers providing quick and low-cost access to experts worldwide.

In a similar vein, there are websites that host bulletin boards where a question can be posed and someone will pick it up and provide an answer or a lead. Take a look at **www.freepint.com**, which is a kind of market researcher's bar on the internet. You can drop by and talk to people in the bar or leave a message to see if anyone can help. A surprisingly large variety of technical subjects are answered, and some of the past questions and answers make interesting reading. User groups specific to an industry or a subject can be employed in a similar way to pose questions and seek leads.

SUMMARY

The market research industry has changed dramatically over the last 50 years, with a move from face-to-face interviewing to telephone interviewing and latterly to online surveys.

The early days of online research involved sending self-completion questionnaires to e-mail addresses. The speed and simplicity of the approach led to overindulgence and as a result response rates to unsolicited e-mail surveys achieve very low responses. Exceptions are staff surveys and customer surveys where there is high engagement with respondents.

Most online research today is carried out through specialist panel companies that have recruited people to take part in surveys. The panel companies preserve the anonymity of their respondents and experience shows that high-quality responses can be achieved. Research carried out in this way is generally quicker and cheaper than that collected by any other means. It has given rise to a new breed of research technician – script writers who programme online surveys making them attractive, interesting and easy to complete.

The internet has opened up other opportunities for online research. Focus groups can now be carried out online and this enables researchers to bring together respondents who are spread over a wide geographical area. The quality of online focus groups is high and respondents give good consideration and well-balanced views over the two days that they are run.

We can expect the internet to bring still further changes to the market research industry. In the future there will be more surveys carried out over mobile phones.

Google can be expected to build upon its early start in offering inexpensive, short and quick surveys to a much wider audience.

Data analysis

Towards the end of a market research project, the fieldwork is completed and the data must be analysed. Faced with a pile of data, it is not unusual for a market researcher to be subject to 'paralysis through analysis'.

Most market research surveys of 200 or more interviews are entered into computers and analysed on proprietary software that simplifies cross-analysis. This produces tables showing the numbers and percentages of people who answered each question for the whole sample, as well as the results for groups of special interest, for example male respondents versus female, different age groups, different income groups and so on. This cross-analysis of questions cannot easily be carried out on Excel spreadsheets. A typical page from a set of cross-analysis tables is shown in Figure 16.1. The table presents results from one question out of many that were asked in a readership survey of a company magazine mailed to customers. The total column shows that of the 176 respondents, most people flick through the magazine and do not read any of the articles. Looking across the 'cross-breaks' or 'banners' that analyse the results for certain groups of respondents, there are no obvious differences amongst the industry groups but it seems that small companies and younger respondents are more likely to read the magazine (or ignore it). After a couple of minutes examining the data, it does not look so daunting, as patterns of response show through that enable us to make observations and arrive at findings.

We will return to cross-tabulations later after we have looked at the principles of analysis of closed questions.

The analysis of closed questions

A closed question is one that requires respondents to choose an answer that is presented to them in the interview. We will begin with a closed question that requires a single choice – only one response can be chosen out of the five options that are in the question.

FIGURE 16.1 Cross-tab from house magazine readership study

House Magazine Readership Study – JN229

Table 13 (continuation)
Q14 Which of the following statements best describes the degree to which you might have looked at it?
Base: All who have received the July edition of The Magazine

	Total	Q56 What is the principal nature of your business								No of employees						Age			
		Manufac-turing	Distribu-tion	Retailing	Services	Govmt	Leisure Industry	Agri-culture	Other	Less than 25	25–50	51–150	151–250	251–750	750+	Less than 35	35–44	45–54	55+
Base	176	76	8	3	27	32	8	2	14	30	23	43	14	25	40	28	49	58	40
I have read over half	9 / 5%	3 / 4%	1 / 13%	0 / 0%	1 / 4%	2 / 6%	0 / 0%	0 / 0%	2 / 14%	3 / 10%	1 / 4%	2 / 5%	0 / 0%	2 / 8%	1 / 3%	3 / 11%	2 / 4%	2 / 3%	2 / 5%
I have read a couple of articles	38 / 22%	17 / 22%	2 / 25%	1 / 33%	5 / 19%	8 / 25%	0 / 0%	0 / 0%	2 / 14%	8 / 27%	5 / 22%	6 / 14%	1 / 7%	5 / 20%	13 / 33%	9 / 32%	12 / 24%	13 / 22%	4 / 10%
I have read one article	15 / 9%	7 / 9%	0 / 0%	0 / 0%	2 / 7%	3 / 9%	1 / 13%	0 / 0%	2 / 14%	3 / 10%	1 / 4%	5 / 12%	0 / 0%	2 / 8%	4 / 10%	2 / 7%	4 / 8%	7 / 12%	2 / 5%
I have flicked through it but not read anything in any detail	62 / 35%	28 / 37%	3 / 38%	1 / 33%	9 / 33%	13 / 41%	2 / 25%	0 / 0%	4 / 29%	8 / 27%	10 / 43%	21 / 49%	7 / 50%	7 / 28%	8 / 20%	8 / 29%	17 / 35%	20 / 34%	16 / 40%
I haven't read it yet but I may get around to reading it	35 / 20%	14 / 18%	1 / 13%	0 / 0%	6 / 22%	3 / 9%	4 / 50%	2 / 100%	4 / 29%	2 / 7%	5 / 22%	5 / 12%	5 / 36%	7 / 28%	11 / 28%	2 / 7%	10 / 20%	12 / 21%	11 / 28%
I have not read it and don't intend to do so	15 / 9%	6 / 8%	1 / 13%	1 / 33%	3 / 11%	3 / 9%	1 / 13%	0 / 0%	0 / 0%	6 / 20%	1 / 4%	4 / 9%	0 / 0%	1 / 4%	3 / 8%	3 / 11%	4 / 8%	3 / 5%	5 / 13%
No response	2 / 1%	1 / 1%	0 / 0%	0 / 0%	1 / 4%	0 / 0%	0 / 0%	0 / 0%	0 / 0%	0 / 0%	0 / 0%	0 / 0%	1 / 7%	1 / 4%	0 / 0%	1 / 4%	0 / 0%	1 / 2%	0 / 0%

Q5   How likely are you to buy a new car in the next two years? Would you say you are: READ SCALE. ONE RESPONSE ONLY.

Very likely

Quite likely

Neither likely nor unlikely

Fairly unlikely

Very unlikely

The number of people interviewed in this survey was 200, and the responses can be presented simply as the number giving each response: very likely = 50, fairly likely = 80 and so on. However, it is better to set out the results in a more formal manner, as in Table 16.1. This gives the responses as percentages rather than numbers but the total number of responses on which the percentages are based – the base or sample size – is also shown. The inclusion of the base in a table is essential in presenting survey data as this indicates the accuracy or robustness of the result. Another point to note about Table 16.1 is that it has a clear title and says which respondents are included: in this case the whole sample – all respondents.

TABLE 16.1   Likelihood of buying a new car in the next two years (all respondents)

Likelihood of buying	%
Very likely	25
Fairly likely	40
Neither likely/unlikely	14
Fairly unlikely	18
Very unlikely	3
Total	100
Base	200

TABLE 16.2   Likelihood of buying a new car in the next two years
(owners of company cars)

Likelihood of buying	%
Very likely	40
Fairly likely	0
Neither likely/unlikely	25
Fairly unlikely	30
Very unlikely	5
Total	100
Base	100

Possibly, however, it may be useful to present data for just part of the sample, for example for those respondents who own their own car as opposed to those who drive a company car. In order to obtain this sub-group we filter out those who drive a company car by using the answers to one of the other questions in the survey (see Table 16.2).

In nearly all quantitative market research, we need to compare the results of different groups of people. Table 16.3 shows a simple cross-analysis that compares the likelihood of purchase between private and company car owners together with the breakdown for the whole sample; the data for all respondents (total), private car owners and company car owners are shown as separate columns. Two points to note are that the figures in the column for company car owners are the same as in Table 16.2 and that a base – the number of relevant respondents – is shown for each column. The inclusion of a base for each column is very important in order to judge the reliability of making comparisons between subgroups of the sample – in this case the two subgroups of company car owners and private car owners each have bases of 100 and at this sample size the range of sampling error is high (see Chapter 10).

In Table 16.3 the cross-analysis was very simple. It can be far more complex – for example, the likelihood of buying could be cross-analysed by any number of demographic groupings such as age, sex and income group. This sort of analysis is almost standard in most consumer market research. Other interesting cross-analyses could be achieved using any other question included in the questionnaire (for example, in the survey we looked at the number of miles driven, and this could have an influence on the likelihood of buying a new car).

TABLE 16.3   Likelihood of buying a new car in the next two years (by company and private car owners)

Likelihood of buying	Total %	Company car owners %	Private car owners %
Very likely	25	40	10
Fairly likely	40	0	80
Neither likely/unlikely	15	25	5
Fairly unlikely	18	30	5
Very unlikely	2	5	0
Total	100	100	100
Base	200	100	100

The question we have used is a scalar question, and a common way of presenting the responses from this type of question is by mean scores (average scores) as shown in Table 16.4. Each score (shown for each column) is a weighted average of the numerical values assigned to the pre-coded responses (+2 for 'very likely', +1 for 'fairly likely' and so on) and the numbers of respondents giving each response. The resulting mean score in the example indicates the average likelihood of purchase for the whole sample and for the sub-samples of both company car owners and private car owners; comparisons are easier to make with only one figure per column to look at rather than the whole distribution of responses to the scale. In the table, private owners appear more likely to buy than company car owners – a mean score of +0.95 compared to +0.40.

A mean scores is just a form of average – a way of describing a distribution with a single measure of location. However, when interpreting data it also important to consider its dispersion around the average. The standard deviation is the most commonly used such measure, and is an intermediate step to calculating dispersion in the population from which the sample was drawn – that is, standard error, which can in turn be used to estimate sampling error or compare two measures (for instance, from different sub-samples) for statistical significance. The specialized data analysis computer software calculates the mean scores and other statistics such as the standard deviation and the standard error automatically. Table 16.4 includes both standard deviation and standard error.

TABLE 16.4   Likelihood of buying a new car in the next two years by private and company car owners

Likelihood of buying	Total %	Company car owners %	Private car owners %
Very likely (+2)	25	40	10
Fairly likely (+1)	40	0	80
Neither likely/unlikely (0)	14	25	5
Fairly unlikely (−1)	18	30	5
Very unlikely (−2)	3	5	0
Total	100	100	100
Mean score	+0.66	+0.40	+0.95
Standard deviation	1.14	1.39	0.59
Standard error	0.08	0.14	0.06
Base	200	100	100

Interpreting scalar data just from mean scores does, though, have some dangers and the (contrived) example in Table 16.4 illustrates this. Comparison of the mean scores of company car owners and private car owners suggests that it is private car owners who are most likely to buy a new car. However, if we look at the distribution of responses we see that among company car owners, 40 per cent are very likely to buy compared with only 10 per cent of private car owners, and the higher mean score amongst private car owners is because, compared with company car owners, far fewer gave a fairly/very unlikely response. Which of these two ways of interpreting the data will give a better indication of future purchase intentions? Whatever the answer, it is clear that interpretation based on mean scores alone has limitations, and at the most should be regarded as no more than a useful way of summarizing data.

Drawing inferences from a sample to a population requires that the sample is representative – in other words it mirrors the population in its characteristics. However, often the sample of interviews we achieve is not representative, and it may over- or under-represent population groups. Sometimes this may be by design so that adequate numbers of respondents of each important group are included (to allow for statistically meaningful comparisons). Table 16.5 shows the responses from another

TABLE 16.5   Ownership of an appliance by home tenure: weighted totals (all respondents)

Own appliance	Total unweighted	Weighted	Owner-occupiers %	Tenants %
Yes	43	51	60	25
No	57	49	40	75
Total	100	100	100	100
Base	200	200	100	100
Sample (% across)		100	50	50
Population (% across)		100	75	25
Weighting factor			1.50	0.50

survey, this time asking if people own a particular type of domestic appliance – to which they answered either 'yes' or 'no'. These results were then cross-analysed by household tenure (owner-occupiers and tenants).

It will be seen that in the sample, owner-occupiers and tenants each accounted for 50 per cent of the sample. However, among the population sampled it is known (from other sources) that in fact only 25 per cent are tenants and this group is, therefore, over-represented in the sample (and owner-occupiers under-represented). This was by design to provide an adequate number of both – 100 in each group – because a representative sample of 200 would have yielded only 50 tenants and this is too small a number for analysis. Because of the make-up of the sample, the total ('unweighted') column will not, therefore, be a reliable indication of appliance ownership among the whole population. A solution is to calculate a weighted total column. This is the result of multiplying the responses among owner-occupiers by a weighting factor, adding this to the responses from tenants multiplied by another weighting factor, then re-percentaging the combined values to give the weighted column.

In the example, weighting was a simple calculation based on only one variable – household tenure. However, in practice the sample may differ from the population in a number of important aspects (for instance, age and gender as well as tenure) and several variables may need to be used in weighting to replicate a representative sample. This is a simple task for the market analysis software to perform.

Data analysis of open-ended questions

Up to this point we have considered the analysis of closed questions. However, questionnaires often include open-ended questions of the type shown below. In principle, each response to such a question is unique. The responses given by just nine respondents are shown below the question.

Q. Why would you not consider buying a new car in the next two years? DO NOT PROMPT. RECORD VERBATIM.

Respondent number	Response
1	My existing car is very reliable.
2	I cannot to afford to buy one.
3	They depreciate too quickly and my own car is running well.
4	My life seems uncertain at the moment.
5	We own dogs and they wreck a new car.
6	With only two of us at home we have no need of one.
7	I think that discounts will increase in the future.
8	I may get a car with my job.
9	I don't know really.

With only nine responses it is easy to read through them all and make some generalizations (or not). However, with say 100 respondents, each giving their own reasons for not intending to buy, it is much harder or impossible to see any common pattern. What we need to do is to arrange the individual responses into similar groups. This is illustrated below.

Each response group is designated a code, which is entered into the computer for purposes of analysis. The process of categorizing individual responses to open-ended questions is called coding, and the list of codes is a code frame.

As can be seen in the example, an individual respondent (3) may give a response that falls in two groups. Grouping individual responses in this way involves a certain judgement – in the example, three responses have been grouped as 'monetary reasons'. However, one mentioned being unable to afford a new car, one mentioned depreciation, one mentioned the prospect of better discounts in the future. It may be more useful to group these in different ways (for example, high price issues, depreciation). There is no absolutely right or wrong approach; it all depends on what the information is to be used for.

Code	Response group	Respondents included
1	Satisfaction with current car	1, 5, 6, 3
2	Monetary reasons	2, 3, 7
3	Job uncertainty	4
4	Could get company car	8
5	Don't know	9

It should be clear from this short discussion that producing the most appropriate coding frame requires skill and a holistic understanding of the project. It is a job for the researcher in charge of the project and should not be left to the data preparation team as they may not be aware of all the objectives of the study.

The result of this type of coding can be presented in a table such as Table 16.6. In this case the table shows the responses from 70 respondents (that is, those not intending to buy). Note that the column does not total 100 per cent; this is because of multi-response – some respondents have given reasons for not intending to buy that fall in two or more code categories. Tables showing this type of coded responses to open-ended questions can of course also include cross-analyses.

The coding of open-ended questions in market research is quite a problematical activity. The coding frame itself may be inappropriate and produce a data analysis output that leads to misinterpretation and possibly wrong conclusions. Also, even if the code frame has been well designed, the actual coding process may be poorly done – every response must be related to the frame, the 'correct' grouping selected and the corresponding code assigned. This work is usually carried out by clerical staff (the data preparation team) with little or no understanding of the overall objectives of the research, and even with the right aptitude and effective training, mistakes can be made.

TABLE 16.6   Reasons for not considering buying a new car (those not considering)

Reason	%
High prices/can't afford	55
Satisfaction with current car	35
High depreciation/high insurance	21
Job uncertainty	15
Don't know	10
Total	*
Base	70

*Multi-response and therefore the column does not total 100.

Open-ended questions require coding, which, as we have seen, is very labour-intensive (therefore costly) and highly judgemental. This type of problem does not exist with closed questions. The researcher should think very carefully at the questionnaire design stage whether open-ended questions are really needed, and be certain that using them is not just due to negligence in thinking through and testing possible responses to arrive at a good pre-coded question. In most quantitative surveys, it is generally best to keep open-ended questions to an absolute minimum.

Analysis of numerical responses

A final type of simple analysis is of questions that produce responses in the form of numerical values, for example:

> Q. How much did you pay for this appliance? DO NOT PROMPT.
> RECORD ACTUAL VALUE
> US$...

TABLE 16.7   Amount paid for appliance (those who have bought an appliance in the last two years)

Amount paid $	%
Under 300	3
Over 301–340	19
Over 340–345	54
Over 345–350	13
Over 350	7
Don't know/can't remember	4
Total	100
Base	58

The individual responses can be listed, sorted into order (for instance, by descending values) and then classified into intervals as illustrated in Table 16.7 – analysis software can take the hard work out of this. It will be seen that the intervals are not of equal range, and this is deliberate since most responses fall into the narrow range of US $340–345. The question responses could have been recorded by the interviewers under pre-coded intervals but, without knowing the likely responses, it is possible that the wrong intervals could have been used – for instance, US $340–350 would have accounted for two-thirds of all responses and there would have been no indication of whether most would tend to the top or bottom end of this range.

As well as showing the distribution of numerical values by intervals (as in Table 16.7), various statistics could also be used to describe the responses, including measures of location (descriptive measures such as the mean, median and modal values) or measures of dispersion (showing variability in the range results, using measures such as standard deviation). Such measures are often useful when grossing up from the sample to the total population (for example, having calculated the average consumption of a product among the sample, that of the whole population might be estimated by multiplying this average by the known total population).

A note on data validation

Checking on data quality is vital at all stages of the market research process. Things can go wrong because we interview the wrong person. We can fail to ask them the right question. In the main, however, the quality control process ensures that these mistakes don't happen or that they get spotted early and are corrected. It is in data analysis that mistakes can sometimes be made that may not be noticed. Once the information is entered into computers, it is programmed by the data-processing team and spewed out as tables. An error in the programming of the tables may go unnoticed if the market research executive is working late into the night to complete the project on time. Most of the deeply embarrassing errors in market research work occur in data analysis. Things that can go wrong at this stage are:

- The wrong base size (number of respondents in a cell) is used. For example, in the data analysis tables should respondents who say 'don't know' be included or excluded? In a customer-satisfaction survey there may be a number of potential customers that have been interviewed – should these potential customers be included in the analysis or are we only interested in the views of actual customers?

- The response codes get flipped. In a question that includes scales (such as from 1 to 10, where 1 is not important and 10 is very important), it is not unknown for them to be swapped around so the results that are presented are the exact opposite of what they should be.

- The mean score is thrown out of line by a rogue response. Some surveys allow open-ended responses on quantities consumed. It is not unusual for someone to input a figure that has too many noughts on it, which results in an arithmetic mean that is far too high. For this reason researchers may use the median (half responses are above this figure and a half are below) or the modal value (the most frequently mentioned figure) and not just the arithmetic mean.

- Flatlining has taken place. Sometimes respondents want to get through the interview as quickly as possible and give the same answers again and again (particularly evident in rating questions).

It can be difficult to identify such errors and the analyst may plough on blindly, seeking to rationalize the strange response. A golden rule is that: 'if a response looks peculiar, it probably justifies a deeper examination because it probably is peculiar.'

The first step in checking and validating responses is to obtain an export of the data in the form of a spreadsheet. In this document all the responses are given, row by row. Columns form the questions. From the spreadsheet the analyst can scan the columns and rows of data to spot things that stand out as unusual. The spreadsheet also allows the analyst to check counts of responses and mean scores. If these do not tally with the cross-tabulations, it should flag the need to have a conversation with the data-processing team.

This raises the question of how adept market researchers need to be in manipulating raw data. A good grasp of Excel is certainly an advantage, including the ability to produce pivot tables for sorting, counting and summarizing data from the spreadsheet. Other means of working the data would be to import it into SPSS (originally, Statistical Package for the Social Sciences) for further tests and analysis.

Top tips

- Plan the data analysis early in the project. The analysis specification and the programming for the data tabulations can be prepared before the fieldwork is finished.

- Anticipate how many cross-breaks are required in the analysis so that you don't have to subsequently wait for the data-processing team to provide extra cuts of data.

- Don't rely entirely on the data tabulations – they could be wrong. Obtain an export of the data into Excel. Get your hands dirty on the detail of the data in order to really understand it.

- Look for patterns in the data that make sense, and equally for patterns that don't make sense. If something doesn't look right, it is worth examining in more detail. It probably is wrong.

- Don't leave everything until the last minute. Like most other things in the market research process it is good to look at data and sleep on it. A rushed analysis is likely to be a poorly considered analysis.

- Look at the first 30 verbatim comments when analysing open-ended responses. Use these to develop codes for your coding frame.

- Be prepared to refine the coding frame as you carry on looking through the verbatim comments. If one of your codes is 'Other Comments' and it contains more than 10 per cent of the total responses, review these and either reallocate them or open new codes.

Multivariate analysis

Cross-analysis enables the relationship between two variables or 'dimensions' to be examined – for example, the likelihood of purchasing a new car as in Table 16.3. The relationship between three dimensions can (if with more difficulty) also be examined in a table; we could for example take miles driven each year as the third dimension in Table 16.3 and have for both company car owners and private car owners, sub-columns of three categories of miles driven (say less than 7,000 miles per annum, 7,000 to 15,000 miles per annum and over 15,000 miles per annum).

However, why stop at only three variables? The investigation of relationships between any numbers of variables may be worthwhile, and produce a model (a representation of the reality restricted to selected but critical variables) that offers useful insights into how a market works, and therefore provides guidance to effective marketing. The relationship between more than two or three variables is the outcome of multivariate analysis. In part the uptake of these techniques is because the mechanics of carrying out complex statistical operations has been made so much easier through widely available and user-friendlier software such as SPSS.

The statistical concepts and techniques underlying multivariate analysis are beyond the scope of a general introduction such as this book, and we limit ourselves to merely pointing to a couple of important applications: segmentation and preference analysis.

Marketing planning is now very much based on segmentation; the age of mass markets is waning and increasingly strategies are aimed at influencing specific market segments or niches. Segments can be defined as target groups with common characteristics. Traditionally, demographics have been the standard groupings used for segmentation. However, segments can be found by grouping people according to more subjective factors and especially their needs – these being determined by ratings of attitudinal questions in the interview. By using appropriate questions, any number of such attitude variables can be obtained, but the question then arises as to how these can be used to group consumers into homogeneous segments, based on common needs, that can be addressed through different marketing tactics. Two multivariate techniques used for such segmentation are factor analysis and cluster analysis.

Factor analysis focuses on the attitude attributes themselves and reduces them to a smaller number of component factors: groupings of attitudes that on the basis of responses appear to be empirically linked.

The focus of cluster analysis, on the other hand, is respondents themselves. As the term suggests, they are clustered into relatively homogeneous groups on the basis of their attitudes to the product. In the drinks market for example, one cluster may prefer drinks that are characterized by attributes that can be described as 'sophisticated' whereas another cluster may share attitudes more related to the intoxication effects of the products. Clusters are usually given contrived names to help the non-specialist (for example, 'vintagers' and 'guzzlers') (see also Chapter 10).

One of the most testing challenges faced by market researchers is finding out what is really important to people in driving their purchasing decisions. In interviews we ask people what is important to them, but often the quick response we receive is related to one of the obvious and measurable issues such as price, product performance or delivery. Of course these things are important, but we know that people who claim that they are driven by price in choosing a supplier or brand often stay loyal to that brand for years, despite the fact that there are many cheaper products around. Something else must be influencing them that they are not articulating.

An alternative to simply asking for 'stated' importance is to link preferences for whole products (which can be purely artificial constructs of attribute bundles) or brands to the way these are described by respondents (in terms of attributes). The importance of the attributes is then derived from the two sets of data at the analysis stage. A widely used multivariate technique to achieve this is conjoint analysis, which calculates 'utility values' for attributes. Trade-off analysis is a variant of this, based on respondents giving preferences for pairs of attributes. A major benefit of conjoint analysis is that it allows the researcher to carry out simulations and forecast the likely effect of changing attributes and, therefore, components of a product mix. This can include the effect of pricing changes; conjoint analysis is often used in pricing studies (see also Chapter 11).

Multivariate analysis is also used in statistical forecasting, with the relationship between a dependent variable (what is to be forecast: for example, market size, brand shares) linked to a number of other variables and possibly with time-lags considered (the effect of changes taking some time to work through to the dependent variable). Often such forecasting is carried out with data other than that produced in primary research (for instance, using published macroeconomic variables), although it can be a useful technique in the analysis of continuous research programmes.

All multivariate analysis, and for that matter all market research analysis, seeks to represent key characteristics of markets and how they relate to each other. In other words data analysis is a form of statistical model building that helps us to understand how markets work, and can often be used to make predictions of the effects of taking certain marketing actions by asking 'what if' questions. But the output needs interpreting, particularly for the benefit of decision makers for whom the techniques may be a mystery. In turn this requires a real understanding of what is being done to the data and what the output actually means. Multivariate analysis, therefore, requires more than just acquaintance with the terminology. Statistical experts cannot always be relied on to interpret the output of the analysis in a useful and practical way. Finally, it should be borne in mind that the most sophisticated analysis is not necessarily the best. Simple cross-analysis often produces adequate results and ones that decision makers can feel confident to use.

Qualitative data analysis

In qualitative research, the samples are smaller than in quantitative surveys and the data is more subtle and complex. It is likely for example that the questions will be mainly open-ended and the interviewer will have prompted for full responses. Also the interview or discussion may be unstructured, with the sequence and even the range of topics varying between different respondents.

Some of the types of data analysis already discussed for quantitative research may also have a place in qualitative research. However, coding open-ended responses is seldom appropriate since too much detail is lost in this way, and it is more usual to list and compare full responses.

If the numbers of responses are few enough, it may be sufficient just to read through the relevant parts of the questionnaires or other records. It is also often useful to enter the verbatim responses into an Excel spreadsheet, together with a code or identifier that enables them to be sorted by different types of respondent.

Often in the report produced of the research it will be appropriate to illustrate with verbatim quotations from individual respondents, and sorting in this way will make this easier. There are a few software packages around that aim to help in the process of sorting and analysing qualitative data by means of counting the frequency of mention of different words or word strings. However, the infinitely wide range of words and combinations of words that can be used to answer a question limits these.

Where interviews or focus groups have been recorded – and this is common practice in qualitative research – it is generally considered good practice to transcribe them into typed-up text and carry out analysis with this material. It will be obvious that while recording interviews is a highly efficient means of capturing what is said at the interview, it imposes much additional work afterwards, and this is one reason why qualitative research is expensive.

Qualitative researchers still have to rely on immersing themselves in the scripts by thoroughly reading the transcripts and making notes on the salient points. This indicates the difficulty of carrying out qualitative research with more than (say) 30 interviews. At or beyond this number, the surfeit of interviews begins to blur and there is a tendency to selectively recall the latest or most impressive interviews that were carried out.

The analysis of qualitative research depends on the flair of practitioners involved, and particularly the interpretation they place on the data. No two qualitative researchers are likely to produce identical outputs from their focus groups or depth interviews. Nor will they analyse and interpret the data in the same way. This is one area of research where the researcher who has carried out the fieldwork should be deeply involved in the analysis, interpretation and presentation, for otherwise much will be lost.

Semiotics and qualitative research

Semiotics is the use of signs and codes and clues that are obtained in qualitative research and that can be used to obtain greater insights into how meaningful things are to consumers. It is based on how we communicate ideas, not just with words but with images, music and all the senses. Semiotics is not so much about the questions that we ask but the way we analyse data that we already have, particularly placing the subject of study within the wider context of the culture within which it resides.

Many consumers argue that 'they know what they like' and 'what you see is what you get'. Consumers are often dismissive about the impact of brands on their buying decisions. However, semiotics recognizes that we are not as self-determined as we like to think that we are and that we are programmed by the culture in which we live.

Culture is defined very broadly, involving everything that we are exposed to in our social, private and public life. It takes into consideration the effect of television, newspapers, the internet, our friends, family and business acquaintances on what we think. We are in essence collectively programmed into a cultural position and this affects our life view.

The semiotician looks beyond the consumer into the cultural background that surrounds him or her, and from this obtains insights into their behaviour and attitudes.

Depth interviewing is one of the tools that researchers use to understand the psychology of the individual, their attitudes, perceptions and emotions. The semiotician considers the results from these interviews but is more interested in the cultural phenomena, the communications from the media that shape these attitudes, and the perceptions and emotions that result from them. In other words, semiotics takes a bird's eye view of the subject and looks at it from the outside in rather than the inside out. It looks for signs and codes and clues that provide this cultural understanding.

Semiotics can be used at different stages in qualitative research. For example, before an advertising campaign is launched, the semiotician could carry out an analysis of the cultural resources that the target audience is subjected to and use these to set up a hypothesis for the ad campaign that would be tested by depth interviews or focus group discussions. Semiotics could also be used following the depth interviews, providing the cultural background that helps explain the findings.

SUMMARY

The final output of fieldwork is data. In quantitative studies, the data-preparation team code and enter the data into computers, and proprietary software enables one question to be analysed in relation to another. This cross-analysis is central to the researcher's task of determining different patterns of response among different groups of people.

The analysis of open-ended questions requires skill, and is costly as all the responses must be slotted into a specially designed coding frame.

Increasing use is being made of statistical and modelling techniques that provide greater insights into the data. Multivariate analysis is used to demonstrate relationships between data, and is used to identify segments and to show how people determine the importance of different issues when they are choosing products or services.

The analysis of qualitative data is in the main handled by the researcher who carried out the focus groups or depth interviews. Using the recordings of the interviews and the transcripts from the groups, the qualitative researcher draws out the findings and develops conclusions with few, if any, analysis tools.

PART FOUR
Using market research

Using market research to segment markets

The marketer's biggest challenge has always been how to get more from less. When promotional budgets are finite, organizations must be disciplined in targeting their resources to parts of their market where the return on investment is greatest. This process of discovering, structuring and serving these pockets of opportunity is the essence of market segmentation.

Evidence of segmentation can be found all around us. The cereal aisle of a typical supermarket may have dozens, if not hundreds of different varieties – each targeted at a highly specific audience. There are vividly coloured, sugary options aimed at children. Organic and high-fibre cereals and muesli attempt to lure the health-conscious. Cereal bars and specially packaged single servings cater for the needs of those 'on the go' or with busy lifestyles. Internationally recognized brands compete with a store's own-label products, recognizing that different groups of the population may have higher or lower incomes.

Underlying each of these product groupings is a common factor – whether it is age, needs, behaviours or disposable income. Segmentation is the art and science of identifying these similarities and developing a marketing strategy that seeks to address them.

Why use market segmentation?

The myriad breakfast options available to consumers in a supermarket are not down to manufacturers' altruistic desire to appeal to everyone's tastes, but the more prosaic imperative of maximizing profits. Segmented marketing is almost always more commercially effective than mass marketing (that is, where everyone is targeted in a uniform way). This is because:

- Buyers are more inclined to select products and services that appear to be crafted to their requirements.

- Companies can better 'cut through' in their marketing if their message resonates and is targeted through relevant channels.

- Companies can be selective and chase only to those parts of the market that they know to be most profitable for them. Choosing exactly who a company wishes (or does not wish) to do business with is perhaps the most important principle of segmentation.

- Some organizations may have a competitive advantage in serving specific parts of the market. For example, national 'flag-carrier' airlines that have access to landing slots at the world's most popular hubs are well-placed to serve the needs of business travellers. By contrast, budget airlines with bases at less-costly provincial or regional airports instead have an advantage in appealing to more price-conscious fliers.

- Segmentation drives innovation. Where the requirements of a segment are not adequately met, having a framework for defining what the market wants or needs catalyses efforts to plug these gaps.

Types of segmentation approach

A market can be segmented in many ways, on a continuum running from simple to complex. We outline below some of the most common approaches (or 'segmentation bases') that are used.

Geo-demographic segmentation

At its simplest, an organization may choose to segment markets based on location. For example, a multinational company may have different marketing strategies for specific countries or regions.

Demographic approaches capture observable or measurable characteristics about individuals or purchasing units that may have implications for how an offer might be perceived (such as age, gender, household income, education level or occupation). These variables can be taken individually, or combined together to form composite descriptions of a target audience (eg 'young, wealthy professionals' or 'middle-aged, male, blue-collar workers'). Within consumer marketing, it is common for demographics to be used as a basis for defining life stage groups that correspond with specific requirements. For instance, car manufacturers focus cheaper, smaller and more stylish models at younger, newly qualified drivers, whereas retirees instead may be targeted with products and messaging around practicality, reliability and fuel economy.

The interface of location and consumer profile gives rise to geodemographic approaches, where specific clusters of demographic characteristics occur in combination with each other. Voting intentions are often linked with age and social class, and so a political party campaigning for public office will closely analyse the demographic composition of a specific electoral area. The soundbites and political policies that are then promoted to the electorate of each region are targeted based on its demographic composition. Messages about schools and childcare will be emphasized where there is a high incidence of families, while there will be a greater focus on healthcare and pensions for areas with older populations.

Several market research and marketing information providers have developed segmentation frameworks that describe populations at the neighbourhood or postal code level. Acorn (in the United Kingdom) and PRIZM (in the United States) are two such commercially available schemes, each with around 60 or 70 distinct segments. This information can be appended to an organization's customer and marketing databases to assist with local targeting of products and services.

Behavioural segmentation

It is often said that actions speak louder than words. This is no less true in the discipline of market segmentation. A buyer's habits and observable behaviours can be very strong predictors of their underlying needs. The analysis of one's behaviour is especially powerful because it can reveal insights that research respondents cannot recall or express through conventional surveys.

Retailers have long recognized the value in mining purchase behaviours. Many supermarkets use loyalty cards to link a customer's purchasing patterns and store usage back to individuals. These enormous internal transactional datasets are then analysed using complex statistical modelling techniques to categorize consumers into segments. This information can then be used to target tailored promotions and special offers at specific groups of shoppers.

Behavioural segmentations tend to be highly 'dynamic' in the sense that the size and nature of segments may constantly be in flux in response to the latest data. This dynamism has been further accelerated by rapid developments in digital technologies. Brands and digital marketing providers (like Google) have access to a huge amount of constantly updated data regarding the online behaviour of individuals. Market research agencies are also now using specialized applications to collect online usage data from opted-in research participants. The data collected from these *passive metering* techniques then forms the basis for segmentation, often as a complement to survey-based research.

At a much simpler level, organizations may also choose to segment their markets based upon the purchasing status of a customer. Those that are current, loyal customers may be grouped and treated differently from recently lost customers, or those whose purchase volumes have steadily decreased over time. For committed customers, the marketer's chief objective will be take advantage of their loyalty – for instance, by encouraging them to refer the brand to a friend or family member. For lapsed customers, the organization will wish to understand how to win this segment back.

Attitudinal and needs-based segmentation

Arguably the most difficult-to-achieve and implement segmentation is one based upon the buyer's opinions and needs. Needs-based market segmentation is notoriously challenging because the requirements or beliefs of an individual constantly change (indeed they may even be different from one day to the next). Customer needs are also very difficult to deduce from afar, making it tricky to allocate current or potential customers to segments unless they are asked questions directly.

For all the potential pitfalls, needs- and attitudinal-approaches are often the most powerful. The brand that is best able to appeal to the deeper-seated feelings, motivations and concerns of the market is the one that will frequently win out.

Many research-driven segmentations have classically been formulated from survey responses to a series of many agree/disagree attitudinal statements that seek to get under the skin of the attitudes of the end-user or buyer. This feedback is often recorded on a 5-, 7- or 10-point Likert scale as in the example below:

TABLE 17.1

Statement	Strongly disagree	Disagree	Neither agree nor disagree	Agree	Strongly agree
Branded products provide better quality	☐	☐	☐	☐	☐
I prefer to buy products online	☐	☐	☐	☐	☐
I try to look for environmentally sustainable options	☐	☐	☐	☐	☐

A significant drawback of this approach is that it is possible for respondents to give similar answers to many of the statements, thus limiting the scope for creating distinct segments. In reality, very few segmentations are based upon attitudes alone.

More often, attitudes are used in combination with other variables such as demographics and behaviours to imbue descriptive segmentation schemes with more character or 'personality'.

When segmenting the **needs** of a market, it is typical to measure this through the use of 'trade-off' exercises. In any purchase decision, buyers will have one or two purchase criteria that are non-negotiable, some which are of secondary importance and others that are merely 'nice to have'. To test this in survey research, a list of between 5 and 10 purchase criteria are identified and then evaluated, either using a simple ranking or through a constant-sum scale or points-spend question – as in this example below:

> Below is a list of factors that others have said are important when choosing a brand. Please spend 100 points across the factors to indicate their importance to you. You can spend your points on as many or as few issues as you prefer.

TABLE 17.2

Factor	Points
Price	....
Availability	....
Range of product functions	....
Reliability/quality	....
Brand reputation	....
After-care and product support	....
Previous experience with the product	....
Aesthetics	....
Total	**100**

The list of purchase factors tested can either be based upon the judgement of the researcher and their client, or it can be informed by prior, exploratory research based upon qualitative methods (such as in-depth interviews or focus groups).

The constant-sum scale question is well suited to needs-based segmentation exercises because it forces respondents to make compromises between their different requirements in a way that simulates real-world purchase decisions. When the sample size is large enough, the data gathered from this question can then be run through cluster analysis in order to identify respondents with similar response patterns. The resulting segments tend to be characterized by high scoring on just one or two of the factors, conferring them a clear and distinct profile. The constant sum question is also able to be used in low-sample surveys as common patterns of response can still be deduced qualitatively in a table or spreadsheet.

Needs-based trade-offs can also be measured using other statistical techniques: For example, MaxDiff questions (see Chapter 11) can be highly effective for segmentation purposes, particularly where a longer list of needs or benefits must be evaluated.

Business segmentations

Much of the preceding is concerned with the segmentation of consumer markets. Even so, many business-to-business organizations use similar principles in order to segment their markets too. Instead of demographics, the B2B organization typically segments based on what are termed 'firmographic' characteristics such as:

- the **size** of the company (judged by number of employees, revenues, sales or profit margins);
- the **industry vertical** of the organization;
- **channel** used to serve the customer (customers served through intermediaries or brokers are usually separated from customers that are sold to directly);
- the future **growth potential** of an account (even small customers may be considered strategically important if their growth trajectory is ahead of the rest of the market).

The very largest customers of a B2B organization are often small in number, but high in complexity. Adopting a sustainable, segmented approach with large accounts is often impractical, as the requirements of these companies are too specific to be generalized under broad labels. Accordingly, many business-to-business firms use dedicated, key account managers to serve these customers, leaving segmentation techniques to divide and conquer their 'longer tail' of smaller companies.

Just as in consumer markets, behavioural and needs-based approaches to segmentation are increasingly being embraced by B2B organizations. The researcher should be mindful, however, not to conflate the personal views and preferences of the business decision maker with those of his or her employer.

Hybrid segmentations

Each of the approaches described above has its advantages and drawbacks. Needs-based techniques are powerful, but are difficult to implement, while demographic-led techniques are simple but easy for competitors to copy. Companies are increasingly using hybrid segmentations that blend the best aspects of each approach.

An effective way of structuring these different segmentation methods is to align them into a grid, where the intersection of different groups of needs, behaviours or demographics defines the segments themselves. This example is based upon a segmentation adopted by a US low-cost airline. Their scheme combines flying behaviour (in the columns) with the key needs of different groups of passengers (in the rows):

TABLE 17.3

Needs from an airline	Flying behaviour		
	Frequent	Occasional	Groups
Very low prices	*Segment A: 'Get me there cheaply'	*Segment C: 'I'll use whichever airline serves the route'	*Segment D: 'Help me with my group trip'
Fewer delays and hassles at the airport	*Segment B: 'Get me there quickly'		
On board catering or other frills	*Segment E: 'Give me an upgraded experience'		
Business or 1st class facilities	Not served by airline		

Key
*High priority for airline (high competitive advantage)

It is notable that the airline elects not to address certain needs because they do not form part of their business model. The company also chooses to prioritize only three segments of the market where it has the greatest competitive advantage – that is, in serving the needs of frequent travellers and coordinating group bookings. To the occasional traveller or those looking for an upgraded experience, the airline is not necessarily any better than its competitors and so it does not actively market to these segments (although it will take bookings from them).

Qualitative/judgement-based approaches

It is often (incorrectly) assumed that segmentations can only be developed from large, quantitative datasets. Earlier in this chapter we described segmentation as both an art and a science in that a good deal of common sense and judgement is often used by the researcher to ensure that the segmentation is practical.

There are circumstances in which a full-blown, quantitative segmentation is not possible – whether due to budget constraints, the availability of market data or because a company only has a small number of customers. In these cases, several options present themselves:

1 **Using qualitative research methods.** In interviewing a small number of buyers in a market, it is usually still possible to identify the main drivers that shape market behaviour and supplier choice. The discussion guide used should cover each of the main segmentation bases described above.

2 **Canvassing views within the client organization or from channel partners.** Many business-to-business organizations forge very close relationships with their customers through their direct sales teams. It is also common for companies to only serve their markets through channel partners. In these cases, obtaining feedback from those serving customers 'at the coalface' can be a very effective shortcut to market segmentation. Internal/channel feedback is usually obtained from depth interviews, self-completion surveys (conducted online) or from focus groups with sales personnel.

3 **Using judgement alone.** This approach dispenses with primary research entirely and relies upon the expertise of the market research consultant, along with input from his or her client. Workshop sessions with teams in the client organization are often used to develop these approaches. These a priori judgements about how a market is segmented may also develop from historic convention. It is important, though, that any hypotheses are periodically challenged by research.

Quantitative methods

The most common approach to segmentation development is through ad hoc quantitative survey research. Although most projects are designed for the express purpose of developing a segmentation, customer satisfaction and usage and attitude (U&A) surveys can also be used to provide the necessary data.

Typical consumer segmentation surveys have relatively large sample sizes. Samples of 10,000 or more are common for international B2C segmentation studies. Large numbers of interviews are required to develop statistically robust models for splitting the market, and to ensure as many analytical routes can be pursued as possible. In quantitative B2B segmentation surveys, it is recommended to work from a base of at least 300 interviews.

The questionnaire that is developed for segmentation is often shaped by prior qualitative research. This is to ensure that all the potentially relevant segmentation bases (like attitudes, needs and behaviours) are included. In addition to segmentation variables, the survey should also include many descriptive variables that will allow for detailed profiling of the segments when they are finalized. These will be used to inform the go-to-market strategy developed for each segment, and could include details about:

- media/promotional channel preferences;
- where products and services are purchased;
- which providers they are likely to consider;
- positioning/opinion of the client organization.

Analysing the data: statistical techniques used in segmentation research

When the data has been collected from the survey, it is then analysed using a variety of statistical techniques in order to determine the most practical or stable model. All of these approaches are multivariate in that several question inputs are simultaneously analysed in order to produce the necessary output. A specialist statistical package (such as SPSS) is used to perform this analysis. The most common statistical techniques used for segmentation are:

- **Factor analysis.** This works out the common linkages that exist between questions. Through this analysis it is possible to distil many variables down to a smaller number of related, but unobservable dimensions called 'factors'. These factors are the elements that best describe the principal themes or drivers of a market. For example, from a battery of 20 or 30 agree/disagree questions, only three or four factors may emerge as being statistically meaningful. Factor analysis is rarely used on its own as a means of segmentation, but is more often an input into *cluster analysis*.

- **Cluster analysis.** This analysis seeks to uncover natural groups or similar patterns of response across a range of input variables.

The example below shows some clusters that are defined on the basis of two inputs: The degree of interest in future potential services and the disposable income of the respondent. The boundaries of response patterns will be fuzzy to some degree and so the clustering program seeks to find the best fit for where the border should lie. It does this by attempting to maximize the distance between the different groups of responses, while ensuring the clusters themselves remain relatively small in size.

FIGURE 17.1   Recognizing clusters based on two factors

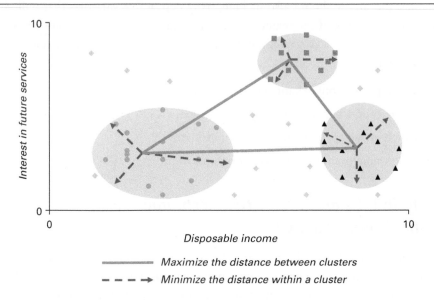

Cluster analysis is, by its very nature, a process of trial and error. In attempting to find the best solution, many dozens or even hundreds of different combinations of inputs may need to be tested. As part of this experimentation process, it may be necessary to take the raw questionnaire response variables and work them into smaller, simpler groups – for instance, age is often banded into only three or four categories for demographic-led segmentations.

In addition to using response data from questions, it is sometimes useful to also construct a dependent variable for the clustering algorithm to analyse. This involves the creation of a composite score that takes inputs from several questions. In the example above, 'interest in future services' might be each respondent's average level of interest (from 0 to 10) in several different service concepts. Utilizing a dependent variable in segmentation is effective because it can be directly linked to a client's objectives (for instance, the identification of segments that represent a high commercial opportunity).

There are several different flavours of cluster analysis that are commonly used in market research. These include:

- K-means clustering
- 2-step clustering
- latent class clustering
- hierarchical clustering
- cluster ensemble analysis

Each of these techniques has its advantages for particular segmentation problems, with latent class modelling (LCM) being the most widely used. Latent class techniques use a mixture of different statistical models and can analyse highly dissimilar types of input variable. This is especially useful for segmentations that mix demographics, behaviours and needs.

Successfully embedding segmentation within a client organization

Once the data collection and statistical analysis have been completed, perhaps the biggest challenge in any segmentation initiative remains: ensuring it is properly implemented. In the rest of this chapter we outline the key characteristics of successful segmentations, and some of the important hurdles that may need to be overcome within the client organization.

Five tenets of successful segmentations

To ensure success, the final segmentation framework should be assessed against the following criteria:

1 **Segment distinctiveness.** Each of the segments should have a clear and distinct 'personality'. If not, then it suggests the segment may not exist within the market in practice.

2 **Segment recognition.** If it is difficult to slot an existing or potential customer into one of the segments, then other, more easily recognizable segments should be developed instead. Being unable to apply or append segments to internal data or processes is one of the most frequent reasons that segmentations fail.

Smart analytics can assist with the task of segment identification. Using discriminant analysis, we can create an 'allocation algorithm' to predict the categorization of new or existing customers, provided we have answers to a select number of survey questions. These inputs are sometimes referred to as 'killer questions'. An agency may develop an allocation or 'typing' tool for use by the client similar to the example below:

FIGURE 17.2   Segment allocation tool

B2B International

Segment Allocation Tool

Profiling Questions

What are the principal activities of your company?	Retail & Wholesale
How many employees do you have?	250 +
Roughly how much does your company spend?	Over £500k
Please tell me about your role in the company. What is your position?	Accounts/finance/ management accountant

Predicted Segment   **General Servicing**

3 Segment durability. Segments must be valid for the long term, or at least as long as is required by the company's marketing strategy, because segmentation frameworks can take years to bed in.

4 Segment size. First, there should not be too many segments. It is an expensive exercise to define and implement a marketing plan for any more than six or seven distinct groups.

Second, segments must be appropriately sized in that they should neither account for too much nor too little of the population. If a single segment is more than 50 per cent of a market, for example, it suggests that further refinement may be needed. Likewise, very small, niche segments are difficult to serve profitably.

5 Actionable segments. The segments need to be straightforward and make sense. If the sales and marketing implications of a segment are not sufficiently clear then a different taxonomy may need to be used.

With segmentation projects, communication is everything

Even the most diligently prepared segmentation studies can be de-railed by poor planning and communication. The client's senior management team must be bought into the segmentation process from the outset in order for the resulting marketing strategy to work.

Tribal and political tensions within an organization can lead to strong resistance to segmentation from certain functions, especially direct sales teams. Salespeople can be defensive because they believe they deeply understand everything there is to know about their accounts.

Segmentation is viewed as a too-vague and too-general framework that fails to capture the unique properties of their customers. This push-back can be mitigated by engaging sales teams in the segmentation design process early, and reassuring them of the benefits of more profitable marketing and service design.

It is vital that segmentation is embarked upon with a clear marketing or operational objective. Too often, segmentation projects are unreasonably regarded as a panacea that will solve all of the organization's problems. The most successful segmentations are those that focus on solving a select number of objectives, such as optimizations to marketing effectiveness, product development or service provision. For the researcher, this is especially pertinent as key project design choices may rest on what the client wishes to achieve. Conducting a workshop with all relevant stakeholders at the beginning of a segmentation study is the best means of ensuring this.

Bringing segments to life

As with other market research projects, segmentation studies usually culminate in a written or PowerPoint report. This, however, is seldom enough to ensure that the framework is implemented and acted upon. Sales and marketing teams need to have lucid descriptions of what each segment looks like, while senior management will expect there to be a clear statement of the impact of the segmentation upon strategy.

Pen portraits or descriptive characterizations of each segment are typically included within the report. The segments are given short, memorable names and augmented with soundbites or imagery that are evocative of how each target audience thinks and acts. Very often, follow-up video interviews and ethnographic sessions are scheduled with members of each group to provide a face to each segment's name. A sample of a single-slide segment description that might be included in a research report is shown below:

FIGURE 17.3 Example of a segment profile: the disengaged

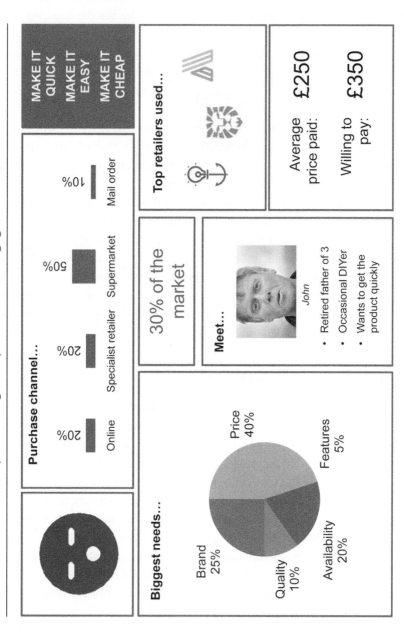

Increasingly, a wide variety of other media are used to communicate segments to teams within client companies, including videos, websites, mobile applications, posters and books.

Detailed marketing plans and strategies to target each of the priority segments will also be developed. Many organizations find it useful to codify their market approach by writing a customer value proposition (or CVP) for each segment. Put simply, this is a statement of how an organization will seek to offer superior perceived value (versus competitors) to those parts of the market that are attractive and potentially profitable. It consists of the following elements:

TABLE 17.4

CVP component	Answers about each segment
Target audience	Who is the segment?
Value	What does the segment value?
Superior	What is the company's unique selling point to this segment?
Profit	Will the segment pay a premium for superior products/services?
Banner headline	What is the elevator pitch for this segment?

Once defined, the segment's CVP then drives other considerations in the marketing mix such as product/service offerings, pricing, routes-to-market and promotional messaging.

Top tips

- Ensure all stakeholders are apprised of the aims and outcomes of the segmentation from the beginning.

- Start with a clear segmentation objective. Keep revisiting it to ensure there is no 'scope creep'.

- Consider conducting qualitative or exploratory research to better understand the market before designing the main questionnaire.

- Have a clear idea of what your main segmentation 'base' will be before designing the study (ie needs, behaviours, demographics). If you need to combine different types of segmentation approach, consider structuring these into a grid.

- The questionnaire should contain as many descriptive/profiling questions as possible to ensure segments can be appropriately categorized.

- Use question types that are well suited to cluster or factor analysis. Likert scales work well for attitudes, while constant-sum scale questions are good for needs-based segmentations.

- When clustering, start with a simple approach and build from there: too many segmentation frameworks are scuppered by becoming overly complex.

- Keep the end application of the segmentation in mind throughout. Challenge yourself with the question 'how will the client be able to use this?'. If you cannot clearly answer this you may need to reconsider your approach.

- Make sure your segments are easy to understand. Bring the segments 'to life' in reports and other deliverables through 'pen portraits' or personas of the relevant target audience.

SUMMARY

Segmentation is an extremely powerful weapon in the marketers' arsenal. A good segmentation helps to improve the return-on-investment of marketing spend and provides a strategic framework for a company to develop and maintain its market position.

All segmentations need to start with a clear objective, as the aims of the initiative will strongly determine the research design of the study. One of the main considerations is whether the segmentation is to be based on demographics, firmographics, behaviours, attitudes or needs. The optimal selection of these different segmentation 'bases' tends to come from experimentation and a close reference to the marketing tools at the disposal of the client.

Segmentation research is often undertaken as a quantitative exercise, but there are occasions where using qualitative techniques are appropriate (for instance, in B2B markets, where customers numbers are smaller). Indeed, some organizations may solely base their segmentation framework on a combination of judgement, internal data and the assistance of external consultants.

Quantitative segmentations almost always involve the use of large sample sizes and advanced, multivariate statistical techniques such as cluster analysis. Many dozens or hundreds of iterations of cluster analysis may be required to arrive at the optimal solution. Good segments are those that are distinct, recognizable, durable, sizable and actionable.

After analysis, segmentations are used to define marketing strategy. Segments are given snappy, memorable names and are cascaded throughout the client organization using various means of multi-media communication. It is important that the client clearly identifies the segments that are its top priority as well as 'de-selecting' any groups that it will choose not to serve. A customer value proposition (CVP) is then drawn up for each of the segments to define the target audience and to summarize and substantiate why a potential customer should buy the organization's product or service.

Using market research to improve a brand position

It has been estimated that up to 30 per cent of the stock market value of the largest corporations is attributable to brand. This makes sense when we consider the role of brands in facilitating purchase decisions in our daily lives: when all other rational factors – such as price and features – have been considered, intangible influences, like brand, tend to be decisive.

Brands are shortcuts that encode a huge amount of information about an organization's values and what a customer should expect from it. Let us take the automotive sector as an example. Developments in engineering and technology mean that most modern cars have very similar levels of performance, economy and reliability. To achieve maximum economies of scale, many of the Volkswagen Group's vehicles are based upon a common chassis across the different ranges it offers. Volkswagen skilfully differentiates these mechanically similar vehicles through branding: Skoda and SEAT appeal to value-conscious consumers, Volkswagen pitches itself as the everyman mass-market choice, while Audi is clearly positioned as a prestige brand.

Although a SEAT Leon, Volkswagen Golf and Audi A3 are substantially the same cars, the Audi commands at least a 20 per cent price premium over the SEAT. Smart brand management allows VW to maximize sales of their products to as many market segments as possible, while also obtaining a premium price from those who 'buy into' the values and experience offered by its more prestigious divisions.

Volkswagen is only able to manage its portfolio of marques in this way through close monitoring and cultivation of its brands. Accordingly, market research is an extremely important tool in helping corporations to establish and maintain their brand's position over time. Research is used throughout the life cycle of a brand, moving from their creation through to the point where they may need to be re-energized, retired or subsumed into another corporate identity. Each of these areas of the brand lifecycle will be covered in this chapter, as well as a consideration of how research can be used to establish a brand's ultimate value (or 'brand equity').

FIGURE 18.1   The brand life cycle

Research at the birth (and re-birth) of a brand

Brands are created all the time. It is easy to think of brands as being the single, corporate identity of a large organization. In fact the vast majority of brands are product brands, created whenever a new offering or proposition is launched by its parent company. The consumer goods manufacturer Unilever, for instance, sells goods under at least 400 different brands worldwide, with many new product marques constantly being added to the portfolio.

Brands are not just the preserve of multinationals, however: any new company, large or small, will be interested in constructing an identity that, in time, will be recognizable, differentiated and which has a clearly articulated vision. Strong brands can also be formed very quickly: many of today's best-known companies such as Google, Facebook and Alibaba are technology firms whose brands were first created within the past 10 to 20 years.

Within the corporate world, most company and product brands are developed with the assistance of a specialist brand strategy consultant. The work of these advisors is often part creative and part research-driven, with the research element either being undertaken internally or in conjunction with a specialist market intelligence company.

Research that contributes towards brand creation is often focused upon **canvassing internal stakeholders** about their ambitions and plans for the brand. For the nascent brand to succeed in the long term, it must align with where key personnel wish to take it. Qualitative research techniques, such as in-depth interviews, focus groups and workshop sessions are used to draw out these opinions and to establish where the consensus lies. The questions that are asked as part of these exercises are often projective and forward-looking, and cover topics such as:

- **ambitions for the brand** – what it should stand for, what its 'big message' is, how it will be different from competitors;

- thinking about the **intended target audience** for the brand and how it should make them think and feel. What is the brand's 'promise' to the market?

- what the **'architecture' of the brands** under development should be – for instance if a new product brand is being created, should it be clearly linked with or endorsed by the corporate or parent brand?

- thoughts on the **visual identity of the brand** – what its logo should be, where its imprint will be seen and how this will be executed.

Aside from internal opinions, external research with the intended target audience may sometimes take place during the brand creation process in order to validate any assumptions and to identify where gaps exist. Again, smaller-scale, qualitative methods tend to be used for this purpose.

In assessing the lie of the land of the market, it may also be prudent to profile the brand image of other players. Desk researching the corporate positioning of major or potential competitors is a low-cost, but very effective means of understanding how any new brand can be placed into the market jigsaw. Gaps in the market can be more easily identified once the corporate imagery, positioning statements and brand values of different competitors have been systematically aligned.

These research activities are vital inputs into the work of the brand strategist. They help with defining a new brand direction that aligns both the ambitions of internal stakeholders and the needs of the market, while avoiding the danger of appearing 'vanilla' and looking like everyone else. Here is a useful framework for locating results from research during new brand development (and brand renewal):

FIGURE 18.2 Viewing a brand from different angles

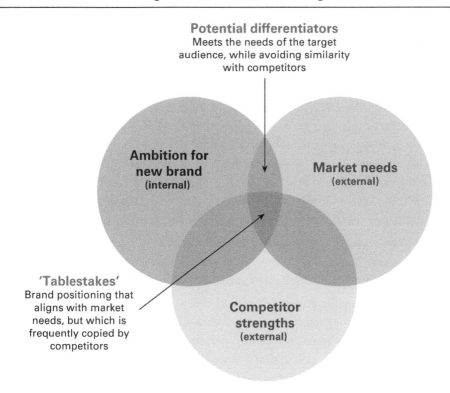

Potential differentiators
Meets the needs of the target
audience, while avoiding similarity
with competitors

**Ambition for
new brand
(internal)**

**Market needs
(external)**

'Tablestakes'
Brand positioning that
aligns with market
needs, but which is
frequently copied by
competitors

**Competitor
strengths
(external)**

From time to time organizations may seek to change an existing brand (either its name, positioning or visual identity). It should also be noted that many of the processes described above are equally relevant when brands are periodically refreshed (or rebranded).

Researching new visual identities

The formulation of a new or refreshed brand will be accompanied by a several potential visual identities that will need to be tested. Central to this is the brand's logo, which is almost always extensively researched before being launched into market. Logo research is most commonly undertaken quantitatively, the aim being to scientifically gauge which of the competing visuals has most appeal to the market. The methods used for logo testing are very similar to those employed in product concept testing.

The evaluation of competing designs within a survey is typically set up in one of several ways:

- **Paired-comparison test.** A straightforward research set-up in which two potential design routes are tested side by side among the entire sample. The winner is the one that gets the most favourable feedback.

- **Monadic testing.** Each respondent is asked for his or her opinions on just one, randomly chosen design option during the survey. So long as there is a sufficiently large, comparable sample for each design tested, then statistically significant differences in opinion can be measured.

  Monadic testing is considered to be the fairest means of testing brand visuals: It replicates the real world, in that only one brand is seen at a time. It also eliminates any bias created from the visual treatment being compared against some other alternative that is under test (eg the existing logo, which might always win due to an incumbency effect). On the downside, monadic testing requires larger sample sizes and so is comparatively expensive to execute.

- **Proto-monadic testing.** Combines a monadic (one at a time) test with a paired comparison later in the interview. By mixing elements of each research design, there is a safety net in case one approach does not suggest a clear winner.

- **Sequential monadic testing.** In essence, this is a series of back-to-back monadic tests for each respondent (ie each design tested individually in turn). This method is used to keep costs down since several designs are evaluated per respondent. The design that is tested first by each respondent is recorded so that the data can still be analysed as if it were a pure monadic test.

Criteria that might be measured as part of a logo/visual identity testing exercise include:

- overall **favourability**/likeability;
- extent to which the visual identity **aligns with desired brand values**;
- whether the logo is **associated** with the brand/category;
- how the logo is **perceived in context** (eg on product packaging, at point of sale, on a corporate website).

Brand health monitoring

If a brand is to adequately fulfil its purpose of driving sales and profitability for a company, its performance must be monitored over time. Classically, this measurement is undertaken with reference to the *brand funnel* framework.

Good performance for a brand at the beginning of the funnel is considered to be a prerequisite for achieving sales and loyal customers. For instance, it is highly unlikely that someone would ever be a user of a brand (and certainly not a *conscious* user) if they were not already aware of it, familiar with it and willing to consider it.

FIGURE 18.3 The brand funnel

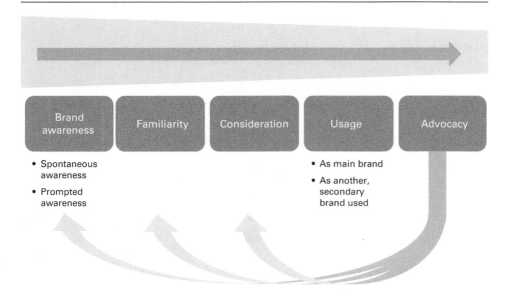

The model is called a funnel because it is assumed that potential buyers within a market will drop out at various stages. So although we might expect awareness for some brands to be very high, when the filters of familiarity and consideration are applied, usage will only ever be a fraction of awareness.

Each of the stages of the funnel can be measured as part of a brand tracking programme. This is a regular survey commissioned on behalf of a brand to understand whether performance of that brand is meeting expectations compared to others in the market. The following measurements are standard components of a quantitative brand tracking study:

- **Awareness.** Respondents are first asked about *spontaneous awareness*. This involves naming, top of mind, all of the brands they associate with a particular category of products or services. For self-completion surveys (such as online surveys), these responses are entered as free text and are then coded for analysis. Spontaneous awareness is seen to be a very good judge of the success of a brand because it relates to how synonymous a brand has become with its category. Related to this, some surveys also measure the brand that is mentioned first on a spontaneous basis.

Awareness is then measured in a *prompted* fashion – either through the interviewer reading out the names of brands or displaying these to the respondent in a self-completion survey. Any spontaneous mentions already recorded will generally be excluded from the list. Prompted and spontaneous awareness are then added together to produce a metric known as *total awareness*.

FIGURE 18.4   Assessing total brand awareness

- **Familiarity (asked of those that are aware).** This stage seeks to measure the 'quality' of one's awareness of a brand (from only having heard the name, through to being 'very familiar'). Familiarity is what distinguishes a brand from just being a label to being a more meaningful locator for aiding purchase decisions.

- **Consideration (asked of those that are aware).** Is the brand among those that the market would seriously consider buying? For many purchases, only a maximum of three or four brands enter into the decision maker's *consideration set*. Accordingly, being within that number is vitally important.

  Some surveys may also seek to understand any brands that would *never* be considered – whether due to previous negative experiences, poor reputation or inappropriate positioning.

- **Usage.** Although a brand could just measure their sales figures, usage is a very important long-term metric to independently track. Understanding the dynamics of competitor brands that are being used and the relative market share that these command are two outputs that internal data alone will not answer. Sometimes secondary usage is asked, particularly in B2B markets where the use of multiple suppliers is common.

A time frame will often be specified to ensure the respondent is only answering about purchases made recently (eg the past 3, 6 or 12 months).

- **Advocacy (asked of those that use).** It pays to understand how well a brand is delivering against its promises. This can be done either with recourse to a satisfaction question, or the buyer's likelihood to recommend a brand to others (on a scale from 0 to 10). Those that give a score of 9 or 10 are then deemed to be 'advocates' for the brand.

Although the brand funnel model appears linear, advocacy is a very powerful feedback loop that can help to positively reinforce earlier stages in the funnel (as shown by the arrows in the funnel diagram earlier in this section). Those that say good things about a brand will raise its awareness levels, make others more familiar with it or encourage people to consider it in future.

Once all measures have been collected from the brand tracking survey, they are presented back in the form of a funnel, with all major brands within the market shown in a single view:

FIGURE 18.5 Example: Four brands compared in a brand funnel

The percentage figures for each phase are on the base of the whole market. This allows a systematic analysis of the loss rate between different stages of the funnel (as shown in the ovals). Transitions that are marked with an upward or downward arrow are where a brand performs relative to its peers. For instance, if we know that a brand would be considered, but is not used, this is likely to be due to problems of availability, pricing or the offering not being attuned to needs. Diagnostic questions to assess the reasons for drop-out between stages of the funnel are often built into brand tracking questionnaires.

Overall conversion efficiency throughout the funnel may also be measured. This is taken to be the percentage of those that are aware of a brand that then go on to be either advocates for or users of that brand. In many ways, this is an overall measure of the success of an organization's brand-building efforts.

Other topics covered as part of brand tracking studies

Aside from measuring funnel items, brand tracking surveys are also used to monitor many other aspects of a brand's performance. Further topics that tend to be included in brand tracking are:

- **Advertising awareness.** Which brands have been seen in promotions? What form of advertising was recalled? What were the messages? Did these communications change the respondent's view of the brand?

  So long as the respondent is not aware of the sponsor of the study, tracking changes in these measures is a good indicator of the effectiveness and reach of advertising.

- **Channel of purchase.** Where did they buy the brand from? When combined with information about the brands used, this gives important intelligence about the channel strategies of competitors.

- **Behaviour during the purchase decision.** For those making a recent purchase, respondents may be asked to report on some of the actions they followed in the build up to the acquisition. Did the buyer refer to information online? Did they look at products in a retail store? Did they get the opinion of others? This information is invaluable in helping marketers to understand where the brand should be prominent in order to positively influence the purchase outcome in their favour.

- **Switching patterns.** Does the buyer intend on staying loyal to the brand? What are their anticipated changes in purchase behaviour? Regularly tracking this can be an early warning of impending defection to competitors.

- **Audience profiling.** Brand tracking is often strongly linked to an organization's segmentation. Accordingly, many tracking surveys ask lots of profiling questions (around demographics/firmographics, attitudes and behaviours) in order to get an up-to-date understanding of their key target audiences.

Research design of brand tracking studies

When designing a brand tracking programme, the researcher should bear in mind several important methodological considerations. The first of these is how **frequently** the survey should run. This tends to range from monthly to every two years. Scheduling of brand tracking research should be based upon when promotional activities are anticipated to fall. For instance, consumer goods manufacturers that run regular advertising campaigns will benefit from more frequent tracking. By contrast, a firm embarking on a large brand repositioning exercise may only be able to fully execute this over a period of several years. In this case, annual tracking may well be more appropriate.

The next critical issue is that of methodological **consistency**. The questions asked from one wave (or iteration) of brand research to the next must either be the same or very similar. All too often, the validity of tracking exercises is spoiled by the client's or researcher's temptation to tweak questions, rendering them incomparable with previously collected data. This applies not just to the headline question, but also the answer options that are shown to respondents (including the number of answer options presented).

In many cases, a brand tracking survey should be 'blind'. In other words, the sponsor of the study should not be disclosed to respondents. At the very least, it should be hidden until the end of the survey. This is to minimize any bias – particularly in terms of brand awareness questions. Linked to this, it is prudent to randomize the order of brand answer lists so that the company behind the research is not given undue prominence (eg by being the first brand in the list). In certain markets, however, it may sometimes be difficult to recruit an adequate sample without first disclosing the sponsor.

For brand monitoring projects the **sample** size must be sufficient to statistically detect any changes from one wave to the next. If the margin of error for a tracking sample is larger than the expected change in the measures that are to be tracked, then more interviews may be required.

Ideally, the sample should be designed so that previous survey participants are excluded from future waves of the tracking survey. This is to avoid them learning who the research sponsor is, as well as ensuring that their answers are not biased from having completed the survey multiple times. There are many markets, however, where the pool of relevant respondents is too small to use sample exclusions for all future iterations of the survey. In these cases, it may be more common for an exclusion to apply for a given time period or number of research waves.

One way of dealing with the challenge of maintaining adequate sample sizes is to group waves together for reporting purposes. For instance, various iterations of the survey may be reported back on annually, twice-yearly or quarterly. To smooth out any changes in brand health measures, 'rolling averages' of sequentially overlapping waves may be used, as in the following example:

→ Wave 1 and 2

→ Wave 2 and 3

→ Wave 3 and 4

Brand tracking survey research may be usefully complemented by research insights from other sources. The **monitoring of brand mentions on social media** is now widely practised by B2C organizations, providing real-time insight into perceptions of brands in whatever online context they are experienced. Using textual and semantic analysis, specialized software can automatically characterize the overall sentiment of comments on social media sites into those that are broadly positive or negative. The net sentiment towards a brand (as well as the number of mentions of it) can be analysed over time through online dashboards or other reporting tools.

Brand positioning

Earlier in this chapter we noted that the most successful brands are those that truly stand for something. While many brands have successfully progressed beyond being a simple label or locator for buying decisions, only a select few have managed to take on a personality; that is to say, a set of values or principles that becomes uniquely and positively associated with that brand.

An organization's current branding position can be expressed neatly with reference to the *brand ladder* framework (Figure 18.6). We may know from brand tracking research that a brand is known or is likely to be considered. But does it really pass muster when it comes to the top three rungs of the ladder?

FIGURE 18.6   Locating a brand's position on the brand ladder

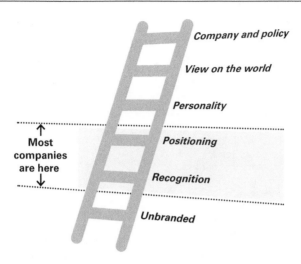

Before embarking on any brand positioning research, it vital to flush out the values that buyers regard as being most relevant. Associative and projective methods are typically used to achieve this. Some techniques are borrowed from the world of psychoanalysis, such as the free association of words or ideas that come to mind when thinking of a brand. Respondents may also be asked to abstract the image of a brand onto other domains: What would this brand wear? What music would it listen to? What animal is it?

Metaphors are very powerful expressions of how buyers subconsciously feel about a brand or category. In the commonly used Zaltman Metaphor Elicitation Technique (or ZMET method), research respondents are invited to express their thoughts about a brand in the form of images. These are selected by the study participant from a range of stimulus material, such as magazines and newspapers. The pictures chosen and the research subject's rationalizations are then thematically analysed to get the underlying values that are being expressed.

Once the audit of relevant brand positions has been completed, the alignment of brands with each of these is then tested through quantitative research. The list of brand values to be evaluated will often consist of both rational attributes and those based on more emotional factors. Figure 18.7 shows some examples of virtuous positions that might be tested as part of brand research:

FIGURE 18.7   Rational and emotional values used in brand research

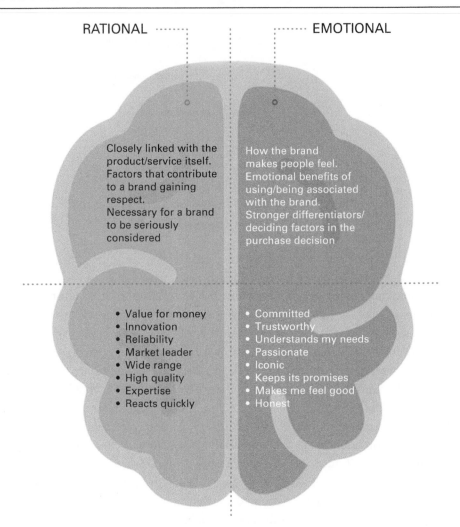

RATIONAL ········⌐   ⌐········ EMOTIONAL

Closely linked with the
product/service itself.
Factors that contribute
to a brand gaining
respect.
Necessary for a brand
to be seriously
considered

How the brand
makes people feel.
Emotional benefits of
using/being associated
with the brand.
Stronger differentiators/
deciding factors in the
purchase decision

- Value for money
- Innovation
- Reliability
- Market leader
- Wide range
- High quality
- Expertise
- Reacts quickly

- Committed
- Trustworthy
- Understands my needs
- Passionate
- Iconic
- Keeps its promises
- Makes me feel good
- Honest

These various brand attributes are then further evaluated to measure their importance to the market. Within the quantitative questionnaire, the respondent is asked
to rank the top three or top five brand positions that are most important to them
when making a purchase decision.

Following this, participants are then asked to state, from the brands of which they
are aware, those that they associate with each of the positions. Below is an example
of a question used for this purpose:

TABLE 18.1

Q   Please indicate for each word or phrase which of the brands shown is associated with that characteristic. MULTIPLE SELECTIONS FOR EACH ROW ARE POSSIBLE.

RANDOMIZED ORDER OF ATTRIBUTES	ONLY SHOW BRANDS RESPONDENT IS AWARE OF					None of these [EXCLUSIVE]
	Brand W	**Brand X**	**Brand Y**	**Brand Z**	...	
Value for money						
Innovation						
Reliability						
Market leader						
Wide range						
High quality						
Expertise						
...						

There are several variations to this question. Sometimes, respondents are asked to name just one brand that is deemed to be most associated with each position, yielding a clearer distinction between brands. Alternatively, a numeric scale running from 1 to 10 may be used to measure the extent to which every brand being tested fits a particular image. It is important always to include the opt-out option, 'none', as there may be few or no brands in the market that are currently associated with a position. Learning about these uncontested brand attributes is itself an important insight and may point toward the 'blue ocean' positions for which brand strategists yearn.

By taking the importance of different brand attributes and aligning these against the degree of association with a specific brand, one can derive a matrix-style assessment of the brand's strengths, weaknesses and areas for improvement:

FIGURE 18.8   Determining drivers of brand performance

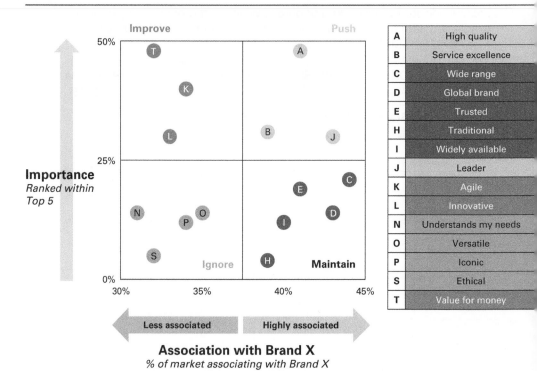

A	High quality
B	Service excellence
C	Wide range
D	Global brand
E	Trusted
H	Traditional
I	Widely available
J	Leader
K	Agile
L	Innovative
N	Understands my needs
O	Versatile
P	Iconic
S	Ethical
T	Value for money

In the above case, Brand X needs to improve the extent to which its brand is perceived as agile, innovative and as providing value for money. These are sought-after properties that this brand is less adept at delivering or communicating.

Of course, missing from this matrix is a third dimension – Brand X's competition. No brand exists in a vacuum and must slot within the existing positioning of its peers. The ultimate aim for a brand is to find values that it can call its own. To this end, a very useful analytical output from brand association data is the brand map. This uses correspondence analysis, a multivariate statistical technique, to evaluate the relative extent to which brands are linked with attributes. It does this by normalizing the effect of brand awareness. Left unchecked, the best-known brand in the market would end up being the most closely associated with different positions in absolute terms. Once this effect has been removed, the statistical analysis then plots the differences in association levels in two-dimensional space:

FIGURE 18.9   Assessing brand positions in a brand map

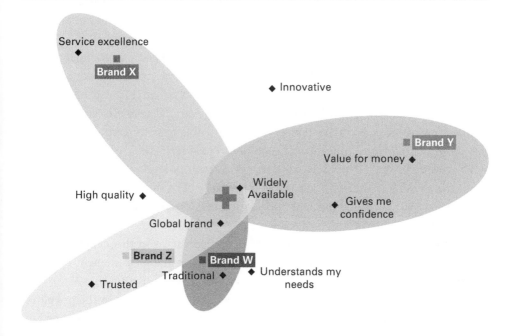

Brands and the brand positions are plotted with reference to a central point (shown as a plus sign above, also known as the 'origin'). Brands and brand positions that are further away from the origin can be deemed to be the most differentiated. In the above example, we can see that Brand X is highly associated with 'Service excellence' and that this is clearly distinct from other market players. The shaded ovals drawn around each brand denote the associations that are more proximate to it. These are determined by sketching an imaginary line between the brand plots and the origin: any positions that are close to these lines are assumed to be closely associated.

In the example provided, some brand positions are hotly contested, such as 'Global brand' and 'Widely available'. Others, such as 'Innovative' and 'High quality' have not yet been claimed by Brand X or its competitors. As a potential strategy, Brand X may therefore wish to claim the tag of being seen as 'Innovative' before Brand Y gets to it first.

Valuing brands/brand equity

If a brand succeeds in being well known and sought after and if it has cachet then its value will inevitably be reflected in the accounts of its parent company. Even in highly commoditized consumer markets, organizations like Apple and Richemont (the holding company behind luxury goods names such as Cartier and Jaeger) can expect to make net profits of 20 per cent or more on the back of their brands' strength. Rivals with less valuable brands will not be able to command anything like the same premium. Using market research and financial analysis to value brands is now widely practised. This has become all the more pertinent now that many listed corporations separate out the value of brands as part of their assets.

At its most basic, the valuation of a brand can be researched by assessing the financial performance of companies operating within the same market. Comparing the profitability of smartphone and tablet sales for Apple (at the top end of the price range) versus Samsung versus the low-cost Chinese manufacturer Xiaomi would tell us about the relative premium that each brand is able to command. By extension, this should also give an indication of each brand's value.

However, this type of analysis relies on good category-level reporting of financial results, something that cannot always be relied upon. For this reason, financial analysis is often paired with additional information from brand tracking research to fill in any gaps in the data.

In addition to the brand measurements described earlier in this chapter, market researchers have developed various tools to assist with the measurement of brand equity. One such technique is called *Brand-Price Trade Off* (or BPTO).

BPTO does what it says: it measures the interrelationship between the price that buyers are willing to pay for different brands when the different options are lined up against each other. BPTO is a simplified form of conjoint analysis that presents survey respondents with a series of hypothetical purchasing scenarios (as in the example below).

FIGURE 18.10   Layout of questions for a brand–price trade-off

The brands and prices shown are randomly rotated (within a pre-defined range) to test buyers' likelihood of purchase. Several iterations of the question, with different

sets of brands and prices, are displayed by a specialized survey program. The most valuable brand is the one that is selected even when it is presented at a higher price than its competitors. Another way of expressing this is to say that the brand (rather than the price) has a strong influence, or utility, in the purchase decision. The 'utility values' derived from this exercise are then proxies for brand valuation.

BPTO works efficiently in consumer packaged goods and commodity markets where products are ostensibly the same. In other circumstances, a full conjoint exercise that includes attributes other than brand and price may need to be considered.

Top tips

- Establish the life-cycle stage and circumstances of the brand that is to be researched. Is it a new brand that is under development? Is it a mature brand that might need refreshing? Is the brand operating in a highly competitive market where its performance requires continual monitoring? The research design required at each of these junctures will be quite different.

- Use qualitative research to answer fundamental questions such as: What are the most significant brands? Do private labels (own-branded products) play a role? What attributes are associated with each of the key brands? How do the main players in the market position themselves? What brand values are important to buyers within the market?

- Establish the objectives of the brand prior to the research: Is the objective to re-position the brand? If so, in what direction? Is the objective to create or consolidate brands? Is the subject of study a product brand or a corporate brand?

- When testing new visual identities for a brand, ensure your research design allows for a fair comparison. Consider testing logos and other collateral in isolation from other options first (ie a monadic design).

- When planning a brand tracking exercise, be clear on the methodology beforehand and try to stick to it throughout subsequent iterations of the study. It will be difficult to accurately track data over time if the questionnaire, the sample frame and quotas are constantly in flux.

- Ensure that your sample sizes are sufficient to detect significant changes in brand health measures.

- In brand tracking, use the brand funnel framework to get a bird's-eye view of the market and then use additional questions or 'deep-dive' studies to further understand specific issues such as brand positioning.

- In assessing a brand's position, try to measure both rational and emotional factors, as each play subtly different roles in shaping purchase decisions.

SUMMARY

Brands are powerful shortcuts that help buyers to make purchase decisions in a world that is burdened by choice. Strong brands allow companies to charge a premium for brand offerings in a way that is not explained by rational factors alone. As a consequence, brand value is increasingly recognized on the balance sheets of the globe's largest corporations. One of the biggest responsibilities of the marketing professional is to maintain and grow the worth and effectiveness of these most important of assets.

Market research is an essential tool for any business with a significant brand portfolio. Research assists at all points of the brand life cycle to ensure that the correct turns are followed during the journey.

When a brand is born or refreshed, researchers work together with brand strategists to ensure that the views of internal stakeholders are aligned with the needs and expectations of the market. This evidential base will cover issues such as visual identity, straplines, brand architecture as well as the brand's 'promise'. Well-executed market research can also identify new positioning possibilities – especially those that competitors have not yet identified.

If a brand experiences turbulence during its life, the fortunes of the parent company will undoubtedly follow suit. It is therefore incumbent on companies to systematically check on the health of their brands at regular intervals. Brand tracking has been a staple of the market research industry since the 1970s and it is still the principal tool for marketers in assessing the vital signs of awareness, familiarity, consideration, usage and advocacy.

Brand tracking studies are often complex undertakings. The researcher needs to be rigorous in their application of good study design as well as being able to react quickly and creatively to evolving circumstances in the brand's market.

Using market research to improve customer satisfaction and loyalty

Defining customer satisfaction and loyalty

Customer satisfaction is an indication of how pleased an individual or organization is with a brand, offering, or aspect of an offer. Usually satisfaction is expressed relative to the expectations of the brand or offering. For instance, a brand that fails to deliver against its promise will most likely receive a low satisfaction score.

Customer loyalty is different from satisfaction. Loyalty is an indication of intent to remain with a particular brand or supplier. This is not to be confused with inertia which is common in markets where there is a perceived difficulty of switching or where there is an expected inconvenience in changing brands or suppliers. Software and banking are examples of markets where inertia is common. In such markets, people are known to stick with a supplier, not necessarily because of high satisfaction or a desire to remain with the same supplier, but because of the anticipated effort in changing. Inertia can also be a stronger driver than loyalty in markets where suppliers are seen as undifferentiated and where there is, therefore, no perceived benefit to switching, such as in the energy market.

The importance of customer satisfaction and loyalty

Very few brands have a true monopoly in a market. This means that suppliers need to work hard to keep their customers satisfied, otherwise a customer could switch to another brand in hopes of greater satisfaction.

Consider these statistics published by Bain & Company:

- A 5 per cent reduction in the customer defection rate will almost certainly increase profits and in certain circumstances could double them.
- A customer can be four times more likely to defect to a competitor if the problem is service-related as opposed to price- or product-related.
- Acquiring a new customer can cost six to seven times more than the costs of retaining an existing customer.

It is thus clear that increasing customer satisfaction and loyalty is financially beneficial, with less customer churn and improved profitability. Furthermore, higher satisfaction and loyalty levels lead to stronger brand reputations and a happier workforce, and the opportunity to increase prices, driving profitability even higher.

Assessing customer satisfaction and loyalty through market research

Market research is a useful tool for measuring customer satisfaction and loyalty. In designing a customer satisfaction and loyalty programme, the following factors need to be taken into consideration:

- target audience
- methodology
- subject matter
- interpretation
- post-research actions

Target audience

For a number of products and services – especially in business-to-business markets – there is more than one individual to research as different people engage with a brand. Some may be involved at the time of specifying the purchase, other people as it is being purchased and yet others when the products or services are used. Commercial flooring, for example, could be sold by distributors, specified by architects, installed by flooring contractors, and used by building owners and tenants. The satisfaction and loyalty levels could be different across the various audiences, and different across functions within the same organization. In the case of commercial flooring, the facilities managers, janitors, and tenants could all rate their satisfaction with the flooring differently, yet all their views are arguably valid and useful.

Determining who to research is, therefore, important when scoping a customer satisfaction and loyalty programme.

The target audience for the research could also be based on their relationship with the brand that is being measured. It is not uncommon to include different types of 'customers' in a study, for example:

- existing customers

- lost customers (those who have switched to another brand)

- lapsed customers (those who have not purchased for a while but are not necessarily lost to a competitor)

- potential customers (where satisfaction and loyalty would be measured on competing brands)

Methodology

This is a book about market research and this chapter is focused on how structured surveys can deliver a customer satisfaction and loyalty programme. However, we shouldn't be precious about using market research alone to test satisfaction and loyalty. A number of other obvious measures could include:

- **Sales volumes.** However, note that these can rise and fall for reasons other than customer satisfaction. For example, a price reduction could generate an increase in sales; competitors introducing new products or lowering their prices could result in a drop in sales.

- **Customer complaints.** These provide important insights but they may reflect the views of only a vociferous minority.

- **Anecdotal feedback** via channel partners and the salesforce. As with customer complaints, this feedback is noteworthy but not representative. It could also be biased, for instance if the sales team deliberately skews or escalates customer feedback.

- **Reviews** (eg online or through warranty cards). Assessing the numbers of stars and reading the comments in Amazon reviews, for example, provide a good indication of satisfaction with a product. However, they are not representative of the total user base as they reflect the feedback of only that part of the population that provides reviews.

- **Social media and blogs.** Various software tools enable an assessment of content on social media sites and other websites. Feedback can be captured on the perceptions and sentiment towards a specific company (including its brand and products), thus indicating customer satisfaction and loyalty.

Although social media monitoring is an important process for understanding the views of a market (especially for mass market consumer brands), it is more useful for assessing brand or product perceptions rather than for measuring customer satisfaction and loyalty levels and the explanations behind these.

While useful, the above sources may not provide a rounded view on satisfaction and loyalty. A more representative sample of a customer base can be achieved through a structured customer satisfaction and loyalty programme. This usually comprises quantitative research where robust sample sizes provide statistically significant measurements and where cross-analysis by demographics can show groups of customers where special attention is required. Typical applications, along with the pros and the cons of the main research methods, are presented below.

Online surveys

Typical use:

- for obtaining quantitative measurements where sufficient e-mail addresses are available
- useful for capturing benchmark and tracking data from wave to wave

Pros:

- low-cost
- easy to administer
- convenient for respondents to complete at a time that suits them
- faster completion rate than other methods
- pictures and diagrams can be shown where necessary

Cons:

- low response rates
- respondent fatigue more likely (potentially resulting in speeding, flatlining etc)
- lower quality open-ended comment compared to administered interviews (eg telephone)
- certain audiences cannot be reached online in sufficient numbers

Telephone surveys

Typical use:

- for obtaining quantitative measurements with some qualitative insights and/or when sufficient e-mail addresses might not be available for an online method
- useful for capturing benchmark and tracking data from wave to wave

Pros:

- more depth of insight possible through interviewer probing
- clearer respondent answers compared to self-completion questionnaires, as a result of interviewer administration
- high control over sample

Cons:

- difficult to reach certain audiences by telephone (especially in over-researched markets like the US)
- longer interview than online
- interviewer bias is possible (eg different interviewer styles may affect answers)

Paper surveys

Typical use:

- for capturing quantitative measurements from hard-to-reach audiences when sufficient e-mail addresses and telephone contacts might not be available
- useful for reaching audiences less likely to participate in online surveys, eg an elderly population, specific ethnicity etc
- useful for capturing benchmark and tracking data from wave to wave

Pros:

- relatively low-cost
- easy for a DIY market researcher
- convenient for respondents to complete at a time that suits them
- pictures and diagrams can be shown where necessary

Cons:

- typically lower response rates than telephone

- additional logistics and costs such as printing of the questionnaires, postage if mailed out and returned, and data entry

- compared to online and telephone surveys, typically shorter in length to avoid respondent fatigue, meaning less data is captured

- respondent handwriting can be challenging to read

Where customer satisfaction and loyalty research comprises regular surveys for tracking purposes (eg for measuring improvements over time), the sample composition should be very similar from wave to wave, ensuring like to like comparisons; otherwise, differences in the sample could explain higher or lower performance scores, as opposed to genuine changes in performance.

Repeat surveys should not be conducted too frequently for this could discourage respondents from participating so soon after they last took part in the research. Furthermore, it takes time to make improvements and for these positive changes to be recognized by customers. Most companies wait at least 6–12 months between waves.

Some surveys are based not on a set timescale but on customer events. These 'pulse' surveys keep a regular check on the health of the brand. Surveys of this kind are triggered by a specific event such as a sales person calling, a delivery, a flight, a vacation, a visit to a hotel. The surveys are relatively short and are focused just on satisfaction with the recent event. If overused, respondents will ignore them and the response levels can be very low.

It could be that qualitative research is required before or after quantitative research. This could include depth telephone interviews or focus groups to explore the necessary attributes to incorporate into the quantitative questionnaire, or to obtain further depth of insight following the quantitative findings.

Subject matter

Satisfaction is measured overall with the brand or supplier, as well as on specific attributes to indicate where improvements might be required. Respondents are asked to give a rating out of 5, 7 or 10, where the higher the score, the higher the satisfaction. Ten-point scales offer more discrimination, allowing respondents to choose from a reasonable range of numbers. In fact, most customers tend to choose scores of 6 or more out of the 10-point scale (which makes sense because if products and services were so poor they attracted scores of below 6 out of 10, they wouldn't last long in the market).

Examples of common attributes tested in business-to-business surveys are listed in Table 19.1.

TABLE 19.1   Attributes common in business-to-business customer satisfaction surveys

Product offering	**Customer service and support**
Reliability	Availability of representatives
Ease of use	Responsiveness of representatives
Durability	Knowledge of representatives
Length of life	Professionalism of representatives
Product range	Problem resolution
Quality consistency	After-sales service
Warranty cover	Technical service
Design/appearance	
Ordering and delivery	**Business relationship**
Lead times	Brand reputation
On-time delivery	Easy to do business with
Speed of delivery	Goes the extra mile
Pricing and payments	
Value for money	
Competitive pricing	
Total cost in use	
Payment terms	

For any detailed attribute that achieved a low satisfaction score (eg 6 out of 10 or below), it is advisable to ask an open-ended question to capture feedback as to why the score is so low.

The most common question in customer loyalty surveys asks respondents how likely they are to recommend the brand or supplier to a friend or colleague out of 10. This indicates the extent to which customers can be expected to act as advocates on behalf of a brand or supplier. Advocacy and loyalty are strongly correlated.

Classification data is important in customer satisfaction and loyalty surveys for cross-analysis of the findings and identifying relationships between demographic, firmographic and behavioural factors and overall satisfaction and loyalty. Classification data are extremely powerful as they will show areas of strengths and weaknesses of a brand in satisfaction and loyalty. Examples of common classification data captured in consumer and B2B surveys are shown in Table 19.2.

TABLE 19.2   Common classification data to capture in customer satisfaction and loyalty research

Consumer data	Business data
Gender	Industry sector
Age	Total number of employees
Marital status	Number of employees at the site
Ethnicity	Annual revenue
Annual household income	Job function of the individual
Number of people in the household	Total spend on the relevant product/service
Employment status	Total consumption of the relevant product/service
Profession	Primary brand used
Geographic location	Length of relationship with each brand
Total spend on the relevant product/service	Geographic locations
Total consumption of the relevant product/service	Number of sites/locations
Primary brand used	Age of business

Interpretation

Customer satisfaction scores are consolidated for the analysis in the form of average (mean) scores. On a 10-point scale, scores of 9 and above are excellent, 8 to 9 is good, 7 to 8 is average and vulnerable, and scores below 7 are poor. Scores of 7 to 8 are considered average as it is relatively easy for a company to achieve a 7 but difficult to score higher. Above a score of 7, a difference of just 0.2 is considered noteworthy, and statistically significant when the base size is $n = 300$ or higher. An improvement of, for example, 7.8 to 8.0 from one wave to the next should be commended. Most customer satisfaction surveys produce a result which is somewhere in the corridor between 7 and 9 out of 10.

Further insights can be obtained through analysis of top box scores, ie the percentage of respondents rating the highest feasible score (top box analysis) or two highest feasible scores (top two box analysis). These top box percentages can be more insightful than average scores which can be skewed by a proportion of very low and/or very high scorers, especially if the base size is on the low side. Moreover, if a company is striving towards customer excellence, it seeks to delight its customers and top box analysis would clearly indicate the extent to which this is the case.

The detailed satisfaction scores should be interpreted within the context of what is important to customers. In other words, the factors considered the most important should be prioritized when assessing satisfaction performance. This can be achieved by plotting all of the detailed satisfaction scores on a matrix such as the chart shown in Figure 19.1, along with importance scores for each attribute, also measured on a 10-point scale. Any attribute rating an 8 and above is considered important, and a satisfaction rating of 7.5 is a typical minimum threshold when assessing satisfaction levels. Attributes falling into the top left quadrant are important but perform relatively poorly on satisfaction, and so this quadrant reflects critical areas to address. Attributes in the top right quadrant are those obtaining high importance and satisfaction scores and are areas where strong performance needs to be maintained.

FIGURE 19.1 Plotting detailed importance and satisfaction scores to identify action areas

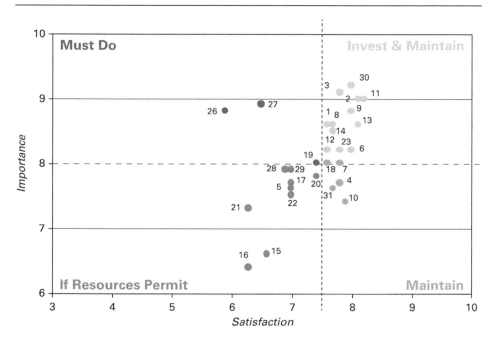

It can be tedious for respondents to rate the importance of numerous attributes in a survey, in addition to the detailed satisfaction scores. Rating questions asking stated importance may not be required, assuming importance levels would be ascertained

by deriving the importance through the statistical technique of correlation analysis. Rather than ask how important attributes are, it is possible to infer the importance of each attribute by correlating the detailed satisfaction score with overall satisfaction, indicating which attributes drive overall satisfaction. The output from this exercise is a list of correlation coefficients, ie scores indicating the relative strength of an attribute in impacting overall satisfaction.

Tips on when to use stated and derived importance

- Stated importance is the level of importance which people say they associate with a particular brand. Stated importance is useful for understanding what attracts customers to a brand. Typically people will say the most important attributes they look for when choosing a brand are price, availability, product quality and the like. These we call hygiene factors or tablestakes. They are essentials if a brand is to play in a particular market.

- Derived importance we obtain by correlating satisfaction ratings with individual attributes and with overall satisfaction. A strong link between attributes and overall satisfaction indicates that the attributes are important – at least they are important in driving satisfaction. These scores of importance are a good indication of what keeps customers loyal. They tend to be softer attributes like brand reputation, ease of doing business with a company, and friendly staff.

High scores on both satisfaction and loyalty are required if a brand is to be successful. A good satisfaction score is not enough as the customer could be drawn too easily to competitors. The 'likelihood to recommend' score is the most important metric in loyalty research. In addition to the average (mean) score, the output from this question leads to the Net Promoter Score – a loyalty measure developed by Fred Reichheld, of Bain & Company and Satmetrix. Respondents are asked to rate a brand or supplier on a 0–10 scale. 'Promoters' are those who provide a rating of 9 or 10 out of 10 as they are the brand advocates likely to recommend the brand or supplier. 'Detractors' are those who rate the brand or supplier a 6 or below as they are unlikely to recommend the brand or supplier and may even spread negative word of mouth on it. Those who rated a score of 7 or 8 are considered 'Passives' as they will most likely do nothing in terms of advocacy as they are neutral in their views. (Please note that there is no difference in results using scales from 1 to 10 or 0 to 10 – the bottom end of the scale being used by customers who are in effect saying 'I am not happy at all.')

The Net Promoter Score is simply the percentage of detractors subtracted from the percentage of promoters. The best possible score is 100 (everyone is a promoter) and the worst possible score is −100 (everyone is a detractor). An NPS of 0 is poor, 20 is quite typical and 30+ is good.

Companies in the USA that are among the best NPS scorers include Apple, Amazon and Southwest Airlines (all with an NPS of more than 60).

The Net Promoter Score is used widely across the world by hundreds of brands. It is acknowledged as a metric guiding growth as customer promoters buy more, stay with a brand for longer, refer friends and colleagues, and provide feedback such as product improvements. A company that seeks to outgrow its competitors on its proportion of promoters will most likely increase its market share.

Post-research actions

Customer satisfaction and loyalty research is useful only if it drives action. Some actions could comprise quick fixes like improvements to communications; other actions could entail longer-term changes like new product opportunities. The following checklist will help ensure that customer satisfaction and loyalty surveys do not gather dust:

- Determine the key drivers of satisfaction and prioritize these. Where does strong performance need to be maintained, and which critical actions are required where satisfaction is low on important attributes? Focusing on just a few important areas will likely have a significantly greater impact on satisfaction than trying to improve everything.

- Set targets on how much to improve on specific attributes. Do not set the bar too high and fail to reach the target in the next wave of the research. Benchmark where possible to set realistic goals by comparing performance to other business units, for example, or to competing brands.

- Develop an action plan and identify who or what department is responsible for each action. People need to take ownership of driving improvements.

- Set a timescale for each action; without a deadline, change might not occur.

- Understand the customer profiles of promoters and detractors. Segmentation lies at the heart of good marketing and it could be that detractors include a disgruntled audience that is not best suited to the brand or product. Target the type of promoter customer more, in order to increase satisfaction with, and loyalty to, the brand.

- Improving customer satisfaction and loyalty should be ingrained within the company culture. A positive change made by some employees could be denigrated by the actions of others within the same company. Everyone needs to embrace improving customer satisfaction and loyalty.

Top tips

- Meticulously kept customer lists with good contact details will yield a high response to customer satisfaction and loyalty surveys.

- Only carry out a customer satisfaction and loyalty survey if there is a genuine commitment within the company to improve products and services. You need buy-in at the top.

- Let customers know that by completing the survey they will not be put under sales pressure. Offer anonymity should it be required.

- Thank customers for taking part in the survey and, wherever possible, provide them with feedback.

- Keep the survey tightly focused on customer satisfaction and loyalty. Don't fall into the 'while you are at it' trap of adding lots of extra questions.

- Don't over-tax customers by carrying out too many customer satisfaction and loyalty surveys.

- Customers get frustrated if they don't see any improvements in your products and services so make sure that your surveys deliver actions.

- Leave sufficient time between surveys for your actions to be recognized in the marketplace.

SUMMARY

Customer satisfaction measures the extent to which customers are pleased with a brand, its offering, or aspects of its product or service.

Customer loyalty is an indication of customers' intent to stick with a particular brand or supplier.

A customer that does not change suppliers cannot be assumed to be a loyal customer. This could be a result of inertia as opposed to a delighted customer who wants to stick with the brand or supplier for the long term.

Most customer satisfaction and loyalty research is quantitative in nature as robust sample sizes provide statistically significant measurements and the ability to analyse the data by subgroup (thus indicating where and among whom actions need to be taken). Whether the research is conducted online, by telephone or on paper depends on various factors, such as the availability of sufficient customer contact records, the numbers of questions to be asked, and budgets available for the research (telephone costs more than online interviewing).

Customer satisfaction needs to be assessed within the context of what is important to customers as this will prioritize actions to be taken. There are two ways of measuring what is important to customers:

- Stated importance captures detailed importance scores which indicate what attracts customers. Attributes relating to price, availability and quality often score highly on stated importance.

- Derived importance correlates the satisfaction scores with individual attributes people look for in a brand with their overall satisfaction with that brand. This indicates which attributes drive satisfaction and therefore how to keep customers. Typically softer attributes like brand reputation, ease of doing business with a company and friendly staff are stronger drivers of satisfaction.

The Net Promoter Score is a tool for measuring loyalty and is based on the proportions of customers who act as brand promoters and brand detractors. The loyalty leaders in an industry are said to outgrow their competitors at a significantly faster rate as promoters buy more, stay with a brand for longer, refer the brand to others, and recommend improvements.

Using market research to achieve optimum pricing

The importance of price

The marketing mix breaks the components of an offer into product, price, place (routes to market) and promotion. Marketers must make informed decisions with respect to each of these, but it is arguably price that is at once the most difficult and the most important of the '4 Ps' to understand.

Price is the currency exchanged for the other three Ps, and a measure of the value a target audience places on the offer. Pricing is not only a crucial marketing decision; it is a fundamental business decision. There are only three ways for a company to increase its profits: sell more, cut costs or raise prices. A well-known study by McKinsey found that for the average company a 1 per cent increase in price would generate an 8 per cent increase in operating profit.

Logically, businesses should devise comprehensive strategies to get their pricing right. In reality, the decision as to how much to charge is frequently neglected by strategic decision makers, poorly implemented by commercial teams or delegated to very inexperienced people. It is estimated that just 1 to 2 per cent of large UK, US and German businesses have written pricing policies against more than 70 per cent who have written promotional plans. Sales people tend to be incentivized by revenue not price, and firms are far better at measuring the revenue – rather than the profits – that employees generate.

While pricing market research is becoming more common, it still represents less than 10 per cent of projects conducted, demonstrating further the view that companies neither emphasize nor understand price sufficiently.

What do we mean by price?

When researching price or setting prices it is essential to be clear on which definition of price we are referring to. Some of the various definitions are explained below.

List price versus transaction price

In many purchase situations (especially in business-to-business markets) the list price is in practice a starting point for negotiation and higher than the actual price that ends up being paid. Discounts are awarded based on factors such as bulk purchase, frequency of purchase and business relationship.

TABLE 20.1

list price	The advertised price for an offer, as communicated by a business's website or price lists
transaction price	The price actually paid for an offer after negotiations and discounts

Price at different stages of the supply chain

The price of a product increases as it moves through the supply chain – for example a manufacturer may sell its product to a distributor, who adds its margin before selling on to an end customer for a higher price.

TABLE 20.2

manufacturer's selling price (MSP)	The price charged by the manufacturer of a product to an end customer, distributor, wholesaler or other customer
wholesale price, distributor's price or trade price	The price charged by a wholesaler or distributor (who will typically add margin to the price they have paid to the manufacturer or other supplier)
retail price	The price charged by a retailer (who will typically add margin to the price they have paid to their supplier)

The impact of taxation

In most countries products and services attract a sales tax, which is added to the price of the product or service. Sales tax can often then be claimed back by the purchaser. Sales taxes reach 20 per cent or more in many countries; hence it is crucial to understand whether this has been added when collating price information.

TABLE 20.3

gross price	Price including sales tax
net price or basic price	Price excluding sales tax

Equating price with value

Price is one of the important means by which customers compare products and services with those of the competition. Take a group of suppliers that sit within a customer's consideration set; some may be supported by strong branding, premium services, guarantees and the like and as such carry a substantial premium. Others could offer low-cost products, stripped of any wrap-around services. Customers recognize the difference in these offers and the value for money they represent. An expensive product with lots of features may be considered to offer fair value for money just as much as one that is cheaper but with fewer frills. In an economist's perfect world, all these products would gravitate towards a point on the value equivalence line that cuts diagonally at 45 degrees from where the X and Y coordinates meet.

FIGURE 20.1   Perceived price, perceived benefits and the value equivalence line (VEL)

However, some suppliers are perceived to be expensive with few benefits, in which case they sit to the left-hand side of the line and can be predicted to lose market share, while others may be considered economically priced with a large number of benefits and so can be expected to win market share. These suppliers sit on the right-hand side of the line. Knowing where a company sits on the value equivalence line is an important requirement of developing a marketing strategy. A company positioned on the right-hand side of the value equivalence line has the option of leaving the price and benefits as they are and enjoying a growth in market share or raising prices and capturing more profit. Similarly, a company to the left-hand side of the value equivalence line knows that it must offer more benefits if it is to succeed or it must reduce its price if it wishes to compete.

Setting price according to business objectives

The starting point for setting prices is to understand the overall objective of the business. Do we want to maximize sales? Do we want to maximize profits? Or do we want to maximize market share? It is almost impossible to achieve all of these objectives at once. Most companies chase profits in the long term; shorter term they may prioritize maximizing sales or market share and be prepared to lower their prices in order to achieve one of these objectives. But lowering price to increase sales or share can result in a decrease in profits – either because distribution, advertising and other costs are incurred in reaching more customers, or simply because the decreased cost does not result in enough extra customers to compensate. It can also set the expectation of further reductions in the future.

A company that does not use its business objectives as the starting point for its pricing strategy will invariably get its pricing wrong and cause damage to its business. A summary of how different business objectives inform different pricing strategies is provided below.

TABLE 20.4

Business objective	Pricing strategy	Definition of pricing strategy
Maximize market share or revenue	Penetration pricing	Pricing low to attract as many customers as possible
Predictable revenue and profits	Cost-plus pricing	Adding a fixed amount to the cost of providing the offer
Predictable revenue and profits	Competitive pricing	Basing prices on what the competition is charging
Maximize profits	Value pricing	Pricing based on the customers' perceived value of the offer
Maximize profits and build exclusive brand	Premium pricing	Pricing high and possibly reducing supply in order to maximize margin per customer
Maximize profits and provide customer choice	Optional pricing	Charge for basic offer and then for additional extras
Maximize revenue	Bundle pricing	Offer discounts for buying more than one product or benefit
Maximize profits	Skimming pricing	Start by charging a high price to those that are willing to pay it. Gradually decrease price to sell to groups with smaller budgets

Using market research to achieve optimum pricing

There are three broad categories of pricing research:

1 research of current prices in a market;

2 research into the potential price that can be charged for an offer (either at market entry or when considering raising prices for an existing offer);

3 research into the value of different aspects of an offer.

Most pricing market research uses quantitative methodologies for the simple reason that the outcome – an empirically justified price level – is a quantitative measure.

Research of current prices in a market

When deciding on the optimum price for an offer it is advisable to research the price of any similar offers in the market. This allows us to benchmark our own potential prices against those of existing offers and decide whether we should align ourselves against them. Market researchers have three main ways of finding out existing market prices:

- Online research into the **price lists** of manufacturers and distributors

- **'Mystery shopping'.** Here the researcher plays the role of a potential customer and contacts the supplier. The supplier treats the researcher as he or she would any other sales prospect and shares prices and specifications

- **Customer interviews.** The market researcher contacts buyers of the product or service in question and asks how much they are spending

The advantage of exploring current prices charged is that the prices are factual, relatively easy to find, and have usually been proven to make companies money. The disadvantage is that current prices can set your expectations too low. Most companies price badly and the majority 'leave money on the table' by focusing on revenue growth rather than profit, or failing to recognize what different customers value. The risk of basing your prices on your competitors is that you repeat other suppliers' mistakes.

Researching the potential price it is possible to charge

Van Westendorp analysis

Van Westendorp analysis identifies the optimum price at which to launch a new offer by asking potential customers at what price would they consider the offer too expensive and at what price it would be too cheap. Responses to both questions are plotted and the optimal price point is the intersection of the two lines – the point at which the proportion of people saying too expensive equals the proportion of people saying too cheap.

In many cases two further questions are asked: at what price would the offer start to get expensive so that the respondent would need to seriously consider whether to buy it; and at what price would the product become a bargain. As illustrated above, these questions allow the researcher to plot the tipping points of too expensive and too cheap (the point of marginal cheapness and the point of marginal expensiveness).

FIGURE 20.2 Output from Van Westendorp questions

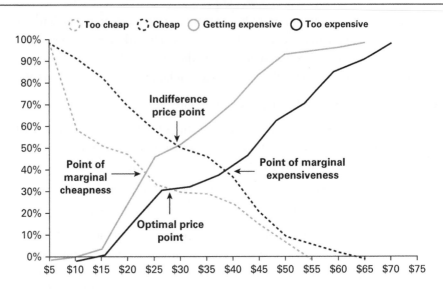

The Van Westendorp method is simple and provides accurate results. As few as 50 interviews can give a true response. The tool can be applied in telephone interviews but it is best used in online surveys where respondents can give due consideration to what they think of different prices. The result can be used as a basis for market entry or as the basis for changing the value proposition in order to charge more.

Gabor Granger analysis and price elasticity

Gabor Granger identifies the optimum price to charge for an existing offer by asking potential customers how likely they would be to buy the offer at different prices. We usually start asking the questions at a high price, lowering them bit by bit until the respondent says they would buy at a certain price. An obvious concern in asking questions in this way is that respondents could realize that the price is continuously being reduced and wait, hoping for it to hit rock bottom. In reality, most respondents play an honest game and the results are believable. Plotting prices from such questions enables us to generate a demand curve and see how much business could be won at different price levels. In many cases the likelihood to purchase scores are 'discounted' in order to best simulate real purchase behaviour. The diagram below shows an offer that 97 per cent of the market would be likely to buy if it was priced at $14, whereas only 3 per cent would buy it at $41. These figures allow us to calculate total revenue at each price point – the optimum price being the point at which most revenue is made and in this case is around $25.

The Gabor Granger question is simple and can be applied to relatively small samples (albeit ideally at least 50). The data can also be used to calculate the elasticity of demand – the implications on revenue of lowering or raising prices.

FIGURE 20.3   Output from Gabor Granger questions

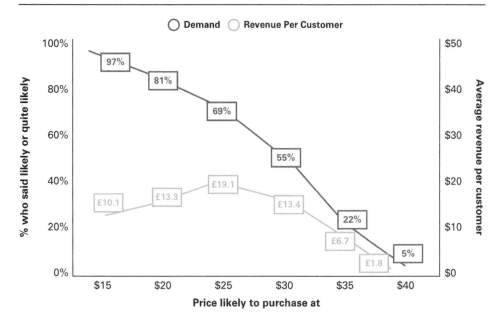

Researching the value of different aspects of the offer

Customers do not buy products or services; they buy the benefits that those products or services provide. A business that wants to extract the maximum value from its customers therefore needs to understand what benefits those customers value, and what value they place on each benefit. This allows the business to charge different customers (or groups of customers) different prices based on the benefits they receive. MaxDiff and conjoint analysis are trade-off techniques that are ideal for anyone who wants to decide on the precise composition of their offer, simulate the likely take-up of different offers or identify target segments.

MaxDiff

A MaxDiff study presents combinations of three to five attributes to a target audience and for each combination of factors asks which they like most and which they like least, as shown in Figure 20.4. When devising the list it is essential to group characteristics around themes so that – for example – functional benefits and emotional benefits do not appear on the same list. This avoids confusing respondents by asking them to make unrealistic trade-offs.

FIGURE 20.4

Please consider the list of 5 characteristics which might influence your choice of notebook computer for use in your business. Please indicate which is the most important factor and which is the least important.

Most Important	Feature	Least Important
O	Long Battery Life	O
O	Low Weight	O
O	Maximum Performance	O
O	Cutting-Edge Style	O
O	Security Features	O

The output of a MaxDiff question is a list of utility scores showing the relative value of all of the characteristics shown on the different lists. MaxDiff also enables the market researcher to segment the market around clusters of needs and create a simulator predicting what different sectors of the market want. MaxDiff does not, however, provide an answer as to the best *combination* of benefits, and a follow-up question (such as Gabor Granger) is needed if a price is to be placed on the combination of benefits identified.

MaxDiff interviews can be conducted online or – provided the lists have no more than five characteristics – over the telephone (more than this and respondents would forget what issues they were trading off). The technique does not need a large quantitative sample – 50 interviews can give clear results.

Conjoint analysis

Whereas MaxDiff requires respondents to compare individual potential components of an offer, *conjoint analysis* requires them to compare grouped packages of benefits with each other at a stated price. It is a technique for a business looking to finalize what its offer should consist of and assess its viability in the marketplace and go-to-market price.

In *choice-based conjoint* a respondent could be asked: Do you prefer 'a flight that has limited leg room, costs $250 and has one stop' or 'a flight that is generous leg room, costs $500 and is direct'? before being asked several more similar questions with different combinations of benefits. Once a statistically significant number of respondents (usually 200 or more) have been asked multiple preference questions, the relative importance of all attributes can be generated and the conjoint simulator built. The simulator allows the researcher to simulate the market demand and likely revenue of different offers at different price points. Conjoint analysis not only shows the relative importance of different attributes; it also identifies the best combination of attributes.

FIGURE 20.5

	Product 1		Product 2		Product 3	
Brand	Brand A	▽	Brand B	▽	Brand C	▽
Single Or 2-Sided	Single sided only	▽	Single + 2-sided	▽	Single sided only	▽
Printer Price	£499	▽	£599	▽	£599	▽
Cartridge Price	£35	▽	£35	▽	£35	▽
Extra Functions	Print only	▽	Print only	▽	All-in-one	▽
Share Of Preference	32%		48%		20%	

Adaptive conjoint analysis

Adaptive conjoint analysis aims for a more efficient and engaging interview by varying the choices presented to respondents, based on the preferences they express. Each interview focuses on the respondent's preferred feature and levels. See Chapter 11 for more on conjoint analysis.

SIMALTO

SIMALTO stands for Simultaneous Multi-Attribute Level Trade-Off. This technique is ideal for a business considering how to improve its offer. Respondents are presented with a grid of different attributes which improve from left to right. They are asked to indicate what level of product or service they currently receive, what level they would like to receive, and then they are given a number of points to spend across different improvements to show how those improvements are valued (the numbers in the bottom right of each square in the grid).

TABLE 20.5

Attribute	Level 1	Level 2	Level 3	Level 4
Capacity of company to handle the cases	They operate on the edge, almost always at full capacity 10	They work at about 80–90% capacity and can handle some extra work 30	They always have capacity in hand and can deal with a big inflow of business 40	They can quickly install capacity to meet almost any level of business 50
Ability to turn the job around on time	You never know when they will turn the case around and it seems to take forever 0	Between 60–70% of cases are close to the time we require them 5	80–90% of cases are close to the time we require them 15	All cases are delivered to the day, every time without fall 35
Low cost	Their prices are at the level where I wonder if I can afford to use them 5	They are expensive but I think they are worth it 10	They pitch their prices in line with the rest of the market 20	Their prices offer the best value for money in the market 30
Friendliness of staff	They are unhelpful and unfriendly whenever you want them to do something 5	They are a bit cold and they need pushing to provide service support 10	They are friendly and they can provide service support, but they do seem quite stretched 20	They are always cheerful, get back to you immediately and they understand your needs as a customer 25
Access to staff who do the actual work	It is difficult getting through to anyone and if they aren't there, they don't return your call 0	It is difficult to get through to anyone but they are quite good at returning your calls 10	You can get hold of people quite easily in working hours and they are good at returning calls 20	You can always get hold of someone who is dealing with your case at any time, day or night 40

The output from SIMALTO enables us to see what levels of service people receive at present and what level they would like (desired level). The points that people spend to get from one level to another is an indication of the value that they place on these improvements and can be converted to dollar values. SIMALTO can be a useful alternative to conjoint in business to business surveys because it can accommodate a greater range of attributes (SIMALTO can handle up to 20 attributes whereas the maximum for conjoint is around 7 attributes) and smaller sample sizes (in theory, just one respondent could be interviewed and provide a meaningful result in a SIMALTO survey). See Chapter 11 for more on SIMALTO.

BPTO (Brand–Price Trade-Off) analysis

BPTO is useful in any situation where there is a strong interest in the interrelationship between brand and the price of an offer. It is suited to categories where offers are similar and brand is the determining factor behind decision making. Survey respondents are shown a series of branded products or services at once, each with a price associated with it – between three and five 'offers' are typically shown at once. Respondents are asked which of the offers presented is most appealing in a hypothetical buying scenario.

The brand and price preference data is then analysed statistically to derive predicted market shares of each brand at different price points and the relative influence of price and brand in decision making. Read more on brand–price trade-off in Chapter 18.

The challenges of researching price

The challenges of researching price must be acknowledged. First, there is the question whether the price a respondent states he or she is willing to pay reflects the reality. Many market researchers who believe that willingness to pay is overstated by respondents apply a discount percentage to the stated responses to reflect reality more closely.

A limitation of all pricing market research is that it assumes pricing behaviour is rational. A challenge to this assumption is the phenomenon of 'framing'. This refers to the setting of pricing expectations. The company that launches a cheap product or enters a market at a low price will find it extremely difficult to raise prices afterwards. The business that prices high to start with can always bring its prices down, but will often end up with a higher final price point than the company that starts cheap.

Similar to framing is the 'anchoring' that can occur in conducting research. The price range shown and the first values shown can influence perceptions of what is appropriate, or cheap or expensive, particularly in markets where prices are largely unknown such as infrequently purchased or specialist goods.

It can be argued that looking for the 'optimum' price is a simplistic concept. It ignores the role of optional add-ons, for example. In the car industry a single model of car typically comes in literally hundreds of variations in colour, wheel options, upholstery options, technology options and so on. This makes the question 'What does a BMW 3 Series cost?' nonsensical, as there are hundreds of 3 Series and therefore hundreds of prices.

And while 'price' conveys the transfer of currency from the buyer to the seller, it does not take account of the transfer of financial benefits in the other direction. Imagine two alternative industrial pumps that pump gallons of water into a manufacturing plant. Pump 1 costs $50,000 and Pump 2 is significantly more expensive at $150,000. But Pump 2 lasts twice as long, requires half the down time and pumps water 50 per cent more quickly. These three points each have a measurable financial benefit that may well outweigh the price. While Pump 2 may have a higher price, it could have a lower cost in use.

Over recent years we have seen the polarization of customers in many markets towards 'very price-sensitive' and 'premium', with fewer customers occupying the middle ground. This makes segmented pricing very important as suppliers seek to provide Gold, Silver and Bronze offers to different parts of the customer base.

And as pricing information becomes more available we see customers in most markets become ever more demanding, many insisting on receiving more in exchange for paying less. This brings us to the fundamental rule of optimum pricing: don't be afraid to walk away. Pricing at a level that reduces profit can in no way be described as 'optimum'.

Top tips

1 Most people make the mistake of pricing their products too low. Salesmen return from customer visits with stories of buyers telling them that their prices are too high (because that's what buyers are paid to say!). It is worthwhile challenging your pricing strategy and asking yourself 'Am I leaving money on the table?'

2 Wherever possible get a scientific fix on your prices (as near as is possible) using tools such as Gabor Granger or Van Westendorp. Conjoint and SIMALTO can also help you understand the value of your products and services.

3 All customers can be grouped into segments which will have different attitudes to price and value. Make sure that your pricing strategy is designed to meet the needs of these different segments.

4 Remember there is more than one way to optimize the value of an offer other than the price ticket alone. Consider changing the pack size, the warranty, discount levels, terms of payment. They all strongly affect price perceptions.

5 Keep a record of price changes and sales so that over time you build a database that informs you of the price elasticity of your products or services.

Conclusions

Charging the optimum price has a huge impact on business profitability. A 1 per cent rise in the price of an offer could raise business profits by as much as 8 per cent.

The price of an offer changes depending on negotiations, the point in the supply chain and whether it is taxed or not.

Target audiences are willing to pay the price that in their view reflects the value of the benefits being provided. If a company wants to charge more it needs to raise customers' perceptions of the value offered.

In the long term businesses tend to focus on maximizing profit and are willing to accept fewer customers in exchange for a higher price. Short term their objectives might be to maximize market share or revenue, and they may reduce prices (and profits) in order to achieve this.

Current prices in a market can be examined through online research of price lists, mystery shopping or customer interviews

The Gabor Granger methodology involves asking a target audience to what extent they would buy an offer at different price points before constructing a demand curve. The optimum price is the point at which revenue achieved is highest.

According to the Van Westendorp methodology, the optimal price point is where the proportion of people saying an offer is too expensive equals the proportion saying it is too cheap.

Several trade-off techniques analyse value and pricing. Conjoint analysis is the most effective at finding the optimum price point and allows a simulator to be developed of the demand for different offers at different prices.

Using market research to enter a new market

Market research is used by businesses to inform decision making. It provides objective evidence that can challenge instinct, impulse, supposition, emotion and perceived wisdom and ensure that decisions are based on rational, clearly justified criteria. The more strategically important or expensive the decision, the greater the risk to the business, and the more important market research becomes in managing that risk.

Entering a new market is one of the biggest risks and biggest investments a company can take. The financial rewards of successfully entering a new market can run into the billions of dollars; conversely billions of dollars can be wasted if the market entry is unsuccessful. The ROI (return on investment) of market entry research can therefore be immense.

Why enter a new market?

The decision to enter a new market can be understood through the prism of the Ansoff matrix. In his article 'Strategies for diversification' Igor Ansoff stated that there are four strategies a company can undertake if it wishes to grow its revenue and profits.

Ansoff's matrix (Figure 2.1) looks at growth strategy by plotting existing or new products and services against existing or new markets. By 'markets' we mean distinct target audiences – for example different industry sectors or countries.

The safest approach to growth is usually **market penetration** – to try to sell more and more existing products to your company's existing target market. A **product development** growth strategy involves providing new products to your existing markets, and is most successful when the needs of customers are changing. The **diversification** strategy is the most risky strategy for growth. Targeting an audience with

FIGURE 21.1   Understanding growth through the Ansoff Matrix

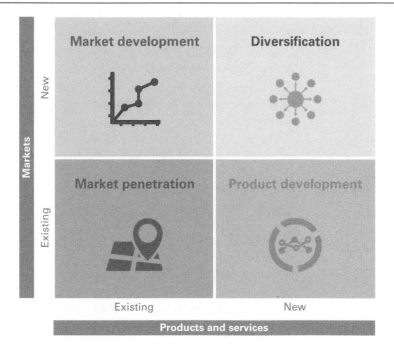

which you are not familiar with an offering you have not previously sold is difficult to get right.

Ansoff referred to entering a new market with an existing offer as **market development**. This typically comes about when a business senses that its growth aspirations cannot be achieved in its current market alone. If other markets exist with similar needs, there may be an opportunity to sell a similar offer to a new group of customers. This strategy is the main focus of this chapter.

So the overriding reasons companies enter a new market is that **they want to grow revenue and profitability**. Market entry works best when the product or service is performing well and new markets with similar needs can be identified.

Challenges when entering a new market

Many market entry challenges depend on the mode of market entry chosen. There are also numerous challenges that are universal. These are summarized by the CAGE distance framework, developed by Pankaj Ghemawat of the University of Navarra – IESE Business School in Barcelona. The framework identifies four differences between countries which represent challenges when doing business and which should be explored fully in a market entry research study.

TABLE 21.1   CAGE distance framework

Type of challenge	Description and example
Cultural	Societal norms, history, language and religious beliefs all affect people's behaviour and habits. For example, in China there is a greater tendency to do business outside the working environment (over dinner, playing golf) than in the West. A Western business person could easily cause offence or lose a deal by turning down a request to socialize, when their intention is to avoid imposing on someone's personal time.
Administrative and political	Historical or political associations between the home country and the target country have a strong bearing on how easy it is to enter a new market. When the two countries have (for example) the same currency, similar laws, similar understandings of law and historical links, the chances of succeeding in the target market are far greater. For example, companies from the US and from the British Commonwealth have a strong record at investing in each other's countries.
Geographical	When the target country is geographically close to the home country, has strong transport links and infrastructure and a moderate climate, it is easier and cheaper to do business there. For this and other reasons Canadian companies are more likely to do business in the US than anywhere else.
Economic	Economic distance includes disparities in wealth between the home country and target country, and the availability of financial and human resources. Western companies often struggle to sell their products for the same price or in the same quantities in developing countries as the people of those countries cannot afford them.

Ways of entering a new market

Market entry can take many forms. Generally the term is used to describe a situation in which the provider establishes a physical presence such as an office or factory in a new country, and bases employees in that country. Entering a new sector within one's home country can also be regarded as market entry. Focusing on market entry in the generally understood sense of entering a new country, we define and summarize below the pros and cons of different market entry methods.

Exporting

Definition

- Selling and delivering products from one country to another

Advantages

- No investment in new offices or factories needed
- Good quality control as products continue to be manufactured in home location
- A good way of evaluating demand and market challenges before investing more heavily

Disadvantages and challenges

- Difficult to be responsive, making problem solving and technical back-up difficult
- Difficult to control the people selling the products (for example distributors and retailers) as they are not direct employees
- Distance from the customer makes it more difficult to understand what the customer wants
- Lead times to deliver products can be long
- Difficult to convince potential customers that you know the market, that you are close to them, or that you care about them
- Only works for products. Most services cannot be exported

Setting up a sales office

Definition

- Establishing a legal entity, employing a salesperson and conducting sales activities (including invoicing) in the target country

Advantages

- Develop a strong understanding of market needs by having an employee meeting customers
- Much smaller investment than establishing a more comprehensive presence such as manufacturing
- Having a legally registered company is seen as more credible by many customers than exporting

- Makes the company more likely to focus on the market
- A good way of trying out a market before investing heavily
- Relatively easy to withdraw from the market if market entry is unsuccessful

Disadvantages and challenges

- Sales offices usually have no technical support, meaning that responsiveness and problem solving is difficult
- In many markets, sales offices are less credible than fully fledged operations
- Establishing a legal entity brings tax and administrative costs both in the target country and in the home country
- Higher overheads than simply exporting
- Often there are limitations on how many people a sales office can employ
- There are no guarantees a profit will ever be made
- Supervision from the home country is usually needed for several years before the rep office can run on its own

Setting up a wholly foreign owned enterprise (WFOE)

Definition

- Setting up a company that is completely owned by the home headquarters, usually with operations and support rather than simply a sales team

Advantages

- Develop a strong understanding of market needs by having employees meet customers
- Very credible to local customers
- Usually no limits on how many people the company can employ
- Makes the company likely to focus properly on the market

Disadvantages and challenges

- Expensive
- Time taken to make a profit is usually three years or more, and sometimes a profit is never made
- Wide range of staff needed across sales, operations, marketing and technical support – recruiting in an unfamiliar market is difficult

- Supervision from the home country is usually needed for several years before the WFOE can run on its own

Establishing a joint venture

Definition

- Buying shares in a company already in the target market or setting up a new company in shared ownership with another organization

Advantages

- Company likely to have a good understanding of the market
- Credible to local customers
- Usually no limits on how many people the company can employ
- Makes the company likely to focus properly on the market

Disadvantages and challenges

- Expensive
- Difficult to exert control on a company that isn't fully owned (especially if the stake is less than 50 per cent)
- Time taken to make a profit may be five years or more and often a profit is never made
- Finding a company with the right resources and 'fit' is extremely difficult

The role of market research in market entry decision making

Why conduct market entry research?

We began this chapter by stating that market entry research can have a large return on investment, either by validating a lucrative opportunity or by finding out that there is no opportunity, meaning that money is not wasted. The overriding reasons for conducting market entry research are:

- to help decide whether to enter a particular market
- to determine how to enter the market
- to determine what is realistic to achieve and set targets accordingly
- to form the basis of a business plan

Developing a shortlist of target markets

Before conducting or commissioning research, companies should reflect on which markets they can realistically serve and which markets they want to serve. For example, if a US company has no record of selling in China, has never received any interest in its offer from China, knows nothing about China and employs no one from China, it may decide that success is simply unrealistic.

Likewise, if Luxembourg has only half a million inhabitants and Germany has over 80 million inhabitants, a business may decide that whatever the complexities, Germany will always be a more attractive proposition. It is far more economical and useful to research a small number of countries in detail than spread research resources across tens of countries. The sensible company develops a shortlist of interesting countries before starting market research.

Information required from a market entry study

Companies should know and understand as many of the following as possible before entering a new market:

1 The size and nature of the opportunity

2 Market threats, growth and trends

3 Competitive landscape

4 The structure of the supply chain

1 The size and nature of the opportunity

Different measures of market size

The size of the opportunity is often referred to as 'market size', for which there are many definitions. **Total market size** can be defined as *the total volume or value of a particular offering sold in the market, in a given year and at a given point in the supply chain.*

Total market size (sometimes called the Total Available Market or TAM) can therefore be expressed in either units sold or financial value of units sold (in a chosen currency). Once a company understands the total sales per year of offerings similar to its own, it can start to understand the potential to sell its own offer. So, a company with revenues of over $10 billion in its home country may quickly lose interest in a target market if that market's TAM is only $500,000.

However, a large total market size does not necessarily mean a large opportunity. Large swathes of the market may be unwilling or unable to ever buy a company's offering, and the company may be unwilling or unable to serve them. Here, two further definitions of market size come into play.

The **serviceable available market (SAM)** refers to the part of the market that can be served with the company's existing sales channel. So, a company that sells coffee in cups through coffee shops would regard its SAM as the total revenue of all cups of coffee sold in the same way. Ground coffee sold in packets in supermarkets would be part of the total market for coffee, but would not be part of the SAM because the sales channel is different. The SAM is useful for a company that has an established sales channel and wants to stick to that sales channel. The SAM is part of the total market size.

Arguably the most useful measure of market size is the **segment market size** or **target market size**. This refers to the part of the SAM that:

- the company wants to serve
- is likely to be interested in the company's offering
- is likely to be willing and able to pay for the company's offering

The segment market size can be far smaller than the TAM or SAM. This is particularly likely to be the case when a Western company is looking to sell into a developing country such as China. Frequently the total market for an offering is worth billions of dollars, however 95 per cent of the market is unwilling or unable to pay Western prices, meaning the segment market size – the only part of the market in which the company can make any money – is just 5 per cent of the total. Hence, a market that at first glance looks lucrative, eventually looks unappealing to the Western business.

Researching and calculating total market size

Total market size can be calculated in four ways:

- **Demand side.** Identify the number of potential customers and multiply by the estimated average (or median) spend of these customers. The number of potential customers can often be found through business databases; estimating average spend usually requires interviewing a representative sample of the market.

- **Supply side.** Identify the companies supplying the customers (through online search or by speaking to a cross-section of customers) and estimate their revenue in the market of interest, before adding up these estimated revenue figures.

- **Top-down.** Find the market size for a market of which your market is a part (usually through researching publicly available reports), and estimate what proportion of that 'parent market' your market represents (usually by garnering the views of industry experts). For example, the value of the market for cars may enable us to estimate the total market for car engines.

- **By proxy.** Find the market size for a 'parallel' market and make an estimate based on factors that drive the market size in both countries. For example, the market size for new cars in France could allow us to estimate the market size for new cars in the UK, if we could find an appropriate proxy. Examples of proxies could be population (we assume the same expenditure on cars per head in both countries) or size of economy (we assume car sales represent the same percentage of the overall economy in both countries).

All methodologies are sensitive to error, meaning that market researchers tend to calculate market size through at least two of the above methodologies before coming to a conclusion on total market size.

2 Identifying market threats, growth and trends

Threats in the market include issues such as substitute products that are increasing in popularity, competitors that may enter the market or economic turmoil. Threats can be macroeconomic or microeconomic, and can derive from anywhere in the market. Identifying threats requires thorough market research: of publicly available information; (potential) customer surveys; supplier surveys, distributor surveys; interviews with industry experts. Growth and industry trends can occur for many reasons, from changing tastes to underlying economic growth. Again, interviews throughout the market are necessary to identify all of the issues.

3 The competitive landscape

Before entering a market, it is crucial to understand the competition. What are their strengths and weaknesses? How will they respond to your business entering the market? How many competitors are there? How big are they? Market entry studies should deliver three key categories of insight relating to the competition:

Porter's 5 Forces (Figure 21.2) is a useful tool for qualitatively assessing five inter-linked aspects of the competitive landscape. The central force, Competitive Rivalry, is an assessment of the current marketplace – how many competitors are there, what differentiates them and how loyal is the customer base? The four forces impinging on competitive rivalry all have the potential to change the competitive landscape. New entrants could drive down prices or provide a differentiated offer that encourages customers to defect. Substitute products could render existing offers obsolete. The balance of power between suppliers and buyers could raise the prices in the market (if supplier power relatively increases) or reduce the number of offers available (if supplier power relatively decreases). Research throughout the supply chain and with industry experts, followed by qualitative analysis, allows the complex topic of competitive environment to be fully understood before a market entry decision is taken.

FIGURE 21.2   Porter's 5 Forces

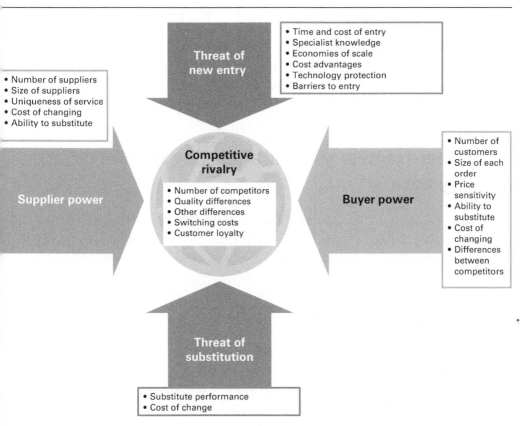

A new entrant to any market should understand in detail how key competitors are set up. How many people do they employ? What locations are they in? Who owns them? What is their financial situation? These and other business fundamentals should be built into detailed company profiles. Company websites are excellent ways of obtaining this information, as are competitor interviews and interviews with industry experts.

Any company entering a new market needs to be differentiated – to offer something of value better than the competition. A survey of competitors' customers is an excellent way of achieving this. The survey should understand target customers' needs, and competitors' performance against these needs. Cross-analysis allows unmet needs and opportunities for differentiation to be identified.

4 The structure of the supply chain

Elsewhere in this book we set out the four Ps of product, price, place and promotion. While product, price and promotion can often be applied to a new market with a few small adjustments, place is often a difficult challenge to overcome. An alcoholic drink that can be freely sold in supermarkets in the UK may have to be sold to government-approved liquor stores in the US. Pharmacies that sell drugs in the UK may have no equivalent in China where drugs are sold through doctors' surgeries. It is important to understand supply-chain differences, and above all, whether those differences make market entry difficult or impossible. Here market research interviews should be carried out throughout the distribution network, particularly with the companies that represent potential routes to market.

Further frameworks for analysing market entry data

Earlier in this chapter we mentioned the CAGE framework and Porter's 5 Forces as useful tools when assessing market entry opportunities. Other frameworks used for turning the findings of a market entry study into a clear decision for market entry are described below.

PEST and PESTLE analysis

PEST analysis is a situation analysis framework through which market challenges and trends are identified. It can be seen as a checklist of challenges and trends that may be present in the market, and which should be researched through desk research and interviews throughout the supply-chain and with experts. The framework identifies four groups of issues: political, economic, socio-cultural and technological. An extended version of the framework is PESTLE analysis, which adds legislative and environmental factors to the list of considerations.

SWOT analysis

SWOT analysis is an action-oriented framework that considers the market entry decision in the context of factors that relate to the business (internal factors) and issues that relate to the market (external factors). The internal factors are strengths and weaknesses. These can be understood based on surveys of potential customers as well as a business's own view of where it performs well and badly. The external factors are termed opportunities and threats and are identified by interviews

TABLE 21.2   PESTLE analysis

P	**Political**	Refers to the political philosophy and policies within a market, as well as the level of political stability
E	**Economic**	Economic policy, economic stability and economic growth
S	**Socio-cultural**	Social norms in the target market, particularly social attitudes to the product category in question
T	**Technological**	Attitude to technology and propensity to adopt technology in the target market
L	**Legislative**	Legislation in the target market, enforcement of legislation, and likelihood of legislation changing.
E	**Environmental**	Issues such as climate, weather and geographical location that relate to the target market

throughout the supply chain and with experts, as well as businesses' own experiences of opportunities and threats. SWOT analysis helps the market researcher define strategies for successful market entry as illustrated below.

TABLE 21.3   SWOT analysis

		S Strengths	**W** Weaknesses
O	**Opportunities**	Strategies that use strengths to maximize opportunities **Example:** *Heavily promoting your fast delivery times in a market where delivery standards are low*	Strategies that minimize weaknesses by taking advantage of opportunities **Example:** *Extending the product range when the market is asking for something more*
T	**Threats**	Strategies that use strengths to minimize threats **Example:** *Aggressively promoting a strong brand in a commoditized market*	Strategies that minimize weaknesses and avoid threats **Example:** *Keeping away from a segment that is too price-focused for you to serve it economically*

1   Unless you can realistically serve a new market and want to serve that market, there is no point researching it.

2   Before conducting or commissioning market research into potential target countries, build a shortlist of markets based on those which appear attractive (in size, trends, competition and the channel to market) and where your company could have a competitive advantage.

3   Focus on the serviceable available market and don't get distracted or too excited by the total available market.

4   Don't worry about arriving at a market size estimate that is too precise as this will be costly and spurious. Simply determine that the market size is over a size that will accommodate your company's aims.

5   Don't attempt to take on the world when working out a market entry strategy. Focus your market research where your chances of success are high. Use the learnings from a successful market entry for future plans.

6   Use established frameworks such as Porter's 5 Forces, SWOT and PEST to assess the opportunities within new markets.

SUMMARY

Companies enter new markets because they want to increase revenue and profit beyond what can be achieved in their home market. Market research is used to establish the opportunities within a new market and, assuming it is positive, to provide insights that will lead to a successful penetration.

A company entering a new market is likely to face a number of challenges because of different culture, politics, geography and economics.

Entering a new market can be achieved by exporting; setting up a sales office/representative office; creating a wholly foreign owned subsidiary (WFOE); or establishing a joint venture. Exporting is usually considered to be the lowest risk while WFOE is typically seen as risky but potentially the most rewarding.

Market research plays a vital role in identifying new market opportunities. It is used to assess the size and nature of the opportunity, particularly showing the serviceable available market (SAM) against the total available market (TAM). It is the serviceable available market that most companies use to identify the opportunity.

Market research will also show the threats and opportunities within a market. Threats arise from the competition, adverse economic situations, and cultural differences that cannot be reconciled. Opportunities exist if there are gaps in the market that are not served by the competition and if the economic portents are favourable. A SWOT and PEST analysis are useful frameworks for carrying out this assessment.

Finally, a business should thoroughly research the supply chain before developing a market entry plan.

Using market research to test advertising effectiveness

The different types of advertising

The promotional mix is one of the four Ps. It comprises advertising, PR, sales promotion, direct marketing and personal selling.

Advertising is the paid promotion of a brand, product or service and an important investment in building brand equity. There are many different types of advertising platforms, with the main channels as follows:

- **Television and radio advertising:** commercials that range from a few seconds to minutes in length.

- **Infomercials:** long television commercials with detailed information on the advertised product such as demonstrations, user testimonials and third party endorsements, with the end goal of encouraging viewers to make an impulse purchase by telephone or online.

- **Print advertising:** an ad in a portable printed medium such as a newspaper, magazine or flyer.

- **In-store advertising:** Advertisements in a bricks-and-mortar store, such as at-shelf signage and displays, floor graphics and TV monitors.

- **Online advertising:** search engine optimization (eg pay per click), display (eg banner and skyscraper ads), e-mail marketing, social media (eg through Facebook and LinkedIn), mobile and video.

- **Billboard advertising:** large display advertisements in high-traffic and highly populated areas such as by busy roads and in shopping malls.

FIGURE 22.1   Comparing promotions on consumer versus industrial goods

There are various other advertising platforms such as product placements (for instance when a brand is featured on a TV show but not as an explicit advertisement), cinema, street and aerial advertising (eg blimps) among others.

As shown in Figure 22.1, advertising is much more common among consumer as opposed to industrial markets. Consumer brands have substantially higher advertising budgets and a much larger target audience that can be reached through mass market communications.

Why test advertising effectiveness?

The largest companies typically spend 2 per cent of revenue on advertising. Automotive, pharmaceutical and retail are among the highest spending industries on advertising, driven by the frequent launch of new products and the need to differentiate against competitors. P&G spends the most on advertising with an expenditure of £2.6 billion in 2015 alone. With such a high advertising expenditure, advertising sponsors need to ensure that their budgets are spent effectively. As the politician and merchant John Wanamaker said: 'I know that half of my advertising is wasted, but I don't know which half.' Market research helps companies understand how well advertising works, so that promotional spend can be maximized and costly mistakes avoided.

Before designing and running an advertising campaign, it is important to consider the goal of the campaign given that advertising can serve different purposes. An ad might fail in its effectiveness, not because it was a weak ad, but because the wrong communications channel or messaging was used for the advertising objective.

Looking at a broader brand perspective, a brand can be measured on efficiency by assessing the proportion of those aware that go on to be advocates of the brand. This is the percentage shown at the far right of the brand funnel in Figure 22.2. The funnel starts with awareness which is the critical foundation for brand equity. Following awareness, it is necessary to generate interest in the brand in order that it enters the consideration set. Penetration represents the percentage using the brand, and advocacy is the proportion of an audience that would recommend the brand and therefore act as an advocate on its behalf.

FIGURE 22.2   The brand funnel

	Awareness	Consideration	Usage	Advocacy	Brand efficiency
Brand 1	90%	72%	61%	45%	50%
Brand 2	45%	24%	18%	12%	26%
Brand 3	88%	55%	38%	22%	25%

Table 22.1 provides examples of how advertising can be used across each stage of the brand funnel, and the different purpose of advertising at each stage, from longer-term brand-building efforts to short-term tactics aimed at triggering a quick purchase.

TABLE 22.1   Advertising across each stage of the brand funnel

	Key goal of advertising	Examples of ad campaigns
Awareness	Raise awareness of the brand	A banner ad to get the brand noticed among a specific audience; a print ad communicating a brand's commitment to sustainability; a billboard advertising a nearby store
Consideration	Communicate the brand difference so that it enters the consideration set	A TV commercial on a drug; a street ad about a new car; an informative e-mail campaign about IT security software

TABLE 22.1 *Continued*

	Key goal of advertising	Examples of ad campaigns
Usage	Push the compelling features and value drivers so that it is the chosen brand to purchase	A point of purchase campaign promoting a buy-one-get-one free offer; an infomercial demonstrating a product in use
Advocacy	Build the brand to reinforce its position and strengths	An e-mail campaign to encourage a repeat purchase; a TV commercial featuring the latest smartphone

Advertising that drives higher performance levels across the brand funnel can be considered effective. For many brands – especially those with a relatively small share of voice – increasing awareness levels has a positive impact through the rest of the brand funnel, and in particular on brand efficiency.

Top tips

- Don't expect too much from one ad. It might require a suite of ads to build momentum and drive recognition and recall.

- Ensure consistency in brand image and brand voice throughout all ads. This will ensure that the brand remains distinct and recognizable.

- Don't assume that an ad has failed if results in the brand funnel barely change or drop in performance. Other factors can affect a brand's efficiency and are out of the brand's control, such as distributors pushing alternative brands, and competitors ramping up their promotional efforts and stealing share of voice.

How to test advertising effectiveness

Whatever the research method employed, there are four important measures of advertising effectiveness that should be assessed in market research:

- **resonance** (it is compelling, ie it resonates with the individual)
- **relevance** (it is relevant to the individual/business)

- **brand fit** (it fits with the advertising brand's identity)
- **clarity** (it is clear in terms of the message and the design)

The use of qualitative research for ad testing

Qualitative research is sometimes used to explore the market's views on an ad concept and to assess whether the message, content and design are optimal for the advertising objectives. This is typically carried out through focus groups or online communities where the group dynamic can stimulate debate and therefore generate more interesting insights. This gives the advertiser an opportunity to refine the ad, as well as optimize the campaign such as the best media through which to run it. Examples of the types of questions asked in qualitative research are:

- What is the main message this ad is communicating to you?
- What does the ad want you to know or do?
- What first caught your attention in the ad?
- How clear is the ad?
- How relevant is this ad to you/your company?
- What appeals to you the most in this ad?
- Does this ad change your views on the brand or product?
- How well does the ad fit with the brand as you know it?
- What do you believe you are encouraged to think or do as a result of the ad?
- How likely are you to take action as a result of the ad?
- Is there anything missing in the ad that could prevent you from taking action?
- Where would you be most likely to notice this ad?

The use of quantitative research for ad testing

There is usually a desire to quantify the effectiveness of an advertising campaign in order to measure the return on investment on the promotional spend. Quantitative market research typically takes the form of pre- and post-advertising studies with similar questions in each wave for benchmarking. These cover the various stages of the brand funnel, in particular awareness (unprompted and prompted), consideration of each known brand for future purchases and the proportion using each brand.

In addition, it is important to measure unprompted and prompted word associations with the advertising brand, as this indicates whether the advertisement changed brand perceptions in any way.

The post-campaign study incorporates additional questions to obtain a more detailed assessment of the advertising impact. This includes the unprompted recall of ads, such as the brands recalled, the marketing channels through which they advertised and recall of the communications or messages (specific words, visual components etc). Given that the awareness of a lot of advertising is subliminal, brand and advertising recall are also measured prompted.

Another important line of questioning included in the post-campaign study is the call-to-action as a result of the ad. For instance, in the case of a banner ad, did it inspire a click-through, or in the case of a direct mail campaign with a money-off coupon, did it trigger a purchase?

Pre- and post-advertising studies can be expensive as two studies are required, both of which need to comprise a large sample size to ensure that any changes in the measurements are genuine and not the result of a statistical quirk. A sample size of $n = 400$ provides a statistical error of +/–4 per cent at 90 per cent confidence limits. This means there is a range of up to 8 per cent where, if the changes from pre- to post-assessment fall within this range, the findings would not be statistically significant. This accuracy does, however, assume a worst-case scenario of a 50–50 response distribution to a question (eg 50 per cent unprompted awareness of a specific brand pre-campaign, versus 59 per cent awareness post-campaign, which would be statistically significant as it exceeds the 8 per cent delta.)

Top tips

- Trust unprompted awareness and recall more than prompted awareness and recall. Research participants are much more likely to claim they are aware, or recall a brand or ad, if it is mentioned to them prompted in the survey, given that recognition (be it real or fake) is far easier than recall.

- Establish a sample size for each wave that is sufficient to capture anticipated changes in awareness with statistical accuracy. In other words, if the goal is for the ad to increase awareness by a certain per cent, ensure that this per cent change does not fall within the margin of statistical error.

- Where the pre- and post-campaign surveys are only a few months apart, avoid returning to the same survey participants in the post-campaign wave. This will eliminate the probability of respondent bias as a result of heightened brand awareness from the first wave of the research.

- Online surveys are the quickest and most cost-effective method for pre- and post-advertising surveys. However, for very targeted audiences such as B2B buyers in niche markets or individuals located in specific geographic areas, telephone surveys would be the more feasible approach.

The use of web analytics

The rise of digital marketing has made measurement of ad effectiveness much easier and more cost-effective. For example, it is possible to measure the effectiveness of digital advertising such as an online ad campaign by assessing the numbers of impressions (views) and click-through rates. While this is highly insightful, the analytics only measure digital marketing efforts, unless the more traditional advertising like print ads or direct mail campaigns are integrated with an online platform.

Web analytics can be incorporated into a market research program through tools such as cookie tracking of digital campaigns. This involves installing hidden cookies into a digital campaign, and visitors of the campaign are then surveyed in order to obtain a deep understanding of the audience. This includes profiling the audience that engaged with the campaign, assessing whether the digital communications are reaching the right audience, the effect of the communications etc. Note that the survey participants have already opted into cookie tracking as they are members of an online research panel for this very purpose.

SUMMARY

Advertising is the paid promotion of a brand, product or service. There are many types of advertising which tend to be employed more by consumer as opposed to B2B brands given the high costs of advertising – especially the more traditional advertising media such as television and print ads. Indeed the larger consumer brands spend several hundred million dollars annually on advertising.

Advertisements serve different purposes, from raising awareness to driving appeal to brand building. An ad might fail in its effectiveness, purely because the wrong communications channel or messaging was used for the advertising objective. Market research can optimize the message, content and design, as well as indicate the optimum channels through which to place ads.

There are typically three research goals of quantitative ad testing: measuring brand efficiency, brand perceptions and message recall. Quantitative sample sizes need to be sufficiently large in order that changes in awareness and other metrics are not the result of a statistical quirk.

Whatever the research method, the four most important measures of ad effectiveness are resonance, relevance, brand fit and clarity.

Using market research to launch a new product

Why launching new products is important

Innovation is a key growth driver in business and industry. New product development fuels future revenue for it is said that at least 30 per cent of a company's products have typically been developed within the past five years.

In addition to driving organic growth, innovation is a source of differentiation. When a company introduces a new product, it is considered forward looking with an improved offering. Innovation can be as much about building a brand as about refreshing, expanding or creating a product portfolio.

Defining a new product

There are three types of new products, as shown in Figure 23.1. Breakthroughs are market-leading innovations and are the most challenging to generate as they are brand new and never been seen before. Line extensions are additional products within a product family or range. Product refreshes are next generation products that are usually improved in some way, either for the user and/or for the manufacturer. Line extensions and product refreshes are much easier and quicker to create and they tend to respond to market demand.

In addition to internal product development initiatives and consumer demand, various forces impact on new product development such as competitors with their latest products, or raw material suppliers with substitute products or shortages.

FIGURE 23.1 The three types of new product

The role of market research in new product development

Given the importance of new product development, most large companies allocate substantial budgets to research and development. Electronics companies may have an R&D budget equal to 7 per cent of their sales but this is necessary to cope with the rapid pace of technological change. For most companies, the expenditure on R&D is somewhere between 2 and 5 per cent of sales.

A system is usually required to control the development of new products. The Stage-Gate idea-to-launch model is an example of a structured approach used by hundreds of companies for assessing the viability of a new product from the idea stage through to the fully developed product. A typical Stage-Gate process is shown in Figure 23.2.

Idea screen

A study by Professor Eric von Hippel, an economist at MIT Sloan School of Management, found that 80 per cent of industrial innovations came from customers themselves. Such innovations are most likely to have been created by the manufacturer as a result of customer feedback. However, customers and internal knowledge are not the only sources of new ideas. As shown in Figure 23.1, new products can be influenced by external forces such as raw material shortages or generated from the availability of substitutes. In fact, new ideas can come from virtually anywhere.

IGURE 23.2 Example of a Stage-Gate process

rocess

Idea generation

| Gate 1 | Gate 2 | Gate 3 | Gate 4 | Gate 5 |

Idea screen

Stage 1: Concept creation

Stage 2: Business case

Stage 3: Product development

Stage 4: Test and validation

Stage 5: Launch and monitor

Market search nput

Discovery and exploration

Concept testing

Opportunity analysis

Product assessment

Product trials

Tracking

---

10 ways to source new product ideas

1 **Internal resources.** In addition to the R&D and technical departments, ask the sales and marketing teams, account managers, customer service reps, and any other role that is customer facing.

2 **Customers.** Watch the products in use. Note whether consumers modify them to make them more useful in some way. Ask about pain points with the product to determine potential improvements.

3 **Extreme users.** Observe those who use products excessively as their behaviours could suggest new product opportunities. Also learn from the outliers – those who use a product for unconventional applications.

4 **External partners.** Seek a viable partner for inspiration and support, such as a design or engineering firm, research agency, university etc.

5 **Competitors.** Research the Internet to learn from their websites, PR articles, annual reports, and shareholder presentations. Visit their booths at exhibitions.

6 **The channel.** Talk to the raw material suppliers, distributors and other players in the value chain.

7 **Substitutes and complimentary products.** Assess alternative products that could act as a substitute, as well as complementary products that deliver a total system or solution.

8 **Patent applications.** Look into where patents are registered and what they are for.

9 **Crowdsourcing.** Tap into the wisdom of the crowd by asking for the input of those eager to share their ideas and opinions in online communities.

10 **Foreign sources.** Explore foreign markets for a different perspective. Significant differences across countries impact the demand for products, how they are used, when they are used etc., given socio-cultural, legislative, environmental and political influences.

Stage 1: Concept creation

In order for an idea to succeed throughout the Stage-Gate process, it may need to be developed into a concept and tested in concept form. When presenting a concept to a potential user, the concept should clearly state the overall purpose of the offer, the problem it addresses and/or solution it offers and the key benefits provided.

Concept testing should assess the following among the target audience:

- First impressions
- Likes and dislikes
- Believability
- Uniqueness
- Overall appeal
- Price perceptions
- Intent to purchase

Top tips: Creating a concept

- Ensure the concept is written in a language appropriate for the target audience. For example, communicate the benefits as opposed to the technical features.

- Include an image or demonstration (where applicable and feasible).

- Provide sufficient evidence behind marketing claims likely to be questioned on believability.

Stage 2: Business case

Most companies require a business case to push a new product forward and receive funding for necessary resources.

A business case typically covers the following:

1 Product description – an explanation of the product including the problem it addresses and solution it provides, technical specifications, market drivers, barriers, the competitive environment etc.

2 Nature and size of the opportunity – a breakdown of the market size and potential in terms of:

    a the total available market (the notional spend from all target audiences who could be consumers of the new product);

    b the served available market (the current spend on all products with which the new product would compete);

    c pricing strategy, revenue potential and profitability.

3 Project plan – criteria for a successful product launch, such as the technical and manufacturing feasibility, CAPEX requirements, risks, timelines, route to market and annual sales targets.

Market research is often used in this stage of the product development process for calculating the market size and potential for the new product. There are three approaches to market sizing:

- **Top-down approach.** Using published data and reports to obtain a macro view of the market

- **Demand-side assessment.** Grossing up survey data to achieve the market size

- **Supply-side assessment.** Assessing the size of all suppliers to the market and summing this to arrive at the market size

Assuming the concept testing comprised a quantitative sample, the revenue potential can be estimated by taking the proportion of respondents expressing purchase intent, and applying a percentage filter to arrive at the proportion expected to purchase in reality. The percentage filter depends on a number of factors such as the pricing strategy and planned promotional investment.

Stage 3: Product development

At this stage in the product development process, prototypes are manufactured. Market research is less common in this early phase of manufacturing, but in some cases, a quick and small-scale customer review of the prototype is useful for identifying any major pitfalls, allowing for product changes before a full-scale production run.

Stage 4: Test and validation

Once the prototype has met the quality standards, it is recommended that it is tested among the target audience. Product trials enable the user to provide valuable feedback indicating necessary changes to the physical product, as well as informing marketing and pricing strategies.

The research objectives of product trials are very similar to those of concept tests. It is beneficial in product trials to also explore comparisons with current products used in order to determine the biggest differentiators of the new offering. In business-to-business markets, this often requires research with the users of the product who may be a separate audience from the decision makers. While decision makers have the final say, users know the products the best and can have a substantial influence on their managers.

Stage 5: Launch and monitor

The final stage entails the full-scale production and launch of the new product. The success of the new product is as much down to the channel, pricing and promotional strategies as it is to the features of the product itself. Market research can be used post launch to monitor the product's performance beyond the sales figures. In such tracking research, key objectives comprise:

- understanding what attracted people to the new product
- determining what encouraged people to switch
- assessing satisfaction with the product overall and on a number of performance attributes
- measuring how likely people would be to recommend the product

Developing success criteria for new product development

Qualitative research is useful for generating new product ideas and for exploring the concepts. However, many companies require a more structured mechanism for assessing both concepts and prototypes through quantitative research. Success criteria with benchmarks suitable for a particular market provide a means of measuring the performance of a concept or prototype with a standard tool across a whole company, ensuring that all new products are assessed equally.

The success criteria are usually based on a purchase intent question asked to market research participants in the form of a five-point Likert scale, as shown in Table 23.1.

TABLE 23.1 The purchase intent question

Assuming the product was offered at a price considered acceptable, which of the following best describes your intent to purchase it?	
Definitely would buy	O
Probably would buy	O
Might or might not buy	O
Probably would not buy	O
Definitely would not buy	O

Two key metrics stem from this question:

- the top box score, ie the percentage of respondents stating 'Definitely would buy';
- the top two box score, ie the sum of the percentage of respondents stating 'Definitely would buy' and 'Probably would buy'.

To pass through the Stage-Gate process, the concept or prototype needs to reach the required metric on purchase intent for either the top box or top two box hurdle, as per the success criteria.

TABLE 23.2 Example of a B2B manufacturing company's success criteria for prototype testing

Success criteria		Top box hurdle	Top box result	Top 2 box hurdle	Top 2 box result
Intent to buy	Standard	31%–34%	33%	60%	59%
	Good	35%–44%		70%	
	Excellent	45%+		80%	

In the example shown above, the prototype received a green light to proceed having achieved a top box score that fell within the standard.

- Develop the success criteria only upon completion of at least a handful of concept or/and prototype tests. The threshold can then be set using relevant data to the business and its objectives.

- Monitor the success criteria over time based on the numbers of 'go' and 'kill' outcomes. It may be necessary to change the criteria, for instance if too many concepts pass through the gate and there is limited R&D budget for prototype development.

- Acknowledge cultural differences when establishing the success criteria. For example, some companies set lower thresholds for Western European versus North American data given that Western Europeans tend to be less enthusiastic in scalar survey responses compared to their North American counterparts.

SUMMARY

Every product has a life cycle from birth to youth to maturity to old age. Sales of an established product typically peak between the maturity and old age phases, and then sales start to fall. Unless the product is rejuvenated, sales continue to decline as substitutes and new innovations eclipse the stagnating product. New products are, therefore, the lifeblood of a company and it is not surprising that between 2 per cent and 7 per cent of sales in large companies is pumped back into R&D.

Market research can play a vital role throughout the whole product development process, including the generation of new ideas for the innovation pipeline, assessing the performance of concepts and prototypes, and monitoring the performance of a product post-launch.

Market research reduces the risk of failure as the discovery of product flaws in research findings is far less costly to remedy during the product development process, compared to post-launch. In addition to this quasi insurance, market research can provide useful intelligence for developing a compelling business case, such as an optimum price point and target audience, and the size of the opportunity.

It is advisable to use success criteria for filtering concepts and prototypes. Not only does this streamline decision making; it also increases the chances of new product success as the success criteria independently ensure that only the best performing concepts and prototypes are selected for development.

While new product development may seem a daunting and costly task, it need not focus exclusively on the product. Improvements to packaging or new services could have just as big an impact as enhancing the physical product itself.

Reporting

Market research reporting has changed over the years. The traditional 10,000 to 15,000-word written reports have almost disappeared, replaced by content-heavy PowerPoint presentations. These are too often laden with spurious graphics and images thought to brighten the page but that look cheesy and add nothing. Data is presented in slides that are too complicated for a reader to work out what is going on without the researcher being there to explain. Some are just not relevant to the objectives. It is not uncommon for report decks to run to over 100 pages. These reports should be the crowning glory of the huge amount of time and money that has been invested in the research and yet so often the results are disastrous.

Data is the problem. Often there is so much information it is difficult to work out what to include and exclude, and making sense of it is not so easy. The report and the way it is presented leaves a lasting impression of the project and the researchers and it requires time and effort to get it right.

Common rules for both written reports and presentations

- Meet the needs of the audience.
- Get the structure right.
- Pay attention to detail with painstaking checking and editing.
- Make it look good.

Meet the needs of the audience

Reports have two purposes – they are prepared as an aid to the presentation and also as a lasting record that people will read, digest and use to develop action plans for the future. Fulfilling both these needs – presentation and report – with the same document can be difficult.

Targeting mixed audiences who want different things from the study can also be a problem. Audiences are often varied and their needs can differ greatly. Typical audiences for research reports consist of product managers, marketing managers, sales managers, market research managers, business development people, technical development managers and of course the 'C-suite' of top executives. A researcher needs to balance the needs of these groups within the report.

The job responsibilities of the audience will strongly influence the specific intelligence they look for from the report. Salespeople want to know specifics such as what each of their customers, and especially potential customers, is thinking and doing. Communications managers are interested in different things, such as which journals people read, which websites they visit and what messages are effective. Technical staff are likely to be interested in which product features are valued.

Overlying the different interests of people with their specific job interests are the personal requirements that people have from a report. Without exception, everyone seeks clarity and insights. Most want to know from the beginning where the report is going and what it has found out, and so an executive summary is appreciated. All reports are expected to give clear direction on the threats and opportunities, though sometimes the researchers are asked to refrain from making recommendations as they may not have all the 'internal' facts that allow them to do so.

Diverse interests mean that it is especially important for there to be close communication with the research sponsor to find out at what level to pitch the report. Different reports may be required for different audiences.

Get the structure right

The key to good market research reporting is structure. Structure is apparent throughout the research process. It is there at the beginning in the listing of the research aims and objectives laid out in the proposal. It exists in the questionnaire used to collect the data. Market research is systematic and organized, and structure lies at the heart of the process. Without structure, the mass of data could get lost and the huge amount of effort that went into the project will not be appreciated.

It may sound as if it is jumping the gun, but it is important to have a feel for the conclusions before the structure of the report is developed. Undoubtedly the researcher preparing the report will have been steeped in the data as the survey has progressed and will have a sense of the impending result. Also, the proposal and the brief that laid out the plan for the project at the beginning will be a reminder as to what is expected from the report. The structure of the questionnaire offers a potential framework for the report but it also brings with it the danger of following the sequence of the interview, which might not be the best line for the report itself. It is crucial at the outset of the reporting stage to map out a structure that drives towards

FIGURE 24.1   Arriving at a report structure by procedure and analysis

The procedural approach to structure

Section A		Section B		Section C
Desk research	⟹	Qualitative findings	⟹	Quantitative findings

The analytical approach to structure

Chapter 1		Chapter 2		Chapter 3		Chapter 4
Market size	⟹	Market structure	⟹	Buying behaviour	⟹	Trends in the market
(From Section A)		(From Section A)		(From Section B+C)		(From Section A+B+C)

a conclusion in a clear and logical way, for otherwise a question-by-question analysis may look like a data dump.

Most market researchers work for survey organizations and it is the results of surveys that are reported. However, survey findings do not stand in isolation and there may be contextual data that could be woven into the structure. Internal data from the sponsoring client could be used to set the scene. Desk research could provide a big picture that can be set alongside the survey data. There may be a mixture of qualitative and quantitative findings to be reported.

Ken Follett is a master storyteller and has sold over 130 million books around the world. His books are meticulously researched and extremely well written. A critical part of his success is the clear structure of his stories. Before beginning one of his epic novels, Follett maps out the story in brief, chapter by chapter, and follows this structure religiously as he writes. We researchers should do the same, recognizing that there will be scope when the report is finally edited to move slides around and improve the logic of the structure.

The reference to Ken Follett and storytelling has an important parallel in reporting market research findings. A market research report should be like a story: it should have a beginning, middle and end. It should have a strong theme that runs right through it. It is often the conclusions where there are most failures in reporting. A hundred pages of good analysis should not end up with only three pages of conclusions that are no more than a summary of the findings. This reinforces the importance of the researcher knowing where the report is going and this requires a report structure that is developed before the writing has begun.

The first section of the report, the start of the story, consists of an introduction to the market and background to the study. The middle part of the report, usually the bulk of it, contains the detail of the findings and is where researchers usually do a good job. In this lengthy middle section, each chapter should link to the next as the thread of the story is followed and it builds towards the conclusion.

The outline of the questionnaire offers a guideline as to the structure of the report but it need not be followed religiously. Using the example of a customer-satisfaction survey, it is likely that towards the beginning of the questionnaire there will have been some questions to find out which suppliers are known and which have been used. This may be followed by questions that determine how suppliers are chosen. Then there may be questions that rate suppliers on factors such as product, price, delivery, customer service and support. There is nothing inherently wrong with this structure and it provides a good starting point. However, it may be better to regroup the data into a story about loyalty and how it can be improved. For example:

Chapter 1. Introduction

Chapter 2. Executive summary

Chapter 3. The problem of customer churn

- The effects of high customer turnover for our company.
- Levels of customer churn in our industry.
- Trends in customer churn.

Chapter 4. Factors building loyalty amongst customers

- Examples from other industries that drive customer loyalty.
- The 'must haves': hygiene factors driving loyalty in the industry.
- Differentiating factors driving loyalty in the industry.
- Summary of factors driving loyalty in the industry.

Chapter 5. The company's performance in driving loyalty

- Levels of satisfaction and loyalty amongst customers.
- Levels of satisfaction and loyalty for competing suppliers.
- Factors that drive loyalty and satisfaction with the company.

Chapter 6. Conclusions

- Summary of findings.
- An analysis of the strengths and weaknesses of our company.
- The opportunities and threats in the market.
- What actions could be taken to engender loyalty by improving:
  - the product (the customer value proposition);
  - the place (the channel to market);
  - the price (the way that value is captured);
  - the promotion (the messages that resonate with the market).

This is a structure built around the subject of customer loyalty. It focuses on the interpretation of the data and the translation of customer satisfaction to loyalty.

Writing, checking and editing

A writing style for narrative reports and presentations needs to be developed to communicate data quickly and clearly. The report must have impact so that a busy reader can quickly 'gut it' for content. Some rules in relation to the style and layout of a report are:

- Break the report into chapters (partitions) that link logically and build the story.

- Give every slide a heading that draws the reader into the slide and communicates what the reader can expect to learn. Researchers have varying opinions on whether headings should be short and snappy or long and discursive. If in doubt, use a short heading of fewer than 10 words with a subheading to add clarification if necessary.

- In the body of the slide use bullets, short paragraphs and notes in text boxes to quickly communicate ideas.

- Avoid heavy text and use graphics and diagrams wherever possible.

- Tables are an excellent means of presenting complicated data. Ensure that the rows and columns of data in the tables are in declining order of importance. Highlight key figures in the table and use text boxes to provide explanations.

- Clearly label all diagrams with headings (as well as sources of data). Consistency is again important here, with the use of an appropriate colour palette, plain fonts and font sizes.

- Avoid complicated words, jargon and slang.

- Avoid long sections of written prose.

- Pay attention to points of detail and little things because these indicate to the reader that care and attention has been given to the whole survey process.

After the report has been drafted, the author checks its structure, readability and content. It may be that some slides need moving around to enhance the flow.

Data must be checked carefully for accuracy. Is the information correct, does it make sense, has it been communicated in the most appropriate way?

Sub-plots can enhance a good story and so too a presentation can have information that is interesting in its own right but not necessarily a key to the bigger plot. If these sub-plots are too tangential to the story, they could be placed in an appendix.

This editing stage requires a ruthless hand, and it is the time to abandon superfluous data that do not support the conclusions and recommendations. When carrying out the edit, it should be borne in mind that there are three key requirements of a good report: it must meet the objectives, it must clearly present the data, and it should drive towards action. If it fails on any of these three requirements, a strong edit is needed.

It is also worth facing up to the 30 per cent challenge. Look through the report and see if you can reduce its length by a third. The likelihood is that in doing so there will be a minimal loss of critical data and the story will be tightened and made more readable. However, the researcher who has spent time and effort constructing the beloved report may not be the one to take an axe to 30 per cent. It may need the hand of a strong editor.

Final edits (there may be more than one) will be required as checks are made on aspects of detail such as the spelling, grammar, labelling of charts, indexing and readability. These edits must be the responsibility of the author of the report but it can be helpful if it is also proofread by an independent person who may spot and challenge things that may not be clear to someone less deeply involved than the author.

Make it look good

We have argued above that different audiences may require different reports. A master report could be developed to tell the whole story and be sufficiently comprehensive to make sense to someone picking it up and reading it without the benefit of the presenter explaining every slide. The second report could be a shorter version, with fewer words per slide, that is more suited to a presentation delivered on a screen.

These reports will be critically examined in every way and must be 'window dressed' to look good. A house style that is consistent will enhance its look and feel.

A checklist of things to look for when window dressing the report are as follows:

- There should be a title page that describes the content of the report and a date that states when it was presented, and names the author(s).
- Include a table of contents or an agenda slide so that people know what the report contains.
- Keep it simple (no fussy design background, borders or colourful templates). The plainer the better.
- Stick carefully to the colour palette that fits in with the PowerPoint design and theme (subtle colours work better than a mishmash of garish colours).
- Use page numbers.
- Label all slides and charts.
- Be consistent in all aspects of the layout – margins, fonts, heading styles, table labelling.
- Do not cram too much on a page – make effective use of white space.
- If in doubt, leave it out.

Reporting qualitative data

Qualitative research reports are harder to write than those based on quantitative data. It is especially important to develop a tight structure for a qualitative study, otherwise it can spin off in many directions. One of the many established analytical frameworks from the social sciences or behavioural economics could be used to guide the overall structure.

The qualitative information itself can be presented through text, flow diagrams and video clips (frequently referred to as 'talking heads'). Verbatim comments can add emphasis as they are the words of the customer, not the researcher. These direct quotes will underline or add to a point that is being made. In order for the reader to understand who made a comment, it is usual to attribute a quote to a type of individual (eg female, 25 to 35 years, affluent) but without giving away anything that would identify them personally.

Summary points when preparing qualitative reports:

- Data should be located in a clear framework.
- Findings can be presented diagrammatically as well as in text.
- Video clips and photographs are very powerful ways of communicating points.
- Direct quotes, when used, should illustrate and expand research findings.
- Quotes should be grammatically 'doctored' to make sense.
- Quotes should respect the confidentiality of respondents.
- It is important that the qualitative researcher preparing the report makes it clear what is his or her interpretation and what is fact.

FIGURE 24.2   Using verbatim comments to communicate a point

I like to do DIY at home, especially wallpapering. I have tried plastering but the plaster dried in the bucket before I could get it into the room to the wall. So I wasn't very successful with that! I like to try anything that needs doing at home. I haven't tried plumbing. I can mend things when they go wrong in the house but I haven't tried anything serious, as I would call it. (Female, 35, affluent)

I am as enthusiastic as I can be really. I don't touch electrics because that's a bit dodgy. I've blown myself up a couple of times. I'm a keen DIY enthusiast but I know my limits. (Male, 65, retired)

Reporting quantitative data

Quantitative information, by its very nature, has more structure than qualitative data. For most types of quantitative findings, there are several options available for presenting the data:

Charts and diagrams

PowerPoint is both a blessing and a curse to market researchers. It provides standard charts and diagrams including 'SmartArt' for instant graphics. These can offer inspiration on how to present data but they can look like a lazy solution. Original thinking is to be encouraged.

There are numerous options for presenting the data and it is worthwhile considering which could be most appropriate.

Pie charts and doughnuts are used where the data must add up to 100 per cent. They are used to show:

- Classification data: who took part in the survey, their age, gender etc.

- Market-size data: the share of the market, sales within a sector of the market.

- Brand shares.

FIGURE 24.3   Pie chart to show market segments or shares

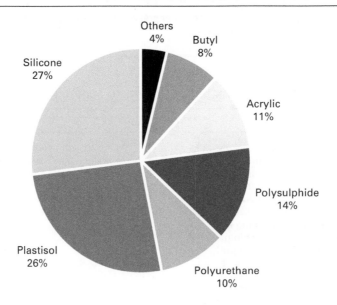

Spider charts are used to present numerical data. In Figure 24.4, by way of example, we see satisfaction levels with a supplier on six attributes across three different countries. It allows the presentation of complex, comparative data so that differences quickly become apparent.

FIGURE 24.4   Spider chart showing satisfaction with a supplier

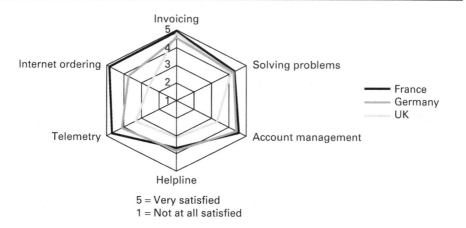

The bar chart

Bar charts are the most commonly used method of displaying data in quantitative studies. There are several different types of bar charts to choose from, depending on the type of data to be presented. They can be horizontal, vertical or divided. It is important that for most data the bars are presented in descending order of importance, except where the scale is an important variable such as age or likelihood to buy (see Figure 24.5).

FIGURE 24.5   Horizontal bar chart showing likelihood of purchase

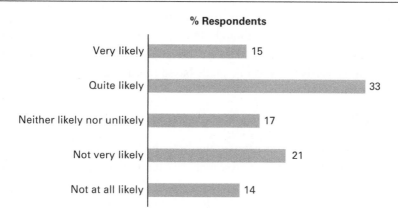

The horizontal bar chart is commonly used to present customer satisfaction and answers to attitudinal questions. The key requirement is to display clearly the rated scale, either by mean scores or the percentage rating at a particular level, again in declining order of importance.

It is also possible to compare the ratings of several groups of respondents on one chart; for example, when examining the attractiveness of a new concept, the reactions of men and women can be plotted against each other for comparison.

Vertical bar charts are commonly used where a measure of size or volume is needed, for example in market sizing. Charts can be split to display the component parts or divisions and trends within a group, for example sales trends over time (see Figure 24.6).

FIGURE 24.6   Vertical bar chart showing sales of carpet designs

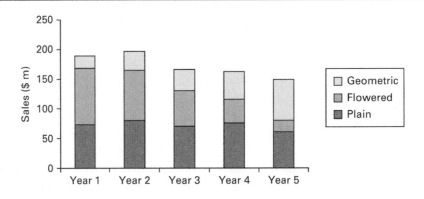

Mekko charts (or to be more correct Marimekko charts – named after the originator) are a useful means of depicting market-size data along two dimensions simultaneously. For example market segments can be shown along the x-axis with the width of each column corresponding to the size of the segment, and within each segment or column the market share of individual brands can then be displayed (see Figure 24.7).

Graphs are used to present trends in numbers over a given period. They perform the same function as bar charts, though they are often used where the prediction of a trend is required, for example sales trends, population trends, economic trends. From line graphs, predictions can be made based on the trend (see Figure 24.8).

Using tables

If the message requires the precision of numbers and text labels to identify what they are, a table could be the best way of presenting the data. Tables quickly communicate data, and can readily be used to display patterns within the data (see Table 24.1 on page 324). Here are some rules on constructing tables to maximize their effectiveness:

FIGURE 24.7   Mekko chart showing market segments and market shares

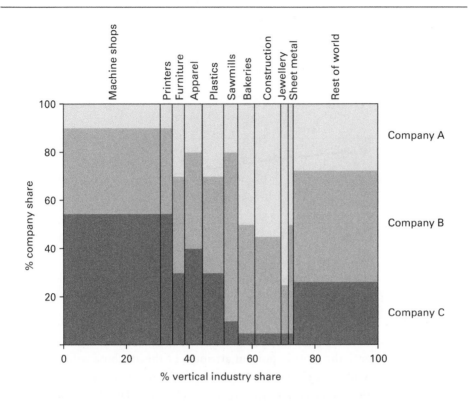

- *Simplicity*: Tables are read from top to bottom and left to right and so they are normally laid out with rows and columns in descending order of importance. Conditional formatting in Excel is a quick and easy way to show any patterns of data by highlighting them in different colours.

- *Labelling*: tables should have clear headings identifying what the table is about. Columns should state their content along with the unit of measurement, indicating whether numbers, percentages, weights or units, monetary values and so on. If appropriate, the question itself should be displayed as a heading and the sample sizes should be stated so the reader can judge the accuracy. Short labels and titles are the rule as long as they make sense.

- *Displaying the totals*: tables should have a total column and a total row as these are reference points against which other data in the table can be compared.

- *Rounding the figures*: in most cases figures in tables should be rounded. This makes it easier for the reader to relate one figure to another. Of course, there

FIGURE 24.8 Line graph showing trends in card and cheque payments

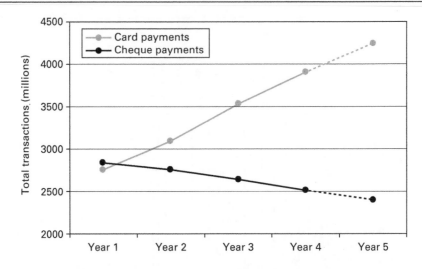

are instances where numbers should not be rounded and decimal places are important (for example, a table of currency conversion rates).

- *Ordering rows and columns*: tables and charts that are organized in increasing or decreasing size make it easier for the reader to interpret the data. In general, the most important attribute or the attribute with the highest response should be at the top of the table and the others in declining order. This draws the reader's eye to the order as well as the data. Where several columns of data are used, the order may be determined by the 'total' or the most important data column. As with charts, the exception to this rule is with ordinal scales (those that are placed in an order) such as 'very likely', 'quite likely', 'not very likely' and 'not at all likely'. The sequence of these scales should be presented in the same way whatever the result.

- *Format of the table*: several techniques can be used to present tables in a manner that easily separates the rows and/or columns, and current word processing and report writing packages have made this much simpler for the writer. The main method of making the data easily readable in tables involves the use of lines, text and colour. Most software packages have a range of automatically formatted tables available that incorporate the use of all these elements.

Using flow diagrams

Flow diagrams are a simple and effective means of presenting organizational data. Such data can relate to anything from how the market is structured to how an

TABLE 24.1 Table to show satisfaction with a supplier

	Impact on satisfaction	Average satisfaction with supplier*
Delivery of product	36%	4.1
Price	28%	4.2
Product	15%	4.6
Customer support	14%	3.8
Technical service and maintenance	7%	4.2
TOTAL	100%	4.3

* 1 is not at all satisfied and 5 is extremely satisfied

organization operates, to how an individual makes decisions. The key issue for the development of a flow chart is the structure of a process. Rather like a maze, the reader should be able to start at one point and follow the flow of the diagram to the end, no matter how many diversions and alternative routes there may be. Figure 24.9

FIGURE 24.9 Flow diagram showing route to market for shower manufacturers displays the complex route to market from shower manufacturers to end users. This single chart has a far greater impact in describing this market than any number of words and paragraphs.

Drawing conclusions

The conclusions and recommendations section of a report is, arguably, the most important. Market research is commissioned to help confirm how to manage change, to re-evaluate the way things are done and make informed decisions about the future. The report has to leave the client feeling they have information that gives a clear way forward.

It is helpful to use frameworks in the conclusions of a report. These locate the problem in a context and bring the detail back into a bigger picture. There are a number of business and marketing frameworks that can be used to do this in market research. These frameworks offer a theory for showing how things work and are well documented in business literature. There are three broad classifications into which these frameworks fall, regardless of the methodologies adopted in the research design. Table 24.2 displays the classifications for drawing conclusions and making recommendations, and the frameworks that fall into them.

TABLE 24.2   Three classifications of frameworks for drawing conclusions and making recommendations

Section of conclusions	Purpose of the section	Examples of frameworks
Situation analysis	To summarize the key issues and bring them together	SWOT, life cycle, Ansoff grid, decision-making models
Marketing and business goals	To show what can be achieved	Porter's generic strategies, Rogers' adoption model for new technology, hierarchical communication models (eg AIDA)
Recommendations	To show what action is required	Four Ps, XY grids, flow models process

Making a presentation

Throughout this chapter we have made a strong link between the market research report and the physical presentation of the findings. Reporting and presenting for many market researchers are one and the same thing.

The presentation of a market research study will normally last up to two hours. The PowerPoint slides may be supported by other materials such as video and audio clips. Audiences of up to 20 people are the norm. As is the case when preparing the report itself, it is useful to know in advance of the presentation the roles and responsibilities of those who will be attending so as to give the researcher a chance to accommodate their different needs.

The biggest determinant of a good presentation is a good presenter. Market research presentations are usually heavy on information and this cannot be avoided. The presentation is not a pitch for a job or aimed at selling a company; rather it is to communicate findings from the study. The content of the slides therefore play a more important role than in a 'pitch' presentation as they are the synthesis of the data.

This said, the presentation itself creates the opportunity to make a good impression, and the polishing of the researcher's skills in communication is essential. Skills of presenters are individual and dependent, to a large extent, on the personality of the presenter. However, there are some imperatives that can be learned.

Preparation is the key. The audience wants to hear the presenter and their views and they presume that they will know the data inside out and backwards. They do not want to see the researcher stand in front of a screen reading aloud from the slides. They are eager for insights on the slides. It is important therefore that the presenter describes the data on the slide and talks around it, expanding on points, pulling out key data and making links with previous slides (or even future slides, if appropriate). In most market research presentations the relatively small audiences encourages a discussion of the findings, which quite clearly will require the researcher to be steeped in the data and prepared to answer questions that inevitably will arise.

It is good practice for the researcher to have rehearsed what will be said on each slide, with notes and prompts as reminders. With an intimate knowledge of the data and the deck, the researcher should be able to face the audience and refer to the slide to emphasize points. In the inevitable discussion it will be the researcher's responsibility to manage the timing, bringing the discussion back to the presentation and make a strong link with what has been said so that things can smoothly move on.

The research industry employs many young people who may feel intimidated presenting to older and senior audiences. Presenting research findings for the first time is a nerve-racking experience and the novice presenter will need to rehearse and practice time and again before they are totally confident and accomplished.

Here are some preparation pointers for a good performance:

- Know the data inside out.
- Know the presentation structure inside out – which slides come next.
- Memorize the slides and the background to the points being made on the slides.
- Practise the presentation and what will be said on the day.

It is perfectly normal to feel nervous before a presentation. Experience and practice are the key requirements of becoming a good presenter. Finding the right occasions on which to practice may not be so easy. Presenting to colleagues and taking minor slots in a big presentation are a necessary step in building skills. Watching experienced presenters both in the workplace and on television will provide tips on how to improve presentation skills.

Some simple considerations are as follows:

1   Dress for the occasion.

2   Control your nerves in a way that works for you. Introduce yourself to the audience as they enter the room and settle down.

3   Draw a quick plan of the seating arrangements, marking who is sitting at each place so that they can be addressed by name during the presentation.

4   Prepare the introduction and set the scene on timing and content. Do not spend long on the objectives and methods and get quickly into the meat of the findings.

5   Look pleased and happy to be presenting rather than someone who wants to sit down as quickly as possible.

6   Use confident and open body language, facing the audience and engaging with them rather than turning your back to them or pressing yourself against the wall.

7   Sweep the room constantly with eye contact, engaging everyone in the audience.

8   Avoid 'dog' words and phrases – those that unconsciously are repeated and that can distract an audience.

9   Speak clearly and confidently and use intonation in your voice.

10   Use people's names (making sure they are correct!).

11   Address audience members' concerns and questions honestly.

12   Pace yourself and the presentation, all the time watching the timing. You will not be criticized for a presentation that finishes early. Encourage

discussion but be prepared to grab back control. You know how long the presentation will take better than the audience, and enough time must be left for the conclusions, recommendations and feedback at the end.

13 Just as you have thought through what you want to say at the beginning, plan what you want to say as concluding remarks.

14 There will almost certainly be some questions that are raised in the discussion and cannot be answered there and then because they require further analysis. Make a note of these and remember to feed them back as soon as possible after the presentation.

Top tips

- Start to think about the final report at the very start of the project. Don't leave it until the end.

- Build your report around a hypothesis or the overarching objective of the study. Make it a story that builds to a strong conclusion. Break the story into chapters.

- All the data in the report should be referenced so that people know its validity. All argumentation should be supported by strong logic.

- If a page of the report doesn't add anything to the report, delete it. If in doubt, miss it out!

- Consider the nature of your audience when preparing the report. Who is it addressed to and what will they be expecting?

- It may be necessary to prepare more than one report. A report of 40 to 50 PowerPoint slides is ideal for the presentation, and a larger report can be submitted for the file copy.

- Make sure that the report is flawless in its consistency of both formatting and data, and without typos.

- Brighten the report with relevant pictures and diagrams and don't cheapen it with cheesy graphics.

- Prepare for the presentation and treat it as the big day that it is. Practise what you want to say using the PowerPoint deck as supporting evidence. Engage strongly with the audience with your knowledge of the subject and your authority.

- Encourage questions and manage the time slot that you have been given. Ensure that you leave sufficient time at the end for the conclusions and a final wrap up.

SUMMARY

Reporting market research findings is the conclusion of a considerable amount of work and it is the occasion on which the findings are presented to the client. It is a great opportunity for the market researcher to impress by communicating findings that meet the objectives of the study, that are clear and interesting, and that lead to actions.

Most reports are prepared in PowerPoint. This is an excellent medium for creating slides to support a narrative that is usually presented face to face. The charts need to fulfil a dual role of supporting the presentation as well as making sense to someone reading them as a stand-alone report.

Clear reporting requires a logical structure that tells a story and that meets the objectives of the study. It needs to be built up from all the different pieces of intelligence that have been collected in the research programme and will comprise a mixture of text, tables, charts, diagrams and graphics.

Reports are judged not only by their content but also by consistent formatting, the use of the right types of charts, and assiduous attention to detail.

Most reports are presented orally and this can be nerve-racking to a junior researcher. Audiences attending presentations may have mixed needs, and the researcher should know what these are and bear them in mind.

Good presenters make good presentations and they are supported by good slides. Presentation skills are honed by diligent preparation and repeated practice.

PART FIVE
The market research industry

International market research

Seeing things more clearly

It has never been easier for a company to market its products and services internationally. A small company can use a website to position itself globally and can draw customers from far afield. Products can be packaged and dispatched by courier to distant corners of the earth. Air travel is cheap and English is the universal language of business, so in theory there is little to stop companies expanding their geographical horizons.

International marketing brings with it a number of complexities. The exporter must know the legal factors operating in the countries where it wishes to sell its products. There are tariffs to take into consideration. In new territories there could be different channels to market, and a business needs to know which will be most effective. International marketing may require different pricing strategies for different countries and local communication plans for different cultures. The marketing world has plenty of examples of companies that have blindly attempted to sell their products in the international marketplace without a solid understanding of local conditions and suffered embarrassing and costly failures.

In their book *International Marketing Research*, Craig and Douglas identify three phases for the use of market research in international strategies:

Phase 1   Information for international market entry. Before entering a new
           market a company needs to understand all the basics about that market
           – its size, its growth, the competitive environment, the legal framework
           of the country and the markets, local prices, routes to market etc.
Phase 2   Information for local market planning. Once a company is committed
           to a market it requires a market plan. It must have a full understanding
           of the type of products which are bought within the country, the prices
           that are charged, the route to market and the communications that are
           necessary to build awareness and interest. In other words it needs to
           have a plan for the 4Ps based on reliable data. It must also be able to

recognize different groups of customers within the market so that it can direct its products to those where it is likely to be more successful. In this phase the company needs a detailed understanding of potential customers in terms of their demographics, their behaviour and their attitudes.

Phase 3   Information for global rationalization. As a company develops its international markets there will be a stage at which it needs to rationalize its global marketing strategy. It is in this phase that the company will require international comparisons for each country so that it can group its markets together and coordinate regional marketing programmes. The market intelligence here will be used for strategic decision making rather than determining marketing tactics.

The structure of the global market research industry

In many respects the market research industry is as old as the hills. People have always asked sensible questions about their customers' needs and the competition. However, in its formal sense, where the collection and interpretation of data is carried out in an organized and independent way to meet specific objectives, the market research industry is only just over a hundred years old.

Market research had its origins in the 19th century. In the 1820s some American newspapers published straw polls that informally surveyed public opinion as a way of testing the direction of the political winds. In 1879 there is reference to a nationwide market research survey into grain production carried out by advertisers NW Ayer & Son in the United States. However, it is from the 1930s onwards that the market research industry became organized and grew. At this time the audit firms of Nielsen and Attwood developed techniques for measuring sales of consumer goods through retailers. Subscribers to these audits were able to see the size of the market for their products and calculate their market shares. Since then the market research industry has benefited from advances in psychology, sociology and technology. The development of marketing has also had an important impact on the development of both market and social research. The result is that market and social research now encompass a wide range of quick and reliable ways of gathering information to help to improve decision making.

Today market research is bought by companies that are selling their goods and services and require intelligence to help them make effective business decisions. To this we can add governments and other organizations that buy market research to help them in their policy making. According to ESOMAR, the global market research industry is worth around $40 billion per annum. This is money spent with market research companies and consultants and doesn't take into consideration in-house market research or the suppliers of software to the industry, the panel companies and all the other suppliers that would significantly add to the value of this figure. The vast majority of market research (three-quarters) is spent within Europe and North America, where the industry has matured and is likely to grow at a steady 2 to 3 per cent per annum. In the developing markets of Latin America, Middle East and Asia Pacific, growth rates will most likely be 5 to 10 per cent per annum.

The focus of international market research changes depending on the interest of the commissioning company. North America and Europe remain strong favourites for multi-country studies, and increasingly China, India and Brazil are included. Over the next few years we can expect to see a huge growth in market research in Russia and Asia.

The market research industry is highly fragmented, with many small players. Quirk's, the marketing research media directory, lists more than 7,000 companies in the United States providing market research services of one kind or another. In the UK there are more than 400 market research suppliers. There has been considerable consolidation amongst the larger groups in the last decade, and on the global stage six companies now represent 40 per cent of the market research industry – Nielsen, Kantar, IMS Health, Ipsos, GfK and Gartner.

Despite the growth of larger agencies, both organically and by acquisition, market research remains an industry typified by small businesses, most of which are owned and managed by the consultants that established them. Quite a few of the larger research companies, although operated as independent companies, are members of larger groups.

There are a relatively small number (well, a few hundred) of organizations that each spend several millions of dollars annually on market research. These include the very largest commercial companies and governments. Research buyers on this scale often have central market research departments that act as service providers to line management throughout their organizations. These departments not only act as professional buyers of market research but also carry out much work themselves, including analysing, interpreting and communicating data. Even the largest departments, however, are seldom involved directly in data collection, which is usually left to outside agencies.

In addition to the organizations that buy and use market research to help them improve their marketing decision making, there is a significant spend by advertising agencies who commission research on behalf of their clients and themselves to test advertising concepts and campaigns. The very largest advertising agencies often have their own research departments.

Quantitative market research dominates the methods of data collection, accounting for three-quarters of all spend, while just less than a fifth goes to qualitative research, most of which is focus group discussions. The balance is made up of consultancy, desk research and special analytics.

In quantitative research there has been a rapid swing towards online studies, which have now overtaken telephone and face-to-face methods (see Figure 25.1). Online research accounts for around half of all the quantitative market research carried out throughout the world. The online research spend is certain to grow still further over the next few years. In parallel with the growth of online studies has been the emergence of specialist companies that own and recruit panels of respondents who have opted in to taking part in online surveys. These companies make their panels available to market research agencies, who specify how many online interviews they require and what criteria respondents should meet in terms of their gender, age, location, income and other factors that may be relevant to the survey in question.

A significant amount of quantitative research is made up of continuous programmes involving the provision of data from respondent panels and retail audits. Continuous research is mainly sold on a syndicated basis, with a number of clients contributing towards the costly projects. This stands in contrast to ad hoc research, which is the mainstay for the large majority of market research companies. Ad hoc projects are carried out for individual clients and designed as one-off programmes to meet specific needs and objectives. Because ad hoc market research companies usually work closely with clients and involve themselves in the full background of the research requirement, their service is very closely aligned with management consultancy.

FIGURE 25.1 Global spend on market research by research method

Response rates internationally

The research industry is now mature. It is no longer a novelty to be phoned or contacted by a market research company to ask for your views. Some people would argue that the research industry has become its own worst enemy by designing long and tedious questionnaires that put people off participating in studies. There is no doubt that we are in danger of becoming an over-researched world.

A corollary of this argument is that in those countries of the world where market research is relatively novel, and people haven't been subjected to tortuous and tedious interviews, they are usually happy to participate in surveys. It is also widely acknowledged that interviewer engagement and the perceived legitimacy of the survey can markedly affect response rates.

Response rates vary enormously depending on the subject, the means of engagement and the source of the enquiry. In the hard-bitten developed market of the United States, response rates from a general list of e-mail addresses are likely to be less than 2 per cent. However, a more targeted e-survey, aimed at customers with high engagement with a supplier, could yield a 30 per cent response.

In most of the developed world the response rates to telephone surveys are between 10 per cent and 50 per cent.

These relatively low response rates to surveys of all kinds are worrying. They potentially affect the accuracy of the survey, as we must ask ourselves whether the people that take part are biased in some way. Equally, are those who do not take part different from those who do? Furthermore, the large rejection rate significantly increases the cost of market research. It is reassuring to know that Holbrook, Krosnick and Pfent (2007), who looked at 81 national surveys with response rates varying from 5 per cent to 54 per cent, claimed that surveys with low response rates were only minimally less accurate than those with higher ones.

Measuring attitudes across nations

Helped by the internet, McDonald's, Disney and CNN, populations worldwide are becoming exposed to a common set of values and expectations. Young people especially are more global in their views, with converging tastes in music, clothing and fashion. This said, every market researcher knows that cultural backgrounds can influence people's responses to questions, particularly attitudinal ones. In general, respondents from developing countries tend to have a more optimistic and positive response to questions than those in developed (and arguably more cynical) countries. In a paper published by ESOMAR and written by Jon Puleston and Duncan Rintoul, 15 multi-country studies were analysed to see how responses to questions with agree/

FIGURE 25.2 Variable results to similar questions across countries

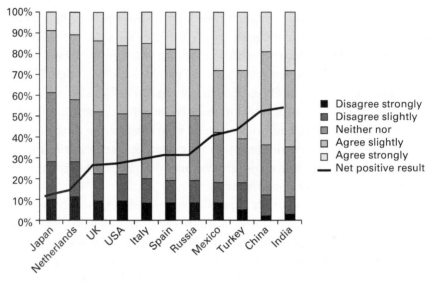

(Based on: 'Can survey gaming techniques cross continents?' Jon Puleston and Duncan Rintoul ESOMAR Publications Series Volume S253 – April 2012)

disagree scales vary by country. The analysis suggests that Indian respondents are five times more likely to agree with statements than Japanese respondents.

The authors postulate that, quite apart from the true difference in the phenomenon that is being measured, there could be other factors that are responsible for these huge variations in the positive and negative responses. Language and translation issues can make a difference. The phrasing of questions can have an influence. Even within the English language, Americans are more comfortable saying that they 'love' a brand than Australians or British, who may find that word too endearing. The word 'okay' to some people may mean that it is acceptable while to others it could mean that it is not good enough.

Now consider the difficulties of designing a questionnaire in one language and translating it into 14 others. There are sure to be some words that are difficult to translate precisely. Imagine a question like the following:

> Thinking of the product that you use most regularly, would you say that it is significantly better, somewhat better, about the same, somewhat worse or significantly worse than other products that you are aware of?

There are potential problems with translating 'significantly' and 'somewhat' as the meaning of these words could vary considerably between languages. So too, a word such as 'quite', which is used frequently by market researchers, is descriptive and could have a range of meaning in different languages – even with the English language it will have different meanings to different people.

Researchers like to use numeric scales, such as those that ask for ratings from 1 to 10 to establish people's satisfaction with a product or service. Although numbers don't need translating, the way people use the scale could be very different. It is not unusual for southern European respondents to give a score that is 10 to 15 per cent higher than their northern European counterparts when using a scale from 1 to 10 when in fact both are saying the same thing – ie that they like product or service to the same degree.

It is also possible that there are different types and levels of truthfulness across cultures and that the small incentives for completing online questionnaires may encourage people to take part in surveys for which they are not qualified. Panel companies protect the identity of their respondents, so a company commissioning the interviews cannot verify the authenticity of the respondent whereas this is easily possible in telephone or face-to-face interviews. Anyone carrying out a panel survey today has to keep an eagle eye on the quality of responses (see Chapter 15).

In some cultures respondents may seek to please interviewers or try and impress them by exaggerating their answers. Anecdotally this is believed to be more common in developing countries than in the more developed countries where respondents don't feel the same pressure to ingratiate.

These variations across different countries and the difficulties that they present are not there to trip us up or stop us doing international research. Indeed, there is no doubt that the commissioning of multi-country studies is likely to increase. Nor is it easy to normalize responses to try and account for some of the cultural differences. Assuming that weighting factors could be applied, they themselves would be subject to error and debate. On balance it is better to work with raw scores and deal with the differences in a discursive way. Over time, a library of understanding will be built up for different countries, providing benchmarks and anchor points that help compare results within a culture or nation.

In many respects qualitative research offers a number of advantages to international market researchers as the approach allows flexibility in both the interviewing and the interpretation of the answers. A local moderator will understand the situational and contextual factors and therefore be able to adapt more readily than a quantitative researcher who has to find a single question that will work across a number of different countries.

Coordinating multi-country studies

International market research studies are likely to require the assistance of a number of research partners. One company may coordinate the research, designing the questionnaire and arranging for translations. Fieldwork partners or panel companies would then carry out the interviews in the different countries, feeding the completed interviews back to the managing company for analysis.

The variations in fieldwork methods and quality control in different countries need careful scrutiny. In North America it may be most appropriate to carry out the interviews online, but this may not be a suitable method in countries where there are low levels of computer ownership and panel companies have not yet built up representative databases. In some countries there could be poor sample frames and literacy problems. Some studies suggest that over 70 per cent of the adult population now has access to a mobile phone, though getting hold of lists of mobile numbers is another problem. Face-to-face interviewing across large geographical expanses is for most companies unrealistically expensive. In countries that are spread across a large geographical area and where telephone penetration is low or difficult to access, the only practical proposition may be to concentrate the data collection in large cities. Mixing research methods and collecting data from a range of different countries will make for some difficulties in terms of quality control and inter-country comparisons.

It is not unusual for an international study covering a number of different countries to require up to three months to complete. The timescale is significantly longer than for a single-country study because questionnaires have to be translated and checked. Questionnaires must be scripted in the different languages and the routing needs checking to ensure that respondents are always directed to the correct questions.

The quality of the lists from which the sample is selected in a particular country will be another important variable. Cooperation rates vary from country to country. Holidays take place at different times around the world and can interrupt a fieldwork programme. It is evident therefore that an international study requires a highly efficient research manager to plan and control the fieldwork programme.

It should be clear from this discussion that international research is significantly more expensive than single-country research. The larger sample sizes covering different countries, the translation costs of the questionnaire, the complexity of coordinating different country studies and the costs of buying in fieldwork from fieldwork agencies will usually take the costs to well in excess of six figures.

Top tips

- Give yourself more time for an international project. You will need it for the more complicated fieldwork. A project that would take eight weeks in just one country can be expected to take 10 to 12 weeks across a number of countries.

- Foreign translations of questionnaires need great care. Use professional translators rather than foreign interviewers. It may be necessary and relevant that the translations are checked by members of the research sponsor's team. Make sure that suggested changes are genuine and not petty arguments about style (or even worse, suggested changes to the questions themselves).

- Interviews (by telephone or face to face) should be carried out by nationals of a country in their mother tongue.

- If the fieldwork is subcontracted to a number of agencies in different countries, keep a very tight rein on both the quality of the interviews and the timetable. Ask to see a sample of the early interviews from each agency and give feedback on the quality.

- Don't assume that respondents in different countries of the world will answer questions in the same way. In developing countries there is a much higher level of agreement with questions than in fully developed countries. When making inter-country comparisons of the data, you will have to take this into consideration.

- Take care when choosing panel companies for online research in international markets. The research quality will be determined by the quality of the panel.

Using desk research (secondary research) to carry out international market research

Whereas surveys are expensive and time-consuming when they cover multiple countries, desk research is, by comparison, relatively easy. Today we are blessed with websites that allow inter-country comparisons at the click of a button. Some of these are government sponsored:

- The CIA (Central Intelligence Agency) is an independent US government agency and produces *The World Factbook*, which provides information on 267 countries around the world. It is an excellent source of statistics on their history, people, government, economy and geography. See **https://www.cia.gov/library/publications/the-world-factbook**.

- The OECD (The Organisation for Economic Cooperation and Development) provides copious statistics on many developing countries. It also has a fact book that can be downloaded with statistics on population, income, prices, energy and transportation, education, public finance and health. See **http://www.oecd.org/statistics/**.

- The United Nations collects statistics and has many publications providing comparable figures for countries throughout the world. See **http://unstats.un.org/unsd/default.htm**. It has a specific website called

UN Comtrade (United Nations Commodity Trade Statistics Database), which provides statistics on over 170 different countries, allowing researchers to interrogate imports and exports of numerous different products and commodities from each country. See **http://comtrade.un.org/db/default.aspx**.

- Eurostat is the statistical office of the European Union and provides volumes of statistics at European level that enable comparisons between countries and regions. See **http://epp.eurostat.ec.europa.eu/portal/page/portal/ eurostat/home/**.

- Every country has its own government statistical department with a website that provides detailed statistics. Independent websites also bring together these international statistics and can be a useful starting point for desk research. One such website is NationMaster, which draws on the CIA World Factbook, the UN and the OECD to generate maps and graphs of all kinds that can readily be downloaded. See **http://www.nationmaster.com/ index.php**.

See also Chapter 5 for more on desk research.

These sites are excellent starting points for obtaining data that help with the assessment of the size of a market – a fundamental requirement for many international marketing plans. In considering the opportunity for a product or service in different countries around the world, it is necessary to have a reasonable estimate of the market size and what drives it. Whatever drives the market size can be used to 'model' the market by applying the drivers across different geographies. For example, an obvious driver of the market for workplace gloves is the number of workers in an industry. In addition to knowing the number of workers in an industry, it would also be necessary to have other inputs such as the proportion of those workers who actually wear gloves and how long they wear them before they are thrown away. Different estimates can be put into the model to see their effect.

Market-size modelling is best done in the first instance in a geography where there is good data on the drivers of the market. Such data enable the researcher to assess the model and the algorithm before it is applied to other countries. Applying the algorithm to another country might require ratios and weightings to account for a lower level of development or different levels of product consumption. For example, it may be possible to apply a market research algorithm developed in the United States to similar developed countries such as Canada or countries in north-west Europe. However, the algorithm may require some adjustments to take account of local characteristics in developing countries. In the example that was given about workplace gloves, an adjustment would have to be made to the model if applied to China, where fewer people wear gloves in the workplace, the gloves cost less and, when they are worn, they are worn for a longer period of time.

In addition to the picture that can be developed of the market-size opportunity around the world, desk research can also provide intelligence on the competition, different types of products used within a market, prices, distribution routes etc. Company websites, articles and published market research reports can all be worthwhile sources of data in building up an understanding of global markets. The use of desk research for these purposes is discussed in more detail in Chapter 5.

SUMMARY

The market research industry began in the United States, which still accounts for nearly 40 per cent of the global market research spend. The market research industry has become more international and it is estimated that around $40 billion is spent on surveys around the world every year.

Six companies now account for around half of all the surveys that are carried out. Despite this domination by the big six, there are thousands of specialist market research companies throughout the world, many of them offering their services only within their local markets.

Online surveys are now more important than telephone and face-to-face interviews combined, and are likely to grow still further in importance as the panel companies that provide access to respondents build stronger positions in developing countries.

Market researchers coordinating multi-country studies are faced with a number of challenges. Cultural differences result in variable answers to the same questions and it is not unusual to have significantly more positive answers to questions from respondents in developing countries. Managing different research methods, organizing multiple translations and keeping multi-country studies on track requires a longer timeline than a study that takes place in just one country.

There are lots of opportunities for using desk research to carry out multi-country studies, especially for assessing market potential and competitive analysis.

Research trends

Drivers of change

The pace of change has increased in every industry, and in the market research industry it has moved like a whirlwind. It seems only a few years ago that the industry thought that punched cards were a major advance in the analysis of data. Today, data is analysed in the blink of an eye. The two biggest impacts on the market research world in the last few years have been the continued move towards globalization and the digital revolution. It is no surprise therefore that both these events have not only affected but transformed the market research industry.

In Chapter 25 we discussed international research and made the point that even the smallest company nowadays can have a website that attracts an international audience. Market researchers working within companies can quickly and inexpensively use the internet to build an understanding of international markets, and online surveys can quickly and relatively inexpensively poll buying habits and attitudes around the world. The digital revolution has resulted in individuals and businesses being more connected than ever, especially through the use of smartphones and tablet computers and the rollout of larger bandwidth networks. These changes, along with the burgeoning use of social media, have generated still more data for market research analysts, to the point where we are challenged to find the nuggets of intelligence in the mass of data that is available. The market research industry has responded to these pressures with new tools and services. These trends have affected both qualitative and quantitative research techniques.

Trends in quantitative research

Passive research techniques

With the recent advances in computing, communications and data storage, there has been a mushrooming of data (often referred to as 'big data' – data sets too big to be analysed on conventional data management programmes such as Excel and Access).

This data can vary from picture sharing and videos to wall-posting and instant messaging and is created through web logs (blogs) and social media sites, with Twitter, Facebook, LinkedIn and YouTube currently being the most popular.

This wealth of information at researchers' fingertips has resulted in an increase in 'passive' or 'inferred' research techniques. Passive research information is gained without asking questions and includes techniques such as internet tracking using cookies and mobile research. These days mobile devices are everyday objects across the world, and thus are capable of providing a constant flow of passive data that can help track people, transactions, and website and social network connections (including length of duration and activities carried out). Cookie analysis is only possible if consent is given by the device user. This can be done through an application (or 'tracker') that is downloaded and installed by those respondents recruited, and all participants need to opt in to having their online data recorded even though all responses are anonymous. This tracker application then collects data about what respondents do online. It can show which articles or websites a respondent has viewed, which products they've looked at or purchased, which search queries they've entered and also which adverts the respondents have been exposed to.

The frightening amount of knowledge that is being picked up on our activities will be used for personal communications as we do our daily round. In the supermarket we may be reminded on a video screen of a special offer that is ideally suited to us because computers have picked up that we are in the store and they know from the data that they hold what products we like. In the same way we could be walking down the street and be enticed into a store by a special offer as Big Brother knows where we are and our predilections. Scary it may be, but we can expect to see more passive research being used to profile our needs and sell us closely targeted products.

Social media monitoring

The subject of social media has already been touched upon in the previous paragraphs. 'Social media' is a term that encompasses a wide range of media forms where the content is generated by individuals and companies and includes internet forums, blogs, social networks, podcasts and video. In its essence it is the bringing together of these different types of media through web and mobile-based technology to assist interaction and communication.

Traditional surveys and focus groups are, of course, vital components of any researcher's toolkit. However, as with all traditional methods, customer opinion is gathered after the event and thus a customer is already satisfied or dissatisfied. Social media monitoring mines data 'of the moment'. This new source of data is growing at an exponential rate. It is real-time information that allows businesses to watch customer trends and behaviours.

The things that people talk about on Twitter, blogs and Facebook can be classified as positive and negative comment. Algorithms can automatically classify comments into different 'sentiments' that can be tracked to see if there is anything that needs a quick reaction. Negative comment can be quickly headed off with some appropriate PR. Positive comment could be used to determine what people are enjoying about a product or service and ensure that they get more of it. Tapping into social media provides an instant pulse reading that shows the health of a brand. It doesn't give all the answers but it does provide clues that cost very little to collect and are 'of the moment'.

We have to be careful of assuming that many market research questions can be answered by an analysis of social media. It is largely made up of banal snippets of conversations and we have to accept that most of it is trivial or even useless. Furthermore, the references that people make to different brands may be indiscriminate or confused. People may spell words incorrectly or use them out of context as they type them into Twitter or on a blog. For example, if we are tracking references to Barclays (the bank), anyone called Barclay or anyone referring to Barclays Premier league could be picked up, and these may not have any relevance to the banking or financial operation in which we are interested. These factors can generally be managed by using Boolean characters to make sure that anything other than references to Barclays and banking and finance is excluded.

We researchers are only just getting to grips with how social media is impacting on us as individuals and businesses, and this will continue to evolve over the next few years. We can expect to see more specialist software designed to sort out the wheat from the chaff in social media with the result that it is sure to become an important and standard tool in our kit bag.

Data mining and analytics

The use of computers for analysing huge sets of data is not new in market research. However, advances are taking place by the day in the way that data can easily be analysed by people without any formal statistical training. The ability to 'mine' data, analyse it, and squeeze more meaning from it, is now much easier. There are quite sophisticated statistical capabilities within Microsoft Excel and many other proprietary software programs that allow market researchers to extract more from their data sets.

Just a few years ago market research presentations were made up of horizontal bar chart after horizontal bar chart. Simple but boring descriptive charts reported what percentage of people gave answers to questions. Today we can quickly and easily map the responses to two different questions in a survey to reveal a more insightful result. Consider a survey in which the market researchers asks the question: 'How likely are you to recommend this company to a colleague or friend?' Elsewhere in the questionnaire there could be a question that asks: 'What share of your spend went on this particular brand?' By plotting the answers to the two questions on an X–Y graph we can quickly see the 'share of wallet' the brand is achieving amongst its loyal and not so loyal customers (as determined by the 'how likely are you to recommend' question). Suddenly we have a result that could lead to a course of marketing action by identifying groups of people who need different types of attention in order to increase their spend on the brand. We can expect to see analytics play a much larger role in market research in the years to come.

Automated surveys

The market research industry has always been labour intensive. Lots of interviewers were needed to carry out face-to-face or telephone interviews. There also had to be data processors and analysts to examine the data and prepare the reports.

The digital revolution has already removed a significant amount of labour from the fieldwork and potentially it could do so from the analysis and reporting. A report template can be set up for tracking surveys to which new data is easily added with very little labour. It may not be long before interpretative text can automatically be added to explain the meaning of the data.

Inevitably this automation will lead to the further commoditization of the research process. The good news for buyers of market research is that it should be possible to carry out surveys more quickly and cheaply. Market researchers will have to respond by using their skills as advisers and consultants, and move away from being 'number jocks'. In truth, market researchers have had this ambition for some years and it is still to be realized.

Trends in qualitative research

The shift in trends is not just towards more quantitative techniques; qualitative research has also seen a number of changes.

Online communities

Online communities are different from online panels in that they are more collaborative by design and are used to engage with customers in a continuous fashion rather than in an ad-hoc way like panel surveys.

Respondents are recruited to take part in an online community based on either their usage or engagement with a particular product or service, or their demographics. The community is therefore a closed network of like-minded respondents that can interact with each other around given subject matter. They develop their views and share their views within the community, so providing expert guidance to the market researchers.

Online communities vary in size; business communities typically have between 50 and 500 members whereas consumer communities can be as large as a few thousand. They straddle the ground between qualitative and quantitative studies.

Even though online communities can be made up of a few thousand members, they are fundamentally a qualitative solution that stimulates both organic and researcher-led conversations. They are typically suited to obtaining quick insights into a subject. They can provide rapid feedback on promotional campaigns. They can be used to check out potential new products or services. They can report on changing trends in terms of attitudes and behaviour.

We can expect online communities to become more popular in the future amongst those companies that have a continuous requirement for market research, especially those that need 'dipstick' surveys and need to be tuned in to an audience so that they can respond to a sudden change of direction.

Text analytics

Verbatim comments and open-ended text are the food and drink of qualitative researchers. Open-ended questions are often included in quantitative surveys, though they are analysed in a quite different way from the free text from focus groups. The verbatim comments to an open question in a semi-structured questionnaire are analysed by developing a coding frame from the first 50 or so responses. Then, reading through all the answers to the question, each is assigned the appropriate code so that a count can be carried out to see what proportion has each comment.

Free text that is generated in depth interviews or focus groups is more difficult to analyse. Market researchers usually replay the recorded interview or read through the transcript, soaking themselves in the responses and making notes that then become the basis of the analysis. This is a major task if there are more than four focus groups or more than 30 depth interviews.

The analysis of such data has challenged market researchers for some time. Software has long been around that does simple things such as measure the frequency with which certain words are mentioned. Word clouds are another way of illustrating the frequency with which words are used, and can be produced at the press of a button to provide a quick visual picture of the things people are saying.

Such aids to analysis, useful as they are, cannot cover the many expressions that can be used to communicate a feeling or emotion. We are not yet at the point where intelligent software can recognize nuances of meaning that would help us more quickly understand word strings and how these link to other subjects in the discussion. This is something that surely will be developed within the next decade.

Making questionnaires more engaging

Gamification

Traditionally, market research has been a structured process in which questions are asked and answers are garnered, whether in a qualitative or quantitative setting. As it becomes more difficult to engage with respondents, it becomes increasingly important to make market research interviews more interesting and exciting. Gamification is the application of game design to questionnaire design to do just that.

In its simplest form, gamification could simply be a change in wording. Most people are familiar with the *Dragons' Den* in the UK or *Shark Tank* in the United States, in which would-be entrepreneurs present their ideas for business to a panel of rich and successful people who are prepared to put money into a scheme they think is viable. Imagine now a question in an online survey that shows a cartoon panel depicting rich and successful people who are judging an idea and you are invited to be one of the panel. Presenting a question in this way could generate additional interest and a new dimension to the way a respondent looks at the subject.

Design and visuals used within questionnaires can also increase engagement and response rates in online surveys through the use of interactive rating scales (drag & drop) and inventive use of video, images and graphics.

It could be argued that qualitative research has always been about gamification; after all, interesting questions and projective techniques are part and parcel of being a qualitative researcher. However, with the development of the online environment through social media, companies have used this to their advantage in gathering customer preferences through gamification on their Facebook page. A well-known US doughnut company designed a game that asked customers to create their perfect drink, with variations of size and different flavours. At first sight it appears to be just an interactive game, but it enabled the company to understand what trade-offs customers make when choosing a drink, and consequently it helped develop new products based on preferences.

Just changing the words of a question can make a difference to the response. For example, a simple question such as 'Make a list of your favourite foods' would typically receive fewer than 10 mentions per response. Changing the question to 'You have one minute to make a list of your favourite foods' is likely to deliver twice as many responses. In the future we can expect to see market researchers using more imagination in the design of their questionnaires to help achieve higher response rates and a better quality of response.

Top tips

- Challenge yourself constantly about the way you carry out your research. Is there a better method? Could the questions be asked in a better way? Are you getting as much as possible from the data?

- Make interviewing more fun for respondents. This may mean shortening questionnaires and/or making questions interactive.

- Be prepared to receive intelligence from as many different sources as possible. Don't rely on a 'big bang' survey to deliver all that you need.

- Be brave and experiment. Try new ways of obtaining data, analysing data and reporting data.

- As well as keeping an open mind for new ideas in market research, don't forget what is tried and tested. It may be old fashioned but it usually works if you ask the right question of the right person.

- Get involved in the research process. Don't abdicate responsibility for obtaining intelligence – it is a vital success factor for any organization.

Trends among users of market research

Market research has for many years been the province of the big and rich companies. This is in part because large companies operate over such a wide territory that they need the help of market researchers to provide a picture of what is going on. They are big enough to afford what has historically been an expensive process. Large companies also recruit business school graduates who have been trained to use market research to minimize the risk of large business decisions. It may not occur to a small company that market research is either possible or necessary.

This is changing. The relative cost of carrying out market research has fallen considerably over the last few decades. Efficiencies in faster and cheaper methods of data collection and analysis mean that market research is now accessible to smaller companies. As has been described in this chapter, market research need not necessarily be the formal and structured approach that it used to be. The founders of the Innocent smoothie drink started selling their products at a music festival in 1999. They put up a sign asking people if they thought they should give up their day jobs to make smoothies and had two bins for the empties in front of the stall, one saying 'yes' and one saying 'no'. At the end of the weekend the 'yes' bin was full. Richard

Reed, Adam Balon and Jon Wright gave up their jobs in advertising and consulting to start the Innocent Drinks Company, which they subsequently sold for many millions to the Coca-Cola Company.

In line with this trend we can also expect to see more and more people within companies having an appreciation of market research so that it is commissioned directly by the person requiring the study rather than through a specialized market research manager. A few years ago large companies had sizeable market research departments that managed the commissioning of market research surveys. As market research has become a commonplace business activity, there is no need for internal specialists to design and manage the relationship with external market research companies.

Specialization in market research skills

The market research industry has grown up. It is no longer a cottage industry employing part-timers; it is made up of international companies with dedicated staff and rigorous processes that are scrutinized and checked for quality. The consolidation of the market research industry will continue, with the big players becoming even more powerful through acquisition. Alongside this consolidation we can also expect small companies to regularly arise to provide personal and specialized services. The cost of entering the market for qualitative market researchers or those providing statistical services is quite small. The market research industry of the future will be polarized, with a small number of huge players on one side and a myriad of small ones on the other.

Within market research companies, the role of market researchers is changing. A few years ago market researchers were expected to know everything about the subject whereas today this is not possible. Market research agencies employ specialists who work in data processing, possibly even in just one area of data processing such as scripting questionnaires. Other people may specialize in online surveys or manage the CATI systems (computer-aided telephone interviewing). There may well be a statistics department that manages conjoint and segmentation studies. It is not unusual for a market research company to employ visualization experts who ensure that presentations and reports are slick and engaging.

In addition to the specialized skill sets that are becoming more important in the market research industry, research analysts often specialize in different subjects. Some may be experts in pharmaceutical research, others in retail markets or electronics. Now the industry has reached maturity we can expect to see more and more specialization take place.

Summary

Globalization and the digital revolution have resulted in major changes to the market research industry. Quantitative research can now be carried out relatively inexpensively across a number of different countries at a speed and costs far less than those that historically made it prohibitive to all but the largest of companies.

The digital revolution has also made possible many new techniques, and market researchers have become more imaginative about the way that questions can be asked. New technology enables market researchers to improve the look and feel of their questionnaires so that they are more fun and connect more closely with our daily lives. These are changes that are likely to become more prevalent in the future, though they will not replace the tried and tested methods that are time-served and proven.

In the future we can expect the market researcher to have new tools such as social media monitoring that deliver a better understanding of the changing market place.

Along with this expansion of research tools there will inevitably be more specialization amongst the market researchers that work in the industry.

Ethics in market research

The importance of ethics in market research

The purpose of market research is to arrive at the truth; to arrive at an understanding of what is actually happening or could happen in a market. In many aspects of market research, judgement is required on the part of the market researcher in deciding what the truth is. Collecting and analysing data to guide decisions of various kinds is a big responsibility and it is essential that the researchers' work is trusted. Ethics determine trust because ethics ensure that absolute honesty is applied at all stages of the project and that no harm will come to anyone from taking part in the project.

Ethics are not legal requirements (although in many societies there is legislation to ensure that things are done the right way). Physicians, dentists, lawyers and journalists operate within a legislative framework but they also are bound by a strong ethical code. In the case of market researchers, the purpose of the ethical code is to safeguard quality, to achieve better evidence and ultimately to win the confidence of both research sponsors and respondents.

There is a difference between ethics and morals. Ethics are rules of conduct which we should adopt as market researchers. Morals are opinions which we market researchers may hold and which may influence our view as to what is right or wrong. For example, you may think it is morally wrong to carry out market research on behalf of a cigarette manufacturer as this could lead to the sale of more cigarettes and therefore more associated disease. Whether it is right or wrong to carry out such research is not the concern of this chapter. Our concern is with the rules that guide market researchers in carrying out surveys and arriving at the truth – irrespective of the purpose of the survey itself.

Examples of ethical dilemmas for market researchers

It may be helpful at the outset to think about some frequently occurring ethical dilemmas faced by market researchers:

- The sponsor of a market research study insists on knowing the contact details of who has participated in the research.
- A market research consultant is asked to find out the results of new product development trials being carried out by a company.
- A respondent is offered $200 to take part in a market research survey.
- A market research company is asked to carry out a mystery shop of a competitor's customers.
- A market researcher chooses to ignore responses from certain respondents when analysing the data.

We will return to these dilemmas later in the chapter and consider how they should be dealt with by professional market researchers.

Principles guiding the ethics of market researchers

There are two basic principles guiding the ethics of market researchers:

1 Researchers should ensure that respondents taking part in market research surveys are in no way harmed or adversely affected by their participation.

2 Researchers should be honest and transparent in all their dealings both with clients and respondents.

The first of these principles is crucial as it means respecting the rights of all respondents. It also demands that researchers maintain the privacy of respondents because once data have been collected and passed into the hands of others, there is no knowing what it could be used for. A respondent could decide to take part in a survey and provide data on their circumstances, attitudes and behaviour which, if passed back to an organization, could be manipulated to sell them something that they don't really want. Data privacy laws exist in many countries and there is a legal requirement of market researcher's to comply with them. Where data privacy laws do not exist, or are lax, the researcher should always act in the best interests of respondents and treat all specific respondent data as confidential. Specific data on respondents can only be passed back to a sponsoring organization if all the following conditions are met:

- The respondent is told the true purpose of the study; that it is for market research purposes only and that no sales pressure will be exerted as a result of taking part in the study.
- The respondent is told the identity of the research sponsor.
- The respondent agrees that the survey data can be passed to the sponsor.

In all other cases the research sponsor should only receive pooled data.

If data is collected directly by the research sponsor, respondents who take part in a survey will know that their answers will be fed directly to that organization. The respondent has been informed of who is seeking the information and what it will be used for and consented to the submission. Equally, a market research company, acting on behalf of a research sponsor, could make it clear to respondents that the data will be passed directly to that sponsor. In such a case, the sponsor should be clearly identified and not hide under some cloak of anonymity so that respondents know where the intelligence is going and what it will be used for. They are then in an informed position to decide whether or not they take part in the study.

One important reason for data privacy in market research surveys is to protect respondents from the unscrupulous use of surveys that are not really surveys at all. It is not unknown for companies to pretend to be carrying out market research when in fact they are seeking data specifically to gain access to potential customers to sell their products or services. This misrepresentation of the purpose of the survey is dishonoring the principle that researchers should at all times be transparent in their dealings with respondents. A respondent who thinks that they are contributing to a survey in the hope that the results will be used to make better products and services, does not want that data to be used against them in a sales situation. Market researchers refer to this as selling under the guise of market research or SUGGING. Honesty as to the true purpose of the survey is fundamental to the professionalism of market researchers.

Mystery shopping is a specialist field of market research in which researchers pretend to be customers or potential customers of an organization in order to assess its performance. If, during the mystery shop, the researcher buys a product, such action would be considered ethical. However, if the researcher poses as a customer and has no intention of buying a product (for example visits car showrooms and pretends to be interested in buying a car) then it would be a flagrant waste of the dealers' time. This type of research would be ethical if the mystery shop is with the research sponsors' dealers but unethical if the mystery shop is with dealers of competitor companies.

Market researchers provide competitive intelligence. However, this has to be within the confines of the ethics that guide the market researcher. For example, it would be unethical for a market researcher to pretend to be a student, a customer or a journalist (that is someone other than a market researcher) in an attempt to infiltrate a company in order to find out something that is not already in the public domain. To obtain such intelligence by subterfuge would not only be unethical, it would also be illegal.

Incentivizing respondents for research

It is commonplace (and entirely legal) for respondents to be offered compensation for giving up their time to take part in market research studies. People who are members of market research panels receive points which accumulate and which can be converted to cash or goods. People attending focus groups receive an honorarium to cover their travel costs and time. In medical studies physicians receive payment for taking part in surveys. In some business to business market research studies, respondents may receive a sum of money or an Amazon gift token as an incentive or a thank you for completing an interview.

Paying respondents incentives raises ethical issues. First of all, how big is the incentive? The general public taking part in consumer surveys (for example in a panel survey) would normally receive an award of much less than a dollar. In telephone surveys respondents normally do not receive incentives except perhaps the vague promise that their help will result in improved products and services. However, in business to business and medical research, respondents may receive between $100 and $200 if they are hard to get hold of and their opinions are much valued.

It could be argued that paying respondents is potentially biasing their views as they may feel pressure to make up answers or pretend that they are in a decision-making capacity when in fact they are not. If the respondent is told the identity of the sponsor of the research study, it could be claimed that the payment is in some way a bribe, encouraging that person to think more positively of the research sponsor. Furthermore, these payments in theory carry a tax liability though in reality this is the ethical dilemma of the respondent who should decide whether or not to admit it on their tax return.

Often market researchers provide respondents with the opportunity to donate the incentive to a charitable cause if they do not want to accept it themselves.

Giving a respondent sample goods made by the research sponsor might be seen as unethical in that by so doing the research could be viewed as 'placing products' (as in a promotion) rather than collecting data.

It is quite common in some surveys for respondents to be incentivized by a free prize drawing instead of a monetary payment to each participant. As with individual incentives, this is an ethical means of promoting the survey as long as a number of rules and conditions are adhered to. For more information on this subject the reader is encouraged to refer to the website of the Market Research Society. (See the paper *MRS Regulations for Administering Incentives and Free Prize Draws*.)

Returning to the ethical dilemmas

Thinking back to the ethical dilemmas posed earlier in this chapter, let us consider how they should be viewed by market researchers.

TABLE 27.1   Ethical dilemmas from the perspective of market researchers

The dilemma	The ethical response
The sponsor of a market research study insists on knowing the contact details of who has taken part in the research.	The only occasion in which specific data on a respondent can be fed back to the research sponsor is when the sponsor's identity is known to the respondent and the purpose of the research has been explained and the respondent gives express permission for the feedback.
A market research consultant is asked to find out the results of new product development trials being carried out by a company.	If any such data is not in the public domain then it should be deemed as confidential and market researchers should not report it – even if they were to obtain the information by eavesdropping on a conversation in a bar or on a train.
A respondent is offered $200 to take part in a market research survey.	It is an established practice in market research (and completely legal) that respondents can be offered an honorarium for taking part in research studies as long as there is total transparency as to the purpose of the research. Of course, there is no compulsion for respondents to take the incentive.
A market research company is asked to carry out a mystery shop of a competitor's customers.	The mystery shop would be acceptable if the goods or services are paid for (for example a mystery shopper paid for and stayed in a competitor's hotel). It would be unethical if there is no intention to actually buy a competitor's product or service for in such cases it would be wasting someone's time.
A market researcher chooses to ignore responses from certain respondents when analysing the data.	It would be acceptable and ethical to ignore responses which are known to be 'rogue' or wrong. It would be unacceptable to ignore data that tells the truth but is hidden because it is unpalatable.

Top tips

- Familiarize yourself with the Market Research Society's *Code Of Conduct*. Live by it.

- Let other people you are working with know the ethical rules. Be clear about these because everyone will have their own interpretation of them.

- Be firm and do not give in to pressure to compromise your ethics.

- Be responsible. If you say you are going to do something, do it so that people learn to trust you.

- When asked to carry out a survey, ask yourself two questions: 'Will anyone be harmed?', 'In carrying out a survey can I be totally honest and transparent?'. If the answer to the first question is yes and the answer to the second question is no, the survey could be unethical.

- If in doubt 'protect the source'. Data privacy of respondents is really important.

- Put yourself in respondents' shoes. If the shoes feel comfortable, what you are doing is probably ethical.

SUMMARY

Integrity is a watchword for market researchers. Market researchers are commissioned to find out the truth by collecting and analyzing data. They have a responsibility to respondents who provide data and clients and sponsors who pay for the studies.

Integrity requires an ethical approach to market research. Underpinning this approach is the requirement for market researchers to be honest and transparent in everything they do related to the collection and reporting of data. What is more, they should never indulge in practices which could harm or mislead respondents or research sponsors.

The key principles of the market researcher's code of conduct are:

1 Taking part in market research surveys is entirely voluntary and based on informed consent.

2 Researchers should be honest and transparent in relationships with both clients and respondents.

3 Researchers should be transparent as to the subject and purpose of data collection.

4 Researchers should respect the confidentiality of information collected and the data privacy of respondents should be honored at all times.

5 Researchers should respect the rights and well-being of all respondents.

6 Researchers should ensure that respondents are not harmed or adversely affected by taking part in market research projects.

7 Researchers shall balance the needs of respondents, research sponsors with their best professional judgment.

8 Researchers shall use their expert professional judgment in the design, conduct and reporting of the research projects.

9 Research projects shall be carried out by people with appropriate training, qualifications and experience.

10 Researchers shall at all times consider their reputation and the integrity of the profession when designing, carrying out and reporting market research studies.

A useful summary of the code of conduct for market researchers can be found on the Market Research Society's website **www.mrs.org.uk**.

BIBLIOGRAPHY

Chapter 1: Introduction

Aaker, D A, Kumar, V and Day, G S (2000) *Market Research*, 7th Edition, John Wiley, Chichester

Alvi, M and Siddiqui, B (2013) *An Empirical Analysis of New Product by Using Models of Market Research*, MPRA, Munich

Baines, P and Chanarker, B (2002) *Introducing Marketing Research*, John Wiley, Chichester

Bell, E and Bryman, A (2015) *Business Research Methods*, 4th Edition, Oxford University Press

Birn, R (ed) (2002) *The International Handbook of Market Research Techniques*, 2nd Edition, Kogan Page, London

Bradley, N (2010) *Marketing Research: Tools and techniques*, Oxford University Press

Crimp, M and Wright, L T (1995) An introduction to the marketing research process, in *The Marketing Research Process*, 4th Edition, 1–19, Prentice-Hall, London

Goffin, K, Varnes, C J, van der Hoven, C and Koners, U (2012) Beyond the voice of the customer: ethnographic market research, *Research-Technology Management*, 55 (4), 45–54

Hague, P (2002) *Marketing Research*, 3rd Edition, Kogan Page, London

Hague, P and Jackson, P (1992) *Marketing Research In Practice*, Kogan Page, London

Holbrook, Morris B (1999) *Consumer Value: A framework for analysis and research*, Routledge, London

Jackson, P (1994) *Buying Market Research*, Kogan Page, London

Jackson, P (1997) *Quality in Market Research*, Kogan Page, London

Kent, R (1993) Perspectives on marketing research, in *Marketing Research in Action*, 1–21, Routledge, London

McGivern, Y (2002) *The Practice of Market and Social Research: An introduction*, FT Prentice-Hall, London

McNeil, Ruth (2005) *Business to Business Market Research: Understanding and measuring business markets*, Kogan Page, London

Proctor, T (2000) *Essentials of Market Research*, Pearson Education, Essex

Punch, Keith F (2005) *Introduction to Social Research*, Sage, London

Smith, D V L and Fletcher, J H (2001) *Inside Information: Making use of marketing data*, John Wiley, Chichester

Zikmund, W, Babin, B, Carr, J, and Griffin, M (2012) *Business Research Methods*, Cengage Learning, Boston

Chapter 2: Uses of market research

Beall, Anne E (2010) *Strategic Market Research: A guide to conducting research that drives businesses*, iUniverse, Bloomington, USA

Birn, R J (2004) *The Effective Use of Market Research: How to drive and focus better business decisions*, 4th Edition, Kogan Page, London

Brown, Lyndon (2008) *Market Research and Analysis*, Wildside Press, Rockville, USA

Callingham, Martin (2004) *Market Intelligence: How and why organizations use market research*, Kogan Page, London

Grover and Vriens (2006) *The Handbook of Marketing Research: Uses, misuses, and future advances*, Sage, London

Kapferer, J N (2012) *The New Strategic Brand Management: Advanced insights and strategic thinking*, Kogan Page, London

Møller Bjerrisgaard, S and Kjeldgaard, D (2013) How market research shapes market spatiality: A global governmentality perspective, *Journal of Macromarketing*, 33 (1), 29–40

Valos, M, Ball, D, Callaghan, W (2007) The impact of Porter's strategy types on the role of market research and customer relationship management, *Marketing Intelligence & Planning*, 25 (2), 147–56

Wedel, M and Kamakura, W (2012) Market segmentation: Conceptual and methodological foundations Vol 8, Springer Science & Business Media, Berlin

Chapter 3: Market research design

Chisnall, P M (2001) *Marketing Research*, McGraw-Hill Education, Europe

Goodyear, M J (1990) Qualitative research, in *A Handbook of Market Research Techniques*, ed Birn, R, Hague, P and Vangelder, P, Kogan Page, London

Gray, D E (2013) *Doing Research in the Real World*, Sage, New York

Hair, J, Bush, R and Ortinau, D (2002) *Marketing Research*, McGraw-Hill Education, Europe

Hair Jr, J F, Wolfinbarger, M, Money, A H, Samouel, P, and Page, M J (2015) *Essentials of Business Research Methods*, Routledge, New York

Hyman, M and Sierra, J (2010) *Market Research Kit for Dummies*, Wiley Publishing, Indiana

Price, R A, Wrigley, C and Straker, K (2015) Not just what they want, but why they want it: Traditional market research to deep customer insights, *Qualitative Market Research*, 18 (2), 230–48

Takhar-Lail, A and Ghorbani, A (2015) *Market Research Methodologies: Multi-method and qualitative*

Wilson, A (2006) *Marketing Research: An integrated approach*, Pearson, London

Chapter 4: Qualitative research

Ereaut, G, Imms, M and Callingham M (2002) *Qualitative Market Research: Principle and practice*, 3rd Edition, Sage, California

Flick, U (2014) An Introduction to Qualitative Research, 5th Edition Sage, California

Guercini, S (2014) New qualitative research methodologies in management, *Management Decision*, **52** (4), 662–74

Keegan, S (2009) *Qualitative Research: Good decision making through understanding people, cultures and markets*, Kogan Page, London

Krueger, R A and Casey M A (2008) *Focus Groups: A practical guide for applied research*, 4th Edition, Sage, California

Merriam, S B and Tisdell, E J (2015) *Qualitative Research: A guide to design and implementation*, 4th Edition, Jossey-Bass, San Francisco

Stewart, D W, Shamdasani, P N and Rook, D W (2015) *Focus Groups: Theory and practice*, 3rd Edition Sage, California

Taylor, G R (2005) *Integrating Quantitative and Qualitative Methods in Research*, 2nd Edition, University Press of America, Lanham, Maryland

Tracy, S J (2013) *Qualitative Research Methods: Collecting evidence, crafting analysis, communicating impact*, Wiley-Blackwell, West Sussex

Chapter 5: Desk research

Beri, G C (2013) *Marketing Research*, Tata McGraw-Hill Education, Noida

Jackson, P (1994) *Desk Research*, Kogan Page, London

Jacob, F and Weiber, R (2015) Business market research, in *Fundamentals of Business-to-Business Marketing*, Springer International Publishing, 275–325

Rahman, M I, Alarifi, A, Eden, R, and Sedera, D (2014) Archival analysis of service desk research: New perspectives on design and delivery, 25th Australasian Conference on Information Systems, Auckland

Van der Hoven, C, Michea, A, Varnes, C, and Goffin, K (2013) Giving the customer a voice: A study of market research methods and their perceived effectiveness in NPD, 20th International Product Development Management Conference, Cranfield

Chapter 6: Focus groups

Bristol, T and Fern, E (2003) The effects of interaction on consumers' attitudes in focus groups, *Psychology and Marketing*, **20** (5), 433–54

Budden, M (1999) Focus groups: theory and practice, *Psychology and Marketing*, 16 (4)

Edmunds, H (1999) *The Focus Group Research Handbook*, NTC, Lincolnwood, Illinois

Ereaut, G, Imms, M and Callingham, M (eds) (2002) *Qualitative Market Research: Principle and practice*, Sage, London

Esser, W (1995) From the 'triad' to a 'quadriga': A systematic qualitative marketing research programme for the Far East, *Marketing and Research Today*, **23** (1), 20–24

Gabriel, C (1990) The validity of qualitative market research, *Journal of the Market Research Society*, (32) 507–20

Gray, D E (2013) *Doing Research in the Real World*, Sage, New York

Greenbaum, T L (2000) *Moderating Focus Groups: A practical guide for group facilitation*, Sage, London

Griggs, S (1987) Analysing qualitative data, *Journal of the Market Research Society*, **29** (1), 15–34

Hague, P (2002) *Market Research*, 3rd Edition, Kogan Page, London

Hall, J (2000) Moderators must motivate focus groups, *Marketing News*, **34** (19)

Kreugar, R A (1998) *Developing Questions for Focus Groups* (Focus Group Kit 3), Sage, California

Kreugar, R A (1998) *Moderating Focus Groups* (Focus Group Kit 4), Sage, California

Kreugar, R A (1998) *Analyzing and Reporting Focus Group Results* (Focus Group Kit 6), Sage, California

Kreugar, R A and Casey, M A (2000) *Focus Groups: A practical guide for applied research*, 3rd Edition, Sage, California

Lazarsfeld, P (1972) *Qualitative Analysis: Historical and critical essays*, Allyn & Bacon, Boston

Lazarsfeld, P (1986) *The Art of Asking Why*, Advertising Research Foundation, New York, (original work produced in 1934 in the National Marketing Review)

Lesley, Y (2001) Focus group results rule changes, *Marketing Magazine*, **106** (9)

Mariampolski, H (2001) *Qualitative Market Research: A comprehensive guide*, Sage, London

McQuarrie, E F (1996) *The Market Research Toolbox: A concise guide for beginners*, Sage, California

Merton, R K and Kendall, P L (1946) The focused interview, *American Journal of Sociology* (51) 541–57

Morgan, D L (1998) *The Focus Group Guidebook* (Focus Group Kit 1), Sage, California

Patino, A, Pitta, D A and Quinones, R (2012) Social media's emerging importance in market research, *Journal of Consumer Marketing*, **29** (3), 233–37

Stewart, D W and Shamdasani, P N (2014) *Focus Groups: Theory and practice* (Vol 20), Sage, New York

Van der Hoven, C, Michea, A, Varnes, C, and Goffin, K (2013) Giving the customer a voice: A study of market research methods and their perceived effectiveness in NPD, 20th International Product Development Management Conference, Cranfield

Warren, M and Craig, A (1991) Qualitative research product and policy, *Marketing and Research Today*, **19** (1), 43–49

Chapter 7: Depth interviews

Chirban, J T (1996) *Interviewing in Depth: The interactive-relational approach*, Sage, London

Goldman, A E (1987) *The Group Depth Interview: Principles and practice*, Prentice-Hall International, London

Gummesson, E (2000) *Qualitative Methods in Management Research*, 2nd Edition, Sage, California

Gummitt, J (1980) *Interviewing Skills*, Industrial Society, London

Kahn, R and Cannel, C (1957) *The Dynamics of Interviewing*, John Wiley, New York and Chichester

Ormston, R, Spencer, L, Barnard, M and Snape, D (2013), The foundations of qualitative research, in *Qualitative research practice: A guide for social science students and researchers*, Sage

Robson, C (2001) *Real World Research*, Blackwell, Oxford

Sarstedt, M and Mooi, E (2014) The market research process, in *A Concise Guide to Market Research* 11–23, Springer Berlin Heidelberg

Silverman, D (1998) *Qualitative Research, Theory, Method and Practice*, Sage, London

Witell, L, Kristensson, P, Gustafsson, A and Löfgren, M (2011) Idea generation: Customer co-creation versus traditional market research techniques, *Journal of Service Management*, **22** (2), 140–59

Chapter 8: Observation and ethnography

Ackroyd, S and Hughes, J (1992) *Data Collection in Context*, 2nd Edition, Longman, London

Boote, J and Mathews, A (1999) Saying is one thing; doing is another: The role of observation in marketing research, *Qualitative Market Research*, **2** (1), 15–21

Bryman, A and Bell, E (2015) *Business Research Methods*, Oxford University Press

Buck, S (1990) Peoplemeters, in *A Handbook of Market Research Techniques*, ed Birn, R, Hague, P and Vangelder, P, Kogan Page, London

Cayla, J and Arnould, E (2013) Ethnographic stories for market learning, *Journal of Marketing*, **77** (4), 1–16

Croft, Boddy and Pentucci (2007) Say what you mean, mean what you say: An ethnographic approach to male and female conversations, *International Journal of Market Research*, **6** (49)

Fox, K (2005) *Watching the English: The hidden rules of English behaviour*, Hodder & Stoughton, London

Gillham, B (2008) *Observation Techniques: Structured and unstructured approaches*, Continuum International Publishing, London

Goffin, K, Varnes, C J, van der Hoven, C and Koners, U (2012) Beyond the voice of the customer: ethnographic market research, *Research-Technology Management*, 55 (4), 45–54

Gray, D E (2013) *Doing Research in the Real World*, Sage, New York

Mariampolski, H (2006) *Ethnography for Marketers: A guide to consumer immersion*, Sage, London

Takhar-Lail, A, and Ghorbani, A (2015) *Market Research Methodologies: Multi-method and qualitative*, n.p., n.d.

Chapter 9: Quantitative research

Balnaves M, Caputi, P (2001) *Introduction to Quantitative Research Methods: An investigation approach*, Sage, London

Bock, T and Sergeant, J (2002) Small sample market research, *International Journal of Market Research*, **44** (2), 235–44

Curwin, J and Slater, R (2007) *Quantitative Methods For Business Decisions*, 6th Edition, Thomson Learning, London

Evans, J R and Mathur A (2005) The value of online surveys, *Internet Research*, **15** (2) 195–219

Martin, W E and Birdgmon, K D (2012) *Quantitative and Statistical Research Methods: From hypothesis to results*, John Wiley, Hoboken, New Jersey

Sarstedt, M and Mooi, E (2014) *A Concise Guide to Market Research: The process, data and methods using IBM SPSS statistics*, Springer-Verlag, Berlin

Taylor, G R (2005) *Integrating Quantitative and Qualitative Methods in Research*, 2nd Edition, University Press of America, Lanham, Maryland

Chapter 10: Sampling and statistics

Baker, M J (1991) Sampling, in *Research for Marketing*, 100–31, Macmillan, London

Brown, P J B (1991) Exploring geodemographics, in *Handling Geographical Information*, ed Masser, I and Blakemore, M, Longman, London

Cowan, C D (1991) Using multiple sample frames to improve survey coverage, quality, and costs, *Marketing Research*, 3(4), 66–69

Crimp, M and Wright, L T (1995) Sampling in survey research, in *The Marketing Research Process*, 4th Edition, Prentice-Hall, London

Denscombe, M (2014) *The Good Research Guide: For small-scale social research projects*, McGraw-Hill Education (UK)

Dent, T (1992) How to design for a more reliable customer sample, *Business Marketing*, **17** (2), 73–77

Evans, N and Webber, R (1995) Geodemographic profiling: MOSAIC and EuroMOSAIC, in *The Market Research Process*, 4th Edition, ed Crimp, M and Wright, L T, Prentice-Hall, London

Ghorbani, A, Moridsadat, H, and Jafarzadeh, F (2014) *Market Research Methodologies: Multi-method and qualitative approaches*, Business Science References, Hershey

Gy, P M (1998) *Sampling for Analytical Purposes*, (trans A G Royle), John Wiley, Chichester

Hague, P and Harris, P (1993) *Sampling and Statistics*, Kogan Page, London

Hair Jr, J F, Wolfinbarger, M, Money, A H, Samouel, P, and Page, M J (2015) *Essentials Of Business Research Methods*, Routledge, London

Leventhal, B (1990) Geodemographics, in *A Handbook of Market Research Techniques*, ed Birn, R, Hague, P and Vangelder, P, Kogan Page, London

Marsh, C and Scarborough, E (1990) Testing nine hypothesis about quota sampling, *Journal of the Market Research Society* (32) 485–506

Sarstedt, M and Mooi, E (2014) *A Concise Guide to Market Research: The process, data and methods using IBM SPSS statistics*, Springer-Verlag, Berlin

Semon, T T (1994b) Save a few bucks on sample size, risk millions in opportunity loss, *Marketing News*, 28 (1), 19

Shiffler, R E and Adams, A J (1987) A correction for biasing effects of pilot sample size on sample size determination, *Journal of Marketing Research*, 24 (3), 319–21

Sleight, P (1993) *Targeting Customers: How to use geodemographics and lifestyle data in your business*, NTC Publications, Henley-on-Thames

Sleight, P and Leventhal, B (1989) Applications of geodemographics to research and marketing, *Journal of the Market Research Society*, 31, 75–101

Swan, J E, O'Connor, S J and Seung, D L (1991) A framework for testing sampling bias and methods of bias reduction in a telephone survey, *Marketing Research*, 3 (4), 23–34

Watson, M A (1992) Researching minorities, *Journal of the Market Research Society*, 34 (4), 337–44

Whitlark, D, Geurts, M D, Christensen, H B, Kays, M A and Lawrence, K D (1993) Selecting sample sizes for marketing research surveys: Advantages of using the coefficient of variation, *Marketing and Research Today*, 21 (1), 50–54

Zikmund, W, Babin, B, Carr, J, and Griffin, M (2012) *Business Research Methods*, Cengage Learning, Boston

Chapter 11: Questionnaire design

Bolton, R (1993) Pretesting questionnaires: Content analyses of respondents' concurrent verbal protocols, *Marketing Science*, 12 (3), 280–303

Brace, Ian (2008) *Questionnaire Design: How to plan, structure and write survey material for effective market research*, Kogan Page London

Bradburn, Sudman, Wansink (2004) *Asking Questions: The definitive guide to questionnaire design – for market research, political polls, and social and health questionnaires*, J Wiley, San Francisco

Crimp, M and Wright, L T (1995) Questionnaire design, in *The Marketing Research Process*, 4th Edition, 132–62, Prentice-Hall, London

De Vaus, D (2013) *Surveys In Social Research*, Routledge, London

Diamontopoulos, A, Reynolds, N and Schlegelmilch, B (1994) Pretesting in questionnaire design: The impact of respondent characteristics on error detection, *Journal of the Market Research Society*, (36) 295–313

Douglas, V (1995) Questionnaire too long? Try variable, *Marketing News*, **29** (5), 38

Fink, A (1995a) *How to Ask Survey Questions*, Sage, California

Fink, A (1995b) *The Survey Handbook*, Sage, California

Foddy, W (1994) *Constructing Questions for Interviews and Questionnaires*, Cambridge University Press

Fowler Jr, F J (2013) *Survey Research Methods*, Sage, New York

Frazer, L (2000), *Questionnaire Design and Administration: A practical guide*, John Wiley, Brisbane

Gillham, B (2007) *Developing a Questionnaire*, Continuum International Publishing, London

Hague, P (1993) *Questionnaire Design*, Kogan Page, London

Hair Jr, J F, Wolfinbarger, M, Money, A H, Samouel, P and Page, M J (2015) *Essentials of Business Research Methods*, Routledge, London

Holbrook, A L (2014) *Introduction to Questionnaire Design*, Survey Research Laboratory

Makienko, I, and Bernard, E K (2012) Teaching applied value of marketing research: A questionnaire design project, *The International Journal of Management Education*, 10 (2), 139–45

Martin-Williams, J (1986) Questionnaire design, in *Consumer Market Research Handbook*, 3rd Edition, ed Worcester, R and Downham, J, ESOMAR, McGraw-Hill, London

Oppenheim, A (1970), *Questionnaire Design and Attitude Measurement*, Heinemann Educational, London

Payne, S (1951) *The Art of Asking Questions*, Princeton University Press, Princeton, New Jersey

Peterson, Robert (2000) *Constructing Effective Questionnaires*, Sage, London

Prunk, T (1994) The value of questionnaires, *Target Marketing*, **17** (10), 37–40

Sudman, S and Bradburn, N M (1982) *Asking Questions: A practical guide to questionnaire design*, Jossey-Bass, Chichester

Vittles, P (1994) Question time, *Health Service Journal* (May), 34–34

Wilson, N (1994) *Questionnaire Design: A practical introduction*, University of Ulster, Newtown Abbey

Chapter 12: Face-to-face interviewing

Chrzanowska, J (2002) *Interviewing Groups and Individuals in Qualitative Market Research*, Sage, London

Eboli, L and Mazzulla, G (2012) Transit passenger perceptions: Face-to-face versus web-based survey, in *Journal of the Transportation Research Forum*, 50 (1)

Guengel, P C, Berchman, T R, and Cannell, C E (1983) *General Interviewing Techniques: A self-instructional workbook for telephone and personal interviewer training*, Survey Research Centre, University of Michigan, Ann Arbor

Holbrook, A L and Green, M C (2003) Telephone vs face-to-face interviewing of national probability samples with long questionnaires: Comparisons of respondent satisficing and social desirability response bias, *Public Opinion Quarterly*, **67**, 79–125

Kim, W C and Mauborgne, R (2015) *Blue Ocean Strategy: How to create uncontested market space and make the competition irrelevant*, Expanded Edition, Harvard Business Review Press

Rowley, J (2012) Conducting research interviews, *Management Research Review*, 35 (3/4), 260–71

Torrington, D (1991) *Management Face to Face*, Prentice-Hall, London

West, B T, Kreuter, F, and Jaenichen, U (2013) 'Interviewer' effects in face-to-face surveys: A function of sampling, measurement error, or nonresponse?, *Journal of Official Statistics*, 29 (2)

Chapter 13: Telephone interviewing

Collins, M, Sykes, W, Wilson, P and Blackshaw, N (1988) Non-response: The UK experience, in *Telephone Survey Methodology*, ed Groves, R M *et al*, John Wiley, New York

Curry, J (1990) Interviewing by PC: What we could not do before, *Applied Marketing Research*, 30 (1), 30–37

DePaulo, P and Weitzer, R (1994) Interactive phone technology delivers survey data quickly, *Marketing News*, 28 (1), p 15

Dickson, J R, Faria, A J and Frieson, D (1994) Live v automated telephone interviewing, *Marketing Research*, 6 (1), 28–35

Fowler Jr, F J (2013) *Survey Research Methods*, Sage, New York

Havice, M J and Banks, M J (1991) Live and automated telephone surveys: A comparison of human interviews and an automated technique, *Journal of the Market Research Society*, 33, 91–102

Mattila, M M (2013) SMS feedback against phone interview as advertising follow-up measuring tools, in *Proceedings in GV-Global Virtual Conference* (No 1)

O'Rourke, D and Blair, J (1983) Improving random respondent selection in telephone interviews, *Journal of Marketing Research*, 20, 428–32

Perkins, W S and Roundy, J (1993) Discrete choice surveys by telephone, *Journal of the Academy of Marketing Science*, 21 (1), 33–38

Zikmund, W, Babin, B, Carr, J and Griffin, M (2012) *Business Research Methods*, Cengage Learning, Boston

Chapter 14: Self-completion questionnaires

Anja S Göritz, (2004) The impact of material incentives on response quantity, response quality, sample composition, survey outcome, and cost in online access panels, *International Journal of Market Research*, 46 Quarter 3

Blyth, W (1990) Panels and diaries, in *A Handbook of Market Research Techniques*, ed Birn, R, Hague, P and Vangelder, P, Kogan Page, London

Brehm, J (1994) Stubbing our toes for a foot in the door? Incentives and survey response, *International Journal of Public Opinion Research*, 6 (1), 45–64

Brown, M (1994) What price response?, *Journal of the Market Research Society*, 36, 227–44

Bryman, A, and Bell, E (2015) *Business Research Methods*, Oxford University Press

Denscombe, M (2014) *The Good Research Guide: For small-scale social research projects*, McGraw-Hill Education (UK)

Gaynor, J (1994) An experiment with cash incentives on a personal interview survey, *Journal of the Market Research Society*, 36, 360–65

Helgeson, J G (1994) Receiving and responding to a mail survey: A phenomenological examination, *Journal of the Market Research Society*, 36, 339–47

Jacob, F, and Weiber, R (2015) Business Market Research, in *Fundamentals of Business-to-Business Marketing*, Springer International Publishing

Kamins, M A (1989) The enhancement of response rates to a mail survey through a labelled probe foot-in-the-door approach, *Journal of the Market Research Society*, 31 (2), 273–83

Martin, C L (1994) The impact of topic interest on mail survey response behaviour, *Journal of the Market Research Society*, 36, 327–38

Mason, N (1990) EPOS, in *A Handbook of Market Research Techniques*, ed Birn, R, Hague, P and Vangelder, P, Kogan Page, London

Meier, E (1991) Response rate trends in Britain, *Admap*, 26 (11), 41–44

Stoop, I, and Harrison, E (2012) Classification of Surveys, in *Handbook of Survey Methodology for the Social Sciences*, Springer, New York

Swires-Hennessy, E and Drake, M (1992) The optimum time at which to conduct survey interviews, *Journal of the Market Research Society*, 34 (1), 61–78

Tse, A, Ching, R, Ding, Y, Fong, R, Yeung, E and Au, A (1994) A comparison of the effectiveness of mail and facsimile as a survey media on response rate, speed and quality, *Journal of the Market Research Society*, 36, 349–55

Chapter 15: Online research

Alan, W, and Nial, L (2003) Internet based marketing research: A serious alternative to traditional research methods?, *Marketing Intelligence & Planning*, 21 (2)

Callegaro, M, Baker, R P, Bethlehem, J, Göritz, A S, Krosnick, J A and Lavrakas, P J (2014) *Online panel research: A data quality perspective*, John Wiley, New York

Coomber, R (1997) Using the internet for survey research, *Sociological Research Online*, 2 (2) [Online] www.socresonlineorguk/socresonline/2/2/2html

Dillman, D A and Andrew, D (1999) *Mail and Internet Surveys: The tailored design method*, 2nd Edition, John Wiley, New York and Chichester

Dodd, J (1998) Market research on the internet: Threat or opportunity?, *Marketing and Research Today*, (February) 60–66

Gray, D E (2013) *Doing Research in the Real World*, Sage, New York

Hair Jr, J F, Wolfinbarger, M, Money, A H, Samouel, P and Page, M J (2015) *Essentials of Business Research Methods*, Routledge, London

Michael, M A and Mavros, D A (2015) Adapting to change, *Research World*, (50) 54–56

Poynter R (2010) *The Handbook of Online and Social Media Research: Tools and techniques for market researchers*, John Wiley, Chichester

Schon, N, Mulders, S, and Dren, R (2002) Online qualitative market research: Interviewing the world at a fingertip, *Qualitative Market Research*, 5(3)

Schonlau, M (2002) *Conducting Research Surveys via E-Mail and the Web*, Rand, Santa Monica

Witmer, D F, Coleman, R W and Katzman, S L (1999) From paper and pen to screen and keyboard: Towards a methodology for survey research on the internet, in *Doing Internet Research*, ed Jones, S, 145–62, Sage, California

Chapter 16: Data analysis

Alt, M (1990) *Exploring Hyperspace: A non-mathematical explanation of multivariate analysis*, McGraw-Hill, London

Balnaves, M and Caputi, P (2001) *Introduction to Quantitative Research Methods: An investigative approach*, Sage, London

Blamires, C (1990) Segmentation, in *A Handbook of Market Research Techniques*, ed Birn, R, Hague, P and Vangelder, P, Kogan Page, London

Byrne, D (2002) *Interpreting Quantitative Data*, Sage, London

Catterall, M and Maclaren, P (1998) Using computer software for the analysis of qualitative market research data, *Journal of the Market Research Society*, **40** (3), 207–22

Charnes, A, Cooper, W W, Lewin, A Y, and Seiford, L M (2013) *Data Envelopment Analysis: Theory, methodology, and applications*, Springer Science & Business Media, Berlin

Davies, R (1993) Statistical modelling for survey analysis, *Journal of the Market Research Society*, **35** (3), 235–47

Dey, I (1993) *Qualitative Data Analysis*, Routledge, London

Diamantopoulos, A (1997), *Taking the Fear out of Data Analysis: A step-by-step approach*, Dryden Press, London

Fox, J, and Long, J S (eds) (1990) *Modern Methods of Data Analysis*, Sage, Newbury Park, California

Gatty, R (1966) *Multivariate Analysis for Marketing Research: An evaluation*, Applied Statistics (Series C), **15** (3)

Hague, P and Harris, P (1993) *Sampling and Statistics*, Kogan Page, London

Holmes, C (1986) Multivariate analysis of market research data, in *Consumer Market Research Handbook*, ed Worcester, R and Downham, J, McGraw-Hill, London

Hooley, G (1980) A guide to the use of quantitative techniques in marketing, *European Journal of Marketing*, **14** (7)

Jackling, P (1990) Analysing data-tabulations, in *A Handbook of Market Research Techniques*, ed Birn, R, Hague, P and Vangelder, P, Kogan Page, London

Kent, R (1993) *Marketing Research in Action*, Routledge, London

Michell, V W (1994) How to identify psychographic segments: Parts 1 & 2, *Marketing Intelligence & Planning*, **12** (7), 4–16

Miles, M B and Huberman, A M (1994) *Qualitative Data Analysis*, Sage, California

Moore, K, Burbach, R and Heeler, R (1995) Using neural nets to analyze qualitative data, *Marketing Research*, **7** (1), 34–39

Morgan, R (1990) Modelling: Conjoint analysis, in *A Handbook of Market Research Techniques*, ed Birn, R, Hague, P and Vangelder, P, Kogan Page, London

Punj, G and Stewart, D W (1983) Cluster analysis in market research: Review and suggestions for application, *Journal of Marketing Research*, **20**

Robson, S (1993) Analysis and interpretation of qualitative findings, *Journal of the Market Research Society*, 35(1), 23–35

Sarstedt, M and Mooi, E (2014) *A Concise Guide to Market Research: The process, data and methods using IBM SPSS statistics*, Springer-Verlag, Berlin

Treiman, D J (2014) *Quantitative Data Analysis: Doing social research to test ideas*, John Wiley, New York

Zhu, J (2014) *Quantitative models for performance evaluation and benchmarking: Data envelopment analysis with spreadsheets* (Vol 213), Springer, Berlin

Chapter 17: Using market research to segment markets

Albert, T C (2003) Need-based segmentation and customized communication strategies in a complex-commodity industry: A supply chain study, *Industrial Marketing Management*, **32** (4) 281–90

Assael, H (1997) *Consumer Behaviour and Marketing Action*, 6th Edition, South-Western, Nashville, Tennessee

Blamires, C (1990) Segmentation, in *A Handbook of Market Research Techniques*, ed Birn, R, Hague, P and Vangelder, P, Kogan Page, London

Cross, J C, Belich, T J and Rudelius, W (2014) How marketing managers use market segmentation: An exploratory study, Proceedings of the 1990 Academy of Marketing Science (AMS) Annual Conference, 531–36

Ferrell, O C, Lucas Jr, G H and Bush, A J (2015) Distinguishing market segments to assess price responsiveness, Proceedings of the 1988 Academy of Marketing Science (AMS) Annual Conference, 261–65

Funkhouser, G R, Chatterjee, A and Parker, R (1994) Segmenting samples, *Marketing Research*, **6** (1), 40–46

Michell, V W (1994) How to identify psychographic segments: Parts 1 & 2, *Marketing Intelligence & Planning*, **12** (7), 4–16

Wedel, M and Kamakura W (2000) *Market Segmentation: Conceptual and methodological foundations*, 2nd Edition, Kluwer Academic Publishers, Boston

Chapter 18: Using market research to improve a brand position

Aaker, D A and Joachimsthaler, E (2000) *Brand Leadership*, The Free Press, New York

Chaudhuri, A and Holbrook, M (2001) The chain of effects from brand trust and brand affect to brand performance: the role of brand loyalty, *Journal of Marketing*, 65 (2), 81–93

Kapferer, J N (2012) *The New Strategic Brand Management Advanced Insights and Strategic Thinking*, 5th Edition, Kogan Page, London

Keller, K L (2011) *Strategic Brand Management: Building, measuring and managing brand equity*, 3rd Edition, Pearson Education, India

Kim, W C and Mauborgne R (2015) *Blue Ocean Strategy: How to create uncontested market space and make the competition irrelevant*, Expanded Edition, Harvard Business School Press

Lehmann, D R Keller, K L and Farley, J U (*2008*) The structure of survey-based brand metrics, *Journal of International Marketing*, **16** (4) 29–56

Chapter 19: Using market research to improve customer satisfaction and loyalty

Brandi J (2001) *Building Customer Loyalty: 21 essential elements in action*, The Walk The Talk Company, Bedford, Texas

Evanschitzky, H, Ramaseshan B, Woisetshläger Richelsen, V, Blut, M and Backhaus, C (2012) Consequences of customer loyalty to the loyalty program and to the company, *Journal of the Academy of Marketing Science*, **40** (5), 625–38

Johnson M D and Gustafsson A (2000) *Improving Customer Satisfaction, Loyalty And Profit: An integrated measurement and management system*, Jossey-Bass, San Francisco

Rust, R T and Zahorik A J (1993) Customer satisfaction, customer retention and market share, *Journal of Retailing*, **69** (2), 193–215

Sachs J (2013) *Customer Loyalty: Top strategies for increasing your company's bottom-line*, Motivational Press, Carlsbad, California

Szwarc P (2005) *Researching Customer Satisfaction and Loyalty: How to find out what people really think*, Kogan Page, London

Veloustou C (2015) Brand evaluation, satisfaction and trust as predictors of brand loyalty: The mediator-moderator effect of brand relationships, *Journal of Consumer Marketing*, **32** (6) 405–21

Chapter 20: Using market research to achieve optimum pricing

Brown, M (1994) What price response?, *Journal of the Market Research Society*, **36**, 227–44

Baker R J (2006) *Pricing on Purpose: Creating and capturing value*, John Wiley, Hoboken, New Jersey

Baker R J (2011) *Implementing Value Pricing: A radical business model for professional firms*, John Wiley, Hoboken, New Jersey

Schindler, R M (2012) *Pricing Strategies: A marketing approach*, Sage, California

Smith T J (2012) *Pricing Strategy: Setting price levels, managing price discounts and establishing price structures*, South-Western, Mason, Ohio

When, C S, Hoppe, C and Gregoriou, G N (2013) *Rethinking Valuation and Pricing Models*, Elsevier, Oxford

Chapter 21: Using market research to enter a new market

Alexander, C (2008) *Market Risk Analysis: Practical financial econometrics*, John Wiley, Hoboken, New Jersey

Couturier, J and Sola, D (2010) International market entry decisions: The role of local market factors, *Journal of General Management*, **35** (4) 45–63

Kenny, G (2009) *Diversification Strategy: How to grow a business by diversifying successfully*, Kogan Page, London

Lee, G K and Lieberman, M B (2010) Acquisition vs internal development as modes of market entry, *Strategic Management Journal*, **31** (2) 140–58

Morschett, D, Schramm-Klein, H and Swoboda, B (2010) Decades of research on market entry modes: What do we really know about external antecedents of entry mode choice?, *Journal of International Management*, **16** (1) 60–77

Chapter 22: Using market research to test advertising effectiveness

Brettel, M and Spilker-Attig, A (2010) Online advertising effectiveness: A cross-cultural comparison, *Journal of Research in Interactive Marketing*, **4** (3) 176–96

Heerde, H J Gijsenberg, M J Dekimpe, M G and Steenkamp J E M (2013) Price and advertising effectiveness over the business cycle, *Journal of Market Research*, **50** (2), 177–93

Johnson, B G (2015) *Trust Funnel: Leverage today's online currency to grab attention, drive and convert traffic, and live a fabulous wealthy life*, Morgan James Publishing, New York

Macfarlane, H (2003) *The Leaky Funnel: Earn more customers by aligning sales and marketing to the way businesses buy*, 3rd Edition MathMarketing, Australia

Mitchell, A A (2013) *Advertising Exposure, Memory and Choice,* Lawrence Erlbaum Associates Inc, Hillsdale, New Jersey

Moriarty, S, Mitchell, N D and Wells, W D (2014) *Advertising and IMC: Principles and practice*, 10th Edition, Pearson Education, Australia

Morrison, M A, Haley, E, Sheehan, K B and Taylor, R E (2012) *Using Qualitative Research In Advertising: Strategies, techniques and applications*, 2nd Edition Sage, California

Sethuraman, R Tellis, G J and Briesch, R A (2011) How well does advertising work? Generalizations from meta-analysis of brand advertising elasicities, *Journal of Market Research*, **48** (3), 457–71

Wells, W D (2014) *Measuring Advertising Effectiveness*, Lawrence Erlbaum Associates Inc, New York

Chapter 23: Using market research to launch new products

Annacchino, MA (2007) *The Pursuit of New Development: The business development process*, Butterworth-Heinemann, Oxford

Bragg, A and Bragg, M (2005) *Developing New Business Ideas: A step-by-step guide to creating new business ideas worth backing*, Pearson Education, Harlow

Desouza, K C (2013) *Intrapreneurship: Managing ideas within your organisation*, University of Toronto Press

Lager, T (2011) *Managing Process Innovation: From idea generation to implementation*, Imperial College Press, Singapore

Muhdi, L, Daiber, M, Friesike, S and Boutellier, R (2011) The crowdsourcing approach process: An intermediary mediated idea generation approach in the early phas of innovation, *International Journal of Entrepreneurship and Innovation Management*, **14** (4), 315–32

Poetz, M K and Schreier M (2012) The value of crowdsourcing: Can users really compete with professionals in generating new product ideas?, *Journal of Product Innovation Management*, **29** (2), 245–56

Tuara, T and Nagai, Y (2013) *Concept Generation for Design Creativity: A systemized theory and methodology*, Springer-Verlag, London

Witell, L, Kristensson, P, Gustafsson, A and Lögren, M (2011) *Idea Generation: Customer co-creation versus traditional market research techniques*, Journal of Service Management, **22** (2) 140–59

Chapter 24: Reporting

Britt, S H (1971) The writing of readable research reports, *Journal of Marketing* (May)

Davies, M B and Hughes, N (2014) *Doing a Successful Research Project: Using qualitative or quantitative methods*, Palgrave Macmillan, London

De Vaus, D (2013) *Surveys in Social Research*, Routledge, London

Hague, P and Roberts, C (1994) *Presentations and Report Writing*, Kogan Page, London

Hausman, J A (2012) *Contingent Valuation: A critical assessment*, Elsevier, Amsterdam

Joseph, A (1998), Put it in Writing: Learn how to write clearly, quickly, and persuasively, McGraw-Hill, New York and London

Lane, J (1999) *Writing Clearly: An editing guide*, 2nd Edition, Heinle & Heinle, Pacific Grove, California

Leigh, A (1997) Persuasive Reports and Proposals, Institute of Personnel and Development, London

Mohn, N C (1989) How to present marketing research results effectively, *Marketing and Research Today*, **17** (2), 115–18

Newman, Richard (2010) *The 'It' Factor: Your guide to unlocking greater success in your business and your personal life*, UK Body Talk Ltd, Buckinghamshire

Roman, K and Raphaelson, J (1985) *Writing That Works*, HarperCollins, New York

Smith, D and Fletcher, J (2004) *The Art & Science of Interpreting Market Research Evidence*, John Wiley, Chichester

Sussmans, J (1991) *How to Write Effective Reports*, Gower, Aldershot

Tufte, E R (1983) *The Visual Display of Quantitative Information*, CT Graphics Press, Cheshire

Van Embden, J (1987) *Report Writing*, McGraw-Hill, London

Zwlazny, G (1991) *Say It With Charts*, Business One Irwin, Holmwood, Illinois

Chapter 25: International market research

Bahadir, S C, Bharadwaj, S G and Srivastava, R K (2015) Marketing mix and brand sales in global markets: Examining the contingent role of country-market characteristics, *Journal of International Business Studies*

Birn, R (2002) *The International Handbook of Market Research Techniques*, Kogan Page, London

Bowman, J (2012) A world of difference, Research World No 35, September

Cavusgil, Knight, Riesenberger, Yaprak (2009) *Conducting Market Research for International Business*, Business Expert Press, New York

Craig and Douglas (2005) *International Marketing Research*, 3rd Edition, John Wiley and Sons Ltd London

ESOMAR Industry Report (2014) Global Market Research

Holbrook, A, Krosnick J, and Pfent A (2007) in *Advances in Telephone Survey Methodology* Wiley, New York

Karakaya, F and Stahl, M J (2015) Global Barriers to Market Entry for Developing Country Businesses, in Proceedings of the 1993 World Marketing Congress, Springer International Publishing, 208–212

Papadopoulos, N, & Martín Martín, O (2011) International market selection and segmentation: perspectives and challenges, International Marketing Review, **28** (2), 132–49

Puleston, J and Rintoul, D (April 2012) Can survey gaming techniques cross continents? Examining cross cultural reactions to creative questioning techniques, ESOMAR, Amsterdam

Roster, Albaum and Rogers (2006) Can cross national/cultural studies presume etic equivalency in respondent's use of extreme categories of Likert scales?, *International Journal of Market Research*, **48** (6)

Synodinos and Kobayashi (2008) Marketing research in Japan: From its emergence to the present, *International Journal of Market Research*, **50** (1)

Wilcock, C (2014) Comparing Apples to Pommes, ESOMAR B2B Forum 2014

Chapter 26: Research trends

Baird, C (2012) Irrevocable Change: The digital revolution is transforming the marketplace, *Research World*, **32** January/February

Bhargava, R (2012) *15 Marketing Trends In 2013: And how your business can use them*, Partnership Publishing

Huijzer, Kok-Jensen and Sceats (2012) Shaken, not stirred: New methods for a changing world, *Research World*, **37** November/December

Lindkvist, M (2009) *Everything We Know Is Wrong: The invisible trends that shape business, society and life*

Minelli, M (2013) *Big Data, Big Analytics: Emerging business intelligence and analytic trends for today's businesses*, John Wiley, New Jersey

Watson, G F, Worm, S, Palmatier, R W and Ganesan, S (2015) The evolution of marketing channels: Trends and research directions, *Journal of Retailing*, Elsevier

Chapter 27: Ethics in market research

Alexander, Matthew (2014) Ethics in qualitative research, 2nd Edition, *Journal of the Market Research Society*, **56** (5), 571–90

Kimmel, A J (2007) *Ethical Issues in Behavioural Research: Basic and applied perspectives*, 2nd Edition, Blackwell Publishing, Australia

Miller, T Birch, M Mauthner, M and Jessop, J (2008) *Ethics in Qualitative Research*, Sage Publishing, London

Nuan, D and Di Domenico, M (2013) Market research and the ethics of big data, *International Journal of Market Research*, **55** (4) 505–20

Singh R (Editor), Wright G (Editor) (2014) Sustainability and marketing to socially connected consumers, *Marketing Intelligence & Planning*, **32** (5)

Van Den Hoonard, W C (2003) Is anonymity an artefact in ethnographic research?, **1** (2), 141–51

Walther, J B (2002) Research ethics in internet-enabled research: Human subjects issues and methodological myopia, *Ethics and Information Technology*, **4** (3), 205–16

Wilson, A M (2001) Mystery shopping: Using deception to measure service performance, *Psychology & Marketing*, **18** (7) 721–34

Zikmund, Z and Babin, B (2013) *Essentials of Market Research*, 5th Edition South-Western, Mason, Ohio

INDEX

Page numbers in *italic* indicate figures or tables